VOLUME 2: COMPREHENSIVE GUIDE TO PHARMACEUTICAL REGULATORY AFFAIRS

GLOBAL REGULATIONS AND ADVANCED TOPICS

VEERAREDDY PRABHAKAR REDDY,
MURALIDHAR RAO AKKALADEVI

Contents

Contents

(EMA)

Chapter 4: Clinical Research Related Guidelines

4.1 Good Clinical Practice Guidelines (ICH GCP E6) 4.2 Indian GCP Guidelines 4.3 ICMR Ethical Guidelines for Biomedical Research 4.4 CDSCO Guidelines 4.5 GHTF Study Group 5 Guidance Documents 4.6 ICH Guidelines on Efficacy and Safety (E4, E7, E8, E10, E11) 4.7 General Biostatistics Principles Applied in Clinical Research

Chapter 5: USA Guidance

5.1 Organization Structure and Functions of FDA 5.2 Federal Register and Code of Federal Regulations (CFR) 5.3 History and Evolution of the United States Federal, Food, Drug, and Cosmetic Act (FFDCA) 5.4 Hatch Waxman Act and Orange Book, Purple Book 5.5 Drug Master Files (DMF) System in the USA 5.6 Regulatory Approval Process for IND, NDA, ANDA, SNDA 5.7 Regulatory Requirements for Orphan Drugs and Combination Products 5.8 Regulatory Considerations for Manufacturing, Packaging, and Labeling of Pharmaceuticals in the USA 5.9 Legislation and Regulations for Import, Manufacture, Distribution, and Sale of Cosmetics in the USA

5.10 FDA Guidance on Human Subject Protection, Financial Disclosure, IND Application, NDA Application, Bioavailability and Bioequivalence Requirements, Investigational Device Exemptions, Post-Market Surveillance 5.11 FDA Safety Reporting Requirements for INDs and BA/BE Studies 5.12 FDA MedWatch and Good Pharmacovigilance Practices

Chapter 6: Australia Regulations

6.1 Introduction 6.2 The application 6.3 Relevant Provisions of the Act 6.4 Commissions Assessment of Application 6.5 Public Detriment 6.6 Public Benefits 6.7 Conclusion on application 6.8 Consideration of Undertakings 6.9 Determination

Chapter 7: European Union (EU) Regulations

7.1 Organization and Structure of EMA & EDQM 7.2 General Guidelines and Active Substance Master Files (ASMF) System in the EU 7.3 Content and Approval Process of IMPD 7.4 Marketing Authorization Procedures in the EU 7.5 Regulatory Considerations for Manufacturing, Packaging, and Labeling of Pharmaceuticals in the EU 7.6 Eudralex Directives for Human Medicines 7.7 Variations & Extensions, Compliance of European Pharmacopoeia (CEP/CoS) 7.8 Marketing Authorization (MA) Transfers and Qualified Person (QP) in the EU 7.9 Legislation and Regulations for Import, Manufacture, Distribution, and Sale of Cosmetics in the EU 7.10 EU Directives and EudraLex Volume 3 and 9A 7.11EU Annual Safety Report and EU MDD 7.12 ISO 14155

Chapter 8: Japan Regulations

8.1 Organization of the PMDA 8.2 Pharmaceutical Laws and Regulations in Japan 8.3 Types of Registration Applications and DMF System in Japan 8.4 Drug Regulatory Approval Process in Japan 8.5 Regulatory Considerations for Manufacturing, Packaging, and Labeling of Pharmaceuticals in Japan 8.6 Post-Marketing Surveillance in Japan 8.7 Legislation and Regulations for Import, Manufacture, Distribution, and Sale of Cosmetics in Japan

Chapter 9: Emerging Markets

9.1 Introduction to Emerging Markets 9.2 Study of Various Committees Across the Globe (ASEAN, APEC, EAC, GCC, PANDRH, SADC) 9.3 WHO GMP and Regulatory Requirements for Registration of Drugs and Post-Approval Requirements in WHO 9.4 Certificate of Pharmaceutical Product (CoPP) - General and Country Specific (South Africa, Egypt, Algeria, Morocco, Nigeria, Kenya, Botswana)

Chapter 10: Brazil, ASEAN, CIS, and GCC Countries

10.1 Introduction to ACTD and Regulatory Requirements in China and South Korea 10.2 Regulatory Requirements for Drugs and Post-Approval Requirements in ASEAN Region (Vietnam, Malaysia, Philippines, Singapore, Thailand) 10.3 Regulatory Requirements for Marketing Authorization in CIS Countries (Russia, Kazakhstan, Ukraine) 10.4 Regulatory Requirements for Marketing Authorization in GCC (Saudi Arabia, UAE) 10.5 Legislation and Regulations for Import, Manufacture, Distribution, and Sale of Cosmetics in Brazil, ASEAN, CIS, and GCC Countries

Chapter 11: Regulatory Aspects of Drugs and Cosmetics

11.1 Drug Regulatory Framework in Different Countries 11.2 Requirements for Drug Approval and Marketing Authorization 11.3 Regulations for Over-the-Counter (OTC) Drugs and Prescription Drugs 11.4 Regulatory Requirements for Cosmetics 11.5 Labeling and Packaging Requirements for Drugs and Cosmetics 11.6 Post-Marketing Surveillance and Pharmacovigilance

Chapter 12: Regulatory Aspects of Herbals and Biologicals

12.1 Regulatory Requirements for Herbal Medicines 12.2 Quality, Safety, and Efficacy of Herbal Products 12.3 Regulatory Framework for Biological Products 12.4 Development and Approval of Biosimilars 12.5 Stability and Safety Testing of Biologicals 12.6 Labeling and Packaging

Requirements for Herbal and Biological Products

Chapter 13: Regulatory Aspects of Medical Devices

13.1 Introduction to Medical Devices and IVDs 13.2 Risk-Based Classification of Medical Devices 13.3 Regulatory Approval Process for Medical Devices 13.4 Quality System Requirements for Medical Devices 13.5 Post-Marketing Surveillance of Medical Devices 13.6 Adverse Event Reporting and Unique Device Identification (UDI)

Chapter 14: Regulatory Aspects of Food and Nutraceuticals

14.1 Regulatory Requirements for Food Products and Nutraceuticals 14.2 Quality and Safety Standards for Food and Nutraceuticals 14.3 Labeling and Packaging Requirements for Food and Nutraceuticals 14.4 Global Regulatory Framework for Nutraceuticals 14.5 Post-Marketing Surveillance and Compliance for Nutraceuticals

Chapter 15: Quality Management Systems

15.1 Quality Control and Quality Assurance in Pharmaceutical Industry 15.2 Total Quality Management (TQM) 15.3 Quality by Design (QbD) 15.4 Six Sigma and Lean Manufacturing 15.5 Out of Specifications (OOS) and Change Control 15.6 Validation and Qualification in Pharmaceutical Industry 15.7 Regulatory Guidelines for Quality Management Systems

Chapter 16: Future Trends in Pharmaceutical Regulatory Affairs

16.1 Emerging Trends in Drug Regulation 16.2 Advances in Regulatory Science 16.3 Role of Technology in Regulatory Affairs 16.4 Global Harmonization and Regulatory Convergence 16.5 Challenges and Opportunities in Regulatory Affairs

Chapter 17: Intellectual Property Rights

17.1 Introduction to Intellectual Property Rights (IPR) 17.2 Patents and Copyrights in Pharmaceutical Industry 17.3 Regulatory Framework for IPR in Different Countries 17.4 Data Exclusivity and Market Exclusivity 17.5 Patent Linkage and Evergreening Strategies 17.6 Challenges and Opportunities in IPR

Chapter 18: Indian Drug Regulatory Agencies and Guidelines

18.1 Introduction to Indian Drug Regulatory System 18.2 Central Drugs Standard Control Organization (CDSCO) 18.3 Schedule Y and Other Drug Regulations in India 18.4 Guidelines for Clinical Trials, Market Authorization, and Post-Marketing Surveillance 18.5 Guidelines for the Manufacture, Distribution, and Sale of Drugs and Cosmetics 18.6 Good Manufacturing Practices (GMP) and Good Distribution Practices (GDP) in India 18.7 Quality Control and Quality Assurance Requirements in India

Volume 2: Comprehensive Guide To Pharmaceutical Regulatory Affairs

Global Regulations and Advanced Topics
EDITED BY
Dr. Prabhakar Reddy Veerareddy
Head, University College of Pharmaceutical Sciences,
Palamuru University,
Mahabubnagar, Telangana, India
Dr. Muralidhar Rao Akkaladevi
Principal, St. Mary's College of Pharmacy,
Secunderabad, Telangana, India
Published by Notion Press
Notion Press, Inc.
800, West El Camino Real #180,
California, USA 94040
Notion Press Media Pvt Ltd
#7, Red Cross Road,
Egmore, Chennai, Tamil Nadu 600008
Email ID: publish@notionpress.com
Phone Number: +91 44 46315631

Preface

The pharmaceutical industry operates in an environment where compliance with regulatory standards is critical for the development, approval, and distribution of products that directly affect human health. The global nature of pharmaceutical operations, combined with rapidly evolving regulations, demands a comprehensive understanding of both international and regional guidelines. In this context, *Volume 2: Comprehensive Guide to Pharmaceutical Regulatory Affairs: Global Regulations and Advanced Topics* by Veerareddy Prabhakar Reddy and Muralidhar Rao Akkaladevi provides an all-encompassing resource designed to address the complex landscape of regulatory affairs.

This volume offers a deep dive into the wide variety of topics central to the pharmaceutical regulatory world. Covering diverse areas, it explores the **clinical drug development process**, from early-phase studies to post-marketing surveillance, providing insights into every step of bringing a new drug to market. Detailed chapters on the **ethics of clinical research** guide professionals through essential standards like the Nuremberg Code and the Declaration of Helsinki, while also covering modern ethical concerns, including the role of placebos, informed consent, and the unique ethical challenges of working with special populations.

The book further explores **regulations governing clinical trials** across different global regions, including **India, the USA, the European Union, and Japan**, with a focus on the variations and similarities in each regulatory framework. This global perspective is particularly valuable for companies and professionals working across borders, helping them navigate the distinct requirements of various regulatory bodies like the **FDA, EMA, PMDA**, and **CDSCO**.

Special attention is also given to **medical device regulations**, reflecting the growing convergence of pharmaceutical and medical technology sectors. The risk-based classification, quality systems, and post-marketing surveillance of medical devices and IVDs are meticulously discussed, ensuring a thorough understanding of this increasingly important area.

Other significant topics covered in the book include **intellectual property rights (IPR)**, focusing on patent laws, data exclusivity, and market exclusivity across different countries. Regulatory frameworks for **cosmetics, herbals, biologicals**, and **nutraceuticals** are also explored, providing readers with guidance on these rapidly growing segments of the healthcare market.

Additionally, this volume covers key areas like **pharmacovigilance, post-marketing safety surveillance**, and **quality management systems,** which are essential for maintaining product safety and efficacy throughout a product's lifecycle. There is also a deep examination of regulatory trends in **emerging markets** such as ASEAN, GCC, and CIS countries, offering valuable insights into opportunities and challenges in these regions.

This guide aims to serve a wide audience, including regulatory professionals, pharmaceutical companies, students, and academic researchers. Its practical approach ensures that readers not only understand regulatory requirements but also know how to apply them effectively in their professional environments.

With its broad coverage of topics and global perspective, this volume offers a unique and invaluable resource for anyone involved in pharmaceutical regulatory affairs. It provides the knowledge and tools needed to navigate the complex, interconnected world of pharmaceutical regulations, helping readers stay compliant and ahead in an ever-evolving industry.

We hope that this book serves as an essential reference, supporting professionals and students alike in understanding the intricacies of global regulatory frameworks and advanced topics in pharmaceutical regulatory affairs.

Clinical Drug Development Process

The **Clinical Drug Development Process** is one of the most crucial aspects of pharmaceutical innovation, providing the framework by which new drugs are brought from the laboratory to patients. This chapter delves into the intricate journey of clinical trials, beginning with early exploratory studies and culminating in post-marketing surveillance. Each phase of clinical trials, from Phase 0 to Phase IV, plays a distinct role in ensuring that therapeutic agents are safe, effective, and suitable for human use. This process not only involves the evaluation of the drug's efficacy but also an extensive investigation into its pharmacokinetics, pharmacodynamics, safety profiles, and potential side effects.

The journey is marked by stringent regulatory oversight, with each phase having specific objectives. **Phase 0 studies**, for example, focus on gaining early insights into the pharmacokinetics of the drug, while **Phase I studies** examine safety in small groups of healthy volunteers. **Phase II and III studies** shift attention to establishing efficacy and comparing the drug to standard treatments across larger and more diverse patient populations. These phases are critical for acquiring robust data needed for drug registration. **Post-marketing studies (Phase IV)** further assess long-term safety and effectiveness in real-world settings.

This chapter also sheds light on the evolving nature of clinical trials, including innovative designs such as **adaptive trials** and the increasing use of **biomarkers** to refine patient selection. By understanding these key phases and the intricacies involved, professionals gain a comprehensive view of how clinical trials drive the development of safe and effective drugs while navigating complex global regulations.

1.1 Different Types of Clinical Studies

Clinical studies are a critical part of the drug development process, providing the necessary data to ensure that new pharmaceutical interventions are both **safe** and **effective**. The variety of **clinical studies** conducted during this process allows for a comprehensive evaluation of a drug's effects on humans. Clinical studies typically fall into different categories based on their purpose, design, and methodology. These categories include **interventional studies, observational studies**, and **randomized controlled trials (RCTs)**, each offering unique insights into the drug's performance.

Interventional Studies

In an **interventional study**, participants are assigned to receive specific interventions, such as a new drug or a different treatment. The purpose of this study type is to investigate how the intervention affects a particular health outcome. These studies are often referred to as **clinical trials** and are the most common form of drug testing in clinical research.

One significant form of interventional study is the **randomized controlled trial (RCT)**, where participants are randomly assigned to receive either the investigational drug or a control treatment, often a **placebo** or an existing therapy. This randomization helps minimize **bias** and ensures that any differences observed between the groups can be attributed to the intervention itself. RCTs are the gold standard for evaluating a drug's efficacy and safety, often involving thousands of participants across multiple **clinical sites**. For instance, in large-scale trials for cardiovascular drugs, studies can include over **10,000** participants, spanning **multiple countries** to gather diverse data.

Interventional studies are typically conducted in **four phases. Phase I** trials, usually involving fewer than **100** participants, focus on evaluating a drug's safety and pharmacokinetics. **Phase II** trials, involving **100 to 300** participants, assess the drug's efficacy and further explore its safety profile. In **Phase III** trials, thousands of participants are recruited to provide more comprehensive data on efficacy and safety. Finally, **Phase IV** trials occur after the drug has been approved for marketing and continue to monitor long-term safety and effectiveness in broader populations.

Observational Studies

Unlike interventional studies, **observational studies** do not involve specific interventions. Instead, researchers observe participants in their natural settings, collecting data on health outcomes without manipulating variables. These studies can offer valuable insights into real-world drug use, safety, and effectiveness, especially when ethical or logistical constraints make conducting **randomized controlled trials** impractical.

One common type of observational study is the **cohort study**, where a group of individuals who have been exposed to a particular drug or treatment is followed over time and compared to a non-exposed group. For example, a cohort study investigating the long-term effects of a **statin** (a cholesterol-lowering drug) might track thousands of patients for over a decade to observe outcomes like the incidence of **cardiovascular events**. Cohort studies can be **prospective**, where the participants are followed from the present into the future, or **retrospective**, where data from past records are analyzed.

Another observational study design is the **case-control study**, where researchers compare individuals with a specific outcome (cases) to those without it (controls). These studies are often used to identify potential risk factors for rare diseases or adverse drug reactions. For instance, case-control studies have been instrumental in identifying risk factors for **adverse drug reactions** associated with certain cancer treatments.

Randomized Controlled Trials (RCTs)

As mentioned, **RCTs** are the backbone of interventional studies. The **randomization** process ensures that participants have an equal chance of being assigned to the treatment group or the control group, which helps eliminate selection bias. RCTs are highly structured, often double-blind, meaning neither the participants nor the researchers know who is receiving the investigational drug. This structure ensures objectivity in reporting results.

RCTs typically generate quantitative data, with results analyzed using statistical methods to determine the significance of the findings. For example, a **p-value** less than **0.05** often indicates that the results are statistically significant, meaning the observed effects are unlikely to be due to chance. Furthermore, **confidence intervals (CIs)** are often reported alongside p-values to provide an estimate of the precision of the results. For instance, a **95% CI** means there is a 95% chance that the true effect lies within the given range.

RCTs can be conducted in multiple phases, each serving a distinct purpose in the clinical development process. **Phase I** trials are typically conducted on a small number of healthy volunteers, often fewer than **50**, to assess the safety profile of a drug. **Phase II** trials expand the study population to include **100-300** patients and focus on evaluating the drug's efficacy while continuing to monitor for side effects. In **Phase III**, the study population grows further, often encompassing **1,000 to 3,000** patients, with the primary aim of confirming the drug's effectiveness and monitoring for adverse events. These large-scale studies provide the data necessary for regulatory approval. **Phase IV** trials, or post-marketing studies, are conducted after a drug has been approved by regulatory authorities and continue to monitor the drug's long-term safety and effectiveness in a larger, more diverse population.

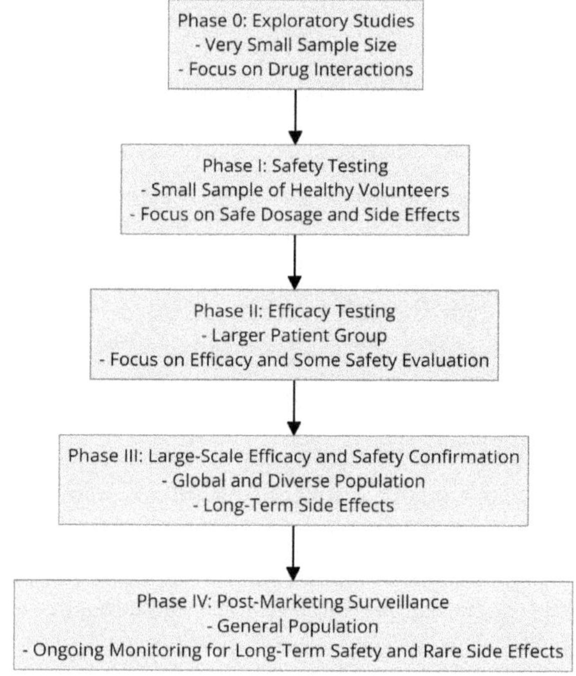

Comprehensive Overview of Safety and Efficacy Testing Across Clinical Trial Phases

Crossover and Adaptive Trials

In addition to traditional **RCTs**, more sophisticated trial designs, such as **crossover trials** and **adaptive trials**, are increasingly used in drug development. In a **crossover trial**, participants receive both the investigational drug and the control treatment at different times during the study. This design allows researchers to compare the effects of the drug within the same individual, which can reduce the variability in the data. Crossover trials are especially useful when studying **chronic conditions**, where long-term management is required.

Adaptive trials, on the other hand, are flexible in their design, allowing modifications to the trial protocol based on interim results. For example, an adaptive trial may increase the sample size or adjust the dosing regimen if early results suggest that the initial protocol is not optimal. These trials can lead to more efficient use of resources and faster decision-making. Adaptive trials have gained popularity in recent years, particularly in **oncology**, where new treatments are constantly evolving.

1.2 Phases of Clinical Trials

Clinical trials are conducted in distinct **phases**, each with a unique objective aimed at ensuring that a new drug is both **safe** and **effective** for human use. These phases systematically build upon each other, starting with small-scale studies focused on safety and culminating in large-scale trials aimed at confirming the drug's efficacy across a broad population. The information gathered in these trials is crucial for obtaining regulatory approval and ensuring that the drug performs as expected in the real world. Clinical trials typically progress through **four phases**, each playing a vital role in the drug development process.

Phase I: Safety and Dosage Evaluation

The primary goal of **Phase I trials** is to evaluate the safety of a drug in humans for the first time. These trials are conducted on a small number of **healthy volunteers** or, in some cases, patients with the condition the drug aims to treat. The typical sample size for a Phase I trial ranges from **20 to 100 participants**. In this phase, researchers focus on determining the **optimal dosage** of the drug and assessing its **pharmacokinetics** (how the drug is absorbed, distributed, metabolized, and excreted by the body).

During Phase I, participants may receive a single dose or multiple doses over a short period to monitor how their bodies respond. The study often starts with **subtherapeutic doses**, which are gradually increased to determine the **maximum tolerated dose (MTD)**—the highest dose at which no severe adverse effects are observed. For example, in oncology drug development, the MTD is a crucial parameter since cancer treatments often have narrow therapeutic windows.

One of the key measurements in Phase I is the drug's **half-life**, which indicates how long it takes for the concentration of the drug in the bloodstream to reduce by half. For instance, if a new drug has a half-life of **6**

hours, this information helps in deciding the appropriate dosing frequency for later trials. **Adverse events** such as nausea, headache, or fatigue are meticulously recorded to establish the drug's initial safety profile.

Phase II: Efficacy and Side Effects

Once a drug has been deemed safe in Phase I, it moves on to **Phase II trials**, where the focus shifts from safety to efficacy. These trials typically involve **100 to 300 participants** who have the medical condition that the drug is intended to treat. The objective is to gather preliminary data on the **effectiveness** of the drug, as well as continue monitoring for side effects. Phase II trials are often referred to as **proof-of-concept** studies.

In this phase, participants are usually divided into two groups: one receiving the investigational drug and the other receiving either a **placebo** or the current **standard of care**. For example, a Phase II trial for a new diabetes medication might compare the blood sugar levels of patients receiving the new drug to those receiving an existing treatment. Efficacy measures, such as reductions in **HbA1c levels** (a marker of blood sugar control), are used to determine whether the drug has the desired effect.

Phase II trials are often divided into two sub-phases: **Phase IIa**, focusing on dosing requirements, and **Phase IIb**, which is more focused on efficacy. For instance, Phase IIa might explore different doses of the drug to identify which dose provides the optimal balance between efficacy and side effects, while Phase IIb would seek to confirm these findings in a larger population. During this phase, **common side effects**, such as mild gastrointestinal disturbances, are closely monitored to ensure they are manageable and acceptable in the target patient population.

Phase III: Large-Scale Confirmation

Phase III trials are the most extensive and often involve **1,000 to 3,000 participants** or even more, depending on the medical condition being treated. These trials aim to confirm the drug's efficacy and monitor side effects in a larger, more diverse population. The results of Phase III trials form the basis for **regulatory approval** by agencies such as the **Food and Drug Administration (FDA)** in the United States or the **European Medicines Agency (EMA)** in Europe.

These trials are usually **randomized, double-blind,** and **placebo-controlled**, meaning neither the participants nor the researchers know who is receiving the investigational drug versus the placebo. This design helps to eliminate **bias** and ensures the results are as objective as possible. For example, in a Phase III trial for a new **antihypertensive drug**, participants might be followed for **12 to 24 months** to track changes in **blood pressure** and monitor for any long-term side effects like **dizziness** or **fatigue**.

The results of Phase III trials are critical because they provide the most robust data on the drug's effectiveness. Regulatory bodies require substantial evidence from these trials before a drug can be approved for **commercial use**. For example, a new **cancer therapy** might be approved based on a Phase III trial that demonstrates a significant improvement in **overall survival rates** compared to the existing standard treatment.

Additionally, **adverse events** that were not seen in earlier, smaller trials might become apparent in Phase III due to the larger number of participants. For instance, a rare but severe side effect affecting **1 in 10,000 patients** might only become evident when tested in larger populations. Therefore, the safety profile of the drug continues to be rigorously assessed at this stage.

Phase IV: Post-Marketing Surveillance

Once a drug has been approved for use, it enters **Phase IV trials**, also known as **post-marketing surveillance studies**. These trials are designed to monitor the long-term safety and effectiveness of the drug in a real-world setting. They often involve **thousands of patients** over several years, allowing researchers to detect **rare adverse effects** that might not have been evident during the earlier phases of clinical development.

For example, after the approval of the **COX-2 inhibitors** for pain relief, **Phase IV studies** uncovered an increased risk of **cardiovascular events**, leading to the withdrawal of some drugs in this class. In addition, Phase IV trials provide an opportunity to study how the drug interacts with other medications commonly used in the general population, an area that might not have been fully explored during earlier trials.

Another purpose of Phase IV trials is to explore **new indications** for the drug. A medication initially approved to treat **hypertension** may, through post-marketing research, be found to have beneficial effects on related conditions such as **chronic kidney disease**. In such cases, the drug's labeling may be updated to reflect these additional benefits.

1.3 Clinical Trial Protocol

A **clinical trial protocol** is a comprehensive document that outlines the detailed plan for conducting a clinical study. It serves as the blueprint that guides investigators, clinical staff, and regulatory authorities throughout the trial, ensuring that the study is conducted in a consistent, ethical, and scientifically sound manner. The protocol must meet stringent requirements set by regulatory bodies such as the **Food and Drug Administration (FDA)** in the United States, the **European Medicines Agency (EMA)**, and other international regulatory agencies.

The protocol not only defines the objectives of the trial but also provides detailed procedures for every aspect of the study, including participant recruitment, treatment plans, data collection, and analysis methods. It is designed to safeguard the **rights, safety, and well-being** of the participants while ensuring the collection of **high-quality, reliable data**. The **International Council for Harmonisation (ICH) Guidelines** serve as a global standard for developing and implementing a clinical trial protocol.

Key Components of a Clinical Trial Protocol

A clinical trial protocol typically contains several key sections, each of which plays a critical role in ensuring the success of the study:

1.3.1 Objectives and Purpose

The protocol begins by clearly stating the **objectives** and **purpose** of the clinical trial. This section defines what the trial aims to achieve, whether it is evaluating the **efficacy** of a new drug, assessing its **safety**, or studying specific **outcomes** in different patient populations. For instance, in a clinical trial for a new diabetes medication, the primary objective might be to evaluate the drug's ability to lower **HbA1c levels** over a six-month period. Secondary objectives might include assessing the drug's impact on **weight loss, insulin resistance**, or **cholesterol levels**.

1.3.2 Study Design

The **study design** section outlines the overall structure of the clinical trial. This includes details such as whether the trial is **randomized, double-blind**, or **placebo-controlled**. For example, in a **double-blind randomized controlled trial (RCT)**, neither the participants nor the researchers know who is receiving the investigational drug versus a placebo. This design helps eliminate **bias** and ensures the results are as objective as possible.

Additionally, the study design specifies the number of **treatment groups**, how participants will be **randomly assigned** to these groups, and the **duration** of the study. For instance, in a cardiovascular study, participants might be assigned to either a new **antihypertensive drug** group or a placebo group, with the study lasting for **12 to 24 months** to assess long-term outcomes.

1.3.3 Participant Selection and Inclusion/Exclusion Criteria

The protocol clearly defines the criteria for **participant selection**, including both **inclusion** and **exclusion criteria**. This ensures that only individuals who meet specific medical, demographic, and other relevant criteria are included in the study, thereby minimizing variability and ensuring that the results are applicable to the target population.

For example, in a study for a **new cancer therapy**, the inclusion criteria might specify that participants must have been diagnosed with a certain type of **stage III cancer**, be within a particular age range (e.g., **40 to 65 years**), and have a **life expectancy** of at least six months. On the other hand, exclusion criteria might disqualify individuals with certain **comorbidities** such as **severe cardiovascular disease**, as these conditions might interfere with the interpretation of the study's results.

1.3.4 Treatment Plan

The **treatment plan** describes the investigational product being tested, including its **dosage**, **route of administration**, and the **schedule** for taking the drug. For instance, in a Phase II trial for a new oral medication, participants might be instructed to take **100 mg** of the drug twice daily with food. The plan also outlines the duration of treatment, which could range from a few weeks to several months or even years.

In some trials, participants may receive **different doses** of the investigational drug to determine the **optimal dose** that provides the maximum therapeutic benefit with minimal side effects. This is particularly common in **oncology** and **cardiovascular** drug trials, where precise dosing is critical.

1.3.5 Outcome Measures

The protocol defines both **primary** and **secondary outcome measures**, which are used to evaluate the effectiveness and safety of the investigational product. The **primary outcome measure** is the main result the trial is designed to assess, such as a reduction in **tumor size** in a cancer study or a decrease in **blood pressure** in a hypertension trial.

Secondary outcome measures provide additional data on other aspects of the drug's performance. For example, in a diabetes study, while the primary outcome might be the reduction in **HbA1c**, secondary outcomes could include changes in **fasting blood glucose levels**, **body weight**, or **lipid profiles**.

Outcome measures must be clearly defined, and the protocol specifies how these will be **assessed**, **measured**, and **recorded**. For example, the reduction in tumor size might be measured using **CT scans** every **three months** and compared with baseline measurements.

1.3.6 Data Collection and Monitoring

Accurate and consistent **data collection** is critical for the success of a clinical trial. The protocol provides detailed instructions for collecting, recording, and monitoring all relevant data throughout the study. This section also outlines how **adverse events** and **serious adverse events** (SAEs) will be reported and managed, as well as the procedures for **data verification** and **quality control**.

Clinical trials often use **electronic data capture (EDC) systems** to collect and manage data in real-time. These systems are designed to reduce **human error** and ensure that data are entered correctly and consistently. Data monitoring is typically conducted by an independent **data safety monitoring board (DSMB)**, which reviews the data periodically to ensure the safety of participants and the integrity of the trial.

1.3.7 Statistical Analysis Plan

The **statistical analysis plan** (SAP) is a critical component of the clinical trial protocol. It outlines the **statistical methods** that will be used to analyze the data, including how the **sample size** was determined, the type of **statistical tests** that will be used, and how missing data will be handled.

For example, in a study testing the efficacy of a new cholesterol-lowering drug, the statistical plan might specify that the primary outcome (change in **LDL cholesterol levels**) will be analyzed using a **two-sample t-test** to compare the treatment group with the placebo group. The plan may also specify the use of **confidence intervals** and **p-values** to determine whether the results are statistically significant. A typical clinical trial will aim for a **p-value of less than 0.05** to indicate statistical significance.

1.3.8 Ethical Considerations

Ethical considerations are paramount in any clinical trial. The protocol outlines the measures taken to ensure that the trial is conducted in an ethical manner, in compliance with **Good Clinical Practice (GCP)** guidelines and **local regulatory requirements**. This section covers important aspects such as **informed consent**, **confidentiality**, and **participant safety**.

Before enrolling in the trial, participants must be provided with clear and detailed information about the study, including its purpose, procedures, potential risks, and benefits. They must voluntarily agree to participate by signing an **informed consent form**. The protocol also describes how participants' **confidentiality** will be protected, typically through the use of **coded identifiers** rather than personal information in study records.

In addition, the trial must be approved by an **Institutional Review Board (IRB)** or **Ethics Committee** before it can begin. These independent bodies review the study protocol to ensure that it adheres to ethical standards and that the rights and welfare of the participants are protected.

1.4 Phase 0 Studies

Phase 0 studies, also known as **microdosing studies**, represent the earliest step in the clinical development of a drug. These studies are not as widely recognized as the traditional **Phase I to IV** trials, but they play a crucial role in providing preliminary data about a drug's **pharmacokinetics** (how the drug is absorbed, distributed, metabolized, and excreted in the body) and **pharmacodynamics** (how the drug affects the body). Phase 0 studies are designed to minimize risk to participants while maximizing early insights into the drug's behavior in humans.

Phase 0 studies are typically conducted before **Phase I** trials and involve administering very small doses—referred to as **subtherapeutic doses** or **microdoses**—of the investigational drug to a limited number of **healthy volunteers** or, in some cases, patients with the condition the drug aims to treat. The **doses** used in Phase 0 studies are often less than **1% of the dose** that is expected to produce a therapeutic effect, which significantly reduces the risk of adverse effects. This allows researchers to gather critical data about the drug's behavior without exposing participants to the full effects of the drug.

1.4.1 Objectives of Phase 0 Studies

The primary objective of **Phase 0 studies** is to gain early insights into the drug's pharmacokinetics and pharmacodynamics, helping researchers decide whether the drug is worth pursuing in subsequent clinical trials. These studies are particularly useful for **screening multiple drug candidates** at an early stage, allowing pharmaceutical companies to prioritize the most promising compounds for further development.

For example, if a company is developing several similar compounds targeting a specific cancer, Phase 0 studies can help determine which compound has the best **absorption** profile or the most favorable **half-life**. This early data helps in making informed decisions about which candidate should move forward into **Phase I** trials, where safety and dosage are more thoroughly evaluated.

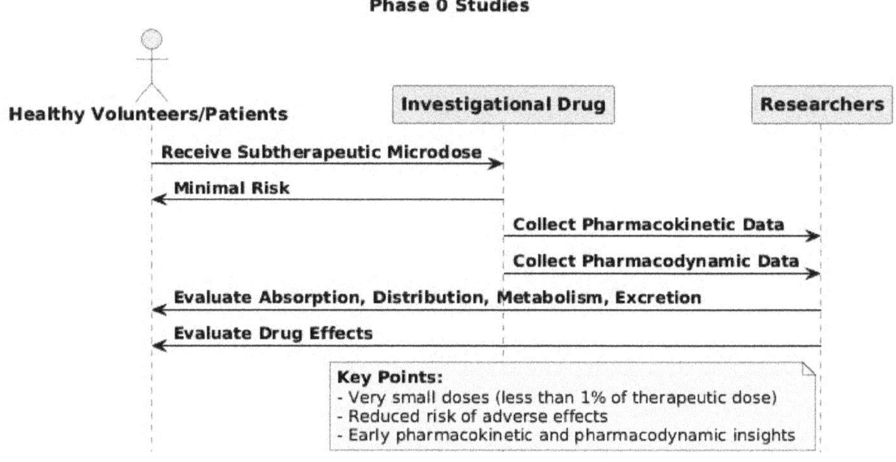

Phase 0 Studies

1.4.2 Participant Selection and Dosage

Phase 0 studies involve a very small number of participants, typically **10 to 15 individuals**. The participants are usually **healthy volunteers**, although in some cases, patients with the disease being studied may be included, especially in the context of **oncology** or other severe conditions where rapid results are needed. The doses administered in these studies are extremely low—generally **1% or less** of the dose expected to have a therapeutic effect. This is why the term **microdosing** is often used in relation to Phase 0 studies.

The goal is not to observe therapeutic effects but to assess how the drug behaves in the human body at very low doses. **Pharmacokinetic parameters,** such as **absorption rates, distribution in tissues, metabolism, and excretion,** are measured using **sensitive analytical techniques** like **liquid chromatography-tandem mass spectrometry (LC-MS/MS)**, which can detect very low concentrations of the drug in the body.

1.4.3 Advantages of Phase 0 Studies

One of the key advantages of **Phase 0 studies** is that they allow researchers to **eliminate ineffective drugs** early in the development process, saving time and resources. By providing early data on a drug's **pharmacokinetics** and **pharmacodynamics**, Phase 0 studies can help identify potential issues that might arise in later phases of clinical trials.

For instance, if a drug has poor bioavailability or is rapidly metabolized and excreted, it may not be suitable for further development, and the company can focus its resources on other drug candidates.

Phase 0 studies are particularly beneficial in **oncology**, where traditional drug development can be long and complex. For example, in a Phase 0 study of a new cancer drug, researchers might administer a microdose to patients with advanced cancer to determine whether the drug reaches the tumor site in sufficient concentrations. If the drug fails to reach the tumor, the company can reconsider its approach before investing in larger and more expensive trials.

Another advantage of Phase 0 studies is the **reduced regulatory burden**. Since the doses are so small, the safety risks are minimal, and the **regulatory requirements** are less stringent than for traditional clinical trials. This allows companies to begin testing their drugs in humans earlier and with fewer administrative delays.

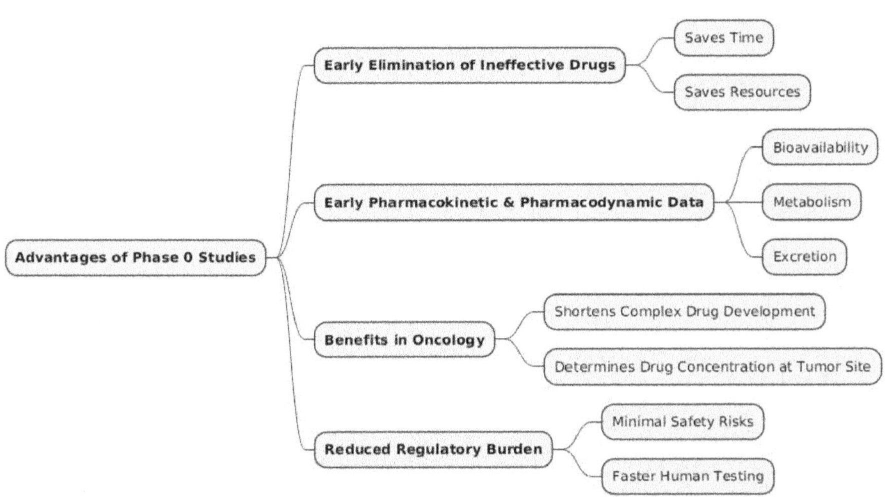

Advantages of Phase 0 Studies

1.4.4 Limitations of Phase 0 Studies

Despite their advantages, **Phase 0 studies** have certain limitations. Since the doses administered are far below therapeutic levels, these studies do not provide information about the drug's **safety** or **efficacy** at higher doses. For example, while a Phase 0 study might show that a drug is well absorbed and distributed in the body, it cannot predict whether the drug will cause side effects at therapeutic doses or whether it will effectively treat the targeted disease.

Another limitation is that the **microdoses** used in Phase 0 studies may not fully represent how the drug behaves at higher doses. In some cases, drugs may exhibit **non-linear pharmacokinetics**, meaning that their behavior changes significantly at higher concentrations. This can limit the usefulness of Phase 0 data in predicting how the drug will perform in later-phase trials.

Additionally, **Phase 0 studies** are not suitable for all drugs. They are most commonly used in **oncology** and for drugs that target severe conditions where time is of the essence. For other types of drugs, where the therapeutic window is wider or where traditional early-phase trials are feasible, Phase 0 studies may not provide enough added value to justify their use.

Limitation	Description
Lack of Safety and Efficacy Data	Due to the very low (subtherapeutic) doses used, Phase 0 studies do not provide information on drug safety or efficacy at therapeutic levels.
Non-Linear Pharmacokinetics	Microdoses may not fully represent the drug's behavior at higher doses, particularly if the drug exhibits non-linear pharmacokinetics, limiting predictive value for later trials.
Limited Application	Phase 0 studies are mainly useful for oncology and other severe conditions, but may not add significant value for drugs where traditional early-phase trials are feasible.
Unsuitability for All Drug Types	Not all drugs are appropriate for Phase 0 studies, especially those with wider therapeutic windows where higher doses need to be evaluated early on.

Limitations of Phase 0 Studies

1.4.5 Regulatory and Ethical Considerations

Although **Phase 0 studies** involve very low doses and minimal risk to participants, they are still subject to **regulatory oversight**. In the United States, Phase 0 studies must comply with **FDA regulations** and **Good Clinical Practice (GCP)** guidelines. The **European Medicines Agency (EMA)** has similar requirements in Europe. The **ethical considerations** for Phase 0 studies are also critical, particularly when patients with severe diseases are involved. Participants must provide **informed consent**, and they must be made fully aware that the doses being administered are not expected to provide therapeutic benefits.

In many cases, the **Institutional Review Board (IRB)** or **Ethics Committee** overseeing the study will require additional safeguards to ensure that participants are not exposed to unnecessary risks, even if the doses are extremely low. For example, in Phase 0 studies involving cancer patients, the ethical committee may require ongoing monitoring to ensure that the disease does not progress rapidly while the patients are on the study.

Phase 0 studies offer a valuable tool in the early stages of drug development, providing critical data about a drug's pharmacokinetics and pharmacodynamics at very low doses. While they do not replace traditional **Phase I** studies in terms of assessing safety and efficacy, they allow researchers to make more informed decisions about which drug candidates should proceed to further testing. Although they have limitations, particularly in predicting drug behavior at therapeutic doses, their ability to provide early insights while minimizing risk makes them an essential part of modern clinical research, particularly in areas like **oncology**.

1.5 Phase I Studies

Phase I studies mark the first time that a new drug is tested in humans, primarily to evaluate its **safety, tolerability,** and **pharmacokinetics** (PK). These studies are essential for determining the appropriate **dose range** and identifying potential **side effects** of the investigational drug. Unlike Phase 0 studies, which involve microdosing, **Phase I trials** typically test the drug at therapeutic doses to understand how the body handles the drug. The participants in these studies are usually **healthy volunteers**, although in some cases, such as in **oncology** studies, patients with the disease being targeted may be included.

Phase I studies are generally divided into several subtypes based on the specific goals of the trial, including **single ascending dose (SAD)** studies, **multiple ascending dose (MAD)** studies, **dose escalation, food effect studies, drug-drug interaction studies**, and the exploration of **pharmacokinetic endpoints**. Each of these designs plays a key role in providing early information about the drug's performance.

1.5.1 Single Ascending Dose (SAD) Studies

Single ascending dose (SAD) studies are the first type of trial conducted in **Phase I**. In these studies, a small group of participants is given a single dose of the investigational drug. If no serious adverse events occur, a new group of participants is administered a higher dose. This process continues until the **maximum tolerated dose (MTD)** is reached, where the drug starts to produce **unacceptable side effects.**

For example, in a SAD study for a new anti-inflammatory drug, the first cohort of **8 to 12 participants** might receive a dose of **50 mg**, followed by a second cohort receiving **100 mg**, and so on. Throughout the process, participants are closely monitored for adverse reactions, and their **vital signs**, **blood chemistry**, and **urine output** are regularly measured. In some cases, the dose escalation may stop earlier if the drug shows signs of **toxicity** at lower doses.

1.5.2 Multiple Ascending Dose (MAD) Studies

Multiple ascending dose (MAD) studies are conducted after SAD studies and involve administering the investigational drug to participants over several days or weeks. These studies help researchers understand how the drug behaves with **repeated dosing**, which is critical for drugs intended for **chronic conditions** such as diabetes or hypertension.

In MAD studies, participants receive a fixed dose of the drug for a specified period, and the dosage is increased for each new group. For instance, in a MAD study for a cholesterol-lowering drug, the first group might receive **50 mg once daily** for **7 days**, while the next group receives **100 mg once daily** for the same duration. This design helps to identify **cumulative side effects** and determine whether the drug **accumulates in the body** over time, which is particularly important for drugs with longer half-lives.

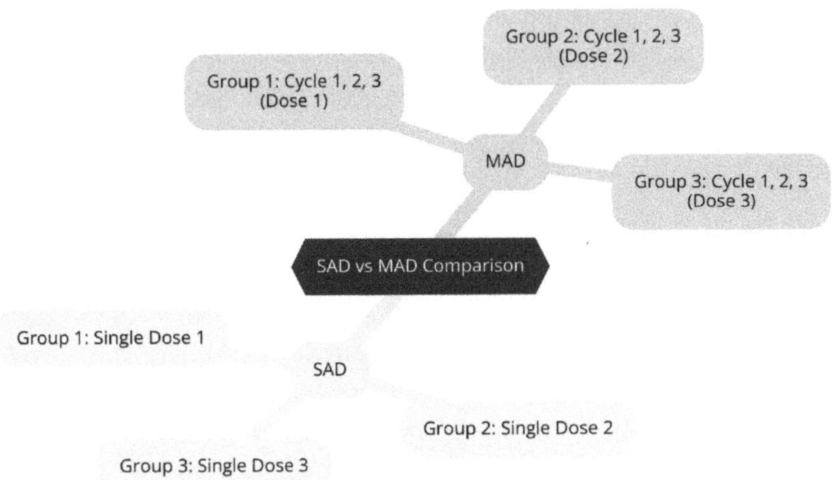

Diagram illustrating the comparison between Single Ascending Dose (SAD) and Multiple Ascending Dose (MAD) studies

1.5.3 Dose Escalation

Dose escalation is a fundamental component of both SAD and MAD studies. The aim is to determine the **optimal dose** that provides the desired therapeutic effect while minimizing the risk of adverse effects. In dose-escalation studies, researchers use a variety of methods to increase the dose in a safe and controlled manner.

One common approach is the **3+3 design**, where three participants are given a certain dose. If none of them experience dose-limiting toxicity (DLT), the dose is increased for the next group of participants. If one participant experiences a DLT, an additional three participants are enrolled at the same dose level. If two or more participants experience a DLT, the dose escalation is stopped, and the previous dose is considered the **maximum tolerated dose (MTD)**.

For example, in cancer research, dose escalation might involve increasing the dose of a chemotherapeutic agent by **25% increments** until the MTD is reached. The goal is to find the highest dose that can be safely administered without causing severe **toxicity**.

1.5.4 Methods in Phase I Studies

The methods used in **Phase I studies** are designed to ensure that the drug's effects are thoroughly evaluated in a safe and ethical manner. These studies are typically conducted in a **clinical research unit (CRU)**, where participants can be closely monitored by medical professionals.

Data collection in Phase I studies includes measurements of **vital signs** (e.g., heart rate, blood pressure), **laboratory tests** (e.g., liver function tests, kidney function tests), and **pharmacokinetic sampling** (e.g., blood and urine samples to measure drug concentrations). The study may also include **electrocardiograms (ECGs)** to monitor heart function and other specialized assessments depending on the drug's mechanism of action.

Blinding and **randomization** are often used to minimize bias, although not all Phase I studies are blinded. In some cases, an **open-label design** is used, especially when the primary focus is on safety rather than efficacy.

1.5.5 Food Effect Studies

Food effect studies are a critical part of Phase I, as they help determine how the presence of food affects the drug's absorption and bioavailability. Many drugs exhibit differences in their **pharmacokinetic profiles** depending on whether they are taken with or without food.

For example, in a food effect study, participants might be given a **single dose** of the drug after fasting overnight, followed by a second dose taken after consuming a standardized meal. The differences in **Cmax** (maximum concentration of the drug in the blood) and **AUC** (area under the curve, which represents the overall drug exposure) are then compared. In some cases, food may increase or decrease drug absorption, which will inform recommendations on whether the drug should be taken with meals.

A drug that shows a **40% increase in AUC** when taken with food might require specific dosing instructions to avoid overdosing or underdosing.

1.5.6 Drug-Drug Interaction Studies

Phase I studies also include **drug-drug interaction (DDI) studies**, which are essential for understanding how the investigational drug interacts with other commonly used medications. These studies are especially important for drugs that are metabolized by the **cytochrome P450 (CYP)** enzymes in the liver, as many drugs can inhibit or induce these enzymes, leading to altered drug levels.

For instance, a drug that is primarily metabolized by **CYP3A4** may interact with medications such as **ketoconazole**, a potent **CYP3A4 inhibitor**, leading to increased drug levels and a higher risk of toxicity. Conversely, a drug may be metabolized more quickly when co-administered with a **CYP3A4 inducer** like **rifampin**, resulting in reduced efficacy. DDI studies help establish guidelines for **co-administration** of drugs and provide safety information for physicians and patients.

1.5.7 Pharmacokinetic (PK) Endpoints

In **Phase I studies, pharmacokinetic (PK) endpoints** are among the most important measurements. PK endpoints provide insights into how the drug is processed by the body, which is critical for determining the appropriate dosage and frequency of administration.

The key PK endpoints include:

- **Cmax**: The maximum concentration of the drug in the blood.
- **Tmax**: The time it takes to reach Cmax.
- **AUC**: The total exposure to the drug over time.
- **Half-life (t½)**: The time it takes for the concentration of the drug to decrease by half in the bloodstream.
- **Clearance (CL)**: The rate at which the drug is eliminated from the body.
- **Volume of distribution (Vd)**: A measure of how extensively the drug is distributed throughout the body's tissues.

For example, a drug with a **half-life of 8 hours** may require dosing every **12 hours** to maintain therapeutic levels, whereas a drug with a **half-life of 24 hours** might only need to be dosed once daily. Understanding these PK parameters is essential for optimizing the dosing regimen and ensuring that the drug reaches the desired therapeutic effect without causing toxicity.

Phase I studies are the foundation of clinical drug development, providing critical data on the drug's **safety, tolerability**, and **pharmacokinetics**. By conducting **SAD, MAD, dose escalation, food effect, drug-drug interaction**, and PK endpoint studies, researchers can gather the necessary information to move forward with larger, more complex trials in **Phase II**. These early trials ensure that the drug can be safely administered to humans while identifying any potential risks or interactions that could affect its overall success.

1.6 Phase II Studies (Proof of Concept or Principle Studies to Establish Efficacy)

Phase II studies play a pivotal role in drug development as they are designed to evaluate the **efficacy** of an investigational drug for the first time in patients who have the target condition. These studies are commonly referred to as **proof of concept** or **proof of principle** studies, as they aim to establish whether the drug produces the intended therapeutic effect. **Phase II trials** also continue to assess the drug's **safety profile**, though the primary focus is on demonstrating **efficacy**. Typically, these studies involve a larger number of participants than Phase I studies, with **100 to 300 patients**, depending on the condition being treated.

The results of Phase II studies are crucial in determining whether the drug should proceed to **Phase III trials**, which involve even larger patient populations and longer treatment periods. If Phase II results show promising efficacy and acceptable safety, the drug has the potential to move forward in the clinical development process.

1.6.1 Objectives of Phase II Studies

The primary objective of **Phase II studies** is to determine whether the investigational drug is effective in treating the target condition. The study design usually involves comparing the **active drug** to a **placebo** or, in some cases, an **active comparator** (another drug that is already approved for the same condition). By comparing the drug's performance against a placebo or another treatment, researchers can assess its **therapeutic potential**.

For example, in a Phase II study for a new drug to treat **type 2 diabetes**, the primary objective might be to evaluate how well the drug reduces **HbA1c levels** (a marker of blood sugar control) over a period of **12 to 24 weeks**. Secondary objectives might include assessing the drug's impact on **fasting blood glucose, body weight**, or **lipid levels**.

In addition to efficacy, **Phase II trials** continue to monitor the drug's **safety profile**, focusing on identifying any adverse effects that may occur when the drug is administered over a longer period or to a larger number of patients. Safety data from Phase II studies help inform dosing recommendations and provide insights into potential **risk-benefit** ratios.

1.6.2 Study Design in Phase II Trials

Phase II trials are usually designed as **randomized controlled trials (RCTs)**, where patients are randomly assigned to receive the investigational drug, a placebo, or an active comparator. This design helps ensure that the results are objective and that differences in outcomes can be attributed to the drug rather than other factors. **Blinding** is often used, meaning that neither the participants nor the researchers know which treatment is being administered, further reducing bias.

The number of participants in a Phase II trial depends on the condition being studied. For **rare diseases**, Phase II studies may involve as few as **50 to 100 patients**, while studies for more common conditions like hypertension or diabetes may include **200 to 300 patients**. The duration of the trial also varies, with most Phase II studies lasting between **several months to a year**, depending on the nature of the disease and the endpoints being measured.

1.6.3 Dose Selection and Optimization

Another key aspect of **Phase II studies** is determining the **optimal dose** of the investigational drug. During **Phase I**, researchers typically identify a **range of safe doses**, but Phase II studies are needed to confirm which dose is most effective. **Dose-ranging studies** are common in Phase II, where different groups of participants receive different doses of the drug to identify the dose that provides the best balance between **efficacy** and **tolerability**.

For example, in a Phase II study for a new **antidepressant**, participants might be assigned to receive **50 mg**, **100 mg**, or **150 mg** of the drug daily. Researchers would then compare the **response rates** (e.g., improvement in depression scores) across these dose groups to determine which dose offers the most benefit with the fewest side effects. The results of these dose-ranging studies are critical for informing the design of **Phase III trials** and for developing dosing guidelines that will be used if the drug is approved.

1.6.4 Proof of Concept (PoC) Studies

Proof of Concept (PoC) studies are a subtype of **Phase II trials** that aim to provide early evidence that the investigational drug works as intended. PoC studies are usually conducted with a smaller number of participants and are designed to answer a specific question about the drug's mechanism of action or its ability to impact a particular outcome.

For instance, in a PoC study for a new **immunotherapy** drug for cancer, researchers might focus on whether the drug can stimulate the immune system to attack tumor cells. The study might measure specific **biomarkers**, such as the activation of certain **immune cells**, or look for signs of tumor shrinkage. If the PoC study shows positive results, it provides a strong rationale for conducting larger Phase IIb or **Phase III trials** to confirm these findings in a broader patient population.

1.6.5 Phase IIa and Phase IIb Studies

Phase II studies are often divided into two sub-phases: **Phase IIa** and **Phase IIb**.

- **Phase IIa studies** are typically smaller and are focused on **exploring dosing regimens** and gathering early data on efficacy. These studies are more exploratory in nature and are designed to help refine the drug's dosing strategy.

- **Phase IIb studies** are larger and more focused on confirming the drug's **efficacy** in a well-defined patient population. These studies are often referred to as **pivotal trials**, as they provide the key data needed to move the drug into **Phase III**.

For example, in the development of a new **asthma medication**, a **Phase IIa study** might explore the impact of different dosing regimens (e.g., once daily vs. twice daily), while a **Phase IIb study** would focus on confirming whether the selected dose improves **lung function** (e.g., measured by **FEV1** – forced expiratory volume) in a larger group of patients.

1.6.6 Safety Monitoring and Adverse Events

Although the primary focus of **Phase II studies** is on efficacy, safety continues to be a critical consideration. Participants in Phase II trials are closely monitored for **adverse events (AEs)**, particularly those that were not detected in the smaller Phase I studies. Researchers also keep track of **serious adverse events (SAEs)**, which could lead to the trial being halted if the risks outweigh the potential benefits.

For example, in a Phase II trial for a new **cardiovascular drug**, patients might be monitored for changes in **blood pressure, heart rate**, and **electrocardiogram (ECG)** readings to detect any early signs of **cardiotoxicity**. If any participants experience significant side effects, such as **arrhythmias** or **heart failure**, the study might be paused or terminated, depending on the severity and frequency of the adverse events.

1.6.7 Statistical Considerations in Phase II Studies

The results of **Phase II studies** are analyzed using various **statistical methods** to determine whether the investigational drug has a statistically significant effect compared to the placebo or comparator. Common statistical endpoints include **p-values** and **confidence intervals**, which help researchers assess whether the observed effects are likely to be real or due to chance.

For instance, in a Phase II study for a new **antiviral drug**, researchers might use a **p-value of less than 0.05** to determine whether the reduction in **viral load** observed in the treatment group is statistically significant compared to the placebo group. Confidence intervals might be used to estimate the precision of the drug's effect, such as a **95% confidence interval** for the percentage reduction in viral load.

Phase II studies are a critical step in drug development, providing the first evidence that a new drug can be effective in treating the target condition. By carefully evaluating efficacy, dose response, and safety, these studies lay the foundation for **Phase III trials**, which will ultimately determine whether the drug can be approved for use in clinical practice. The success of a drug in **Phase II** often determines whether it will proceed to the later stages of development, making these studies a key milestone in the clinical trial process.

1.7 Phase III Studies (Multi-Ethnicity, Global Clinical Trial, Registration Studies)

Phase III studies represent a critical stage in the drug development process, often referred to as **pivotal trials** or **registration studies**. These large-scale trials are designed to confirm the **efficacy** and **safety** of a drug in a broad and diverse population, providing the data needed for **regulatory approval**. Unlike earlier phases, which focus on safety and preliminary efficacy in smaller groups of patients, Phase III trials involve **thousands of participants** and are conducted across multiple clinical sites, often spanning several countries. These trials provide the robust data required to support the marketing and use of the drug in the general population.

Phase III studies are particularly important because they are often the final step before a drug is submitted for approval to regulatory authorities such as the **Food and Drug Administration (FDA)**, **European Medicines Agency (EMA)**, and other global regulatory bodies. The success of a drug in Phase III trials largely determines whether it will receive approval for widespread clinical use.

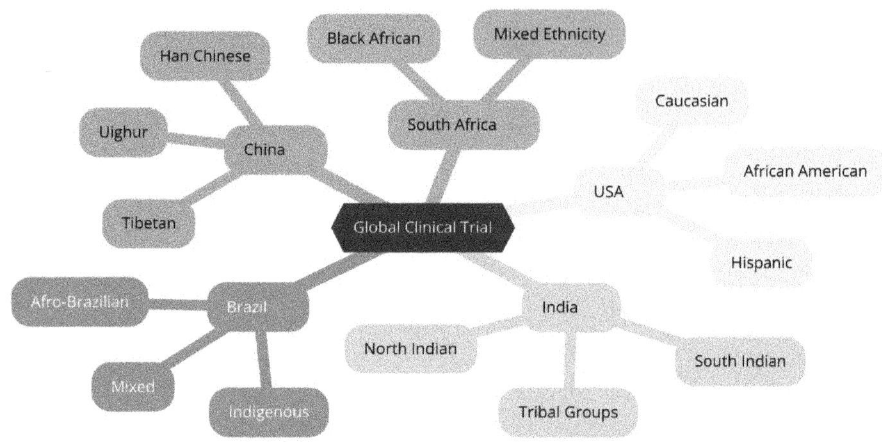

A visual representation of a global clinical trial with different countries, showing the multi-ethnic populations involved in the process.

1.7.1 Multi-Ethnicity in Phase III Trials

One of the key features of **Phase III trials** is the inclusion of participants from diverse **ethnic** and **demographic** backgrounds. This is critical because drugs can sometimes behave differently in different populations due to factors such as **genetic variations, dietary habits, environmental factors,** and **cultural practices.** For instance, certain **genetic polymorphisms** that affect drug metabolism are more common in specific ethnic groups, which can influence the drug's efficacy or safety profile in those populations.

Including participants from various ethnicities helps ensure that the drug will be effective and safe across a broad range of patients once it is approved. For example, a **hypertension drug** might have different effects in **Caucasian, African-American,** and **Asian** populations due to differences in genetic expression of certain enzymes involved in blood pressure regulation. By including participants from these diverse groups in Phase III trials, researchers can assess whether the drug's efficacy and safety are consistent across different ethnicities.

In some cases, regulatory agencies like the **FDA** or **EMA** may require that Phase III trials specifically include patients from certain populations to ensure that the drug is appropriate for **multi-ethnic use.** For instance, if a drug is being developed for **diabetes**, which has a high prevalence in **South Asian** and **Hispanic** populations, the trial might specifically recruit participants from these groups to gather data on how the drug performs in these populations.

1.7.2 Global Clinical Trials

Phase III studies are often conducted as **global clinical trials**, involving multiple countries and regions around the world. Global trials help ensure that the data collected is representative of the **global patient population**, which is particularly important for diseases that affect people across different geographic regions. Conducting trials in diverse regions also allows for the collection of data on how factors like **climate, nutrition**, and **local healthcare practices** might impact the drug's efficacy and safety.

Global clinical trials are logistically complex, as they involve coordinating multiple clinical sites across different countries. This requires careful planning and adherence to **Good Clinical Practice (GCP)** guidelines to ensure that the study is conducted consistently across all locations. For example, a Phase III trial for a new **oncology drug** might involve clinical sites in **North America, Europe, Asia**, and **Africa**, with each site following the same study protocol and data collection methods. This global approach provides a more comprehensive understanding of how the drug performs in different environments and healthcare systems.

Regulatory harmonization efforts, such as those led by the **International Council for Harmonisation of Technical Requirements for Pharmaceuticals for Human Use (ICH)**, have facilitated the conduct of global clinical trials by standardizing many aspects of trial design, data collection, and reporting. This allows data from global trials to be used for regulatory submissions in multiple countries, reducing the time and cost of drug development.

1.7.3 Registration Studies

Registration studies are another term for Phase III trials because the data collected from these studies are submitted to regulatory authorities as part of the **New Drug Application (NDA)** or **Marketing Authorization Application (MAA)** process. These studies are the final step before a drug can be approved for marketing and use in the general population. Regulatory agencies like the **FDA, EMA**, and others rely heavily on the results of Phase III trials to determine whether a drug is safe and effective enough to be approved for public use.

The primary endpoints of registration studies are typically focused on **clinical outcomes**, such as improvements in **disease symptoms, survival rates**, or **quality of life**. For instance, in a Phase III trial for a new **antiviral**

medication, the primary endpoint might be the reduction in **viral load** over a period of **12 months**, while secondary endpoints could include measures such as **hospitalization rates** or **adverse event rates.**

Because these trials are conducted on such a large scale, they provide the most reliable data on the drug's **risk-benefit profile.** For example, a Phase III trial involving **5,000 patients** might show that the drug reduces the risk of **stroke** in **80%** of patients compared to a **control group**, while also identifying **rare but serious adverse effects** that were not apparent in earlier trials. This comprehensive data set is critical for regulatory decision-making.

1.7.4 Safety Monitoring and Adverse Event Reporting

Safety remains a top priority during Phase III trials. As more patients are exposed to the drug over a longer period, **adverse events (AEs)** and **serious adverse events (SAEs)** are closely monitored and reported to regulatory authorities. Phase III trials often reveal **rare side effects** that were not detected in smaller Phase I or II studies.

For example, in a Phase III trial for a new **cardiovascular drug**, participants may be monitored for potential **heart-related side effects**, such as **arrhythmias** or **myocardial infarctions**. If a certain percentage of participants experience a severe side effect, the trial may be halted, or the dosing regimen may be adjusted to minimize the risk.

In addition to patient monitoring, Phase III trials often include **Data Safety Monitoring Boards (DSMBs)**, which are independent committees responsible for reviewing safety data during the trial. The DSMB can recommend stopping the trial early if the drug is found to be unsafe or, conversely, if the drug shows overwhelming efficacy, which could justify early approval.

1.7.5 Statistical Analysis and Regulatory Approval

The statistical analysis of **Phase III data** is critical in determining whether the drug meets its **efficacy endpoints** and is safe enough to move forward for regulatory approval. Commonly used statistical measures include **p-values, confidence intervals**, and **hazard ratios**, which help quantify the drug's effect compared to placebo or an active comparator.

For example, a Phase III trial for a new **cancer drug** might show a **p-value of less than 0.01**, indicating a statistically significant reduction in **tumor size** compared to the control group. Confidence intervals provide an estimate of the precision of this effect, while **hazard ratios** can be used to measure the reduction in the risk of disease progression.

The results of Phase III trials are compiled into comprehensive reports that form the basis of the **New Drug Application (NDA)** or **Biologics License Application (BLA)** submitted to regulatory authorities. If the drug meets the required safety and efficacy standards, it can receive **regulatory approval** and be marketed for general use.

1.8 Phase IV Studies (Post Marketing Studies; PSUR)

Phase IV studies, also referred to as **post-marketing surveillance studies**, are critical in the lifecycle of a drug. These studies occur after a drug has been approved by regulatory authorities and is available for use in the general population. The primary purpose of these studies is to gather additional information on the **long-term effectiveness** and **safety profile** of the drug. While clinical trials during the pre-marketing phases (Phase I, II, III) involve relatively small, controlled groups of patients, **Phase IV studies** involve large numbers of patients in real-world settings. These studies may involve **thousands** or even **millions** of patients, depending on the drug and its intended use.

One of the significant aspects of **Phase IV studies** is the detection of **rare adverse effects** that may not have been identified during earlier phases. For instance, a drug might cause an adverse reaction in **1 out of 10,000 patients**, which is not easily detectable in a smaller clinical trial. The broader patient population during this phase helps in identifying such **low-incidence events**. An example of this is the **COX-2 inhibitors**, which, after approval, were found to increase the risk of **cardiovascular events** in a small subset of the population, leading to market withdrawal of some drugs.

Post-Marketing Studies can also help in evaluating the **long-term efficacy** of the drug in diverse populations, as clinical trials typically involve a controlled environment with specific inclusion and exclusion criteria. In real-world settings, patients may have **comorbid conditions** or be taking **concomitant medications**, which can influence how the drug behaves. Therefore, data gathered during this phase is vital for understanding the drug's performance under varying conditions.

In terms of **regulatory requirements**, Periodic Safety Update Reports **(PSUR)** play a crucial role. The **PSUR** is a formal document required by many regulatory bodies, including the **European Medicines Agency (EMA)**, the **US Food and Drug Administration (FDA)**, and others. The report must be submitted at regular intervals (e.g., **every 6 months for the first two years** after approval, then **annually**) to ensure continued safety and to reassess the risk-benefit balance of the drug. A **PSUR** typically includes information on new or ongoing **adverse drug reactions (ADRs)**, **off-label use**, and any emerging **safety concerns**. If significant safety concerns are identified, the regulatory authorities may recommend modifications such as **labeling changes**, **restricted use**, or, in extreme cases, **market withdrawal**.

In addition to safety and efficacy, **Phase IV studies** may focus on gathering data on **cost-effectiveness**, **quality of life outcomes**, and **patient adherence** to medication. These aspects are crucial for healthcare providers, policymakers, and insurers in making informed decisions about drug use in broader healthcare systems.

An example of a successful **Phase IV study** can be seen in the case of **atorvastatin (Lipitor)**, a widely prescribed **statin** used to manage cholesterol levels. After the drug was marketed, **Phase IV studies** demonstrated its effectiveness in reducing the risk of heart disease in a larger, more diverse population than was originally studied, further solidifying its role in clinical practice. These studies also revealed minimal long-term safety concerns, helping to build confidence in the drug's widespread use.

Phase IV studies are essential to fully understand a drug's safety and efficacy in the general population. They provide valuable information on **rare adverse events**, the **real-world performance** of the drug, and the overall risk-benefit balance. Through **PSUR** submissions, regulatory bodies continuously monitor the safety of marketed drugs, ensuring that the benefits continue to outweigh the risks for patients in everyday clinical use.

1.9 Clinical Investigation and Evaluation of Medical Devices & IVDs

The **clinical investigation** and **evaluation of medical devices** and **in vitro diagnostics (IVDs)** play an integral role in ensuring that these products are safe, effective, and suitable for their intended use. Unlike pharmaceuticals, **medical devices** range from **simple bandages** to **complex implantable devices** such as **pacemakers** and **joint prostheses**, while **IVDs** include products like **blood glucose meters**, **pregnancy tests**, and **molecular diagnostic tests**. Given this broad range of complexity, regulatory standards and clinical investigations for these products are tailored to assess specific aspects such as **performance**, **safety**, and **usability**.

Clinical investigations for medical devices are typically conducted to confirm their **clinical performance**, which is defined as the device's ability to achieve the intended purpose under normal conditions of use. For example, a **stent** used to prevent arterial blockages must be evaluated in **clinical trials** to ensure that it effectively prevents blockages while minimizing complications such as **thrombosis**. The investigations may involve **several hundred patients**, depending on the type of device and its risk category.

Medical devices are often categorized based on **risk**—with **Class I devices** being low risk (e.g., bandages) and **Class III devices** being high risk (e.g., heart valves). For high-risk devices, **randomized controlled trials (RCTs)** are often required to rigorously evaluate their safety and effectiveness. For lower-risk devices, **observational studies** or **simulated use tests** may suffice.

In vitro diagnostics (IVDs), on the other hand, are evaluated for their ability to provide accurate, reliable, and reproducible results. The **performance characteristics** of IVDs include **sensitivity, specificity, positive predictive value (PPV)**, and **negative predictive value (NPV)**. For example, an IVD used for **COVID-19 testing** needs to demonstrate that it correctly identifies infected individuals (**sensitivity**) and correctly identifies non-infected individuals (**specificity**). The evaluation of these characteristics is typically performed using **large datasets** involving both positive and negative samples to assess the device's accuracy under various conditions.

Regulatory agencies such as the **FDA** and the **European Medicines Agency (EMA)** have set specific guidelines for conducting clinical investigations of medical devices and IVDs. The **Medical Device Regulation (MDR)** in the European Union and the **FDA's 510(k) clearance** pathway in the United States outline the processes for bringing a device to market. These regulatory pathways require robust clinical evidence to demonstrate that the device is safe and effective for its intended use.

One of the challenges in clinical investigations of medical devices and IVDs is that these products often undergo continuous **technological evolution**. Unlike drugs, where the formulation remains largely the same throughout clinical trials, medical devices may be **redesigned or modified** even during trials. For instance, a **new software version** for an implantable **insulin pump** might be released mid-study, potentially affecting performance. This requires continuous monitoring and **post-market surveillance**.

For high-risk devices, **post-market clinical follow-ups (PMCF)** are often mandatory. These studies monitor long-term safety and effectiveness in the general population. For instance, the **Essure device**, a permanent birth control device, underwent extensive PMCF studies after it was approved. The studies revealed **unanticipated adverse events**, leading to its eventual market withdrawal in several countries.

In terms of **numbers**, a typical clinical investigation for a high-risk device may involve **500–1,000 patients**, while evaluations for IVDs may require **thousands of samples** to ensure adequate **statistical power**. The **sample size** is determined based on factors such as the **prevalence** of the condition being tested and the **expected sensitivity and specificity** of the device.

The evaluation of medical devices and IVDs also considers their **usability** and **ergonomics**. Devices like **infusion pumps** or **surgical instruments** must be designed not only to function effectively but also to be safe and intuitive for healthcare professionals to use. **Human factors engineering** plays a significant role in ensuring that devices are user-friendly and minimize the potential for **human error**.

1.10 Key Concepts of Medical Device Clinical Evaluation and Investigation

The **clinical evaluation** and **investigation of medical devices** are critical processes that ensure the safety, performance, and effectiveness of devices before they are used in patients. These evaluations are regulated through stringent frameworks to assess whether the devices meet the necessary standards for medical use. The clinical evaluation typically includes **clinical investigations**, post-market studies, and continuous monitoring. Understanding the **key concepts** behind these evaluations is essential for medical professionals, regulatory bodies, and manufacturers.

A central concept in medical device clinical evaluation is the **risk-based classification** of devices. Devices are categorized into different **classes** based on their risk to patients. In general, **Class I devices** pose minimal risk (e.g., surgical instruments like scalpels), while **Class III devices** represent high risk (e.g., pacemakers and artificial heart valves). This classification impacts the regulatory requirements for clinical evaluations. For instance, high-risk devices often require **randomized controlled trials (RCTs)**, while lower-risk devices might be approved based on observational studies or literature reviews.

Clinical evidence is the cornerstone of any medical device evaluation. Clinical evidence includes data derived from **clinical investigations**, published literature, and clinical experience with the device. For high-risk devices, clinical trials are mandatory to generate direct evidence of safety and effectiveness. An example of a clinical trial for a medical device is an **RCT** evaluating a **drug-eluting stent** to prevent artery blockages. The study would compare the stent with traditional treatments, assessing key outcomes like **restenosis rates** and **adverse events.**

For many devices, an essential concept is the **equivalence principle**. In cases where a device has already been proven safe and effective, newer devices that are **substantially equivalent** to the previous one may be approved with fewer clinical data requirements. For example, a **new version** of an **insulin pump** might not require extensive new trials if it is functionally similar to an earlier model, assuming the clinical performance remains the same. However, this principle is strictly regulated, and equivalence must be proven with robust evidence.

Safety and performance endpoints are crucial in these investigations. Safety endpoints focus on minimizing the risk of harm to patients, such as **adverse device-related events**, infections, or mechanical failures. Performance endpoints, on the other hand, measure the **effectiveness** of the device in achieving its intended purpose. For instance, in a clinical trial for an artificial heart valve, **safety endpoints** might include the rate of **device failure** or **infection**, while **performance endpoints** might measure the success of maintaining proper blood flow and preventing **blood clots.** Both types of endpoints are necessary to comprehensively evaluate the device.

Another important concept is the evaluation of **real-world evidence** (RWE). RWE refers to data collected from everyday clinical settings, outside of the controlled environment of clinical trials. For instance, after a **hip implant** has been marketed, manufacturers might gather RWE by monitoring patients in hospitals and clinics to track **long-term performance** and **complications** like dislocation or implant wear. Regulatory authorities are increasingly relying on RWE to support device approvals and modifications, as it provides valuable insights into how devices perform under **actual use conditions.**

In addition, **biocompatibility** is a key concern, especially for implantable devices. The materials used in medical devices must not provoke an immune response or cause toxicity. For example, **pacemakers** and **orthopedic implants** must undergo rigorous testing to ensure that they do not induce **inflammatory reactions** or **material degradation** over time. Testing for biocompatibility often involves both **in vitro** and **in vivo** studies to simulate the long-term effects of the device inside the human body.

The concept of **post-market surveillance (PMS)** is also vital in the life cycle of a medical device. Once a device is approved and marketed, manufacturers must continue to monitor its performance through **post-market clinical follow-ups (PMCF)**. This is especially important for high-risk devices, as it helps to identify rare or long-term side effects that may not have been apparent during initial clinical trials. For instance, a **cochlear implant** used to restore hearing in patients may show **excellent short-term results**, but **post-market surveillance** might reveal potential complications such as **device malfunction** or adverse interactions with other implanted devices over time.

In the context of regulatory submissions, manufacturers are required to submit a **clinical evaluation report (CER)**, which compiles all clinical data, safety evidence, and performance results. This report serves as the basis for regulatory decision-making. The **European Medical Device Regulation (MDR)** and the **FDA's 510(k) and PMA pathways** set stringent requirements for the content of these reports. They must include a comprehensive analysis of **clinical risks** and benefits, as well as **justifications** for the device's use in the intended patient population.

Lastly, the importance of **ethical considerations** cannot be overlooked. Clinical investigations involving human subjects must adhere to ethical guidelines such as the **Declaration of Helsinki.** Informed consent, patient safety, and ethical trial designs are mandatory to protect participants and ensure the integrity of the clinical evaluation process.

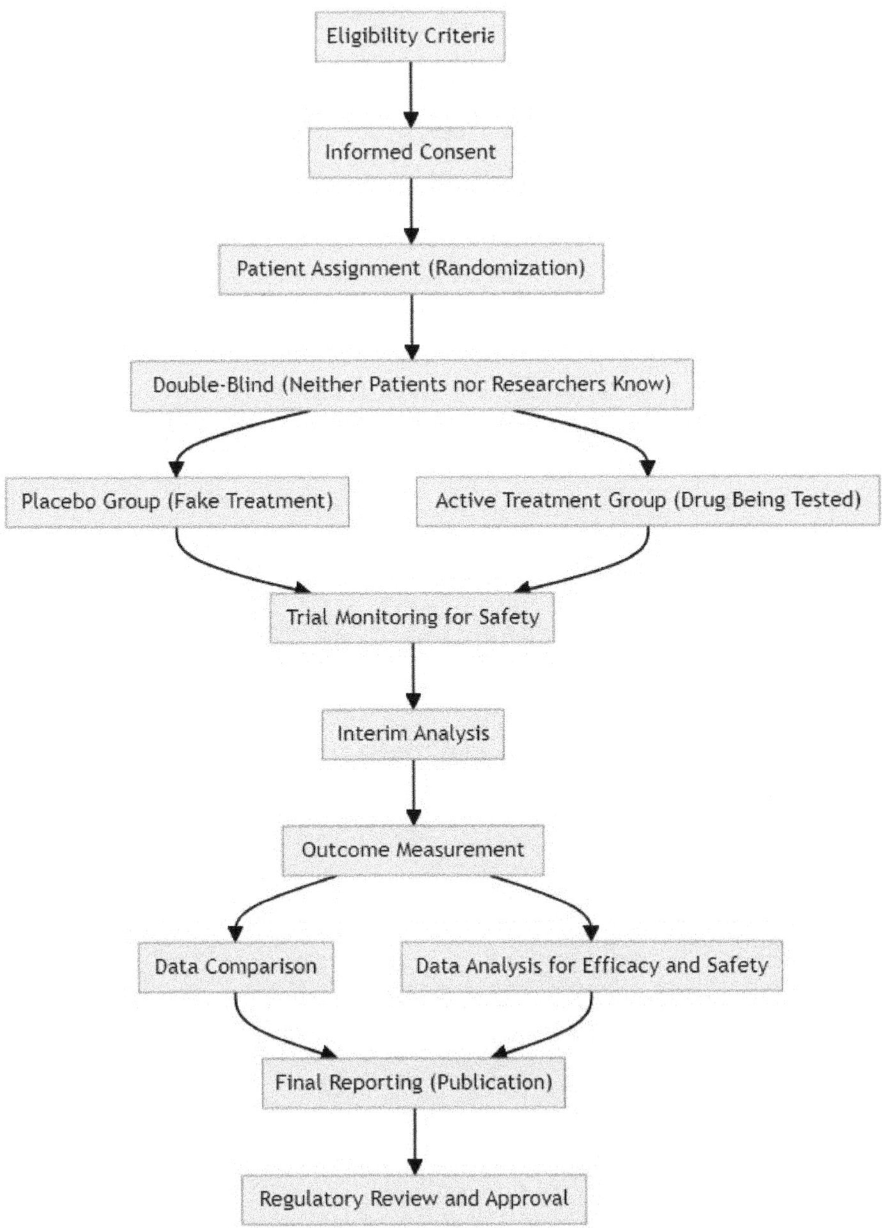

Comprehensive Workflow of Placebo-Controlled Clinical Trials: From Eligibility Screening to Regulatory Approval

CHAPTER TWO

Ethics in Clinical Research

Ethics in clinical research is a key principle and the foundation of the entire drug development process. This chapter discusses the ethical concerns that guide clinical trials, ensuring that human participants receive the highest level of care and respect. Over time, ethical guidelines have changed because of past abuses and scandals, such as the **Tuskegee Syphilis Study** and the **Nuremberg Trials**. These events highlight the need for strict ethical control in research involving humans.

This chapter covers important ethical documents like the **Nuremberg Code**, the **Declaration of Helsinki**, and the **Belmont Report**. These documents focus on key ideas like **informed consent, beneficence,** and **justice**. These principles protect the rights of trial participants and ensure that data collected is honest and valid. Special ethical considerations are also given to vulnerable groups like **children, pregnant women,** and **people with cognitive impairments,** who need extra protection during trials.

A major part of this chapter explains the role of **Institutional Review Boards (IRBs)** or **Ethics Committees (ECs)**. These groups approve and monitor clinical research. They ensure that both international and local ethical standards are followed, which is necessary for the research to remain credible. This chapter explains how ethical principles should be applied at each step of clinical research, from designing the study to reporting the results. It highlights the need for clear communication and responsibility in the global drug development process.

2.1 Historical Perspectives

Nuremberg Code

The Nuremberg Code, established in 1947, was a direct response to the atrocities committed during the Nazi human experiments. It laid the foundation for modern ethical standards in clinical research. The code emphasizes the necessity of voluntary consent, which means participants must be fully informed and agree to participate without any coercion. It also highlights the importance of minimizing harm, ensuring that experiments should not be conducted if there is a priori reason to believe that death or disabling injury will occur. The principles of the Nuremberg Code became a cornerstone for future ethical guidelines, emphasizing the dignity and rights of research subjects.

Thalidomide Study

The Thalidomide tragedy in the late 1950s and early 1960s highlighted the catastrophic consequences of insufficient drug testing and the lack of regulatory oversight. Thalidomide was marketed as a safe sedative for pregnant women but led to severe birth defects in thousands of babies. This disaster prompted stricter regulations and testing requirements for new drugs, leading to the enactment of the Kefauver-Harris Amendment in the United States in 1962. This amendment required drug manufacturers to provide proof of the efficacy and safety of their drugs before approval, significantly strengthening the drug approval process and emphasizing the importance of thorough clinical testing.

Nazi Trials

The Nuremberg Trials, held after World War II, were a series of military tribunals for prominent leaders of Nazi Germany. The Doctors' Trial, one of the twelve trials, specifically prosecuted twenty-three physicians and administrators for their involvement in war crimes and crimes against humanity through inhumane medical experiments. The trials exposed the horrific nature of the experiments conducted on concentration camp prisoners, which included exposing them to extreme conditions, infecting them with diseases, and performing unnecessary surgeries without anesthesia. The trials underscored the need for ethical standards in medical research and contributed to the formulation of the Nuremberg Code.

Tuskegee Syphilis Study

The Tuskegee Syphilis Study, conducted between 1932 and 1972 by the U.S. Public Health Service, is one of the most infamous examples of unethical medical research in history. In this study, 600 African American men, 399 with syphilis and 201 without, were misled and not provided with adequate treatment, even after penicillin became the standard cure for the disease in the 1940s. The participants were told they were receiving free healthcare, but in reality, they were being observed to study the progression of untreated syphilis. This study highlighted severe ethical violations, including lack of informed consent and exploitation of vulnerable populations, leading to significant changes in U.S. law and regulations governing medical research.

The Belmont Report

The Belmont Report, published in 1979, was a response to the ethical failures exemplified by the Tuskegee Syphilis Study. It laid out three fundamental ethical principles for research involving human subjects: respect for persons, beneficence, and justice. Respect for persons involves acknowledging the autonomy of individuals and protecting those with diminished autonomy. Beneficence requires researchers to minimize harm and maximize benefits. Justice ensures that the benefits and burdens of research are distributed fairly. These principles guide the ethical conduct of research and are the basis for federal regulations in the United States, such as the Common Rule, which governs human subjects research.

The Declaration of Helsinki

The Declaration of Helsinki, first adopted by the World Medical Association (WMA) in 1964, provides ethical guidelines for medical research involving human subjects. It builds upon the principles of the Nuremberg Code and addresses issues such as informed consent, the importance of independent review by ethics committees, and the necessity of ensuring that research benefits outweigh risks. The Declaration has undergone several revisions, with the latest update in 2013, reflecting evolving ethical standards and practices. It emphasizes that the well-being of research participants should take precedence over the interests of science and society, underscoring the importance of ethical considerations in medical research.

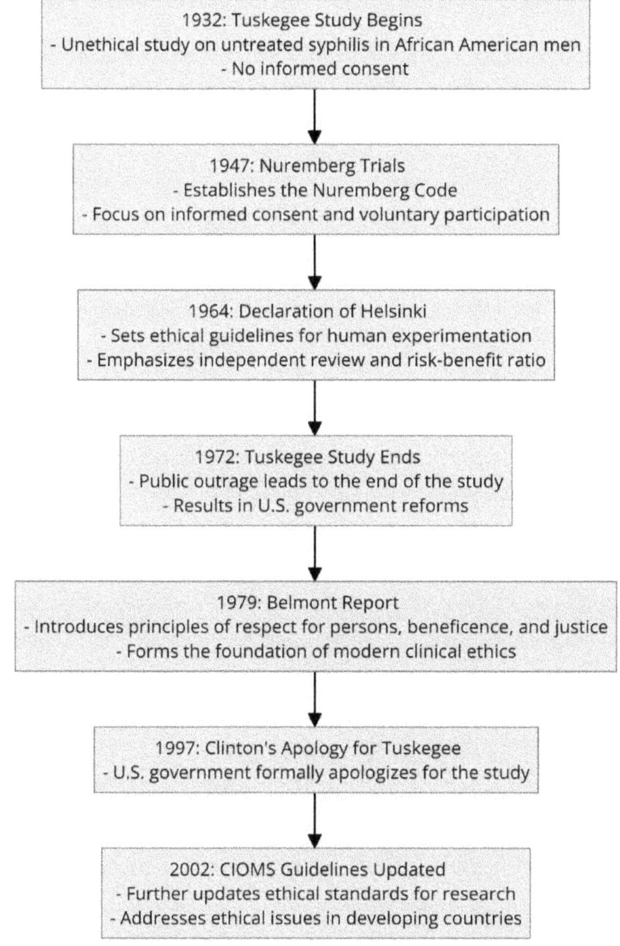

Milestones in Clinical Research Ethics: From the Tuskegee Study to Global Guidelines

2.2 Origin of International Conference on Harmonization - Good Clinical Practice (ICH-GCP) Guidelines

Introduction to ICH-GCP

The International Conference on Harmonization (ICH) was established in 1990 with the primary goal of harmonizing regulatory requirements for pharmaceutical products among Europe, Japan, and the United States. The ICH aimed to ensure that clinical trials are conducted in a consistent manner across different regions, facilitating the global development and approval of new drugs. The Good Clinical Practice (GCP) guidelines, developed by the ICH, provide a unified standard for designing, conducting, recording, and reporting clinical trials. These guidelines ensure that the rights, safety, and well-being of trial participants are protected and that the data generated is credible and accurate.

Historical Context

Before the establishment of the ICH, clinical trial regulations varied significantly between regions, leading to inefficiencies and challenges in the global pharmaceutical industry. Different countries had their own regulatory requirements, which often resulted in duplication of effort and delays in drug development and approval. This lack of harmonization created barriers for the pharmaceutical industry, increasing the time and cost of bringing new drugs to market. The need for a standardized approach to clinical trials became evident as the industry faced growing demands for more efficient drug development processes and enhanced protection for trial participants.

Formation of the ICH

The ICH was formed as a collaborative effort between regulatory authorities and the pharmaceutical industry from Europe, Japan, and the United States. The founding members included the European Medicines Agency (EMA), the United States Food and Drug Administration (FDA), and the Japanese Ministry of Health, Labour, and Welfare (MHLW). The ICH aimed to achieve greater harmonization in the interpretation and application of technical guidelines and requirements for product registration. By bringing together experts from regulatory agencies and the pharmaceutical industry, the ICH sought to address the challenges of divergent regulations and streamline the drug development process.

Development of ICH-GCP Guidelines

The development of the ICH-GCP guidelines was a significant milestone in the history of clinical research. The guidelines were finalized in 1996 and have since become a global standard for conducting clinical trials. The ICH-GCP guidelines outline the responsibilities of sponsors, investigators, and ethics committees, emphasizing the importance of ethical conduct, participant safety, and data integrity. These guidelines are structured to provide comprehensive coverage of all aspects of clinical trials, from planning and initiation to conduct, monitoring, auditing, recording, analysis, and reporting.

Key Principles of ICH-GCP

- **Ethical Conduct:** Clinical trials should be conducted in accordance with ethical principles, including respect for persons, beneficence, and justice, as outlined in the Declaration of Helsinki.
- **Informed Consent:** Participants must provide informed consent, which involves understanding the trial's nature, risks, and benefits and agreeing to participate voluntarily.
- **Protocol Adherence:** Trials must be conducted according to a scientifically and ethically sound protocol, with any deviations documented and justified.
- **Data Integrity:** Accurate and complete data must be recorded and reported, ensuring the credibility of the clinical trial results.
- **Quality Assurance:** Systems with procedures to ensure the quality of every aspect of the trial should be implemented.

Impact of ICH-GCP

The ICH-GCP guidelines have had a profound impact on clinical research worldwide. By providing a unified standard, they have facilitated the global conduct of clinical trials, enabling data from different regions to be compared and combined more easily. This has accelerated the drug development process and improved the efficiency of bringing new treatments to market. The guidelines have also strengthened the protection of trial participants, ensuring that their rights and well-being are prioritized in all clinical research activities. Regulatory authorities across the world now require compliance with ICH-GCP for the approval of new drugs, underscoring the global acceptance and importance of these guidelines.

2.3 The Ethics of Randomized Clinical Trials

Introduction to Randomized Clinical Trials

Randomized Clinical Trials (RCTs) are considered the gold standard in clinical research for evaluating the efficacy and safety of new treatments. In an RCT, participants are randomly assigned to either the treatment group or the control group, which may receive a placebo or standard treatment. This randomization process helps eliminate bias, ensuring that the outcomes can be attributed to the intervention being studied rather than other factors. However, the ethical conduct of RCTs involves several key considerations to ensure that participants' rights, safety, and well-being are protected throughout the study.

Informed Consent

Informed consent is a cornerstone of ethical research, particularly in RCTs. Participants must be fully informed about the nature of the trial, including its purpose, procedures, risks, and potential benefits. They should understand that they may be randomly assigned to different groups and that they have the right to withdraw from the study at any time without any penalty. The informed consent process must be thorough and transparent, ensuring that participants have all the information they need to make an informed decision about their participation.

Balancing Risks and Benefits

One of the primary ethical concerns in RCTs is the balance between risks and benefits. Researchers must ensure that the potential benefits of the study justify any risks to the participants. This involves conducting a thorough risk assessment and implementing measures to minimize potential harms. Ethical review boards or institutional review boards (IRBs) play a crucial role in evaluating the risk-benefit ratio of proposed trials to ensure that participants are not exposed to unnecessary risks.

Equipoise

Equipoise is the ethical principle that there must be genuine uncertainty within the medical community about the comparative therapeutic merits of each arm in a clinical trial. This means that researchers must believe that the new treatment being tested is potentially as effective as the standard treatment or placebo. Equipoise is essential for justifying the random assignment of participants to different treatment groups, as it ensures that no participant is knowingly given an inferior treatment.

Use of Placebos

The use of placebos in RCTs can raise ethical concerns, particularly when effective treatments are available. Placebos are ethically acceptable when no current proven intervention exists, and withholding treatment does not pose a significant risk to participants. In cases where effective treatments are available, placebo use must be carefully justified, and participants should be fully informed about the possibility of receiving a placebo. The ethical use of placebos requires careful consideration to avoid deceiving participants or denying them necessary treatment.

Vulnerable Populations

RCTs often involve vulnerable populations, such as children, pregnant women, or individuals with cognitive impairments. Special ethical considerations must be taken to protect these groups. This includes obtaining consent from legally authorized representatives when participants cannot provide informed consent themselves and ensuring that the research addresses important health issues relevant to these populations. Additional safeguards and ethical oversight are necessary to prevent exploitation and ensure that the research is conducted with the utmost respect for participants' rights and well-being.

Privacy and Confidentiality

Maintaining the privacy and confidentiality of participants is crucial in RCTs. Researchers must implement robust data protection measures to ensure that participants' personal information is securely stored and only accessible to authorized personnel. Participants should be informed about how their data will be used, who will have access to it, and the measures in place to protect their privacy. Ensuring confidentiality helps build trust between researchers and participants and promotes ethical research practices.

2.4 The Role of Placebo in Clinical Trials

Introduction to Placebo Use

A placebo is a substance or treatment with no therapeutic effect, commonly used as a control in clinical trials. Placebos are crucial in determining the efficacy of new treatments by providing a baseline against which the active treatment can be compared. The use of placebos helps to eliminate bias and allows researchers to attribute observed effects specifically to the treatment being tested. However, the ethical use of placebos requires careful consideration, particularly when effective treatments are already available.

Scientific Justification for Placebo Use

The primary scientific justification for using placebos in clinical trials is to provide a control that helps isolate the effect of the investigational treatment. In a placebo-controlled trial, participants are randomly assigned to receive either the experimental treatment or the placebo. This randomization helps ensure that any differences observed between the groups can be attributed to the treatment rather than external factors. Placebos are particularly valuable in early-phase trials, where the goal is to establish the treatment's efficacy and safety profile.

Ethical Considerations

The use of placebos in clinical trials raises significant ethical issues. The key ethical consideration is the principle of "do no harm." Researchers must ensure that participants are not exposed to unnecessary risks, and the use of a placebo must be scientifically and ethically justified. Ethical guidelines, such as those provided by the Declaration of Helsinki, stipulate that placebos can be used when no current proven intervention exists, and withholding treatment does not pose a significant risk to participants.

Informed Consent

Informed consent is crucial when using placebos in clinical trials. Participants must be fully informed about the possibility of receiving a placebo instead of the active treatment. This includes explaining the purpose of the placebo, the probability of being assigned to the placebo group, and the potential risks and benefits. Ensuring that participants understand and voluntarily consent to this aspect of the trial is essential for ethical compliance.

Placebo in the Absence of Effective Treatments

Placebo use is generally considered ethically acceptable when there are no existing effective treatments for the condition being studied. In such cases, the placebo serves as a baseline to evaluate the new treatment's effectiveness. For example, in trials for new pain medications or psychiatric treatments, placebos help distinguish the actual therapeutic effect of the drug from the psychological benefit that patients might experience simply from believing they are receiving treatment.

Placebo in the Presence of Effective Treatments

The ethical justification for placebo use becomes more complex when effective treatments are available. Withholding effective treatment in favor of a placebo can pose significant risks to participants. In these cases, placebo use must be carefully justified, and alternatives, such as active control trials where the new treatment is compared to the existing standard treatment, should be considered. Ethical guidelines recommend that placebos be used only when absolutely necessary and when withholding treatment will not cause harm to participants.

Placebo Effect

The placebo effect is a well-documented phenomenon where participants experience real changes in their health condition despite receiving a placebo. This effect can result from psychological factors, such as the expectation of improvement, and can complicate the interpretation of trial results. Understanding and accounting for the placebo effect is essential in designing and analyzing clinical trials. It underscores the importance of including a placebo group to distinguish between the actual efficacy of the treatment and the psychological impact of receiving any form of intervention.

Regulatory Guidelines

Regulatory agencies, such as the FDA and EMA, provide guidelines for the ethical use of placebos in clinical trials. These guidelines emphasize the importance of scientific justification, informed consent, and minimizing risks to participants. Compliance with these guidelines ensures that the use of placebos is ethically sound and scientifically valid, contributing to the credibility and reliability of clinical research.

2.5 Ethics of Clinical Research in Special Populations

Introduction to Special Populations

Special populations in clinical research include groups such as children, pregnant women, the elderly, and individuals with cognitive impairments or other vulnerabilities. These populations often require additional protections due to their unique physiological, psychological, or social characteristics. Conducting ethical research involving special populations necessitates careful consideration of their specific needs and vulnerabilities to ensure their safety, dignity, and rights are protected throughout the study.

Children in Clinical Research

Children are considered a vulnerable population because they are not legally capable of providing informed consent. Instead, researchers must obtain parental or guardian consent and, when appropriate, assent from the child. Assent involves explaining the study to the child in an age-appropriate manner and obtaining their agreement to participate. The ethical conduct of research involving children requires ensuring that the potential benefits justify any risks and that the research is of minimal risk or offers the prospect of direct benefit to the child.

Key Considerations:

- **Parental Consent and Child Assent:** Both parental consent and child assent must be obtained, ensuring that parents or guardians fully understand the study and its risks and benefits.
- **Minimal Risk:** Research should pose minimal risk to the child, or if greater risk is involved, it should offer the prospect of direct benefit.
- **Ethical Review:** Studies involving children should undergo rigorous ethical review to ensure that the risks are justified and that the study is ethically sound.

Pregnant Women in Clinical Research

Pregnant women are another special population due to the potential risks to both the woman and the fetus. Ethical considerations include assessing the potential risks and benefits for both and ensuring that the research does not harm the fetus. Pregnant women should only be included in clinical trials if the research is likely to provide significant health benefits and if there are no alternative ways to obtain the data.

Key Considerations:

- **Risk-Benefit Assessment:** Thoroughly assess the risks and benefits to both the pregnant woman and the fetus.
- **Informed Consent:** Obtain informed consent that includes a detailed explanation of potential risks and benefits to both the mother and the fetus.
- **Alternative Methods:** Consider alternative methods to obtain the necessary data if possible.

Elderly in Clinical Research

The elderly often have multiple comorbidities and may be taking various medications, which can complicate clinical research. Ethical considerations include ensuring that the study design accounts for these factors and that the potential benefits justify the risks. Additionally, obtaining informed consent from elderly individuals may require special considerations, such as accounting for cognitive impairments.

Key Considerations:

- **Comorbidities and Medications:** Design studies that consider the unique health challenges and medication regimens of elderly participants.
- **Informed Consent:** Ensure that consent processes are adapted to accommodate potential cognitive impairments, using clear and straightforward language.
- **Benefit Justification:** Ensure that the potential benefits of the research justify any risks involved.

Individuals with Cognitive Impairments

Individuals with cognitive impairments may have limited capacity to provide informed consent. Researchers must obtain consent from legally authorized representatives and, when possible, assent from the participants themselves. The ethical conduct of research involving individuals with cognitive impairments requires ensuring that the research is of minimal risk or offers potential benefits that outweigh the risks.

Key Considerations:

- **Legally Authorized Representatives:** Obtain consent from legally authorized representatives when participants cannot provide informed consent.
- **Assent:** Seek assent from participants when possible, using methods appropriate to their level of understanding.
- **Risk Minimization:** Ensure that the research poses minimal risk or offers potential benefits that justify any risks.

Ethical Review and Oversight

Research involving special populations must undergo rigorous ethical review by Institutional Review Boards (IRBs) or Ethics Committees. These bodies are responsible for ensuring that the study design is ethically sound and that appropriate safeguards are in place to protect the rights and welfare of participants. Continuous monitoring throughout the study is also essential to address any emerging ethical concerns and ensure compliance with ethical standards.

2.6 Institutional Review Board/Independent Ethics Committee/ Ethics Committee

Composition

The composition of an Institutional Review Board (IRB), Independent Ethics Committee (IEC), or Ethics Committee (EC) is critical to ensuring a thorough and unbiased review of clinical research proposals. These committees typically include a diverse group of members with varying expertise and backgrounds. This diversity ensures a comprehensive evaluation of the ethical, scientific, and social implications of the research.

Key Members:

- **Medical Professionals:** Physicians, nurses, and other healthcare providers with relevant clinical expertise.
- **Scientific Experts:** Researchers with experience in the specific area of study.

- **Ethicists:** Individuals with expertise in bioethics to provide guidance on ethical considerations.
- **Legal Experts:** Lawyers knowledgeable in healthcare law and regulations.
- **Community Representatives:** Laypersons who can represent the perspectives and concerns of the general public.

Roles and Responsibilities

IRBs, IECs, and ECs have the critical responsibility of protecting the rights, safety, and well-being of research participants. They achieve this by thoroughly reviewing research protocols to ensure ethical and scientific integrity.

Key Responsibilities:

- **Protocol Review:** Evaluating the research protocol to ensure it is ethically and scientifically sound.
- **Informed Consent:** Ensuring that the informed consent process is adequate and that participants are provided with all necessary information.
- **Risk-Benefit Assessment:** Assessing whether the potential benefits of the research justify the risks to participants.
- **Monitoring Compliance:** Ensuring that the research complies with all applicable laws, regulations, and guidelines.

Review and Approval Process

The review and approval process of an IRB/IEC/EC is designed to ensure that research proposals meet the highest ethical and scientific standards. This process involves several key steps:

Submission of Protocol: Researchers submit a detailed research protocol, including informed consent documents, recruitment materials, and any other relevant information.

Initial Review: The committee conducts an initial review to ensure that the submission is complete and that all necessary documents are included.

Full Review: The full committee reviews the protocol in detail, focusing on the ethical and scientific aspects. This includes evaluating the study design, risk-benefit ratio, and informed consent process.

Deliberation and Decision: The committee deliberates on the protocol, discussing any concerns or questions. They may approve the protocol, request modifications, or reject it based on their evaluation.

Communication of Decision: The decision is communicated to the researchers, along with any required modifications or conditions for approval.

Ongoing Monitoring of Safety Data

Ongoing monitoring of safety data is a crucial aspect of the responsibilities of IRBs/IECs/ECs. This continuous oversight ensures that the safety and well-being of participants are maintained throughout the study.

Key Aspects of Ongoing Monitoring:

- **Periodic Reports:** Researchers are required to submit periodic safety reports, including information on any adverse events or unanticipated problems.
- **Site Visits:** The committee may conduct site visits to ensure that the research is being conducted according to the approved protocol and that participants are being adequately protected.
- **Review of Amendments:** Any proposed changes to the protocol must be reviewed and approved by the committee to ensure that they do not compromise participant safety or the integrity of the study.
- **Final Reports:** At the conclusion of the study, researchers must submit a final report summarizing the findings and any safety issues that arose during the study.

2.7 Data Safety Monitoring Boards

Introduction to Data Safety Monitoring Boards

Data Safety Monitoring Boards (DSMBs) are independent groups of experts responsible for ensuring the safety of participants and the integrity of data in clinical trials. DSMBs play a critical role in monitoring ongoing trials, particularly large-scale, multi-center studies, or those involving significant risks. They provide an additional layer of oversight, helping to protect participants and ensure that the study adheres to ethical and scientific standards.

Composition of DSMBs

The composition of DSMBs typically includes experts from various fields relevant to the clinical trial. This diversity ensures that the board has the necessary expertise to evaluate the trial comprehensively.

Key Members:

- **Clinical Experts:** Physicians and healthcare professionals with expertise in the therapeutic area being studied.
- **Biostatisticians:** Experts in statistical methods to analyze and interpret the data.
- **Ethicists:** Individuals with knowledge of ethical principles in clinical research.
- **Pharmacologists:** Specialists in drug actions and interactions, particularly important for trials involving new medications.
- **Lay Representatives:** Members of the public to provide a broader perspective on the trial's conduct and impact.

Roles and Responsibilities of DSMBs

The primary responsibility of a DSMB is to monitor the safety of participants and the integrity of the data throughout the clinical trial. They achieve this through regular review of accumulated data and making recommendations on the continuation, modification, or termination of the trial.

Key Responsibilities:

- **Monitoring Safety Data:** Regularly reviewing safety data, including adverse events and serious adverse events, to identify any trends or concerns.
- **Efficacy Monitoring:** Evaluating interim data to determine if the trial is meeting its efficacy endpoints or if early termination is warranted due to overwhelming evidence of benefit or lack of efficacy.
- **Stopping Rules:** Establishing pre-defined criteria for pausing or stopping the trial, either for safety reasons or because the trial has already achieved its objectives.
- **Data Integrity:** Ensuring that the data collected is accurate, complete, and reliable. This includes verifying that the trial is being conducted according to the approved protocol.
- **Confidentiality:** Maintaining the confidentiality of interim data to avoid introducing bias into the ongoing trial.

Review and Decision-Making Process

The DSMB's review process involves periodic meetings where the board examines accumulated data and makes decisions regarding the trial's conduct. This process is critical to maintaining the trial's integrity and ensuring participant safety.

Review Process:

- **Data Collection:** Data from the trial is collected and periodically submitted to the DSMB for review.
- **Interim Analysis:** The DSMB conducts interim analyses of the data to assess safety and efficacy outcomes.
- **Meetings:** Regular meetings are held to discuss findings and make recommendations. These meetings can be scheduled at predefined intervals or triggered by specific events in the trial.
- **Recommendations:** Based on their review, the DSMB makes recommendations to the trial sponsor regarding the continuation, modification, or termination of the trial. These recommendations are based on the safety and efficacy data, as well as the overall ethical considerations.

Ongoing Monitoring and Reporting

The DSMB's role extends beyond initial reviews and includes ongoing monitoring throughout the trial. This continuous oversight helps ensure that any emerging safety concerns are promptly addressed.

Key Aspects of Ongoing Monitoring:

- **Regular Reports:** The DSMB provides regular reports to the trial sponsor and regulatory authorities, summarizing their findings and recommendations.
- **Adverse Event Reporting:** Detailed analysis of adverse events and serious adverse events to identify any patterns that may indicate a risk to participants.
- **Protocol Adherence:** Monitoring adherence to the trial protocol to ensure that deviations are minimized and justified.

2.8 Responsibilities of Sponsor, CRO, and Investigator in Ethical Conduct of Clinical Research

Introduction

The ethical conduct of clinical research relies on the collaboration and shared responsibilities of various stakeholders, including sponsors, Contract Research Organizations (CROs), and investigators. Each of these parties plays a crucial role in ensuring that clinical trials are conducted with the highest ethical standards, safeguarding the rights, safety, and well-being of participants while ensuring the integrity and validity of the data collected.

Responsibilities of the Sponsor

The sponsor, typically a pharmaceutical company or a research institution, is responsible for the overall design, management, and financing of the clinical trial. Their primary role is to ensure that the trial is scientifically sound and ethically conducted.

Key Responsibilities:

- **Protocol Development:** Designing a scientifically robust and ethically sound study protocol that outlines the objectives, methodology, and procedures of the trial.
- **Regulatory Compliance:** Ensuring that the trial complies with all applicable regulatory requirements, including Good Clinical Practice (GCP) guidelines and local regulations.
- **Funding and Resources:** Providing adequate funding and resources to conduct the trial, including financial support, study materials, and necessary infrastructure.
- **Monitoring and Auditing:** Implementing systems for continuous monitoring and auditing of the trial to ensure compliance with the protocol and regulatory standards.
- **Data Management:** Ensuring proper data collection, storage, and analysis to maintain the integrity and confidentiality of the data.

Responsibilities of the CRO

Contract Research Organizations (CROs) are often hired by sponsors to manage various aspects of the clinical trial. CROs provide specialized services and expertise, facilitating the efficient conduct of the study.

Key Responsibilities:

- **Study Management:** Overseeing the day-to-day operations of the trial, including site selection, initiation, and management.
- **Regulatory Submissions:** Preparing and submitting necessary documents to regulatory authorities for approval and ongoing compliance.
- **Monitoring:** Conducting site monitoring visits to ensure that the trial is being conducted according to the protocol and GCP guidelines.

- **Data Collection and Analysis:** Managing the collection, processing, and analysis of trial data to ensure accuracy and completeness.
- **Training and Support:** Providing training and support to investigators and site staff on the protocol, GCP, and regulatory requirements.

Responsibilities of the Investigator

Investigators, usually physicians or researchers at clinical sites, are responsible for the direct conduct of the trial and the welfare of the participants. Their role is critical in ensuring that the trial is conducted ethically and that participants' rights are protected.

Key Responsibilities:

- **Informed Consent:** Obtaining informed consent from participants, ensuring they fully understand the trial's nature, risks, and benefits.
- **Participant Safety:** Ensuring the safety and well-being of participants, monitoring for adverse events, and taking appropriate actions when necessary.
- **Protocol Adherence:** Conducting the trial strictly according to the approved protocol, documenting any deviations and their justifications.
- **Data Accuracy:** Collecting and recording accurate and complete data, maintaining source documents, and ensuring data integrity.
- **Ethical Conduct:** Upholding ethical principles, including respect for participants, beneficence, and justice, throughout the trial.

Collaboration and Communication

Effective collaboration and communication among sponsors, CROs, and investigators are essential for the ethical conduct of clinical research. Each party must understand and fulfill their respective roles and responsibilities, working together to address any challenges and ensure the trial's success.

Key Aspects of Collaboration:

- **Clear Communication:** Establishing clear lines of communication to ensure that all parties are informed and aligned on the trial's progress and any issues that arise.
- **Regular Meetings:** Conducting regular meetings and updates to discuss the trial's status, address concerns, and make necessary adjustments.
- **Documentation:** Maintaining comprehensive and transparent documentation of all trial activities, decisions, and communications.

2.9 Ethical Principles Governing Informed Consent Process

Introduction

Informed consent is a fundamental ethical requirement in clinical research, ensuring that participants voluntarily agree to participate with a full understanding of the study's nature, risks, benefits, and alternatives. The informed consent process is governed by several ethical principles that aim to respect the autonomy, dignity, and rights of participants while promoting trust and transparency in the research process.

Respect for Autonomy

Respect for autonomy is a core ethical principle that underscores the importance of allowing individuals to make informed and voluntary decisions about their participation in clinical research. This principle mandates that participants are provided with all necessary information to understand the study and its implications, enabling them to make decisions aligned with their values and preferences.

Key Elements:

- **Voluntary Participation:** Ensuring that participation is entirely voluntary, without any form of coercion, undue influence, or manipulation.
- **Comprehensive Information:** Providing complete and understandable information about the study, including its purpose, procedures, risks, benefits, and alternatives.

Beneficence and Non-Maleficence

Beneficence and non-maleficence are ethical principles that require researchers to maximize potential benefits and minimize potential harms to participants. The informed consent process must include a thorough explanation of the potential risks and benefits, enabling participants to make an informed decision about their involvement.

Key Elements:

- **Risk-Benefit Assessment:** Clearly outlining the potential risks and benefits, including any possible discomfort or harm that might arise from participation.
- **Mitigation Measures:** Describing measures in place to mitigate risks and ensure participant safety.

Justice

The principle of justice requires that the benefits and burdens of research be distributed fairly among all groups in society. The informed consent process should ensure that no group is unfairly burdened or excluded from the potential benefits of research.

Key Elements:

- **Equitable Recruitment:** Ensuring fair recruitment practices that do not exploit vulnerable populations or exclude groups without justified reasons.
- **Fair Compensation:** Providing appropriate compensation for participation, considering the time, effort, and any inconvenience to participants.

Informed Consent Process

The informed consent process involves several steps designed to ensure that participants are fully informed and voluntarily agree to participate. This process must be conducted in a transparent and respectful manner, accommodating the needs and understanding levels of participants.

Steps in the Informed Consent Process:

- **Initial Information Session:** Providing potential participants with comprehensive information about the study, typically through an initial meeting or information session.
- **Consent Form:** Offering a written consent form that details the study's purpose, procedures, risks, benefits, and participant rights. This form should be written in clear, simple language.
- **Question and Answer Session:** Allowing participants to ask questions and receive clear, understandable answers to ensure they fully comprehend the information provided.
- **Voluntary Agreement:** Ensuring that participants voluntarily agree to participate by signing the consent form. They should also be informed of their right to withdraw from the study at any time without penalty.

Continuous Process

Informed consent is not a one-time event but an ongoing process throughout the study. Researchers must ensure that participants remain informed about any new information that may affect their willingness to continue in the study.

Key Aspects:

- **Ongoing Communication:** Keeping participants updated about any new findings or changes in the study that might impact their decision to participate.
- **Re-consent:** Obtaining re-consent if significant changes occur in the study protocol or new risks are identified.

Special Considerations

Special considerations must be made for vulnerable populations, such as children, individuals with cognitive impairments, and non-native speakers. These populations may require additional protections and tailored approaches to the informed consent process.

Key Elements:

- **Parental/Guardian Consent:** Obtaining consent from parents or legal guardians for minors or individuals unable to provide informed consent themselves.
- **Assent:** Seeking assent from minors in addition to parental consent, ensuring that they understand and agree to participate.
- **Language and Comprehension:** Providing consent forms and information in the participant's preferred language and ensuring that they understand the content.

2.10 Patient Information Sheet and Informed Consent Form

Introduction

The Patient Information Sheet (PIS) and Informed Consent Form (ICF) are essential documents in clinical research that ensure participants are fully informed about the study and voluntarily agree to participate. These documents are critical for upholding ethical standards and protecting the rights and well-being of research participants. The PIS provides detailed information about the study, while the ICF documents the participant's agreement to join the study after understanding all relevant information.

Patient Information Sheet (PIS)

The PIS is designed to give potential participants a comprehensive overview of the study. It should be written in clear, simple language that is easy to understand, avoiding technical jargon and complex sentences. The aim is to ensure that participants fully comprehend what the study involves before they decide to participate.

Key Components of the PIS:

- **Study Title and Purpose:** Clearly state the title of the study and its primary objectives. Explain why the study is being conducted and what it aims to achieve.
- **Study Procedures:** Describe the procedures involved in the study, including the duration, the frequency of visits, and any interventions or tests that will be conducted.
- **Eligibility Criteria:** Outline the criteria for participation, including any inclusion and exclusion factors. This helps potential participants understand if they qualify for the study.
- **Potential Risks and Benefits:** Provide a detailed explanation of the potential risks and benefits associated with participation. This includes any side effects, discomforts, or advantages that may arise from being part of the study.
- **Confidentiality:** Explain how the participant's data will be kept confidential and what measures are in place to protect their privacy.
- **Voluntary Participation:** Emphasize that participation is voluntary and that participants can withdraw from the study at any time without penalty or loss of benefits.
- **Contact Information:** Provide contact details for the research team and ethics committee, allowing participants to ask questions or express concerns at any time.

Informed Consent Form (ICF)

The ICF is a document that participants sign to indicate their voluntary agreement to participate in the study after reading and understanding the PIS. The ICF must reflect the information provided in the PIS and ensure that participants are making an informed decision.

Key Components of the ICF:

- **Study Title and Purpose:** Reiterate the title and purpose of the study.
- **Study Procedures:** Summarize the procedures involved in the study.
- **Risks and Benefits:** Outline the potential risks and benefits once again.
- **Confidentiality:** Reaffirm the measures taken to ensure confidentiality.

- **Voluntary Participation:** Emphasize the voluntary nature of participation and the right to withdraw.
- **Consent Statement:** Include a statement where participants acknowledge that they have read and understood the PIS and agree to participate in the study.
- **Signature Section:** Provide space for the participant's signature, the date, and, if applicable, the signature of a parent or legal guardian. Also include a section for the researcher to sign, confirming that they have explained the study to the participant.

Ensuring Comprehension and Voluntariness

The process of obtaining informed consent is not merely about having participants sign a form. It involves ensuring that they genuinely understand the information provided and are making an informed, voluntary decision.

Key Strategies:

- **Interactive Discussions:** Engage in discussions with potential participants to answer their questions and clarify any doubts. This helps ensure they understand the study fully.
- **Assessing Understanding:** Ask participants to explain the study in their own words to assess their understanding. This can help identify any areas of confusion.
- **Providing Time:** Allow participants ample time to consider their decision and discuss it with family or friends if they wish.

Special Considerations for Vulnerable Populations

Additional safeguards are necessary when obtaining informed consent from vulnerable populations, such as children, individuals with cognitive impairments, or non-native speakers.

Key Considerations:

- **Simplified Language:** Use language appropriate to the participant's comprehension level.
- **Assent for Minors:** Obtain assent from children in addition to parental consent, ensuring that they understand and agree to participate.
- **Translation Services:** Provide translated documents and interpretation services for participants who do not speak the primary language of the

study.

2.11 The Informed Consent Process and Documentation

Introduction

The informed consent process is a crucial element in clinical research, ensuring that participants are fully informed about the study and voluntarily agree to participate. This process involves providing comprehensive information, assessing participant understanding, and documenting their consent. Proper documentation is essential for maintaining transparency and accountability in clinical research.

The Informed Consent Process

The informed consent process is designed to respect and uphold the autonomy of participants. It involves several key steps to ensure that participants are well-informed and capable of making an informed decision about their participation.

Steps in the Informed Consent Process:

- **Initial Contact:** The process begins with an initial contact where potential participants are introduced to the study. This can occur through various means, such as informational sessions, advertisements, or direct communication from the research team.
- **Information Delivery:** Participants are provided with a Patient Information Sheet (PIS) that details the study's purpose, procedures, risks, benefits, and their rights as participants. The information should be presented in a clear and understandable manner, avoiding technical jargon.
- **Discussion and Clarification:** Researchers engage in a dialogue with potential participants to answer questions and clarify any doubts. This interactive discussion helps ensure that participants fully understand the information provided.
- **Assessment of Understanding:** Researchers may assess participants' understanding by asking them to explain the study in their own words. This step helps identify any areas of confusion that need further clarification.
- **Voluntary Decision:** Participants are given adequate time to consider their decision. They should feel free to discuss their participation with family or friends and are encouraged to ask additional questions.

- **Obtaining Consent:** Once participants have a clear understanding of the study and have decided to participate, they sign the Informed Consent Form (ICF). This form reiterates the key points from the PIS and includes a statement of consent.

Documentation of Informed Consent

Proper documentation of informed consent is vital for ensuring the ethical and legal integrity of the study. The Informed Consent Form serves as a record that participants have been fully informed and have voluntarily agreed to participate.

Key Elements of the Informed Consent Form:

- **Study Title and Purpose:** Clearly state the title and objective of the study.
- **Study Procedures:** Summarize the procedures involved, including what participants will need to do and the duration of their involvement.
- **Risks and Benefits:** Outline the potential risks and benefits associated with participation.
- **Confidentiality:** Describe how participants' data will be protected and confidentiality maintained.
- **Voluntary Participation:** Emphasize that participation is voluntary and that participants can withdraw at any time without penalty.
- **Consent Statement:** Include a statement where participants acknowledge that they have read and understood the information provided and agree to participate.
- **Signatures:** Provide spaces for the signatures of the participant, the researcher obtaining consent, and, if applicable, a witness or legal guardian. The date of signing should also be recorded.

Ongoing Consent and Communication

Informed consent is an ongoing process, not a one-time event. Researchers must continue to provide participants with relevant information as the study progresses, especially if there are significant changes to the study protocol or new findings that may affect participants' willingness to continue.

Key Aspects of Ongoing Consent:

- **Regular Updates:** Keep participants informed about the study's progress and any new information that may impact their participation.
- **Re-consent:** Obtain re-consent if there are significant changes to the study protocol or new risks are identified. This ensures that participants remain fully informed and agree to continue their involvement.
- **Open Communication:** Maintain open lines of communication with participants, allowing them to ask questions and express concerns at any time.

Special Considerations for Vulnerable Populations

Additional safeguards are necessary when obtaining informed consent from vulnerable populations, such as children, individuals with cognitive impairments, or non-native speakers.

Key Considerations:

- **Simplified Information:** Use language and explanations appropriate to the participant's level of understanding.
- **Assent for Minors:** Obtain assent from children, in addition to parental consent, ensuring that they understand and agree to participate.
- **Translation and Interpretation:** Provide translated documents and interpretation services for participants who do not speak the primary language of the study.

Key Points of Chapter 2: Ethics in Clinical Research

- **Historical Perspectives:**

  - Nuremberg Code established post-World War II to emphasize voluntary consent and minimize harm in human experiments.
  - Thalidomide Study led to stricter regulations after causing severe birth defects.
  - Nazi Trials exposed unethical medical experiments during WWII, leading to the formulation of ethical standards.
  - Tuskegee Syphilis Study highlighted severe ethical violations, prompting changes in U.S. research regulations.
  - The Belmont Report outlined principles of respect for persons, beneficence, and justice.

- The Declaration of Helsinki provided ethical guidelines for medical research involving human subjects.

- **Origin of ICH-GCP Guidelines:**

  - International Conference on Harmonization aimed to harmonize regulatory requirements.
  - Good Clinical Practice (GCP) guidelines ensure the protection of participants and data integrity.

- **Ethics of Randomized Clinical Trials:**

  - Ensuring informed consent and balancing risks and benefits.
  - Principle of equipoise to justify random assignment.
  - Ethical considerations of placebo use, particularly when effective treatments exist.

- **Role of Placebo in Clinical Trials:**

  - Placebos as control to isolate treatment effects.
  - Ethical use requires justification, informed consent, and consideration of existing treatments.

- **Ethics of Clinical Research in Special Populations:**

  - Additional protections for children, pregnant women, elderly, and individuals with cognitive impairments.
  - Ensuring informed consent, minimal risk, and fair recruitment practices.

- **IRB/IEC/EC Composition, Roles, and Responsibilities:**

  - Diverse membership including medical professionals, ethicists, and community representatives.
  - Responsibilities include protocol review, risk-benefit assessment, and ongoing monitoring.

- **Data Safety Monitoring Boards:**

- Independent groups ensuring participant safety and data integrity.
- Regular review of safety data, interim analysis, and ongoing monitoring.

- **Responsibilities of Sponsor, CRO, and Investigator:**

  - Sponsors ensure scientific soundness, regulatory compliance, and adequate resources.
  - CROs manage study operations, regulatory submissions, and data management.
  - Investigators obtain informed consent, ensure participant safety, and collect accurate data.

- **Ethical Principles Governing Informed Consent Process:**

  - Respect for autonomy, beneficence, non-maleficence, and justice.
  - Steps include initial information delivery, discussion, understanding assessment, and voluntary agreement.

- **Patient Information Sheet and Informed Consent Form:**

  - PIS provides comprehensive study details in simple language.
  - ICF documents participant agreement after understanding the study.

- **Informed Consent Process and Documentation:**

  - Detailed steps from initial contact to obtaining and documenting consent.
  - Emphasis on ongoing consent and communication, especially for vulnerable populations.

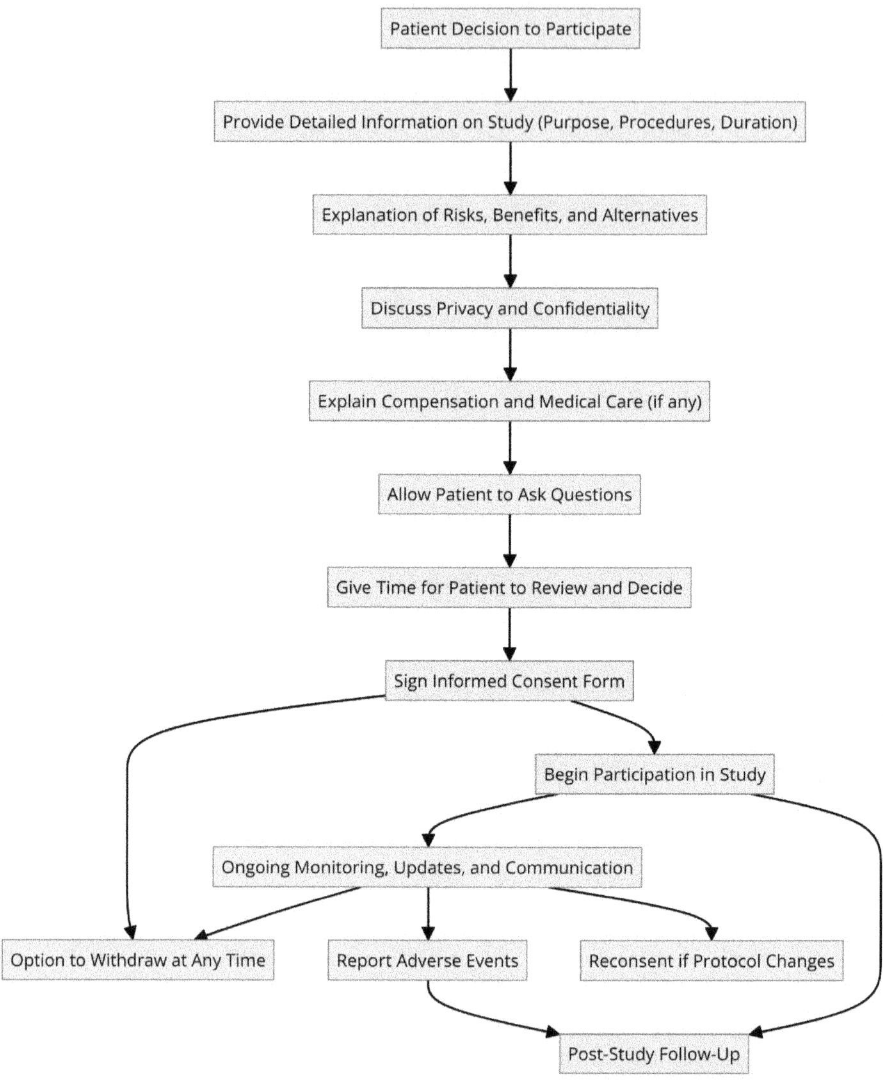

Comprehensive Flow of the Informed Consent Process in Clinical Trials

CHAPTER THREE

Regulations Governing Clinical Trials

Clinical trials are highly regulated processes, with stringent guidelines designed to ensure patient safety and scientific integrity. This chapter focuses on the regulatory frameworks that govern clinical trials, with an emphasis on key regulatory bodies such as the **FDA (USA), EMA (EU),** and **CDSCO (India).** Regulatory agencies play a pivotal role in overseeing the design, conduct, and evaluation of clinical trials, ensuring that they meet high ethical and scientific standards.

The regulatory landscape varies significantly between countries, but the underlying goal remains consistent: to protect human participants and ensure that the data generated are robust and reliable. This chapter provides an in-depth examination of the **Clinical Research Regulations in India,** including **Schedule Y** and the regulatory guidance for conducting trials involving medical devices. In the USA, the **FDA's Code of Federal Regulations (CFR)** outlines the legal requirements for clinical trials, while in the European Union, **EMA** regulations ensure harmonized standards across member states.

Understanding these regulatory requirements is essential for pharmaceutical companies and researchers seeking to navigate the complex approval processes in various regions. This chapter also addresses the growing trend toward **global clinical trials,** where multi-ethnic populations are involved in the research to ensure that drugs are effective across different genetic backgrounds. By mastering the regulatory guidelines of various jurisdictions, professionals can effectively bring new drugs to market while maintaining compliance with local and international laws.

3.1 Clinical Research Regulations in India – Schedule Y & Medical Device Guidance

3.1.1 Introduction to Schedule Y

Schedule Y is a critical component of the Drugs and Cosmetics Act, 1940, which governs clinical trials in India. It outlines the requirements for the import and manufacture of new drugs for sale and for conducting clinical trials. The primary goal of Schedule Y is to ensure that clinical trials are conducted in an ethical manner, protecting the rights, safety, and well-being of trial subjects. It also ensures that the data generated from these trials is credible and scientifically sound. This regulatory framework applies to both pharmaceutical products and medical devices, emphasizing the need for rigorous evaluation before they are introduced to the market.

3.1.2 Key Provisions of Schedule Y

Schedule Y includes several key provisions that detail the steps and standards for conducting clinical trials. One of the primary requirements is obtaining approval from the Drugs Controller General of India (DCGI) before initiating a clinical trial. Additionally, it mandates the submission of detailed information about the investigational product, including pre-clinical data, study protocols, and informed consent documents. Ethical guidelines are also a significant part of Schedule Y, requiring the establishment of Institutional Ethics Committees (IECs) to review and approve trial protocols, ensuring they comply with ethical standards.

3.1.3 Clinical Trial Phases

Clinical trials under Schedule Y are divided into four phases:

- **Phase I**: Involves testing the drug on a small group of healthy volunteers to assess its safety, tolerability, and pharmacokinetics.
- **Phase II**: Focuses on evaluating the drug's efficacy and side effects in a larger group of patients.
- **Phase III**: Conducted on a much larger patient population to confirm the drug's effectiveness, monitor side effects, and compare it with commonly used treatments.
- **Phase IV**: Post-marketing studies conducted after the drug has been approved for public use to gather additional information on its risks, benefits, and optimal use.

Each phase is designed to answer specific research questions and provide comprehensive data on the investigational product.

3.1.4 Medical Device Guidance

In addition to pharmaceuticals, Schedule Y also addresses the regulation of medical devices. The Medical Device Rules, 2017, were introduced to establish a comprehensive framework for the regulation of medical devices in India. These rules categorize medical devices based on their risk levels and specify the requirements for their manufacture, sale, and clinical investigation. For instance, low-risk devices (Class A) have simpler regulatory requirements, while high-risk devices (Class D) are subject to more stringent controls, including rigorous clinical evaluation and post-market surveillance.

3.1.5 Ethical Considerations and Informed Consent

Ethical considerations are paramount in clinical research, and Schedule Y emphasizes the importance of informed consent. Informed consent is a process through which potential trial subjects are provided with comprehensive information about the study, including its purpose, procedures, risks, and benefits. Subjects must voluntarily agree to participate without any coercion. Schedule Y requires that informed consent be documented in writing, and participants must be given adequate time to ask questions and consider their decision. This process ensures respect for the autonomy and rights of the participants.

3.1.6 Institutional Ethics Committees (IECs)

Institutional Ethics Committees play a crucial role in safeguarding the rights and welfare of clinical trial participants. Schedule Y mandates the establishment of IECs at institutions conducting clinical trials. These committees are responsible for reviewing and approving trial protocols, ensuring they comply with ethical standards and regulatory requirements. IECs must be independent and include members with diverse expertise, such as medical professionals, legal experts, and laypersons. Their primary function is to protect trial subjects by ensuring that the study is ethically conducted and that the risks are minimized.

3.2 Regulations to Conduct Drug Studies in the USA (FDA)

3.2.1 Introduction to FDA Regulations

The Food and Drug Administration (FDA) is the primary regulatory body overseeing drug studies in the United States. Established in 1906, the FDA's mission is to protect public health by ensuring the safety, efficacy, and security of drugs, biological products, and medical devices. The regulatory framework set by the FDA is comprehensive and aims to ensure that clinical trials are conducted ethically and that the resulting data is reliable. The regulations are designed to protect the rights, safety, and well-being of trial participants and to ensure that new drugs are thoroughly evaluated before being approved for public use.

3.2.2 Investigational New Drug (IND) Application

Before a new drug can be tested in humans, the sponsor must submit an Investigational New Drug (IND) application to the FDA. The IND application contains detailed information about the drug, including its chemical composition, manufacturing processes, preclinical study results, and proposed clinical trial protocols. The primary purpose of the IND is to ensure that the drug is safe to administer to humans and that the study design is scientifically sound. The FDA reviews the IND to determine whether the potential benefits justify the risks and whether the study can proceed.

3.2.3 Phases of Clinical Trials

Clinical trials in the USA are conducted in three main phases, similar to the process outlined in Schedule Y:

- **Phase I**: These trials involve a small number of healthy volunteers (20-80) and focus on assessing the drug's safety, dosage range, and pharmacokinetics.
- **Phase II**: These studies involve a larger group of patients (100-300) who have the condition the drug is intended to treat. The goal is to evaluate the drug's efficacy and further assess its safety.
- **Phase III**: These are large-scale trials involving several hundred to several thousand patients. They aim to confirm the drug's effectiveness, monitor side effects, compare it with standard treatments, and collect information that will allow the drug to be used safely.

After successful completion of these phases, the sponsor can submit a New Drug Application (NDA) for FDA approval.

3.2.4 New Drug Application (NDA)

The New Drug Application (NDA) is the formal proposal for the FDA to approve a new pharmaceutical for sale and marketing in the United States. The NDA includes all data from the clinical trials, as well as information about the drug's manufacturing, labeling, and proposed use. The FDA's review process involves evaluating the safety and efficacy data, inspecting manufacturing facilities, and assessing the proposed labeling to ensure it provides adequate information for safe use. If the FDA is satisfied with the evidence, it approves the NDA, allowing the drug to be marketed.

3.2.5 Institutional Review Boards (IRBs)

Institutional Review Boards (IRBs) are an essential part of the FDA's regulatory framework. An IRB is a group that has been formally designated to review and monitor biomedical research involving human subjects. IRBs have the authority to approve, require modifications to, or disapprove research. They ensure that the study is ethical and that the rights and welfare of participants are protected. The FDA requires that all clinical trials conducted in the USA be reviewed and approved by an IRB before they begin.

3.2.6 Informed Consent

The FDA places great emphasis on informed consent to protect the rights and safety of trial participants. Informed consent is a process in which participants are provided with comprehensive information about the study, including its purpose, duration, procedures, risks, and benefits. Participants must voluntarily agree to participate and have the right to withdraw from the study at any time without penalty. The informed consent document must be written in plain language and reviewed by the IRB to ensure it is clear and comprehensive.

3.2.7 Good Clinical Practice (GCP) Guidelines

Good Clinical Practice (GCP) guidelines are a set of internationally recognized ethical and scientific quality standards for designing, conducting, recording, and reporting clinical trials. The FDA requires that all clinical trials conducted in the USA adhere to GCP guidelines. These guidelines ensure that the data generated from the trials is credible and accurate, and that the rights, integrity, and confidentiality of trial participants are protected. Compliance with GCP is essential for the acceptance of trial data by regulatory authorities worldwide.

3.3 NDA 505(b)(1) and NDA 505(b)(2) of the FD&C Act

3.3.1 Introduction to the FD&C Act

The Food, Drug, and Cosmetic Act (FD&C Act) is a set of laws passed by Congress in 1938, giving authority to the U.S. Food and Drug Administration (FDA) to oversee the safety of food, drugs, and cosmetics. Within this framework, the New Drug Application (NDA) is a critical process for gaining approval to market new pharmaceutical products. Two important types of NDAs under the FD&C Act are NDA 505(b)(1) and NDA 505(b)(2), each serving different purposes and requirements.

3.3.2 NDA 505(b)(1): Traditional New Drug Application

NDA 505(b)(1) is the standard application pathway for new drug approvals. This type of application is used when the sponsor has conducted all necessary clinical trials to demonstrate the safety and efficacy of the drug. It requires comprehensive data from preclinical studies (animal testing) and clinical trials (human testing) that the sponsor has directly conducted or commissioned.

Key Aspects of NDA 505(b)(1):

- **Full Reports of Safety and Efficacy:** The application must include detailed reports of the studies demonstrating the drug's safety and efficacy.
- **Manufacturing Information:** The sponsor must provide extensive details about the drug's composition, manufacturing processes, and quality control measures.
- **Labeling:** Proposed labeling must be included to ensure it provides adequate directions for use, warnings, and other essential information for safe administration.
- **Administrative Information:** The application includes administrative components like patent information, user fee cover sheet, and financial disclosure information.

3.3.3 NDA 505(b)(2): Alternative Pathway for New Drug Approval

NDA 505(b)(2) provides an alternative regulatory pathway intended to reduce the burden of duplicative research and facilitate drug development. This type of application allows the sponsor to rely, at least in part, on existing clinical data not developed by the applicant. It is often used for drug products that are similar to previously approved drugs but may have differences in formulation, dosage, strength, or route of administration.

Key Aspects of NDA 505(b)(2):

- **Use of Existing Data:** The sponsor can reference published literature or the FDA's findings of safety and effectiveness for an approved drug. This can significantly reduce the need for extensive new clinical trials.
- **Innovative Changes:** NDA 505(b)(2) is often used for drugs that represent modifications of previously approved drugs. These modifications might include new dosage forms, combination products, or new indications.

- **Bridging Studies:** While the sponsor can rely on existing data, bridging studies are typically required to demonstrate that the modifications do not compromise safety or efficacy. These studies help to "bridge" the new product to the existing data.
- **Patent Certification:** The application must include certifications concerning patents listed in the FDA's Orange Book for the reference drug. This may involve certifying that the new product does not infringe on existing patents or that such patents are invalid.

3.3.4 Differences Between NDA 505(b)(1) and NDA 505(b)(2)

The primary difference between NDA 505(b)(1) and NDA 505(b)(2) lies in the source of the data used to support the application. NDA 505(b)(1) relies entirely on data developed by the sponsor, including full reports of clinical trials. In contrast, NDA 505(b)(2) allows the sponsor to use existing data from other sources, which can expedite the development process and reduce costs.

Comparison Summary:

- **Data Requirements:** NDA 505(b)(1) requires comprehensive original data, while NDA 505(b)(2) can leverage existing data from published literature or other studies.
- **Development Time and Cost:** NDA 505(b)(2) can be faster and less expensive due to reduced requirements for new clinical trials.
- **Patent and Exclusivity Issues:** NDA 505(b)(2) involves complex patent certifications and potential challenges, whereas NDA 505(b)(1) focuses on new data and original research.

3.4 ANDA 505(j) of the FD&C Act

The **Abbreviated New Drug Application (ANDA) 505(j)**, as outlined in the **Federal Food, Drug, and Cosmetic Act (FD&C Act)**, is a regulatory pathway designed for the approval of **generic drugs**. This pathway allows manufacturers to market generic versions of already-approved brand-name drugs without having to repeat the extensive clinical trials required for new drugs. The ANDA 505(j) process helps to promote competition in the pharmaceutical industry by offering lower-cost alternatives to brand-name drugs while ensuring that generics are equally safe and effective.

3.4.1 Purpose and Scope of ANDA 505(j)

The purpose of **ANDA 505(j)** is to provide a simplified and faster process for bringing **generic drugs** to the market. Generic drugs are required to be **bioequivalent** to the original **reference listed drug (RLD)**, meaning that they must deliver the same **active ingredient** to the body at the same rate and to the same extent as the original product. Unlike the **NDA 505(b)(1)** pathway for new drugs, the ANDA 505(j) process does not require the generic manufacturer to conduct large-scale **preclinical** and **clinical trials**. Instead, the focus is on demonstrating **bioequivalence**, which significantly reduces the time and cost of bringing generics to the market.

3.4.2 Bioequivalence and Generic Drug Requirements

To gain approval under ANDA 505(j), the generic drug must meet strict **bioequivalence** requirements. This means that the generic product must deliver the **same therapeutic effect** as the brand-name drug when used under the same conditions. The **bioequivalence studies** conducted for ANDA submission are typically **pharmacokinetic studies** that compare the absorption and metabolism of the generic drug to the reference drug. These studies measure key parameters such as the **maximum concentration (Cmax)** and **time to reach maximum concentration (Tmax)** of the drug in the bloodstream.

For example, if a generic manufacturer submits an ANDA for a **generic version** of a widely used **antihypertensive drug**, the bioequivalence study would ensure that the generic drug has similar pharmacokinetic properties to the original drug. If the results show that the generic achieves the same **Cmax** and **Tmax** as the reference drug within a **narrow margin (80% to 125%)**, it is considered bioequivalent, making it eligible for ANDA approval.

3.4.3 ANDA Submission Process

The **ANDA 505(j) submission** requires the generic manufacturer to provide detailed documentation on the **composition, manufacturing process**, and **quality control** of the generic drug. Additionally, the **labeling** of the generic drug must be essentially the same as that of the reference drug, with only minor differences that do not affect safety or efficacy, such as changes in the packaging or company name.

One significant advantage of the ANDA pathway is that it allows generic manufacturers to bypass the costly and time-consuming process of **clinical trials** by relying on the FDA's prior approval of the reference drug. However, the manufacturer must still meet strict **quality standards** and demonstrate that the generic product is manufactured consistently to ensure that it performs the same as the original brand-name product.

3.4.4 Market Exclusivity and Patent Considerations

Patent and exclusivity considerations play a significant role in the **Abbreviated New Drug Application (ANDA)** process. The **Hatch-Waxman Amendments** to the **Federal Food, Drug, and Cosmetic (FD&C) Act** established a regulatory framework that seeks to balance the interests of **brand-name** and **generic drug manufacturers**. This framework is essential for fostering competition while ensuring that innovation in drug development is protected for a certain period. Under this structure, generic manufacturers seeking FDA approval for their products must address any **patents** listed for the **Reference Listed Drug (RLD)** in the FDA's **Orange Book** by providing one of four types of patent certifications, each of which affects the timing and conditions under which a generic drug may be approved and marketed.

- **Paragraph I Certification**: This certification states that **no patent information** has been filed for the RLD. In such cases, the generic manufacturer faces no patent-related barriers to approval and can proceed without the need to address patent challenges.
- **Paragraph II Certification**: This certification applies when the relevant **patent has already expired**. Since there are no valid patents remaining on the RLD, the generic manufacturer can seek immediate approval and market the drug without legal restrictions related to patents.
- **Paragraph III Certification**: In this case, the generic manufacturer acknowledges that a **patent is still in force**, and they agree to delay the marketing of the generic drug until after the patent expires. This certification allows the ANDA to be reviewed and approved by the FDA but delays the commercial launch of the product until the patent protection ends.
- **Paragraph IV Certification**: The **Paragraph IV certification** is the most contentious of the four. It asserts that the patent listed for the RLD is either **invalid, unenforceable**, or that the **generic drug** will not infringe upon the patent. This certification is likely to result in **patent litigation**, as the brand-name company often files a lawsuit against the generic manufacturer for patent infringement. Under the **Hatch-Waxman Act**, the filing of a patent infringement lawsuit triggers an **automatic 30-month stay** on the approval of the ANDA, unless the court resolves the dispute in favor of the generic manufacturer sooner. However, the

first generic manufacturer to submit a substantially complete ANDA with a **Paragraph IV certification** is eligible for **180 days of market exclusivity** upon FDA approval. During this exclusivity period, no other generic version of the drug can enter the market, providing a significant financial incentive for generic companies to challenge patents.

The **180-day exclusivity** is a critical component of the **Hatch-Waxman framework** as it promotes competition among generic manufacturers by offering a reward for the first successful patent challenge. However, the system can also delay generic competition if patent litigation or **settlement agreements**, such as **pay-for-delay** deals, extend the period during which generics are kept off the market. In such cases, the brand-name company compensates the generic manufacturer to delay the launch of their product, maintaining higher drug prices.

3.4.5 Approval Process and Market Entry

Once the ANDA is submitted, the FDA reviews the application to ensure it meets all regulatory requirements. This includes evaluating the bioequivalence data, manufacturing processes, and compliance with labeling requirements. If the application is deemed complete and satisfactory, the FDA grants approval, allowing the generic drug to be marketed in the United States.

The introduction of generic drugs through the ANDA process significantly impacts healthcare by providing more affordable medication options, increasing access to essential drugs, and reducing healthcare costs. The rigorous standards and requirements of the ANDA 505(j) process ensure that generic drugs are as safe and effective as their brand-name counterparts, maintaining public trust in the generic drug market.

3.5 FDA Guidance for Industry - Acceptance of Foreign Clinical Studies

3.5.1 Introduction to FDA Guidance for Foreign Clinical Studies

The U.S. Food and Drug Administration (FDA) provides guidance for the acceptance of foreign clinical studies in support of applications for the marketing of drugs and biologics. This guidance ensures that clinical data generated outside the United States meets the FDA's standards for quality, integrity, and reliability. With the globalization of clinical research, it is common for sponsors to conduct studies in multiple countries. The FDA's guidelines help harmonize international research practices and facilitate the inclusion of foreign data in regulatory submissions.

3.5.2 Regulatory Requirements for Acceptance

For the FDA to accept foreign clinical study data, the studies must comply with Good Clinical Practice (GCP) standards. GCP is an internationally recognized ethical and scientific quality standard for the design, conduct, recording, and reporting of clinical trials. It ensures that the data and reported results are credible and accurate, and that the rights, integrity, and confidentiality of trial subjects are protected.

Key Requirements:

- **Compliance with GCP:** Foreign studies must adhere to GCP guidelines, which encompass ethical principles from the Declaration of Helsinki. These guidelines ensure the safety and rights of participants and the credibility of the data.
- **FDA Inspection:** The FDA reserves the right to inspect the study sites, data, and records to verify compliance with GCP and the reliability of the data.
- **Informed Consent:** Informed consent must be obtained from all participants in a manner that aligns with GCP standards, ensuring that participants are fully aware of the study's nature, risks, and benefits.
- **IRB/IEC Review:** The study must be reviewed and approved by an independent ethics committee or institutional review board (IRB/IEC), which oversees the ethical conduct of the study.

3.5.3 Submission of Foreign Data

When submitting an application that includes foreign clinical study data, sponsors must provide comprehensive documentation demonstrating compliance with FDA requirements. This includes detailed study protocols, informed consent forms, IRB/IEC approvals, and evidence of adherence to GCP standards. The data should be presented in a clear and organized manner, allowing the FDA to evaluate the study's design, conduct, and outcomes effectively.

Required Documentation:

- **Study Protocols:** Detailed descriptions of the study objectives, design, methodology, statistical considerations, and organization.
- **Ethics Committee Approvals:** Documentation of IRB/IEC approvals and continuing reviews.

- **Monitoring and Auditing Reports:** Records of study monitoring and auditing activities to ensure ongoing compliance with GCP.
- **Clinical Study Reports (CSR):** Comprehensive reports summarizing the study's findings, including safety and efficacy data, statistical analyses, and conclusions.

3.5.4 Challenges and Considerations

Sponsors may face challenges when conducting and submitting foreign clinical study data. Differences in regulatory environments, cultural practices, and healthcare systems can impact the conduct and acceptability of studies. It is crucial for sponsors to understand and navigate these differences to ensure that their studies meet FDA standards.

Key Challenges:

- **Regulatory Differences:** Variations in regulatory requirements between countries may complicate the alignment of study protocols with FDA expectations.
- **Cultural Sensitivity:** Understanding cultural differences in informed consent processes and participant interactions is essential for ethical study conduct.
- **Data Integrity:** Ensuring the accuracy, completeness, and reliability of data across different study sites requires robust monitoring and auditing practices.

3.5.5 Benefits of Accepting Foreign Data

Accepting foreign clinical study data has several benefits for drug development and regulatory processes. It allows for a more diverse participant population, which can improve the generalizability of study findings. Additionally, it can expedite the drug development process by leveraging existing studies, reducing the need for redundant trials.

Advantages:

- **Diverse Populations:** Inclusion of diverse populations enhances the understanding of a drug's safety and efficacy across different demographic groups.
- **Accelerated Development:** Utilizing foreign data can streamline the development timeline and bring new therapies to market more quickly.

- **Global Harmonization:** Encouraging compliance with GCP standards worldwide promotes consistency in clinical research practices, benefiting global health.

3.6 FDA Clinical Trials Guidance Document: Good Clinical Practice

3.6.1 Introduction to Good Clinical Practice (GCP)

Good Clinical Practice (GCP) is an internationally recognized standard for the design, conduct, performance, monitoring, auditing, recording, analysis, and reporting of clinical trials. The FDA's guidance on GCP provides detailed instructions and expectations for conducting clinical research to ensure the rights, safety, and well-being of trial participants. GCP guidelines also aim to guarantee the credibility and reliability of data generated from clinical trials, thereby facilitating the approval of new drugs and treatments.

3.6.2 Core Principles of GCP

The core principles of GCP cover various aspects of clinical research, including ethical conduct, protocol adherence, informed consent, and data integrity. These principles ensure that clinical trials are conducted in a manner that respects the rights of participants and produces high-quality, reliable data.

Key Principles:

- **Ethical Conduct:** Clinical trials should be conducted in accordance with ethical principles that have their origin in the Declaration of Helsinki. This includes respect for persons, beneficence, and justice.
- **Protocol Compliance:** Trials must be conducted according to a scientifically and ethically sound study protocol. Any deviations from the protocol must be documented and justified.
- **Informed Consent:** Participants must be fully informed about the trial, including its purpose, procedures, risks, and benefits, and must voluntarily agree to participate.
- **Data Integrity:** Accurate and complete data must be recorded and reported. This includes maintaining proper records and ensuring data security and confidentiality.

3.6.3 Roles and Responsibilities

GCP outlines the roles and responsibilities of various stakeholders involved in clinical trials, including sponsors, investigators, and Institutional

Review Boards (IRBs). Each party has specific duties to ensure the ethical and scientific integrity of the research.

Sponsors:

- **Trial Design and Management:** Sponsors are responsible for designing the trial, selecting qualified investigators, and providing necessary resources and oversight.
- **Regulatory Compliance:** Sponsors must ensure that trials comply with all applicable regulatory requirements and guidelines.
- **Data Monitoring:** Continuous monitoring of trial data is essential to ensure ongoing compliance with the protocol and GCP standards.

Investigators:

- **Participant Safety:** Investigators are responsible for the safety and welfare of trial participants, including obtaining informed consent and reporting adverse events.
- **Protocol Adherence:** Investigators must conduct the trial according to the approved protocol and document any deviations.
- **Data Accuracy:** Accurate and complete recording of trial data is critical for the integrity of the study.

IRBs:

- **Ethical Review:** IRBs are responsible for reviewing and approving the trial protocol to ensure it meets ethical standards.
- **Ongoing Oversight:** IRBs must provide continuous oversight of the trial to ensure compliance with ethical guidelines and regulatory requirements.

3.6.4 Informed Consent Process

The informed consent process is a fundamental aspect of GCP, ensuring that participants are fully aware of the trial's nature, risks, and benefits. This process involves several key steps:

- **Information Disclosure:** Participants must receive comprehensive information about the trial in a language they understand.

- **Comprehension:** Participants should have the opportunity to ask questions and receive clear answers to ensure they fully understand the information provided.
- **Voluntariness:** Consent must be given voluntarily, without coercion or undue influence. Participants should know they can withdraw from the trial at any time without penalty.

3.6.5 Monitoring and Auditing

Continuous monitoring and auditing are crucial for maintaining GCP standards throughout the trial. Monitoring involves regular review of trial conduct and data to ensure compliance with the protocol and GCP guidelines. Auditing is an independent assessment of trial activities and documentation to verify compliance with GCP.

Monitoring:

- **Regular Visits:** Monitors conduct regular site visits to review source documents, verify data accuracy, and ensure protocol adherence.
- **Issue Resolution:** Monitors identify and address any issues or deviations from GCP standards, providing corrective actions as needed.

Auditing:

- **Independent Review:** Audits are conducted by independent auditors who assess the trial's conduct and documentation.
- **Compliance Verification:** Audits verify that the trial complies with GCP guidelines, regulatory requirements, and the approved protocol.

3.7 Clinical Research Regulations in the European Union (EMA)

3.7.1 Introduction to EMA Regulations

The European Medicines Agency (EMA) is the regulatory authority responsible for the scientific evaluation, supervision, and safety monitoring of medicines in the European Union (EU). Established in 1995, the EMA plays a critical role in ensuring that medicines available in the EU are safe, effective, and of high quality. The EMA's regulations for clinical research are designed to harmonize standards across member states, facilitating the conduct of clinical trials and the approval of new drugs within the EU.

3.7.2 Clinical Trials Regulation (CTR) EU No 536/2014

The Clinical Trials Regulation (CTR) EU No 536/2014, which came into effect in January 2022, replaces the previous Clinical Trials Directive 2001/20/EC. The CTR aims to create a more harmonized and efficient framework for clinical trials across the EU, ensuring the protection of participants and the reliability of data.

Key Provisions of the CTR:

- **Single Portal and Database:** The CTR introduces a centralized EU portal and database, known as the Clinical Trials Information System (CTIS). Sponsors can submit clinical trial applications and reports through this single portal, simplifying the process and enhancing transparency.
- **Coordinated Assessment:** The regulation establishes a coordinated assessment procedure for multi-national clinical trials. This involves a single application for trials conducted in multiple member states, with a coordinated evaluation by the concerned national competent authorities.
- **Informed Consent:** The CTR reinforces the importance of informed consent, ensuring that participants receive comprehensive information about the trial, including its objectives, risks, and benefits, in a language they understand.
- **Transparency and Public Access:** The regulation mandates the publication of clinical trial information in the CTIS, making data publicly accessible and enhancing transparency in clinical research.

3.7.3 Good Clinical Practice (GCP) Compliance

The EMA requires that all clinical trials conducted in the EU comply with Good Clinical Practice (GCP) guidelines. GCP is an international ethical and scientific quality standard for the design, conduct, recording, and reporting of clinical trials. Compliance with GCP ensures that the rights, safety, and well-being of trial participants are protected and that the clinical trial data is credible and accurate.

Key Elements of GCP:

- **Ethical Principles:** Trials must adhere to ethical principles, including respect for persons, beneficence, and justice, as outlined in the Declaration of Helsinki.
- **Protocol Adherence:** Clinical trials must be conducted in accordance with a scientifically and ethically sound protocol, with any deviations

documented and justified.

- **Informed Consent:** Participants must provide informed consent, which involves understanding the trial's nature, risks, and benefits and agreeing to participate voluntarily.
- **Data Integrity:** Accurate and complete data must be recorded and reported, with appropriate measures to ensure data security and confidentiality.

3.7.4 Roles and Responsibilities

The EMA outlines specific roles and responsibilities for various stakeholders in clinical trials, including sponsors, investigators, and ethics committees.

Sponsors:

- **Trial Management:** Sponsors are responsible for designing the trial, selecting qualified investigators, and providing the necessary resources and oversight.
- **Regulatory Compliance:** Sponsors must ensure that trials comply with all applicable regulatory requirements and guidelines.
- **Monitoring:** Continuous monitoring of trial data and activities is essential to ensure compliance with the protocol and GCP standards.

Investigators:

- **Participant Safety:** Investigators are responsible for the safety and welfare of trial participants, including obtaining informed consent and reporting adverse events.
- **Protocol Compliance:** Investigators must conduct the trial according to the approved protocol and document any deviations.
- **Data Accuracy:** Accurate and complete recording of trial data is crucial for the integrity of the study.

Ethics Committees:

- **Ethical Review:** Ethics committees review and approve the trial protocol to ensure it meets ethical standards and protects participants.
- **Ongoing Oversight:** Ethics committees provide continuous oversight of the trial to ensure ongoing compliance with ethical guidelines and

regulatory requirements.

3.7.5 Inspections and Audits

The EMA conducts inspections and audits to ensure compliance with regulatory requirements and GCP standards. These inspections are carried out by national competent authorities and can occur at any stage of the clinical trial.

Inspection Focus:

- **Study Sites:** Inspections may involve visits to clinical trial sites to review procedures, data, and documentation.
- **Data Verification:** Inspectors verify the accuracy and completeness of data reported by the sponsor and investigators.
- **GCP Compliance:** Inspections assess compliance with GCP guidelines and identify any deviations or deficiencies that need to be addressed.

CHAPTER FOUR

Clinical Research Related Guidelines

Clinical research is governed by a wide array of guidelines that ensure trials are conducted in a standardized, ethical, and scientifically valid manner. This chapter focuses on the essential guidelines that shape the landscape of clinical trials, such as **Good Clinical Practice (GCP)** and **ICH GCP (E6)**, which serve as global benchmarks for the design and conduct of clinical trials. These guidelines ensure that clinical research is carried out in a manner that prioritizes patient safety and generates high-quality, reliable data.

The **Indian GCP Guidelines** are highlighted for their role in shaping clinical trial conduct within India, alongside the **ICMR Ethical Guidelines for Biomedical Research**, which provide a framework for ethical decision-making in the Indian context. Globally, guidelines developed by organizations such as the **CDSCO** and the **Global Harmonization Task Force (GHTF)** standardize research practices across different regions, ensuring uniformity and consistency in clinical research.

4.1 GOOD CLINICAL PRACTICE GUIDELINES (ICH GCP E6)

The **ICH Good Clinical Practice (GCP) E6** guidelines serve as the global standard for the design, conduct, monitoring, and reporting of clinical trials involving human subjects. These guidelines were developed by the **International Council for Harmonisation (ICH)** to ensure that clinical trials are conducted in a manner that is both scientifically sound and ethically responsible, safeguarding the rights, safety, and well-being of participants while ensuring the integrity of the clinical data.

4.1.1 Overview and Scope

The **ICH GCP E6** guidelines apply to all aspects of clinical trials, from the initial planning to the final reporting of results. These guidelines provide a detailed framework for **sponsors, investigators, monitors,** and **ethics committees** to follow in order to ensure compliance with **ethical standards** and **regulatory requirements.** One of the key principles is that a trial should be scientifically justified and have a clear, well-defined **protocol** that outlines the objectives, design, methodology, and statistical considerations. This ensures that the trial will provide valid and reliable data that can support regulatory decisions.

4.1.2 Ethics and Informed Consent

A cornerstone of **ICH GCP** is the emphasis on ethical conduct, primarily through the protection of **trial participants.** The guidelines mandate that trials must comply with the **Declaration of Helsinki,** which outlines the ethical principles for medical research involving humans. A critical component of this is obtaining **informed consent** from participants. Participants must be fully informed about the nature, purpose, potential risks, and benefits of the trial, and must voluntarily agree to participate. For instance, in a trial testing a new cancer drug, participants must be clearly informed about possible side effects, alternative treatments, and their right to withdraw from the study at any time without any penalty.

4.1.3 Responsibilities of Investigators

The guidelines place significant responsibility on the **principal investigator,** who is tasked with ensuring that the clinical trial is conducted according to the approved **protocol** and GCP standards. Investigators must ensure that all trial procedures are followed accurately and that any deviations are reported. They are also responsible for **participant safety,** including the monitoring and reporting of any **adverse events** that occur during the trial. For example, if a participant experiences an unexpected allergic reaction to the drug being tested, the investigator must document and report this promptly to the **sponsor** and **ethics committee.**

4.1.4 Role of Sponsors

Sponsors play a vital role in ensuring the quality and integrity of the clinical trial data. According to ICH GCP E6, the sponsor must ensure that the trial is well-designed, has adequate **funding,** and is monitored throughout its duration. Sponsors are also responsible for **data management,** ensuring that trial data is collected accurately and analyzed properly to produce reliable results. Furthermore, sponsors must ensure that **trial sites** are adequately equipped and staffed, and they are responsible for selecting qualified investigators and providing the necessary training and resources.

4.1.5 Monitoring and Quality Assurance

Monitoring is a key aspect of the ICH GCP guidelines, and sponsors must ensure that clinical trials are monitored to verify that data is accurate, complete, and consistent with source documents. This includes **on-site monitoring** and **remote monitoring** to ensure compliance with the trial protocol and regulatory requirements. In addition to monitoring, sponsors must establish a system of **quality assurance** to ensure that all processes comply with GCP standards and **Good Manufacturing Practice (GMP)** if applicable. This could involve **audits** of trial sites, review of data integrity, and ensuring that **standard operating procedures (SOPs)** are followed.

4.1.6 Data Handling and Record Keeping

The guidelines emphasize the importance of **data integrity**, requiring that all data from clinical trials must be recorded, handled, and stored in a way that allows for accurate reporting, interpretation, and verification. Investigators are required to maintain **source documents** and **trial records**, ensuring that these are available for inspection by regulatory authorities. For example, all case report forms (CRFs) and patient medical records must be kept securely and must be accessible in the event of an audit.

4.1.7 Adverse Event Reporting and Safety Monitoring

A major component of GCP is the **safety monitoring** of participants throughout the trial. **Adverse events (AEs)** and **serious adverse events (SAEs)** must be reported according to the timelines specified in the protocol and to the relevant regulatory authorities. **Safety monitoring boards** (DSMBs) may be established for higher-risk trials to provide ongoing assessments of participant safety and to determine whether a trial should be modified or discontinued based on safety concerns.

4.2 INDIAN GCP GUIDELINES

The **Good Clinical Practice (GCP) guidelines** in India are designed to ensure the ethical and scientific integrity of **clinical trials** conducted in the country. These guidelines, which align with international standards, provide a framework for conducting clinical research in a manner that prioritizes the safety and well-being of trial participants while ensuring the quality and reliability of data. Indian GCP guidelines focus on the roles and responsibilities of **sponsors, investigators, Institutional Ethics Committees (IECs),** and **regulatory authorities** in overseeing clinical trials.

A key element of the Indian GCP guidelines is the need for **informed consent,** where participants are thoroughly informed about the purpose of the study, potential risks, benefits, and their right to withdraw at any time.

For example, in a trial testing a new **antidiabetic medication**, participants must be fully aware of the possible side effects and alternative treatments available. The guidelines also emphasize the importance of **protocol adherence**, ensuring that clinical trials follow pre-approved procedures and that any deviations are reported to ethics committees. **Data integrity** is another critical component, with strict guidelines for recording and reporting results to avoid manipulation or misinterpretation of trial data.

Additionally, the guidelines cover **adverse event reporting**, mandating timely notification of any harmful effects experienced by trial participants. Overall, the Indian GCP guidelines provide a comprehensive framework for conducting ethical and scientifically sound clinical trials, ensuring that participant rights are protected while generating credible data for regulatory decisions.

4.3 ICMR ETHICAL GUIDELINES FOR BIOMEDICAL RESEARCH

The **Indian Council of Medical Research (ICMR)** developed its **Ethical Guidelines for Biomedical Research** to address ethical issues related to biomedical and health research involving human participants. These guidelines ensure that such research is conducted with respect for human dignity and without exploitation. They cover all aspects of **biomedical research**, from planning and approval to conducting and reporting results.

A major focus of the ICMR guidelines is on ensuring that research participants are treated fairly, with particular attention to vulnerable populations such as **children**, **pregnant women**, and **economically disadvantaged individuals**. For example, in research involving children, both **parental consent** and **child assent** (if the child is old enough) are required. The guidelines also emphasize the need for **confidentiality** and **privacy**, ensuring that participants' personal health information is protected throughout the study.

The ICMR guidelines stress the importance of **community engagement**, especially in research conducted in rural or marginalized communities, ensuring that the benefits of research are shared equitably. **Risk-benefit analysis** is another critical aspect, where researchers must ensure that the potential benefits of a study outweigh any risks to participants. Furthermore, **post-trial access** to effective treatments is encouraged, particularly in cases where the study finds a new drug or intervention that could benefit participants.

4.4 CDSCO GUIDELINES

The **Central Drugs Standard Control Organization (CDSCO)** is the national regulatory body in India responsible for approving and overseeing **clinical trials, drug approvals**, and the regulation of **medical devices**. The **CDSCO guidelines** are crucial for ensuring that medical products in India meet international standards of **safety, quality**, and **efficacy**. These guidelines govern various processes, from the approval of clinical trials to the post-market surveillance of drugs and devices.

The CDSCO guidelines mandate that all new drugs and medical devices undergo thorough clinical trials before they are approved for marketing in India. For example, if a pharmaceutical company wishes to introduce a new **antibiotic**, it must submit data from preclinical studies, followed by multiple phases of clinical trials demonstrating the drug's safety and efficacy. The guidelines ensure that these trials follow **Good Clinical Practice** (GCP) standards and are approved by **Ethics Committees**.

CDSCO also monitors the **pharmacovigilance** of marketed drugs, requiring manufacturers to report **adverse drug reactions (ADRs)** and conduct **post-marketing studies** if necessary. For high-risk products like **biologics** or **medical devices** (e.g., heart stents), the CDSCO guidelines require more stringent testing and post-approval monitoring to ensure long-term safety. Furthermore, the organization has guidelines for **import, manufacturing**, and **sale** of drugs, ensuring that quality control is maintained at every stage.

4.5 GHTF STUDY GROUP 5 GUIDANCE DOCUMENTS

The **Global Harmonization Task Force (GHTF)** was established to promote harmonization in the regulation of medical devices across different countries, ensuring the safety, performance, and quality of medical devices globally. **Study Group 5 (SG5)** of the GHTF focused on **clinical safety and performance** of medical devices, specifically addressing the requirements for clinical evidence, evaluation, and investigations. The **guidance documents** developed by SG5 provide a framework for the **clinical evaluation** of medical devices, which is essential to demonstrate their safety and effectiveness before they can be marketed. These documents are designed to harmonize the regulatory requirements across different jurisdictions and ensure that medical devices meet the necessary standards for patient care.

4.5.1 Clinical Evidence for Medical Devices – Key Concepts

SG5's guidance documents emphasize the importance of **clinical evidence** in supporting the safety and performance of a medical device.

Clinical evidence refers to the information derived from **clinical data** regarding the device's use in humans. This evidence is used to demonstrate that the device achieves its intended purpose without posing undue risk to patients. **Clinical evaluation** is the ongoing process of assessing the clinical data and making conclusions about the device's safety and performance. The GHTF guidance defines **clinical evaluation** as a structured approach to collecting, appraising, and analyzing clinical data.

The key components of **clinical evidence** include **clinical investigations, literature reviews**, and the **post-market surveillance** of similar devices. Clinical investigations involve the collection of data from formal clinical studies conducted on the medical device, while literature reviews analyze relevant existing clinical data from scientific publications. **Post-market surveillance** involves gathering real-world data on the device's performance after it has been introduced to the market, ensuring continuous monitoring of its safety and efficacy.

4.5.2 GHTF/SG5/N1R8:2007 – Clinical Evidence

The guidance document **GHTF/SG5/N1R8:2007** outlines the principles of **clinical evidence** required to support the **regulatory approval** of medical devices. It stresses that the level of clinical evidence should be proportional to the **risk** associated with the device. High-risk devices, such as implantable devices or life-supporting devices, require robust clinical investigations to demonstrate their safety and efficacy. For example, a **cardiac pacemaker** would necessitate extensive clinical trials to ensure that it functions safely and effectively in regulating heart rhythms. Conversely, lower-risk devices, such as a **bandage**, might rely on **literature reviews** and **historical data** from similar products.

The document also emphasizes the role of **equivalence** in clinical evaluations. If a device is substantially similar to an existing product, clinical data from the equivalent device may be used to support the safety and efficacy of the new device. However, it is crucial to ensure that the devices are comparable in terms of **design, materials**, and **intended use**.

4.5.3 GHTF/SG5/N2R8:2007 – Clinical Evaluation

The **GHTF/SG5/N2R8:2007** document provides detailed guidance on conducting a **clinical evaluation** for medical devices. Clinical evaluation is the process of systematically assessing clinical data, and it plays a central role in ensuring that a device meets regulatory requirements for **safety** and **performance**. This document outlines the steps for performing a clinical evaluation, including identifying relevant clinical data, appraising the quality and relevance of the data, and analyzing the data to determine whether the device performs as intended.

For example, a clinical evaluation for a new **orthopedic implant** would include reviewing data from clinical trials where the implant was used in patients with **joint problems**. Researchers would assess whether the implant improved patient outcomes, such as **mobility** and **pain reduction**, while monitoring for potential complications like **infection** or **implant failure**.

4.5.4 GHTF/SG5/N3:2010 – Post-Market Clinical Follow-Up (PMCF)

The **GHTF/SG5/N3:2010** guidance document focuses on the importance of **post-market clinical follow-up (PMCF)**, a key component of **post-market surveillance**. PMCF is conducted to gather additional data on the performance and safety of a device once it has been marketed. This is particularly important for devices that are **high-risk**, have **new technology**, or are used in **diverse patient populations** that may not have been fully represented in pre-market clinical trials.

PMCF activities may include ongoing **clinical studies**, **registries**, or **survey-based data collection** from users. For example, a manufacturer of a new type of **surgical stent** might conduct a PMCF study to track long-term patient outcomes, such as **stent durability** and **rates of restenosis** (narrowing of the blood vessels). This real-world data helps to confirm the long-term **safety** and **efficacy** of the device and can inform any necessary adjustments in its use or design.

4.5.5 GHTF/SG5/N4:2010 – Clinical Investigations

The **GHTF/SG5/N4:2010** guidance outlines the requirements for conducting **clinical investigations** on medical devices. Clinical investigations are formal studies that involve human participants and are designed to gather data on a device's **safety** and **performance** under controlled conditions. This guidance details the need for **ethical considerations**, including obtaining **informed consent** from participants, ensuring the study protocol is scientifically sound, and minimizing risks to patients.

For example, a clinical investigation for a new **diabetes monitoring device** would involve recruiting patients with **diabetes**, obtaining their consent, and monitoring their glucose levels using the new device compared to an existing standard. The study would assess the accuracy, reliability, and ease of use of the new device while also tracking any **adverse events** or complications.

4.6 ICH GUIDELINES ON EFFICACY AND SAFETY (E4, E7, E8, E10, E11)

The **International Council for Harmonisation (ICH)** has established a set of guidelines aimed at harmonizing the development and regulation of pharmaceutical products across different regions. The guidelines pertaining to **efficacy** and **safety** of medical products are crucial for ensuring that drugs and treatments are both effective and safe for the populations they are intended to serve. Five key ICH guidelines that focus on these areas are **E4 (Dose-Response Studies)**, **E7 (Geriatric Populations)**, **E8 (General Considerations for Clinical Trials)**, **E10 (Choice of Control Group in Clinical Trials)**, and **E11 (Clinical Investigation of Medicinal Products in the Pediatric Population)**. These guidelines provide a comprehensive framework for the design, conduct, and analysis of clinical studies to ensure that **regulatory decisions** are based on robust and well-validated data.

4.6.1 ICH E4 – Dose-Response Studies

The **ICH E4 guideline** emphasizes the importance of understanding the relationship between the **dose** of a drug and its **clinical response. Dose-response studies** are fundamental for determining the optimal dose that provides the maximum therapeutic benefit with minimal side effects. The guideline recommends that both **efficacy** and **safety** data be gathered across a range of doses to establish a **dose-response curve**. For instance, in a clinical trial for an anti-hypertensive drug, patients might be given doses of 10 mg, 20 mg, and 40 mg, and the effect on **blood pressure reduction** would be measured. The guideline also highlights the importance of **statistical modeling** to accurately estimate the **therapeutic window**—the range of doses that offer the best balance between efficacy and safety.

4.6.2 ICH E7 – Geriatric Populations

ICH E7 focuses on the inclusion of **geriatric populations** in clinical trials, recognizing that older adults often have different **pharmacokinetic** and **pharmacodynamic** profiles compared to younger adults. The guideline addresses the necessity of studying the **efficacy** and **safety** of drugs specifically in **patients aged 65 and older**, as aging can affect drug absorption, distribution, metabolism, and excretion. For example, older patients may have reduced **renal function**, which can alter the clearance of certain drugs, necessitating dose adjustments. The E7 guideline recommends that clinical trials include sufficient numbers of geriatric patients to identify any differences in **adverse event profiles** or **therapeutic effects**. Moreover, it stresses the need to evaluate **age-related diseases** and conditions that could impact treatment outcomes, such as co-morbidities like diabetes or heart disease.

4.6.3 ICH E8 – General Considerations for Clinical Trials

ICH E8 provides an overarching framework for the design and conduct of **clinical trials**, focusing on ensuring that trials are scientifically sound and ethically conducted. It emphasizes the importance of **trial objectives**, **study design**, and **study population** selection to ensure that the results are generalizable to the intended patient population. The guideline outlines the steps involved in planning a clinical trial, from **defining the study hypothesis** to determining the **appropriate endpoints** and **sample size**. For instance, in a trial evaluating a new cancer treatment, the **primary endpoint** could be **overall survival**, while secondary endpoints might include **progression-free survival** and **quality of life**. ICH E8 also highlights the need for **data integrity** and **quality control** measures throughout the trial process to ensure the reliability of the study outcomes.

4.6.4 ICH E10 – Choice of Control Group in Clinical Trials

The **ICH E10 guideline** focuses on the selection of an appropriate **control group** in clinical trials, which is essential for making valid comparisons between treatments. The guideline provides recommendations on different types of **control groups**, including **placebo-controlled**, **active comparator**, and **historical controls**. The choice of control depends on various factors such as the **disease under study, ethical considerations**, and the **objective of the trial**. For instance, in a trial for a **life-threatening condition**, using a placebo may not be ethical, and an **active control** would be more appropriate. The guideline also discusses the potential for **bias** and the importance of **blinding** in reducing the risk of systematic errors. It ensures that the selection of the control group aligns with the **scientific rationale** of the study, while also safeguarding the rights and well-being of participants.

4.6.5 ICH E11 – Clinical Investigation of Medicinal Products in the Pediatric Population

ICH E11 addresses the specific challenges of conducting clinical research in **pediatric populations**, which have unique physiological and developmental considerations. The guideline recognizes that children cannot simply be treated as "small adults" and that their **response to drugs** may vary significantly depending on their **age, developmental stage**, and **maturity of organs** like the liver and kidneys. The guideline encourages the inclusion of **pediatric patients** in clinical trials whenever possible to ensure that medicines are appropriately tested for **safety, efficacy,** and **dosing** in children. For example, the dosing of an **antibiotic** in a 5-year-old might be based on **body weight** or **body surface area**, and safety assessments would focus on potential **developmental toxicities**. Additionally, the guideline stresses the importance of **ethical considerations** when enrolling children in trials, including the need for **parental consent** and **assent** from older children.

4.7 GENERAL BIOSTATISTICS PRINCIPLES APPLIED IN CLINICAL RESEARCH

Biostatistics plays a critical role in **clinical research** by offering tools to collect, analyze, interpret, and present **medical data**. The principles of biostatistics are essential for understanding the nature of biological variability and ensuring the **reliability and validity** of clinical findings. In clinical research, biostatistical methods guide the process of decision-making, ensuring that the conclusions drawn from medical data are based on **statistical evidence** rather than random variation or bias.

4.7.1 Descriptive Statistics

The first step in any clinical research is to describe the collected data. **Descriptive statistics** summarize the data and give a clear picture of the **sample characteristics**. This includes measures of central tendency such as the **mean** (average value of the data), **median** (the middle value when the data is ordered), and **mode** (the most frequent value). For instance, if the **blood pressure** levels of 100 patients are measured, the mean value might be 120 mmHg, with a median of 118 mmHg, indicating that most patients have a blood pressure level near 120 mmHg. Additionally, measures of **dispersion** like the **range, variance,** and **standard deviation** help us understand the spread of the data. For example, if the **standard deviation** of the blood pressure levels is 10 mmHg, it suggests that most of the patients' blood pressure values lie within 10 mmHg of the mean.

4.7.2 Inferential Statistics

Inferential statistics allow researchers to make generalizations about a population based on sample data. In clinical research, this is crucial when it is not feasible to study the entire population. **Hypothesis testing** is a key part of inferential statistics. Researchers typically start with a **null hypothesis** (H^0), which assumes that there is no effect or difference. A **p-value** is used to determine whether to reject the null hypothesis. For example, in a study comparing the effectiveness of two treatments, if the p-value is less than 0.05 (the commonly accepted significance level), researchers reject the null hypothesis and conclude that there is a statistically significant difference between the two treatments. Another important concept is the **confidence interval** (CI), which gives a range of values within which the true population parameter is likely to lie. A **95% confidence interval** means that we can be 95% confident that the true value lies within that range. For example, if a drug's effectiveness is measured with a mean reduction in symptom severity of 2.5 (95% CI: 2.0 to 3.0), this interval provides an estimate of the drug's real-world effect.

4.7.3 Sampling Methods

Sampling is a fundamental aspect of clinical research as it is often impractical or impossible to study an entire population. Therefore, researchers rely on representative samples to make inferences about the larger population. There are different **sampling methods** such as **random sampling, systematic sampling, stratified sampling,** and **cluster sampling.** **Random sampling** ensures each member of the population has an equal chance of being selected, minimizing bias. For example, in a study on diabetes in adults, a **random sample** of 500 patients might be selected from a population of 10,000 individuals. **Stratified sampling** is useful when the population is heterogeneous; for instance, researchers may divide the population into age groups before sampling to ensure each age group is proportionally represented.

4.7.4 Study Designs

Study design is critical in determining the strength and reliability of the results. The most common designs in clinical research include **randomized controlled trials (RCTs), cohort studies, case-control studies,** and **cross-sectional studies.** RCTs are considered the gold standard for determining the efficacy of interventions. In an RCT, participants are randomly assigned to either the treatment or control group, which reduces selection bias. For instance, in a drug efficacy trial, 500 participants might be randomly assigned to receive either the new drug or a placebo. **Cohort studies** follow a group of people over time to assess the effects of certain exposures, like a study following smokers and non-smokers for 10 years to observe the development of lung disease. **Case-control studies** compare patients with a condition (cases) to those without (controls), while **cross-sectional studies** provide a snapshot of the population at a single point in time.

4.7.5 Bias and Confounding

In clinical research, **bias** and **confounding** are significant challenges that can affect the validity of results. **Selection bias** occurs when the study sample is not representative of the population, while **information bias** happens when data collection methods introduce systematic errors. For example, in a study on heart disease, if younger and healthier participants are more likely to be included, the results may underestimate the true risk in the general population. **Confounding** occurs when a third variable affects both the exposure and outcome, creating a false association. For instance, if a study finds an association between coffee drinking and heart disease, but **smoking** is more prevalent among coffee drinkers, smoking could be a confounder. To address confounding, researchers can use **statistical methods** like **multivariate analysis** to adjust for confounders or **randomization** in RCTs to distribute confounders equally across study groups.

4.7.6 Statistical Power and Sample Size

Statistical power is the probability that a study will detect an effect if there is one to be found. **Power** is influenced by the **sample size, effect size**, and **significance level**. A **high-powered study** reduces the risk of **Type II errors** (failing to reject a false null hypothesis). For example, in a clinical trial with a sample size of 200 patients, if the **power** is calculated to be 80%, there is an 80% chance of detecting a true difference between treatment groups. **Sample size** calculation is crucial because too small a sample may not detect a real difference (underpowered study), while an unnecessarily large sample wastes resources. For instance, using standard sample size formulas, a study might determine that 150 participants are required to detect a clinically significant difference in blood pressure reduction between two treatments.

4.7.7 Ethical Considerations

Ethical principles in clinical research are guided by respect for persons, **beneficence**, and **justice**. Researchers must ensure informed consent, confidentiality, and the protection of vulnerable populations. All clinical trials must be reviewed by an **Institutional Review Board (IRB)** to ensure that the risks to participants are minimized and justified. For instance, in a trial testing a new cancer treatment, the **IRB** would review the study protocol to ensure the potential benefits outweigh the risks to patients. Additionally, researchers must be transparent in their reporting and avoid manipulating data or **p-hacking** to achieve statistically significant results. **Clinical equipoise**, the genuine uncertainty within the expert medical community regarding the superiority of one treatment over another, is also a key ethical consideration in RCTs.

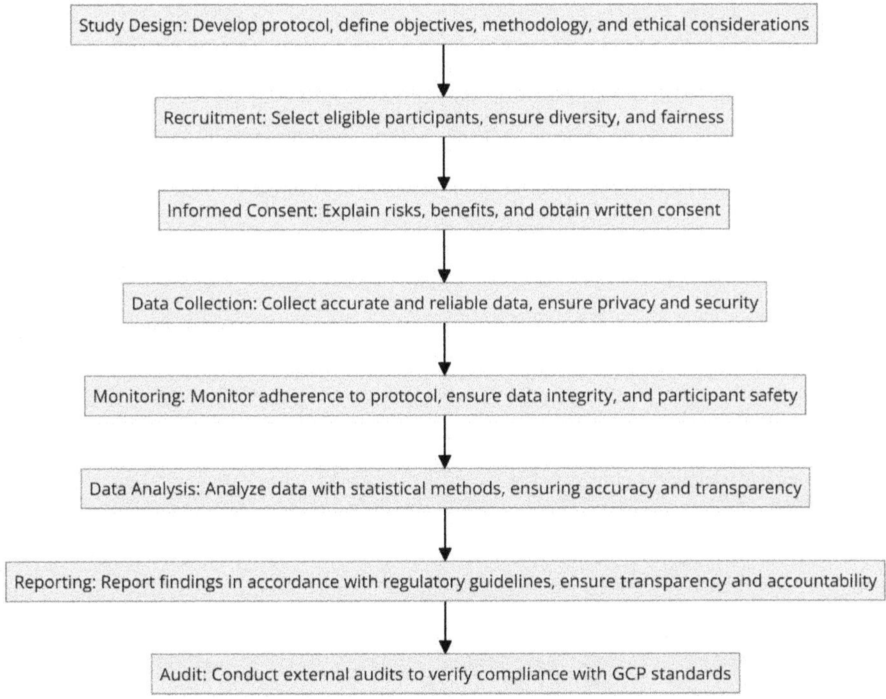

Good Clinical Practice (GCP) Principles

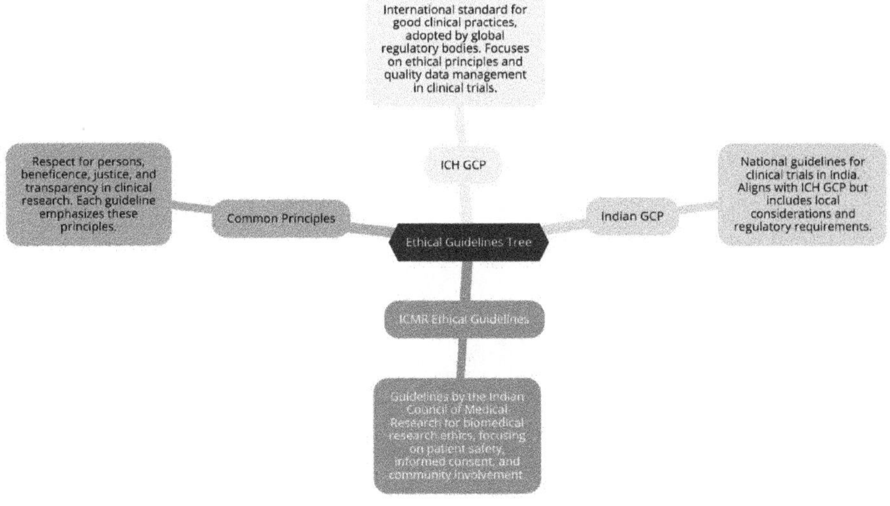

Interconnected Ethical Guidelines in Clinical Research: ICH GCP, Indian GCP, and ICMR

• 94 •

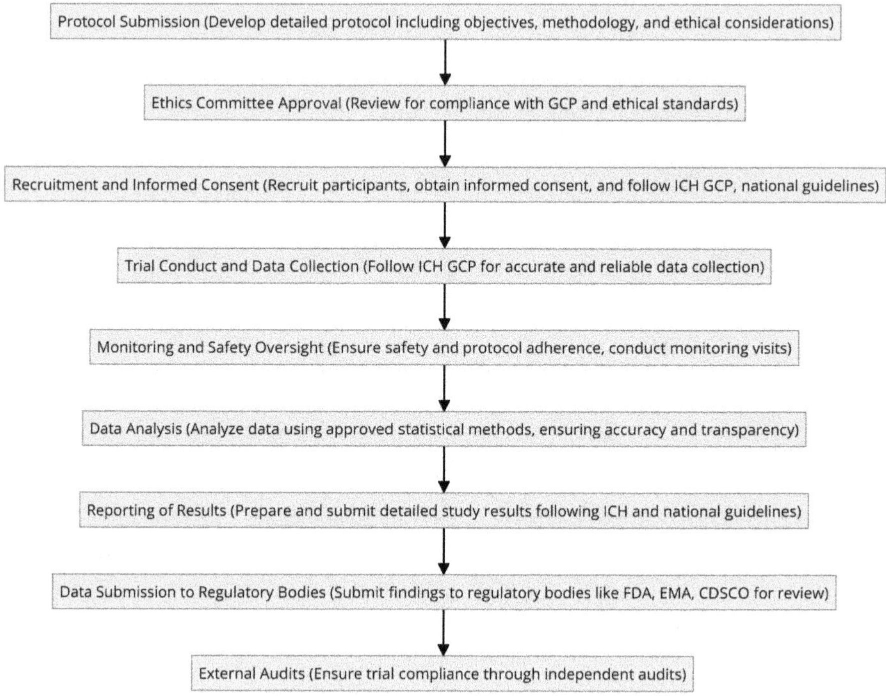

Comprehensive Clinical Trial Process: From Protocol Submission to Regulatory Data Submission

CHAPTER FIVE

USA Guidance

The USA has one of the most comprehensive and stringent regulatory frameworks for pharmaceuticals, overseen by the Food and Drug Administration (FDA). This chapter provides a deep dive into the organization and functions of the FDA, offering a detailed examination of how the agency ensures that drugs, biologics, medical devices, and even cosmetics meet the highest standards of safety, efficacy, and quality before reaching the public.

This chapter also covers the history and evolution of key legislation, such as the Federal Food, Drug, and Cosmetic Act (FFDCA), which lays the groundwork for modern drug regulation in the United States. The Hatch-Waxman Act, which governs the approval of generic drugs through the ANDA (Abbreviated New Drug Application) process, is explored in depth. Similarly, the role of the Drug Master Files (DMF) system is discussed, outlining how companies submit confidential information about the drug's manufacturing process to the FDA.

Other key topics include the Regulatory Approval Processes for IND, NDA, ANDA, and SNDA, as well as the specific regulatory requirements for orphan drugs, combination products, and the import, manufacture, and sale of cosmetics in the USA. The FDA's role extends beyond pre-market approval to post-market surveillance, ensuring that drugs continue to be safe and effective after they have been made available to consumers. This chapter provides essential guidance for those seeking to understand or work within the complex regulatory framework of the United States, offering insights into both the procedural and practical aspects of compliance with FDA standards.

5.1 Organization Structure and Functions of FDA

The **U.S. Food and Drug Administration (FDA)** is a critical regulatory body responsible for safeguarding public health in the United States. The

FDA operates under the **Department of Health and Human Services (HHS)**. Its main functions are ensuring the **safety, efficacy,** and **quality** of **food, drugs, biologics, medical devices, cosmetics,** and **radiation-emitting products.** The FDA also plays a significant role in regulating **tobacco products** and advancing **public health initiatives** through various channels.

The FDA is divided into several **centers** and **offices,** each focusing on different regulatory areas. At the top of the FDA's structure is the **Office of the Commissioner (OC),** headed by the **FDA Commissioner,** who is appointed by the President and confirmed by the Senate. The **Office of the Commissioner** oversees all the centers and ensures that policies and regulatory actions align with the **agency's mission.**

One of the primary divisions under the FDA is the **Center for Drug Evaluation and Research (CDER).** This center is responsible for regulating **prescription** and **over-the-counter drugs.** CDER ensures that drugs marketed in the U.S. are **safe** and **effective.** It reviews **new drug applications (NDAs)** and **investigational new drug (IND) applications.** For instance, CDER evaluates **clinical trial data** and assesses whether a drug's **benefits outweigh its risks** for public use. In 2022, CDER approved over **35 new molecular entities** (NMEs), showing its critical role in drug regulation.

The **Center for Biologics Evaluation and Research (CBER)** is another major division. CBER focuses on the regulation of **biological products,** including **vaccines, blood products,** and **gene therapies.** It ensures the safety of the **nation's blood supply** and approves new **biologics** for public use. For example, during the COVID-19 pandemic, CBER played a key role in the evaluation and approval of **mRNA vaccines** by reviewing data from clinical trials. CBER also collaborates with **international regulatory bodies** to establish **global standards** for biological product safety.

The **Center for Devices and Radiological Health (CDRH)** oversees **medical devices** and **radiation-emitting products.** CDRH evaluates both **pre-market applications** for new devices and **post-market surveillance** to ensure device safety. Devices are classified into different categories, ranging from **Class I** (low risk) to **Class III** (high risk). For instance, CDRH reviews **510(k) submissions** for Class II devices and **Premarket Approval (PMA) applications** for Class III devices. In 2022, CDRH cleared over **3,500 medical devices,** indicating its extensive oversight.

Another important division is the **Center for Food Safety and Applied Nutrition (CFSAN).** CFSAN regulates **food safety,** including food additives and **dietary supplements**. It ensures that food products are free from **contaminants**, properly labeled, and safe for consumption. For example, CFSAN investigates foodborne illnesses and sets regulations for **food manufacturing practices** to prevent contamination. In 2021, CFSAN handled over **700 recalls** related to food safety concerns.

The **Center for Tobacco Products (CTP)** was established following the passage of the **Family Smoking Prevention and Tobacco Control Act of 2009**. The CTP regulates the manufacture, marketing, and distribution of **tobacco products** to protect public health. It reviews new tobacco products through **Premarket Tobacco Product Applications (PMTAs)** and enforces regulations to reduce tobacco use among minors. The **FDA's tobacco regulatory authority** aims to lower tobacco-related illnesses and deaths in the U.S.

In addition to these centers, the **Office of Regulatory Affairs (ORA)** is responsible for **field inspections** and **enforcement activities**. ORA conducts inspections of **manufacturing facilities** to ensure compliance with **current Good Manufacturing Practices (cGMP)**. It also handles product recalls, issues warning letters, and monitors **imports** to prevent the entry of unsafe products. For instance, ORA inspects pharmaceutical manufacturing plants both in the U.S. and abroad to ensure drug safety and quality.

The FDA also has specialized offices like the **Office of Global Policy and Strategy (OGPS)**, which coordinates with **international regulatory agencies**. The **FDA's international collaborations** are crucial for regulating **imported products**, which make up a significant portion of the U.S. market. The OGPS helps align U.S. regulations with global standards to ensure the safety of products from **foreign markets**.

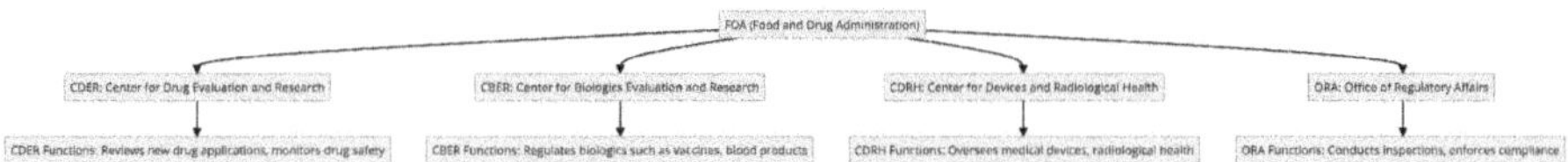

FDA Organizational Structure

5.2 Federal Register and Code of Federal Regulations (CFR)

The **Federal Register** and the **Code of Federal Regulations (CFR)** are two important tools for the dissemination of **rules, regulations,** and **legal guidelines** in the United States. These documents are essential for both regulatory bodies like the **FDA** and industries that must comply with federal laws. Understanding the role and structure of the **Federal Register** and the **CFR** is vital for navigating the regulatory landscape, especially in fields like **pharmaceuticals, medical devices, food safety**, and **public health**.

The **Federal Register** is the official **daily publication** of the U.S. government for **proposed rules, final rules, public notices**, and **presidential documents**. It is published each weekday, except on federal holidays, and serves as the mechanism through which the government communicates with the public and interested stakeholders. Agencies like the **FDA** use the **Federal Register** to announce **proposed regulations**, seek **public comments**, and publish **final rules** once they are approved. Each publication in the **Federal Register** includes a **preamble**, which explains the rationale for the rule, followed by the proposed or final text of the regulation.

For instance, when the FDA wishes to introduce a new regulation regarding **medical device safety**, it first publishes the **proposed rule** in the **Federal Register**. The public is typically given **30 to 90 days** to submit comments, which the FDA then reviews before issuing a final rule. This process ensures **transparency** and allows for public participation in the regulatory process. In 2022, the **Federal Register** contained over **70,000 pages** of regulatory updates, showing its significant role in keeping the public informed about changes in federal law.

Once a rule is finalized, it is codified in the **Code of Federal Regulations (CFR)**. The **CFR** is a **comprehensive set** of rules and regulations organized by subject matter. It is divided into **50 titles**, each representing a broad area of federal regulation. For example, **Title 21** of the **CFR** deals with **food and drugs**, which includes regulations governing the **FDA**. Within Title 21, there are various parts that cover specific topics like **drug approval, medical devices, cosmetics**, and **dietary supplements**.

The **CFR** is updated annually and is an essential reference for industries and regulatory professionals. It provides the **official legal text** of all rules in force, ensuring that regulated entities can stay compliant with federal law. For example, pharmaceutical companies refer to **21 CFR Part 314** for regulations on **new drug applications (NDAs)**, while **medical device manufacturers** consult **21 CFR Part 820** for rules on **quality system regulation**. The FDA itself enforces these regulations during **inspections** and **compliance reviews**.

Another key feature of the **CFR** is its structured format, which makes it easy to navigate. Each **part** within a title is divided into **sections**, which detail specific regulatory requirements. For instance, **21 CFR Part 312** provides detailed guidance on the **investigational new drug (IND) application** process, outlining the requirements for clinical trials, safety reporting, and investigator responsibilities. This structure allows both regulators and industry professionals to quickly find the specific rules that apply to their activities.

The importance of the **CFR** extends beyond U.S. borders, as many other countries model their regulatory frameworks after it. Moreover, U.S. companies that export products must comply with these regulations to ensure that their products are safe and effective, meeting global standards. Non-compliance with **CFR regulations** can lead to serious consequences, including **product recalls, fines,** and **legal actions**.

It is also important to note that the **Federal Register** and **CFR** are publicly accessible. Both are available online, ensuring that businesses, legal professionals, and individuals can access the most up-to-date regulatory information. The **Electronic Code of Federal Regulations (eCFR)** is a popular resource that provides real-time updates on regulatory changes, whereas the **Federal Register** website offers a searchable database of daily publications. In 2022, the eCFR had over **5 million visitors**, showing the demand for up-to-date legal information.

The **Federal Register** serves as the government's method for announcing new regulations and seeking public input, while the **CFR** compiles these rules into an organized legal document. Together, they form the backbone of the U.S. regulatory system, ensuring that all stakeholders have access to transparent, structured, and enforceable laws. Understanding these tools is essential for compliance and navigating the complexities of federal regulation in industries regulated by the **FDA** and other U.S. agencies.

5.3 History and Evolution of the United States Federal, Food, Drug, and Cosmetic Act (FFDCA)

The **United States Federal Food, Drug, and Cosmetic Act (FFDCA)** is a cornerstone of American public health law. Its origins can be traced back to the early 20th century, when growing concerns about the **safety of food** and **drug products** led to demands for stronger federal regulation. The **FFDCA** was officially enacted in **1938**, but its development was shaped by a series of events, legislative changes, and public health crises.

The first major step toward regulating food and drugs occurred with the passage of the **Pure Food and Drug Act of 1906**. This law was prompted by widespread concerns about the **unsanitary conditions** in food production, as well as the sale of **misbranded** and **adulterated drugs**. The publication of **Upton Sinclair's novel "The Jungle"**, which exposed unsafe practices in the meatpacking industry, played a significant role in mobilizing public support for the law. The **1906 Act** was a landmark at the time, giving the government the authority to regulate interstate commerce in food and drugs. However, its limitations quickly became apparent. The law did not require **pre-market approval** of drugs, nor did it set comprehensive safety standards for food and cosmetic products.

The inadequacies of the **1906 Act** became even more evident in the **1930s**, following a tragic incident involving a drug known as **Elixir Sulfanilamide**. In **1937**, the drug was marketed as a treatment for bacterial infections, but it contained **diethylene glycol**, a toxic solvent. The drug caused the deaths of over **100 people**, including many children. This public health disaster prompted the need for stronger drug safety regulations, leading to the creation of the **Federal Food, Drug, and Cosmetic Act of 1938**.

The **FFDCA of 1938** significantly expanded the regulatory authority of the **FDA**. It required that drugs be shown to be **safe** before they could be marketed, establishing a **pre-market approval system** for the first time. This was a major shift from the 1906 law, which had only required drugs to be accurately labeled. In addition, the **1938 Act** extended federal oversight to **cosmetic products** and **medical devices**, areas that were previously unregulated. The law also set new standards for **food safety**, prohibiting the sale of **adulterated** or **misbranded** food products.

The **FFDCA** continued to evolve over the decades as new public health challenges and technological advancements emerged. In **1962**, the **Kefauver-Harris Amendments** were added to the FFDCA in response to the **thalidomide tragedy**, in which thousands of children were born with birth defects after their mothers had taken the drug during pregnancy. These amendments introduced the requirement that drug manufacturers provide evidence not only of **safety** but also of **effectiveness** before receiving FDA approval. This shifted the burden of proof onto the drug companies and significantly strengthened the **drug approval process**.

Another important evolution of the **FFDCA** came in **1976** with the passage of the **Medical Device Amendments**. Prior to this, medical devices were subject to minimal regulation. The amendments established a classification system for devices based on their **risk** and required **premarket approval** for high-risk devices, similar to the system in place for drugs. This was a response to incidents involving defective medical devices, such as the **Dalkon Shield** intrauterine device, which caused serious injuries to thousands of women.

Further amendments to the FFDCA have focused on specific public health concerns. In **1990**, the **Nutrition Labeling and Education Act (NLEA)** was passed, mandating that food products include **detailed nutrition labels**. This helped consumers make informed choices about the food they were consuming and gave the FDA more control over **nutritional claims** made by manufacturers. The **Dietary Supplement Health and Education Act of 1994 (DSHEA)** also modified the FFDCA by establishing specific regulations for **dietary supplements**, allowing them to be sold without FDA pre-market approval, but giving the FDA the authority to take action if products were found to be unsafe.

In more recent years, the **Food Safety Modernization Act (FSMA)** of **2011** further expanded the scope of the FFDCA, particularly in relation to food safety. FSMA shifted the focus of federal regulation from responding to contamination to **preventing** it, granting the FDA greater authority to enforce food safety standards across the supply chain.

The **FFDCA** remains the foundation of the **FDA's regulatory powers** and continues to evolve in response to new scientific knowledge and public health concerns. Today, the **FFDCA** governs a wide array of products, including **prescription drugs**, **biologics**, **vaccines**, **medical devices**, **cosmetics**, and **dietary supplements**. Its provisions are codified in **Title 21** of the **Code of Federal Regulations (CFR)**, which includes detailed rules on product approval processes, labeling, manufacturing standards, and post-market surveillance.

The history of the **FFDCA** illustrates the need for continuous oversight and adaptation to ensure that the products people use are **safe, effective,** and **properly labeled**. Each amendment and regulatory development has addressed specific shortcomings in the system, building a stronger framework for protecting public health in the United States.

5.4 Hatch-Waxman Act and Orange Book, Purple Book

The **Hatch-Waxman Act**, formally known as the **Drug Price Competition and Patent Term Restoration Act of 1984**, was a pivotal piece of legislation that reshaped the pharmaceutical industry in the United

States. The primary goal of the Hatch-Waxman Act was to balance two key objectives: **encouraging innovation** in drug development and **promoting the availability of low-cost generic drugs**. Before this Act, the process of bringing **generic drugs** to market was time-consuming and expensive, as generic manufacturers had to conduct their own **clinical trials** to prove both the safety and effectiveness of their products.

One of the key provisions of the **Hatch-Waxman Act** was the creation of the **Abbreviated New Drug Application (ANDA)** process. This allowed generic drug manufacturers to submit an ANDA instead of a full **New Drug Application (NDA)**. Under an ANDA, generic companies are not required to repeat clinical trials, but must prove that their product is **bioequivalent** to the brand-name drug. This means that the generic drug must deliver the same amount of **active ingredient** into a patient's bloodstream within the same time frame as the original product. This provision significantly reduced the cost and time required to bring generic drugs to market, leading to a rapid increase in the availability of generic alternatives.

The Hatch-Waxman Act also included provisions that allowed **brand-name drug manufacturers** to extend the life of their patents. Specifically, the Act introduced the concept of **patent term restoration**, which compensated for the time a drug spent under **regulatory review** before it could be marketed. Brand-name manufacturers could receive an extension of their **patent life** by up to **five years**, though the total patent protection from the time of the patent filing could not exceed **14 years** post-FDA approval. This provision was designed to ensure that innovators were rewarded for their investments in research and development, even if regulatory delays shortened the time they could exclusively market their products.

Another important feature of the Hatch-Waxman Act was the creation of the **Orange Book**. The **Orange Book**, officially titled the **Approved Drug Products with Therapeutic Equivalence Evaluations**, is a **list of drugs** that the **FDA** has approved, along with patent information and **therapeutic equivalence** ratings. Drugs listed in the Orange Book are categorized based on their patent status and whether they have generic equivalents available. The **therapeutic equivalence codes** in the Orange Book provide guidance on whether a generic drug is equivalent to the brand-name product. For instance, drugs that are **bioequivalent** and **pharmaceutically equivalent** receive an "AB" rating. The Orange Book is an essential reference for **pharmacists, healthcare providers**, and **generic manufacturers**, helping them identify which drugs can be substituted with generic equivalents.

In addition to the Orange Book, the **Purple Book** was introduced in **2014** to provide information on **biological products**. Unlike traditional small-molecule drugs, **biologics** are large, complex molecules that are often produced using living organisms. The **Biologics Price Competition and Innovation Act (BPCIA)** of **2009**, which was part of the Affordable Care Act, created a regulatory pathway for **biosimilars**, similar to how the Hatch-Waxman Act facilitated the approval of generic drugs. The **Purple Book** lists all FDA-approved biologics and biosimilars, along with information on their **interchangeability**. While **generic drugs** are usually interchangeable with their brand-name counterparts, **biosimilars** are not automatically considered interchangeable with the reference product unless specifically designated by the FDA. The Purple Book serves as a key resource for determining which biologic products are available and which biosimilars can be substituted for the reference biologic.

The impact of the **Hatch-Waxman Act** on the pharmaceutical market has been profound. Since its enactment, **generic drug utilization** in the U.S. has skyrocketed, with generic drugs now accounting for **90% of prescriptions** filled in the country. This has resulted in significant cost savings for both consumers and the healthcare system. It is estimated that the availability of generic drugs saves the U.S. healthcare system over **$300 billion annually**. At the same time, the patent extensions provided under the Hatch-Waxman Act have allowed innovator companies to recoup their research investments, fostering continued **drug development** and innovation.

The Hatch-Waxman Act also introduced the concept of **180-day market exclusivity** for the first generic applicant that challenges a brand-name patent through a process known as **Paragraph IV certification**. This exclusivity period encourages generic manufacturers to challenge patents and bring lower-cost alternatives to market more quickly. However, the provision has also led to **litigation** between brand-name and generic manufacturers, as brand-name companies may seek to delay generic entry by filing lawsuits. These **patent challenges** have become a common feature of the U.S. pharmaceutical market, with **brand-name companies** often settling with generic manufacturers to delay the launch of generic products.

The **Hatch-Waxman Act**, along with the creation of the **Orange Book** and **Purple Book**, has transformed the U.S. pharmaceutical landscape. It has struck a delicate balance between **incentivizing innovation** through patent protection and **facilitating access** to affordable medications through the availability of generic drugs and biosimilars. This framework continues to play a critical role in regulating the pharmaceutical industry and ensuring that patients have access to both innovative therapies and affordable alternatives.

5.5 Drug Master Files (DMF) System in the USA

The **Drug Master Files (DMF) system** in the United States is a critical component of the regulatory framework for pharmaceuticals. The **DMF** is a confidential document submitted to the **FDA** by a pharmaceutical manufacturer or supplier to provide detailed information about the facilities, processes, or ingredients used in the manufacturing of a drug product. The purpose of the DMF system is to allow the sharing of proprietary information with the FDA without disclosing it to the drug applicant, thereby protecting the intellectual property of the manufacturer or supplier.

A **Drug Master File** contains important technical data related to **active pharmaceutical ingredients (APIs), excipients, packaging materials**, or **manufacturing processes**. It allows manufacturers to provide this information to the **FDA** while maintaining confidentiality from other parties, such as the drug product manufacturers that may use the same materials in their products. The DMF system is particularly useful for manufacturers that supply materials to multiple drug companies, as it avoids the need to submit the same information multiple times.

There are **five types** of DMFs, each serving a specific purpose:

- **Type I DMF**: This file pertains to the **manufacturing site, facilities, and operating procedures**. It contains information on the location of the manufacturing plant, its layout, and the procedures used to ensure proper operation. Although **Type I DMFs** are rarely submitted today, they were more commonly used in the past to document the general structure of manufacturing facilities.

- **Type II DMF**: This type focuses on **drug substances, drug substance intermediates, and materials used in their preparation**. It contains detailed information about the production process of the **API** and any intermediates. **Type II DMFs** are one of the most commonly submitted files, as they provide comprehensive data on the drug's **quality, purity**, and **stability**. For example, a manufacturer producing an API like **atorvastatin** would submit a **Type II DMF** with detailed information on the synthesis process, quality control measures, and specifications for the API.

- **Type III DMF**: This file relates to **packaging materials** used for drug products. It includes data on the composition, safety, and suitability of the packaging materials, such as **bottles, blisters,** or **capsules**. For example, a **Type III DMF** might contain details about the **plastic resin** used to make tablet bottles, demonstrating that the material does not interact with or degrade the drug product. This ensures the drug remains safe and effective throughout its shelf life.
- **Type IV DMF**: This type covers **excipients, colorants, flavorings,** and **materials used in drug formulations**. For instance, a manufacturer supplying **magnesium stearate** (a common tablet lubricant) would submit a **Type IV DMF** to provide information about the material's purity, origin, and manufacturing process.
- **Type V DMF**: This is a **miscellaneous DMF** and may contain information not covered by the other types, such as **contract manufacturing agreements, quality control agreements,** or **environmental control measures.**

One of the key benefits of the **DMF system** is that it allows manufacturers to **update** their files as new information becomes available, without needing to resubmit a full application. This **flexibility** ensures that the **FDA** always has access to the most up-to-date information. For example, if a supplier changes the manufacturing process for an API, they can submit a **DMF amendment** to reflect the change, ensuring that all stakeholders are aware of the updated process.

While DMFs are not required by law, they are highly encouraged, especially for companies that do not want to disclose proprietary information to drug applicants. **Pharmaceutical companies** often rely on suppliers that have **active DMFs** with the FDA to avoid the complexities of submitting proprietary manufacturing information in their own applications. In return, the **FDA** reviews the DMF during the evaluation of **New Drug Applications (NDAs)** or **Abbreviated New Drug Applications (ANDAs).**

The submission of a DMF does not itself lead to **FDA approval,** nor does it grant the submitter a specific regulatory status. Instead, it provides supporting documentation that is used in the assessment of a drug product's application. When a pharmaceutical company submits an **NDA** or **ANDA,** it can refer to the DMF by providing the **DMF number**. The **FDA** then reviews the referenced DMF alongside the drug application to ensure that all components meet regulatory requirements.

In 2022, the **FDA** received over **3,000 DMF submissions**, reflecting the growing complexity of pharmaceutical supply chains and the increasing reliance on third-party manufacturers. The **globalization** of pharmaceutical manufacturing has further heightened the importance of the DMF system, as many drug ingredients are produced by **foreign suppliers**. The DMF system ensures that the **FDA** can maintain oversight of these suppliers without requiring them to submit full **drug applications**.

DMF system is an essential tool for ensuring the **confidentiality** of proprietary information while facilitating regulatory compliance in the pharmaceutical industry. It provides a structured way for manufacturers to share critical data with the FDA, while protecting their intellectual property from competitors. As pharmaceutical supply chains become more complex and global, the role of DMFs in maintaining drug quality and safety will continue to grow.

5.6 Regulatory Approval Process for IND, NDA, ANDA, SNDA

The **regulatory approval process** in the United States for pharmaceuticals involves several key applications, each serving a distinct purpose in bringing new drugs to the market or making changes to already approved products. The four major applications used in this process are the **Investigational New Drug (IND)** application, **New Drug Application (NDA)**, **Abbreviated New Drug Application (ANDA)**, and **Supplemental New Drug Application (SNDA)**. Each application type corresponds to different stages of drug development, modification, or market entry and must adhere to specific regulatory guidelines established by the **FDA**.

The **IND application** is the first step in the regulatory approval process for any new drug or biological product intended for human use. It is submitted to the **FDA** by a sponsor, usually a pharmaceutical company, before starting **clinical trials** in humans. The **IND** must contain extensive preclinical data, including **animal pharmacology**, **toxicology**, **manufacturing information**, and a detailed **clinical trial protocol**. The goal is to demonstrate that the drug is reasonably safe for initial human testing. There are three types of **INDs**: **commercial INDs**, **investigator INDs**, and **emergency use INDs**. Once submitted, the FDA has **30 days** to review the IND. If the FDA does not place the study on **clinical hold**, the sponsor can begin the **Phase I clinical trials**.

In **2022**, the FDA received approximately **1,400 IND submissions**, reflecting the increasing pace of drug development. After the IND is approved, the drug goes through multiple phases of clinical trials, including **Phase I** (safety), **Phase II** (efficacy), and **Phase III** (confirmation of effectiveness in larger populations). The culmination of the clinical trial process is the submission of the **New Drug Application (NDA)**.

The **NDA** is submitted to the FDA once all clinical trials are completed and the sponsor has gathered sufficient evidence of the drug's **safety, efficacy**, and **quality**. The **NDA** contains detailed data on **clinical trial results, manufacturing processes, drug stability, labeling**, and **proposed usage guidelines**. The review process for an NDA can take anywhere from **6 to 10 months**, depending on the drug's priority status. Drugs that address **serious conditions** or provide **significant improvements** over existing treatments can qualify for **priority review**, shortening the approval timeline. The NDA is a comprehensive document that must convince the FDA that the benefits of the drug outweigh its risks. In **2022**, the FDA approved around **50 new molecular entities (NMEs)**, highlighting the NDA's role in the introduction of new therapeutic options.

The **Abbreviated New Drug Application (ANDA)**, in contrast, is the submission process for **generic drugs**. Unlike an NDA, an ANDA does not require the sponsor to conduct new clinical trials to prove safety and efficacy. Instead, the applicant must demonstrate **bioequivalence** to the **reference listed drug (RLD)**, which is the original brand-name product already approved by the FDA. **Bioequivalence** means that the generic drug delivers the same **amount** of the **active ingredient** into the bloodstream within the same timeframe as the original drug. The ANDA process is streamlined, significantly reducing the time and cost of bringing a generic drug to market. **Generic drugs** account for about **90% of prescriptions** in the U.S., and in **2022**, the FDA approved over **700 ANDAs**. The approval of generic drugs helps reduce healthcare costs and improve patient access to essential medications.

The **Supplemental New Drug Application (SNDA)** is required when the manufacturer of an approved drug seeks to make changes to the product after the NDA has been approved. These changes can include modifications to the **drug formulation, labeling changes, new indications, dosing regimens**, or **manufacturing processes**. The SNDA must provide evidence that the proposed changes will not compromise the **safety, efficacy**, or **quality** of the drug. For example, a company might submit an SNDA to add a **pediatric indication** to a drug initially approved for adult use. In 2022, the FDA approved over **150 SNDAs**, reflecting the ongoing need for manufacturers to adapt and update their products based on new data or changing market needs.

Each of these applications plays a crucial role in the FDA's drug approval process, ensuring that drugs and biologics meet rigorous standards before and after they enter the market. The process ensures that **innovative new treatments, safe and affordable generics**, and **updated formulations** are available to the public in a timely manner.

5.7 Regulatory Requirements for Orphan Drugs and Combination Products

The **regulatory requirements** for **orphan drugs** and **combination products** in the United States are designed to address specific challenges associated with these categories. The **FDA** has established distinct pathways and incentives to promote the development of **orphan drugs** for rare diseases and to ensure that **combination products**, which include a mix of drugs, biologics, and devices, meet rigorous safety and efficacy standards.

Orphan drugs are developed to treat **rare diseases** or conditions, which are defined as affecting fewer than **200,000 people** in the United States. These conditions are often referred to as **orphan diseases** because, due to the small number of patients, drug development is less financially attractive for pharmaceutical companies. Recognizing this gap, the U.S. Congress passed the **Orphan Drug Act (ODA)** in **1983**, which provided several incentives to encourage the development of treatments for rare diseases.

One of the key incentives under the **Orphan Drug Act** is **market exclusivity**. Upon FDA approval, orphan drugs are granted **7 years** of exclusive marketing rights, meaning that no other company can market a **similar drug** for the same indication during this period, even if the original drug's **patent** has expired. This exclusivity encourages pharmaceutical companies to invest in developing treatments for conditions that may not be profitable under normal circumstances. Another benefit includes **tax credits** of up to **25%** for clinical testing costs, further reducing the financial burden on developers. Additionally, companies may receive **waivers** of certain **FDA application fees**, such as those for **New Drug Applications (NDAs)** or **Biologics License Applications (BLAs)**.

The FDA's **Office of Orphan Products Development (OOPD)** oversees the orphan drug program and evaluates applications for **orphan drug designation**. A sponsor must apply for this designation and demonstrate that the drug is intended to treat a rare disease or condition. In **2022**, the FDA granted **orphan drug designation** to more than **500 drugs**, highlighting the growing focus on rare disease treatment. Some of the successful therapies approved for rare diseases include treatments for conditions such as **cystic fibrosis, Huntington's disease**, and **Duchenne muscular dystrophy**.

The development of **combination products**, which incorporate elements of **drugs, biologics**, and **medical devices**, presents unique regulatory challenges because these products must comply with multiple sets of regulations. The FDA defines combination products as therapeutic and diagnostic products that combine two or more types of medical products. For instance, a **drug-eluting stent** that combines a **device** (the stent) with a **drug** that prevents artery blockage is considered a combination product. Other examples include **pre-filled syringes, inhalers** with medication, or a **biologic-device** combination such as an insulin pump.

To regulate **combination products**, the FDA established the **Office of Combination Products (OCP)**, which coordinates between the **Center for Drug Evaluation and Research (CDER)**, the **Center for Devices and Radiological Health (CDRH)**, and the **Center for Biologics Evaluation and Research (CBER)**. The OCP assigns a **primary mode of action (PMOA)** to the combination product, determining which center will have primary jurisdiction over its review. For example, if the drug component is the primary therapeutic mechanism, CDER will take the lead in the review process. Similarly, if the **device** is the primary mechanism, CDRH will handle the evaluation.

Regulatory approval for combination products often requires the submission of multiple applications, such as a **New Drug Application (NDA)** or a **Premarket Approval (PMA)** for devices, depending on the components involved. The complexity of the combination product determines the data required for FDA approval. For instance, if a **biologic** and a **device** are involved, the manufacturer may need to submit a **Biologics License Application (BLA)** alongside a device application to meet all regulatory requirements.

Combination products must meet the safety, effectiveness, and quality standards for each of their components. The FDA ensures that all aspects of a combination product, including the drug or biologic substance and the mechanical aspects of a device, function as intended. This can lead to longer review times and additional scrutiny, especially when the components interact in ways that could affect the product's overall safety or efficacy. For example, a **pre-filled syringe** delivering a drug must meet the **sterility** requirements for the device while also maintaining the **stability** and **potency** of the drug.

In addition to premarket regulation, postmarket requirements for **combination products** are equally stringent. Manufacturers must comply with **Current Good Manufacturing Practices (cGMP)**, **quality system regulations (QSR)** for devices, and applicable drug regulations. Combination products also require **postmarket surveillance**, including **adverse event reporting** for both the drug and device components.

5.8 Regulatory Considerations for Manufacturing, Packaging, and Labeling of Pharmaceuticals in the USA

The **manufacturing, packaging, and labeling** of pharmaceuticals in the USA are subject to stringent regulatory oversight by the **FDA**. These processes are governed by various standards and guidelines to ensure that all pharmaceutical products are of the highest quality, safe for consumption, and effectively labeled to convey important information to healthcare providers and patients. Compliance with **Current Good Manufacturing Practices (cGMP)** is at the core of these regulations, ensuring that every aspect of the pharmaceutical product's lifecycle meets federal standards.

Manufacturing regulations in the U.S. focus on maintaining **quality control** throughout the production process. **Current Good Manufacturing Practices (cGMP)**, outlined in **21 CFR Parts 210 and 211**, specify the minimum requirements for the design, monitoring, and control of manufacturing facilities and processes. These guidelines ensure that drugs are consistently produced and controlled according to quality standards. cGMP regulations cover aspects such as **cleanroom environments, quality assurance systems, raw material testing**, and **production documentation**. For example, drug manufacturers are required to maintain precise documentation of every batch produced, including data on the equipment used, environmental conditions, and quality control tests.

The FDA regularly inspects pharmaceutical manufacturing facilities to verify compliance with **cGMP regulations**. In **2022**, the FDA conducted over **1,400 inspections** of domestic and international facilities, ensuring that products manufactured both within and outside the U.S. meet FDA standards. Non-compliance can result in severe penalties, including **warning letters, product recalls**, and **import bans** for foreign manufacturers. For example, a manufacturer producing sterile injectables must adhere to strict guidelines on **aseptic processing** to prevent contamination. A failure in this process could lead to **FDA enforcement actions** and significant disruptions in the supply chain.

Packaging regulations are equally critical, as they ensure the drug's **stability, protection** from contamination, and **accurate identification**. Under cGMP, pharmaceutical packaging must ensure that the drug remains stable under specified storage conditions, such as **temperature** and **humidity**. For instance, drugs that are sensitive to light or moisture must be packaged in protective materials like **amber-colored glass** or **blister packs** to prevent degradation. Packaging materials must be tested to confirm their **compatibility** with the drug product, ensuring that there are no **interactions** between the packaging material and the drug that could affect its quality or efficacy.

In addition to ensuring product stability, the **packaging** must also protect against tampering and ensure that the product reaches the end user in the same condition as it left the manufacturer. For this reason, the FDA mandates the use of **tamper-evident packaging** for certain types of products, especially **over-the-counter (OTC)** drugs. The packaging must include **indicators** or **barriers** that provide visible evidence of tampering, thereby ensuring product integrity.

Labeling is another crucial aspect of pharmaceutical regulation, governed by **21 CFR Part 201**. The **FDA** requires that drug labels provide clear, accurate, and comprehensive information to ensure the safe and effective use of the drug. The **principal display panel (PDP)** on the drug packaging must include key information such as the **brand name, generic name, dosage strength**, and **quantity** of the drug. For prescription drugs, the label must also contain a **package insert**, which provides detailed information for healthcare professionals, including the drug's **indications, dosage instructions, contraindications, warnings**, and **adverse reactions**.

The FDA also regulates the **format** and **content** of drug labels to ensure clarity and consistency. For example, drug labels must include a **black box warning** if the drug carries significant risks of serious or life-threatening adverse effects. This warning, which is the FDA's strongest alert for drug safety, must be prominently displayed at the top of the label. In **2021**, the FDA added black box warnings to several drugs, emphasizing the need for clear and strong labeling to inform healthcare professionals of critical safety issues.

Another important aspect of **labeling** is ensuring that the information is accessible to **non-English-speaking patients** or patients with low literacy. The FDA encourages the use of **plain language** and **pictograms** where possible, particularly for **over-the-counter (OTC)** products that are used without direct healthcare supervision. In addition, **medication guides** and **patient package inserts (PPI)** must be provided for certain prescription drugs to inform patients about the drug's proper use, risks, and benefits.

The FDA also regulates **promotional labeling**, ensuring that pharmaceutical companies market their products in a way that is truthful and not misleading. Drug advertisements must present a **balanced view** of the drug's risks and benefits, avoiding overstating the drug's efficacy or minimizing potential side effects. In **2022**, the FDA's **Office of Prescription Drug Promotion (OPDP)** issued over **20 warning letters** to pharmaceutical companies for violating promotional labeling regulations, highlighting the FDA's ongoing efforts to ensure honest communication about drug products.

5.9 Legislation and Regulations for Import, Manufacture, Distribution, and Sale of Cosmetics in the USA

The **regulation of cosmetics** in the United States is overseen by the **FDA** under the **Federal Food, Drug, and Cosmetic Act (FFDCA)**. Unlike pharmaceuticals and medical devices, cosmetics are not subject to pre-market approval by the FDA. However, there are strict regulations concerning the **import**, **manufacture**, **distribution**, and **sale** of cosmetics to ensure that these products are safe for consumers and do not contain harmful or **adulterated ingredients**. The FDA's authority over cosmetics extends to labeling, ingredient safety, and good manufacturing practices.

Import regulations for cosmetics require that products entering the United States comply with **FDA standards**. Imported cosmetics must not be **adulterated** or **misbranded**. The term "adulterated" refers to products that contain **harmful ingredients**, are produced under **unsanitary conditions**, or are contaminated with substances that could make them unsafe for use. For example, a cosmetic product contaminated with **bacteria** or **toxic chemicals** during manufacturing could be classified as adulterated. In **2022**, the FDA issued import alerts for over **150 cosmetic products**, barring their entry into the U.S. market due to safety concerns. Importers are responsible for ensuring that their products comply with U.S. laws before shipment, and non-compliant cosmetics may be refused entry or detained by **U.S. Customs and Border Protection (CBP)**.

The **manufacture of cosmetics** in the USA is governed by **Good Manufacturing Practices (GMP)** guidelines, which are designed to ensure that cosmetics are consistently produced and controlled to meet quality standards. Although GMP for cosmetics is not mandatory under the FFDCA, the FDA strongly recommends that manufacturers follow these guidelines. GMP practices cover areas such as **cleanliness, personnel training, equipment maintenance**, and **ingredient testing**. For example, manufacturers must ensure that raw materials used in cosmetics are tested for purity and do not contain **prohibited substances** like **lead** or **mercury**, which have been found in some cosmetics and pose serious health risks.

In terms of **ingredient safety**, the FDA requires manufacturers to ensure that their products are safe for use under labeled or customary conditions. While the FDA does not have the authority to approve cosmetic ingredients (except for **color additives**), it can take action against products that are unsafe or misbranded. The **Voluntary Cosmetic Registration Program (VCRP)** allows manufacturers to register their products and ingredients with the FDA, although participation is voluntary. By **2021**, more than **30,000 cosmetic products** were registered under the VCRP, helping the FDA monitor trends in cosmetic ingredient usage.

The **distribution** and **sale** of cosmetics are also subject to FDA regulations, particularly concerning **labeling**. Cosmetic labels must be clear, truthful, and not misleading. Under **21 CFR Part 701**, labeling regulations specify that cosmetics must include the **name and address** of the manufacturer or distributor, the **net quantity of contents**, and a list of ingredients in descending order by weight. Misleading or incomplete labels can result in the product being classified as **misbranded**, leading to enforcement actions such as product recalls or legal penalties. For instance, a product marketed as "natural" or "organic" must meet specific claims, and the FDA can take action if these claims are found to be deceptive.

In recent years, there has been increasing focus on **cosmetic safety legislation**. The **Personal Care Products Safety Act**, introduced in the U.S. Senate, proposed strengthening the FDA's oversight of cosmetics by requiring manufacturers to register facilities, submit ingredient statements, and report adverse events. This legislation reflects growing concerns about the lack of stringent regulations compared to other consumer products. Additionally, there have been discussions about **banning certain ingredients** that are still allowed in U.S. cosmetics but are prohibited in other countries, such as certain **phthalates** and **parabens**.

Cosmetic manufacturers must also comply with specific regulations for **color additives** used in their products. Unlike other cosmetic ingredients, color additives must be **FDA-approved** before they can be used in products. The **Color Additive Amendments of 1960** gave the FDA authority over the safety of color additives, and manufacturers are required to submit a **Color Additive Petition** to demonstrate that a color is safe for its intended use. In **2022**, the FDA conducted inspections of cosmetic products containing color additives to ensure compliance, with several products being flagged for using unapproved or unsafe colorants.

The **sale of cosmetics** also involves compliance with **advertising regulations** overseen by the **Federal Trade Commission (FTC)**. The FTC ensures that cosmetic advertising is truthful and not misleading. For instance, claims such as "anti-aging" or "wrinkle-reducing" must be backed by scientific evidence, and the FTC can take action against companies that make **false or exaggerated claims** about their products. The FDA and FTC work together to ensure that both labeling and advertising accurately represent the safety and effectiveness of cosmetic products.

5.10 FDA Guidance on Human Subject Protection, Financial Disclosure, IND Application, NDA Application, Bioavailability and Bioequivalence Requirements, Investigational Device Exemptions, Post-Market Surveillance

The **FDA** provides extensive guidance to ensure the ethical and scientific integrity of clinical trials, the approval of drugs and devices, and the monitoring of their safety after they reach the market. These regulatory frameworks cover a wide range of areas, including **human subject protection, financial disclosure, Investigational New Drug (IND) applications, New Drug Applications (NDA), bioavailability** and **bioequivalence** requirements, **Investigational Device Exemptions (IDE),** and **post-market surveillance.** Each of these elements is critical to the development and ongoing evaluation of medical products.

Human subject protection is a fundamental part of the FDA's regulatory process. The FDA ensures that all clinical trials involving human subjects comply with ethical standards and that participants are protected from unnecessary risks. Under **21 CFR Part 50**, the FDA mandates that informed consent be obtained from all participants, ensuring they understand the purpose of the study, potential risks, and benefits. Additionally, clinical trials must be approved by an **Institutional Review Board (IRB)**, which is responsible for reviewing and monitoring the trial to ensure the safety of participants. In 2022, the FDA issued over **150 warning letters** to clinical trial investigators and sponsors for failing to meet human subject protection guidelines, emphasizing the importance of adherence to these regulations.

Financial disclosure is another area where the FDA provides guidance to avoid conflicts of interest that could bias the outcomes of clinical trials. Under **21 CFR Part 54**, sponsors must disclose any financial arrangements between investigators and the sponsor, such as compensation tied to the study outcome or stock ownership in the company. This transparency is crucial for maintaining the integrity of the trial results. Financial conflicts of interest can undermine the credibility of the research, and the FDA has stringent guidelines in place to ensure that such disclosures are made before the trial begins. Sponsors are required to submit financial disclosure forms as part of their **NDA** or **BLA** submissions, and the FDA reviews these documents to ensure compliance.

The **IND application** is the starting point for the FDA's regulatory process for new drugs. Sponsors must submit an **IND** to the FDA before conducting clinical trials in humans. The IND provides the FDA with data from preclinical studies, including animal pharmacology and toxicology, as well as information on the drug's **manufacturing process** and proposed clinical trial protocol. The FDA reviews the IND to ensure that the investigational drug is reasonably safe for use in humans. If no clinical hold is placed, the sponsor can begin Phase I trials. The FDA's guidance on IND submissions emphasizes the need for detailed safety data, and sponsors must also provide information on **Good Laboratory Practice (GLP)** compliance for preclinical studies.

The **NDA application** follows successful clinical trials and is the formal submission to the FDA requesting approval to market a new drug. The **NDA** contains comprehensive data on the drug's **safety, efficacy, pharmacokinetics**, and **manufacturing process**. The FDA reviews the NDA to determine whether the benefits of the drug outweigh its risks for the intended use. The NDA must also include proposed labeling, which details the drug's approved uses, dosage, and potential side effects. In 2022, the FDA approved over **50 new molecular entities** (NMEs) through the NDA process, underscoring the rigor of the drug approval process.

The FDA also provides guidance on **bioavailability (BA)** and **bioequivalence (BE)** requirements, which are crucial for the approval of generic drugs. Under **21 CFR Part 320**, generic drug manufacturers must demonstrate that their product is bioequivalent to the reference listed drug

(RLD). **Bioequivalence** means that the generic drug delivers the same amount of active ingredient into the bloodstream at the same rate as the original drug. This ensures that the generic product is therapeutically equivalent to the brand-name drug. To demonstrate bioequivalence, manufacturers conduct **pharmacokinetic studies** comparing the generic and reference drugs. In 2022, the FDA approved over **700 ANDAs** based on bioequivalence studies, reflecting the importance of these requirements in expanding access to affordable medications.

Investigational Device Exemptions (IDEs) allow medical devices to be used in clinical trials to collect safety and efficacy data. The FDA's guidance on IDEs, outlined in **21 CFR Part 812**, specifies that manufacturers must submit an IDE application to the FDA before testing high-risk devices in humans. The IDE must include data on the device's design, manufacturing process, preclinical testing, and proposed clinical trial protocol. The FDA reviews the IDE to ensure that the device does not pose an unreasonable risk to participants. In 2022, the FDA approved over **100 IDEs** for novel medical devices, ensuring that these devices met safety standards before proceeding to clinical trials.

Finally, **post-market surveillance** is a critical aspect of the FDA's oversight of drugs and medical devices after they are approved and marketed. Post-market surveillance involves monitoring the safety and effectiveness of products in real-world use. Manufacturers are required to report **adverse events** and **product defects** to the FDA under **21 CFR Parts 314** (for drugs) and **803** (for devices). The FDA's **MedWatch** program allows healthcare professionals and consumers to report adverse events, helping the agency identify potential safety concerns. In 2022, the FDA received over **2 million adverse event reports**, leading to product recalls, safety warnings, and, in some cases, market withdrawals.

5.11 FDA Safety Reporting Requirements for INDs and BA/BE Studies

The **FDA's safety reporting requirements** for **Investigational New Drug (IND)** applications and **bioavailability (BA) / bioequivalence (BE)** studies are designed to protect participants in clinical trials by ensuring that any adverse effects or safety issues are promptly reported and addressed. These requirements are outlined in **21 CFR Part 312** for **INDs** and **21 CFR Part 320** for **BA/BE studies**. The FDA mandates strict timelines and protocols for reporting safety information to minimize risks and ensure the well-being of trial participants.

For **IND applications**, the sponsor is required to submit **safety reports** to the FDA if a **serious and unexpected adverse event** occurs during a clinical trial. A **serious adverse event (SAE)** is defined as any event that results in **death**, is **life-threatening**, requires **hospitalization**, or causes significant disability or congenital anomaly. An **unexpected adverse event** is one that is not listed in the investigator's brochure or is more severe than previously observed. Sponsors must report these events to the FDA within **15 calendar days** of becoming aware of the event. However, if the event poses an **immediate hazard** to participants, it must be reported within **7 calendar days**.

In addition to individual adverse event reporting, sponsors are also required to submit **annual reports** during the clinical trial. These reports provide the FDA with a summary of the **safety data** collected over the year, including all **serious adverse events** and **non-serious adverse events** that may have cumulative safety implications. The annual report also includes updates on the overall progress of the trial, any changes in the study protocol, and ongoing risk assessments.

For **bioavailability (BA)** and **bioequivalence (BE)** studies, the safety reporting requirements are similar but slightly adapted to reflect the nature of these trials. Since **BA/BE studies** typically involve healthy volunteers and focus on comparing the **pharmacokinetic profiles** of generic drugs with their reference products, the occurrence of serious adverse events is generally lower. However, sponsors must still report any **serious adverse events** that occur during BA/BE studies, using the same timelines as IND trials (15 days for non-urgent events and 7 days for urgent events).

One of the key components of the FDA's safety reporting framework is ensuring that the **adverse event reports** are complete and contain sufficient detail for the FDA to assess the severity and implications of the event. Reports must include information such as the **subject's demographic data**, details about the **adverse event**, the **suspected cause** (if known), and any actions taken by the sponsor or investigator to mitigate the event. Incomplete or delayed safety reports can result in **FDA enforcement actions**, such as clinical trial suspension or termination.

The FDA also requires sponsors to continuously **monitor** the safety of study participants throughout the trial. Sponsors are encouraged to implement a **data monitoring committee (DMC)** for larger or high-risk trials to independently review safety data and make recommendations regarding trial continuation. This proactive approach to safety monitoring helps identify potential safety concerns early and minimizes risks to participants.

In **2022**, the FDA received over **10,000 safety reports** from ongoing clinical trials, highlighting the importance of vigilant monitoring and prompt reporting. These reports play a critical role in the FDA's oversight of drug development and its ability to ensure that investigational drugs do not pose undue risks to participants.

5.12 FDA MedWatch and Good Pharmacovigilance Practices

The **FDA MedWatch program** and **Good Pharmacovigilance Practices (GVP)** are essential components of the FDA's system for monitoring the safety of pharmaceuticals, medical devices, and other FDA-regulated products. These programs help ensure that **adverse events** and **safety concerns** are promptly reported, evaluated, and addressed to protect public health. Through these systems, the FDA is able to collect and analyze data related to **post-market surveillance**, ensuring that drugs and devices continue to be safe and effective after they have been approved and are widely used.

The **FDA MedWatch program**, established in **1993**, serves as a centralized platform for **healthcare professionals**, **patients**, and **consumers** to report **adverse events** and **product problems** related to FDA-regulated products, including **drugs**, **biologics**, **medical devices**, **dietary supplements**, and **cosmetics**. MedWatch allows for the reporting of **serious adverse events**, **product quality issues**, **device malfunctions**, and **use errors** that could potentially harm users. The program is crucial for identifying safety issues that may not have been evident during pre-market testing.

Adverse events reported through **MedWatch** include any **unexpected side effects**, **injuries**, or **life-threatening reactions** associated with a product's use. These reports are submitted via **Form FDA 3500** for healthcare professionals and consumers or **Form FDA 3500A** for mandatory reports from manufacturers. Reports can be filed online, by mail, or by fax, making it accessible to all users. In **2022**, the FDA received over **2 million MedWatch reports**, highlighting the program's role as a critical tool for ongoing safety surveillance.

The **MedWatch system** is an essential part of the FDA's **pharmacovigilance** efforts. The data collected through MedWatch is analyzed to identify **trends** and **patterns** that may indicate previously unknown risks associated with a product. For example, if several reports indicate a similar adverse event, such as **liver toxicity** associated with a new drug, the FDA may initiate a more in-depth investigation to determine whether the drug poses a significant risk. Based on these findings, the FDA can take appropriate actions, including issuing **safety alerts**, updating **product labels**, or in extreme cases, recommending **market withdrawal** of the product.

Good Pharmacovigilance Practices (GVP) refer to the systematic process that pharmaceutical companies must follow to monitor the safety of their products after they enter the market. These practices are essential for identifying and managing **risks** associated with drug products, particularly those that may not have been detected in clinical trials. The FDA's guidelines for **pharmacovigilance** are outlined in several regulatory documents, including **21 CFR Part 314** for **drugs** and **21 CFR Part 600** for **biologics**.

One of the key components of **GVP** is the establishment of a **pharmacovigilance system** by the drug sponsor. This system includes processes for **adverse event reporting, risk management,** and **periodic safety updates**. Companies are required to submit **periodic adverse drug experience reports (PADERs)** and **Periodic Safety Update Reports (PSURs)**, which provide summaries of the safety data collected over time. These reports allow the FDA to continuously monitor the **risk-benefit profile** of a drug.

Another important aspect of **GVP** is the use of **Risk Evaluation and Mitigation Strategies (REMS)**. In cases where a drug presents specific risks that need to be managed, the FDA may require a REMS program. REMS programs can include elements such as **restricted distribution, patient education,** and **healthcare provider training**. For instance, drugs with a high potential for **abuse** or **serious side effects** may be subject to REMS to ensure that they are used safely. As of **2022**, the FDA had implemented over **80 REMS programs**, demonstrating the role of REMS in enhancing drug safety.

Pharmaceutical companies are also expected to have systems in place to detect **signals**—early indicators that there may be a **safety issue** with a drug. Signal detection involves analyzing data from various sources, including **clinical trials, post-market surveillance,** and **spontaneous reports** like those submitted through MedWatch. When a potential safety signal is identified, companies must investigate and, if necessary, take actions such as updating labeling, issuing warnings, or conducting additional studies to assess the risk.

Post-market surveillance is a critical element of **pharmacovigilance** and involves the ongoing monitoring of drug safety after the product is available to the general public. Companies are required to establish systems to collect, assess, and report adverse events that occur in the **real-world setting**. Unlike the controlled environment of clinical trials, post-market use may involve patients with **comorbid conditions** or those using other medications, revealing risks that were not evident during pre-approval testing.

The FDA's guidance on **GVP** also emphasizes the importance of global cooperation. Since drugs are often marketed in multiple countries, international regulatory bodies collaborate to share safety data and address global safety concerns. The FDA works with agencies like the **European Medicines Agency (EMA)** and the **World Health Organization (WHO)** to harmonize pharmacovigilance standards and improve global public health. This cooperation is especially important for managing adverse event reports related to **biologics** and **biosimilars**, which are becoming more widely used.

CHAPTER SIX

Australia Regulations

Australia has a well-established regulatory system for pharmaceuticals, medical devices, and other therapeutic goods, overseen by the Therapeutic Goods Administration (TGA). This chapter provides a comprehensive overview of Australia's regulatory landscape, focusing on the processes and legal requirements for the approval and monitoring of drugs and medical devices. The TGA operates under the Therapeutic Goods Act, which mandates that all therapeutic goods marketed in Australia meet strict standards of safety, quality, and efficacy.

The chapter emphasizes the importance of understanding the application process, which includes submitting data on the safety, efficacy, and manufacturing of a product. It also discusses the role of the TGA in conducting assessments and reviews to ensure that the product's benefits outweigh any potential risks. This regulatory oversight extends beyond the initial approval process to include ongoing monitoring through post-market surveillance and safety data collection.

In addition to pharmaceuticals, the chapter covers the regulatory framework for nutraceuticals, cosmetics, and medical devices in Australia, highlighting the country's commitment to ensuring public health and safety. For professionals working in the pharmaceutical industry or seeking market entry into Australia, this chapter provides essential knowledge about the regulatory processes and compliance requirements necessary to succeed in this market.

6.1 Introduction

The regulatory framework for pharmaceuticals, medical devices, and therapeutic goods in **Australia** is primarily governed by the **Therapeutic Goods Administration (TGA)**, an agency under the **Australian Government Department of Health and Aged Care**. The **TGA** is responsible for ensuring the safety, efficacy, and quality of therapeutic goods available in Australia. Its regulatory activities cover a wide range of products, including **prescription medicines, over-the-counter (OTC) products, complementary medicines, medical devices**, and **biological products.**

The **TGA's regulatory authority** is established under the **Therapeutic Goods Act 1989**, which serves as the foundation for all regulations related to therapeutic products in Australia. This act outlines the processes for **product registration, safety monitoring, post-market surveillance**, and **compliance enforcement.** The **Therapeutic Goods Regulations 1990** and other subordinate legislation provide detailed guidance on how therapeutic goods should be regulated and managed. For instance, any medicine or medical device marketed in Australia must be included in the **Australian Register of Therapeutic Goods (ARTG)** before it can be sold or distributed. The ARTG is a publicly accessible database that contains information about all therapeutic goods approved for supply in the Australian market.

In terms of **pharmaceutical regulation**, the TGA classifies medicines into different **schedules** based on their safety profile, therapeutic use, and potential for misuse. These schedules determine how a medicine can be supplied to the public. For example, **Schedule 4** medicines, which include most **prescription drugs**, can only be supplied by a pharmacist on a valid prescription from a healthcare provider. **Schedule 3** drugs are available from pharmacists but do not require a prescription, though pharmacist consultation is necessary. The scheduling system helps balance **access** to medicines while ensuring **patient safety.**

The TGA also has an established process for assessing the **safety and efficacy** of new medicines before they are approved for the Australian market. **Clinical trial data, pharmacokinetic studies**, and **toxicological assessments** are reviewed by the TGA's scientific experts, who evaluate whether a drug's benefits outweigh its risks. In **2022**, the TGA approved approximately **40 new medicines** for the Australian market, including innovative treatments for conditions like **cancer, diabetes**, and **rare genetic disorders.** The rigorous evaluation process ensures that only high-quality products are made available to Australian patients.

Post-market monitoring is another crucial aspect of the TGA's regulatory framework. Once a medicine or device is included in the ARTG, the TGA continues to monitor its safety through adverse event reporting and **pharmacovigilance** activities. Healthcare professionals, consumers, and manufacturers are encouraged to report **adverse drug reactions (ADRs)** to the TGA through its **Australian Adverse Drug Reactions Reporting System (ADRS)**. The TGA analyzes these reports to detect potential safety issues and takes appropriate action, such as issuing safety alerts or updating product labeling.

In addition to pharmaceuticals, the TGA also regulates **medical devices** under a risk-based classification system. Devices are classified into **Classes I to III** based on the potential risk they pose to patients. **Class I devices**, such as bandages and surgical instruments, are considered low-risk, while **Class III devices**, like pacemakers and heart valves, are high-risk and require more stringent assessment before approval. In **2022**, the TGA evaluated over **1,200 medical devices**, ensuring that these products met the required safety and performance standards before being made available to the public.

Complementary medicines, which include herbal medicines, vitamins, and supplements, are also regulated by the TGA. These products are typically classified as **low-risk** medicines, but they must still meet **quality standards** and be included in the ARTG. The TGA conducts **random audits** of complementary medicines to ensure they comply with the **Good Manufacturing Practices (GMP)** and do not contain any harmful ingredients or contaminants. For instance, in 2021, the TGA identified several complementary medicines containing **undeclared substances**, leading to product recalls and increased scrutiny of the sector.

In terms of international collaboration, the TGA works closely with regulatory authorities from other countries, including the **U.S. FDA**, the **European Medicines Agency (EMA)**, and the **World Health Organization (WHO)**. This collaboration helps the TGA harmonize its regulations with global standards and share safety information about therapeutic goods. Additionally, the **TGA participates in international working groups**, such as the **International Coalition of Medicines Regulatory Authorities (ICMRA)**, which fosters collaboration on global regulatory challenges and emerging health threats, such as the COVID-19 pandemic.

6.2 The Application

The **application process** for registering pharmaceuticals, medical devices, and other therapeutic goods with the **Therapeutic Goods Administration (TGA)** in Australia is a detailed and structured procedure. The TGA evaluates the **quality, safety, and efficacy** of therapeutic products before they are approved for inclusion in the **Australian Register of Therapeutic Goods (ARTG)**. All medicines and devices, whether manufactured domestically or imported, must go through this application process before being sold or distributed in Australia.

For **pharmaceuticals**, the application process involves submitting a **complete dossier** that contains all relevant information about the drug's **composition, manufacturing process, clinical trial data**, and **safety profile**. This dossier is submitted via the **Electronic Submission Portal (eBS)**, which allows applicants to upload their documentation digitally. The TGA requires detailed information about the **active pharmaceutical ingredients (APIs)**, including **stability studies** and **manufacturing controls**, to ensure that the drug meets **Good Manufacturing Practices (GMP)**.

In addition to providing **preclinical data**, the application must include results from **clinical trials** demonstrating that the drug is effective and safe for its intended use. These clinical trials typically follow the **Phase I to Phase III** structure, with each phase providing progressively more data on the drug's safety and efficacy. The **Phase III trials**, which involve a larger patient population, are especially critical as they provide the TGA with the data needed to assess the drug's performance in real-world scenarios. For example, during the **2021-2022** period, the TGA reviewed over **100 pharmaceutical applications**, many of which involved detailed clinical trial data from both Australian and international studies.

The application process also requires the submission of proposed **product labeling**, which must meet the TGA's guidelines on **clear and accurate information**. The label must include details such as the **drug's name, strength, dosage instructions, contraindications**, and **side effects**. The TGA evaluates whether the label provides sufficient information for both healthcare professionals and consumers to safely use the drug. Any misleading or incomplete labeling can result in delays or rejections during the application review process.

For **medical devices**, the application process is based on a **risk classification system**, where devices are categorized into **Classes I to III** depending on the level of risk they pose to patients. For low-risk devices (Class I), the application process is relatively straightforward, involving self-declaration of compliance with relevant standards. However, for higher-risk devices (Classes IIa, IIb, and III), applicants must provide more detailed documentation, including **design specifications, clinical evaluation reports**, and **evidence of compliance** with international standards, such as those established by the **International Organization for**

Standardization (ISO).

The application for high-risk medical devices must also include a **risk management plan** that details how potential safety issues will be addressed during the device's lifecycle. For example, in 2022, the TGA reviewed applications for several high-risk devices, including **implantable pacemakers** and **artificial joints**, requiring comprehensive data on device durability, performance, and long-term safety.

Applicants for both pharmaceuticals and medical devices must pay an **application fee**, which varies based on the type of product and its classification. For instance, the application fee for a new **prescription medicine** was approximately **AUD 50,000** in 2022, while the fee for a high-risk medical device was around **AUD 8,000**. These fees cover the cost of the TGA's scientific review and administrative processing of the application.

Once an application is submitted, the TGA follows a **multi-step review process**. This process includes an **initial screening** to ensure that all required documents are included, followed by a **scientific evaluation** phase where TGA experts assess the data. The TGA may also request **additional information** from the applicant during the review process if there are any gaps or concerns. On average, the review process for a new pharmaceutical takes between **8 to 12 months**, depending on the complexity of the application and the type of product being evaluated. For medical devices, the review timeline may vary based on the device's risk classification, with low-risk devices often reviewed in a few months, while high-risk devices may take up to **12 months** or more for approval.

If the TGA approves the application, the product is added to the **ARTG**, and the sponsor can begin distributing the product in the Australian market. The TGA then monitors the product through **post-market surveillance** to ensure continued safety and efficacy.

6.3 Relevant Provisions of the Act

The **Therapeutic Goods Act 1989** forms the legal foundation for regulating therapeutic goods in Australia, including pharmaceuticals, medical devices, biologicals, and complementary medicines. This Act outlines the **requirements** for **importing, manufacturing, supplying,** and **advertising** therapeutic goods, as well as ensuring the **safety, quality, and efficacy** of these products. Administered by the **Therapeutic Goods Administration (TGA)**, the Act is designed to protect public health while facilitating access to high-quality therapeutic goods.

One of the central provisions of the Act is the requirement for all therapeutic goods to be included in the **Australian Register of Therapeutic Goods (ARTG)** before they can be legally supplied in Australia. The ARTG serves as a comprehensive database of all products that have been approved for sale, providing information on the product's **composition, intended use, and conditions of approval.** As of **2022**, there were over **90,000 entries** in the ARTG, reflecting the wide range of therapeutic products available in Australia, from prescription medicines to medical devices and over-the-counter products.

Another key provision of the Act relates to **Good Manufacturing Practices (GMP)**, which are mandatory for manufacturers of therapeutic goods. The **GMP guidelines** outlined in the Act require manufacturers to implement quality control systems, conduct regular audits, and ensure that their products are consistently produced to a high standard. For example, manufacturers of **sterile injectable drugs** must adhere to stringent aseptic processing requirements to prevent contamination. The TGA conducts **inspections** of manufacturing facilities, both within Australia and overseas, to ensure compliance with GMP. Non-compliance can result in penalties, including the **suspension** or **cancellation** of the manufacturer's ARTG listing.

The Act also addresses the **scheduling of medicines** through the **Poison Standard (SUSMP)**, which classifies medicines into different **schedules** based on their risk to public health. **Schedule 4** drugs, for example, are prescription-only medicines, while **Schedule 2** drugs can be obtained over the counter without a prescription. This system ensures that medicines are supplied in a manner appropriate to their risk profile, helping to prevent misuse and ensuring that patients receive appropriate medical supervision when required.

In terms of **advertising**, the Act imposes strict regulations on how therapeutic goods can be promoted to the public. **Advertisements** must be truthful, not misleading, and must not imply that a product can be used for purposes that are not supported by evidence. The **TGA Advertising Code** provides specific guidance on acceptable advertising practices, and breaches of this code can result in penalties, including fines or the removal of the product from the ARTG. In **2021**, the TGA issued over **200 compliance notices** related to misleading advertising of therapeutic goods, underscoring the importance of truthful marketing in this sector.

Post-market surveillance is another critical element of the Act, ensuring that therapeutic goods continue to meet safety and efficacy standards after they have been approved. The Act requires manufacturers and sponsors to report any **adverse events** associated with their products through the **Australian Adverse Drug Reaction Reporting System (ADRS)**. This allows the TGA to monitor the real-world performance of therapeutic goods and take corrective action if necessary, such as issuing safety alerts or initiating product recalls. For example, in **2022**, the TGA conducted a review of several **implantable medical devices** following reports of device malfunctions, resulting in enhanced safety warnings for these products.

The Act also empowers the TGA to take enforcement actions in cases where therapeutic goods are found to be **non-compliant**. This includes the authority to **seize products**, issue **recall notices**, and impose **civil penalties** for breaches of the Act. For instance, if a company supplies an unapproved medicine or device, the TGA has the power to remove it from the market and impose fines. The **2022** review of **cosmetic injectables** is an example of how the TGA enforces the Act to ensure that products meet the necessary safety standards.

6.4 Commissions Assessment of Application

The **commission's assessment of applications** for the approval of therapeutic goods in Australia is a key process in ensuring the **safety**, **efficacy**, and **quality** of products that enter the Australian market. The **Therapeutic Goods Administration (TGA)** oversees this assessment, which involves a comprehensive review of the information provided by applicants seeking to register pharmaceuticals, medical devices, and other therapeutic goods. This process is detailed, thorough, and aims to ensure that only safe and effective products are made available to the public.

The assessment process begins with the submission of an application by a **sponsor**. Sponsors are required to provide a **complete dossier** that contains extensive data about the product, including **clinical trial results, manufacturing details**, and **risk management plans**. This dossier is submitted via the **TGA's Electronic Submission Portal (eBS)**. The commission then conducts an **initial screening** to ensure that the application is complete and that all necessary documentation has been provided. This includes information on the product's **formulation, intended use**, and the **scientific data** supporting its use.

Once the initial screening is complete, the commission moves into the **scientific evaluation phase**, where the detailed assessment of the application begins. For **pharmaceuticals**, this phase involves a review of the **pharmacokinetic** and **pharmacodynamic data**, as well as an analysis of the **clinical trial results**. The TGA commission assesses whether the clinical trials were conducted according to **Good Clinical Practice (GCP)** guidelines and whether the data presented demonstrate that the product is both effective for its intended use and safe for consumers. For example, a new **antibiotic** would need to show clear evidence of its effectiveness against specific bacterial strains, along with a thorough risk assessment of potential **adverse reactions**.

For **medical devices**, the assessment process involves a detailed review of the device's **design, manufacturing process**, and the results of any **preclinical testing**. The commission evaluates whether the device meets the necessary **safety standards** and performs its intended function without posing undue risks to patients. Devices classified as **Class III (high-risk devices)**, such as **pacemakers** or **joint implants**, undergo a more rigorous evaluation due to their potential impact on patient health. In **2022**, the TGA commission reviewed over **1,500 medical device applications**, ensuring that these products complied with Australian and international safety standards.

A critical part of the commission's assessment is the review of the product's **risk management plan (RMP)**. The RMP outlines how potential risks associated with the product will be managed throughout its lifecycle. This includes **post-market monitoring, adverse event reporting**, and **recall strategies** if necessary. The commission examines whether the sponsor has robust systems in place to monitor the product's safety after it has been approved and is being used by patients. For instance, a pharmaceutical company must have a system for reporting **serious adverse reactions** to the TGA, which can trigger further investigation or action by the commission if safety concerns arise.

The assessment process also considers **manufacturing quality**, with particular emphasis on compliance with **Good Manufacturing Practices (GMP)**. The TGA commission may conduct inspections of **manufacturing facilities**, both domestically and internationally, to verify that the product is being produced under conditions that meet Australian standards. The **GMP compliance** requirement ensures that therapeutic goods are consistently manufactured to the highest quality, with controls in place to prevent contamination or deviation from approved processes.

After the scientific evaluation is completed, the commission prepares a **report** detailing the findings of the assessment. This report includes recommendations on whether the product should be approved for inclusion in the **Australian Register of Therapeutic Goods (ARTG)**. The TGA may request additional information from the sponsor if there are any concerns or gaps in the data provided. In some cases, the commission may recommend **conditional approval**, where the product is approved with specific conditions, such as further post-market studies to monitor long-term safety.

The time required for the commission to assess an application varies depending on the complexity of the product and the quality of the submitted data. For **new medicines**, the assessment process typically takes between **12 to 18 months**, while lower-risk medical devices may be reviewed in a shorter time frame, such as **6 to 12 months**. However, products that address **urgent public health needs**, such as **vaccines** or treatments for **life-threatening conditions**, may be fast-tracked under the TGA's **priority review pathways**, which shorten the review time to as little as **6 months**.

Once the commission has completed its assessment and approved the product, it is included in the ARTG, and the sponsor is authorized to market and distribute the product in Australia. The commission continues to monitor the product's performance through **post-market surveillance** to ensure that it remains safe and effective for public use.

6.5 Public Detriment

In the context of therapeutic goods regulation, **public detriment** refers to any potential harm or adverse impact on public health that could arise from the use of pharmaceuticals, medical devices, or other therapeutic products that fail to meet safety, efficacy, or quality standards. The **Therapeutic Goods Administration (TGA)** plays a crucial role in minimizing public detriment by ensuring that all therapeutic goods supplied in Australia are thoroughly assessed before being approved for use and that their safety is monitored throughout their lifecycle.

One of the primary ways public detriment can occur is through the **adverse effects** of pharmaceutical products. If a drug causes unexpected **serious adverse reactions**, it can lead to **hospitalization, disability**, or even **death** in some cases. These risks are especially concerning in drugs that are widely used by large patient populations. For example, **nonsteroidal**

anti-inflammatory drugs (NSAIDs) are commonly used for pain relief but have been associated with risks such as **gastrointestinal bleeding** and **cardiovascular events** in certain populations. In 2022, the TGA issued several safety alerts concerning the use of NSAIDs, emphasizing the need for healthcare providers to carefully consider the risks before prescribing these medications to patients with underlying conditions.

Medical devices also pose a significant risk of public detriment if they malfunction or do not perform as intended. For example, **implantable cardiac devices** like **pacemakers** and **defibrillators** can cause serious harm if they fail, as they are critical to maintaining heart function in patients with severe cardiac conditions. In the event of a **device recall**, the TGA works to minimize public detriment by ensuring that affected products are removed from the market and that healthcare providers are informed of alternative treatment options. In 2021, the TGA issued a **recall notice** for a batch of implantable cardiac devices due to manufacturing defects that could lead to **malfunctions**, highlighting the serious consequences that can arise when medical devices fail to meet regulatory standards.

Another area where public detriment can occur is through the **misleading advertising** or **labeling** of therapeutic goods. If products are marketed with exaggerated claims or **misinformation**, consumers may use these products incorrectly, leading to ineffective treatment or worsening of their health condition. For instance, in **2021**, the TGA took enforcement action against several companies that made **false claims** about the effectiveness of their **cosmetic injectables**. The misleading advertising suggested that these products could deliver results far beyond what was scientifically proven, posing a significant risk to consumers who may have unrealistic expectations and engage in risky cosmetic procedures without proper understanding of the potential dangers.

The **distribution of counterfeit** or **unapproved products** also represents a serious risk to public health. Counterfeit medicines, for example, may contain harmful substances, incorrect dosages, or no active ingredients at all. This not only deprives patients of the proper treatment but also exposes them to potentially dangerous substances. In **2022**, the TGA seized several shipments of **counterfeit weight-loss pills** that contained **undeclared toxic substances**, preventing these dangerous products from reaching the Australian market and potentially causing harm.

Additionally, public detriment can arise from **non-compliance with Good Manufacturing Practices (GMP)** by manufacturers of therapeutic goods. Products that are not manufactured under controlled conditions can be contaminated or compromised, leading to reduced efficacy or unsafe products. The TGA conducts routine inspections of manufacturing facilities to ensure compliance with GMP standards. In cases where non-compliance is identified, the TGA may suspend or cancel the manufacturer's license, preventing further distribution of unsafe products. For example, in **2020**, the TGA suspended the license of a manufacturing facility that failed to meet the required standards for the production of sterile injectable products, which could have resulted in contamination and serious patient harm.

Post-market surveillance is an essential component in reducing public detriment. Once a product is approved and enters the market, the TGA monitors its safety and efficacy through adverse event reporting systems such as the **Australian Adverse Drug Reaction Reporting System (ADRS)**. The ADRS allows healthcare providers and consumers to report adverse events, which are then analyzed to identify potential safety signals. In **2021**, the TGA received over **30,000 adverse event reports**, many of which prompted further investigation and safety updates to protect the public from potential harm.

6.6 Public Benefits

The **regulation of therapeutic goods** in Australia, overseen by the **Therapeutic Goods Administration (TGA)**, provides substantial **public benefits** by ensuring that medicines, medical devices, and other therapeutic products meet strict safety, efficacy, and quality standards. This regulatory framework not only safeguards public health but also fosters **public confidence** in the healthcare system, ensuring that individuals have access to high-quality, effective treatments.

One of the key public benefits is the **protection of patient safety**. Through rigorous pre-market evaluations, the TGA ensures that all therapeutic goods are thoroughly tested before they are made available for use. For example, before a new **pharmaceutical product** can be included in the **Australian Register of Therapeutic Goods (ARTG)**, it must undergo extensive clinical trials to demonstrate its **efficacy** and **safety**. This prevents the introduction of harmful or ineffective treatments. In **2022**, the TGA evaluated over **90 new drug applications**, ensuring that these products met stringent safety criteria before they reached Australian consumers.

Medical devices, which can have a direct impact on patient outcomes, are also closely regulated. Devices such as **prosthetics**, **implants**, and

diagnostic tools must meet strict performance and safety standards. By ensuring the availability of reliable and safe medical devices, the TGA enhances the quality of healthcare services. For instance, the introduction of advanced **implantable cardiac devices** that meet TGA standards has improved treatment outcomes for patients with heart conditions, reducing the risk of complications associated with device failures.

Another major public benefit is the **access to affordable and effective medicines**. The TGA's regulation of **generic drugs** plays a significant role in reducing healthcare costs for Australian consumers. Generic drugs, which are bioequivalent to their branded counterparts, offer the same therapeutic benefits but at a lower cost. In **2021**, approximately **85%** of all prescriptions filled in Australia were for generic medicines. The availability of generics allows patients to access necessary treatments without the financial burden that often accompanies brand-name drugs.

The **post-market surveillance** system managed by the TGA further contributes to public safety. By monitoring therapeutic goods after they have been approved, the TGA ensures that any **adverse events** or **safety concerns** are promptly identified and addressed. This system, which includes the **Australian Adverse Drug Reaction Reporting System (ADRS)**, allows healthcare professionals and consumers to report any unexpected side effects associated with therapeutic products. In **2021**, the TGA received over **30,000 adverse event reports**, many of which led to updates in product labeling or additional safety warnings, thereby protecting consumers from potential harm.

Additionally, the TGA's regulation of **complementary medicines** offers public benefits by ensuring that these products, which include **vitamins, herbal supplements**, and **minerals**, meet quality and safety standards. While complementary medicines are often perceived as lower risk, the TGA ensures that they are free from harmful contaminants and accurately labeled, providing consumers with safe alternatives to conventional treatments. For instance, in **2020**, the TGA conducted a review of complementary medicines containing **St. John's Wort**, leading to updated warnings about its potential interactions with other medications, which protected consumers from unintended side effects.

The **therapeutic goods regulatory framework** also benefits the public by fostering **innovation** and **access to new treatments**. The TGA's streamlined processes for assessing innovative therapies, such as **biologics** and **advanced medical devices**, ensure that Australian patients have timely access to cutting-edge treatments. In **2022**, the TGA approved several **novel cancer therapies**, giving patients access to life-saving treatments that were not previously available. The regulation of **biosimilars**, which are biologic medicines highly similar to already approved biologic drugs, also provides a public benefit by offering more affordable options for treating complex diseases such as **rheumatoid arthritis** and **cancer.**

The **TGA's enforcement of advertising regulations** is another area where public benefits are clear. By ensuring that therapeutic goods are marketed accurately and not misleadingly, the TGA helps consumers make informed decisions about their health. Advertisements for medicines and medical devices must comply with the **TGA Advertising Code**, which mandates that claims made about a product's effectiveness must be backed by scientific evidence. This regulation prevents companies from making exaggerated or false claims that could mislead the public. In **2021**, the TGA took enforcement actions against several companies for misleading advertising, protecting consumers from deceptive marketing practices.

International collaboration also brings public benefits. The TGA works closely with regulatory agencies such as the **U.S. FDA**, the **European Medicines Agency (EMA)**, and the **World Health Organization (WHO)** to harmonize standards and ensure the global availability of safe therapeutic goods. This collaboration allows for the sharing of safety data and helps speed up the availability of critical treatments, especially in times of global health crises such as the **COVID-19 pandemic.** The public benefits from access to vaccines and treatments that have been rigorously evaluated and found to be safe by multiple regulatory bodies around the world.

6.7 Conclusion on Application

The **application process** for registering therapeutic goods with the **Therapeutic Goods Administration (TGA)** is comprehensive and designed to ensure that only products that meet stringent standards of **safety, efficacy,** and **quality** are approved for the Australian market. From the initial submission of detailed dossiers to the final decision on inclusion in the **Australian Register of Therapeutic Goods (ARTG)**, the application process plays a critical role in safeguarding public health.

Through the rigorous **scientific evaluation** conducted by the TGA, each product undergoes a thorough assessment, including a review of **clinical trial data, manufacturing practices,** and **post-market surveillance plans.** The inclusion of robust **Risk Management Plans (RMPs)**, adherence to **Good Manufacturing Practices (GMP),** and continuous post-approval monitoring are integral to ensuring that therapeutic goods remain safe for public use throughout their lifecycle. For instance, in **2021**, the TGA's assessment of **novel cancer therapies** resulted in the approval of cutting-edge treatments that adhered to these stringent requirements, demonstrating the importance of a well-regulated application process.

The conclusion of an application is based on the collective findings of the **commission's assessment**, which evaluates whether the benefits of the product outweigh its risks. If the product is deemed to be of sufficient benefit and meets the necessary regulatory criteria, it is granted inclusion in the **ARTG** and authorized for sale. However, the TGA's responsibility does not end with approval; **post-market surveillance** ensures that the product continues to perform as expected, with safety updates issued as needed based on real-world data. In **2022**, several post-market reviews conducted by the TGA led to **updated safety warnings** for approved products, highlighting the ongoing vigilance required to maintain public safety.

6.8 Consideration of Undertakings

During the application review process for therapeutic goods, the **Therapeutic Goods Administration (TGA)** may require the applicant to provide **undertakings** or commitments to ensure that any potential risks associated with the product are effectively managed. These undertakings are critical to addressing concerns raised during the assessment process, particularly if there are uncertainties related to **long-term safety, efficacy,** or **manufacturing consistency**. By requiring undertakings, the TGA can approve a product while ensuring that additional safeguards are in place to protect public health.

An undertaking may involve a commitment to conduct **post-market studies**, such as additional **clinical trials** or **observational studies**, to gather further data on the product's performance in real-world settings. This is especially important for novel therapies or medical devices that may have limited long-term data at the time of approval. For example, in **2021**, several sponsors of new biologics were required to conduct post-market surveillance and submit **annual safety reports** as part of their undertakings to the TGA. These reports allowed the TGA to monitor the long-term safety of these treatments, ensuring that any adverse trends were detected early.

Another type of undertaking could involve **risk management strategies** to mitigate known risks associated with the product. This may include **patient education programs, restricted distribution systems**, or specific training for healthcare providers on the appropriate use of the product. For instance, a pharmaceutical company may be required to implement a **Risk Evaluation and Mitigation Strategy (REMS)** for a high-risk drug, ensuring that only qualified healthcare professionals prescribe it and that patients are fully informed of the potential side effects.

Manufacturing undertakings may also be required if the TGA identifies concerns related to the consistency or quality of the production process. In such cases, the applicant may need to provide regular updates on **manufacturing conditions**, conduct additional **batch testing**, or adhere to specific **quality control measures** to ensure that the product maintains its efficacy and safety throughout its lifecycle. In **2022**, the TGA required a medical device manufacturer to enhance its **quality assurance protocols** as part of the undertaking process after concerns were raised about the device's reliability in long-term use.

The TGA's consideration of undertakings is a flexible approach that allows for **conditional approvals** when the benefits of a therapeutic good outweigh its risks, provided that ongoing safeguards are in place. This process ensures that products can reach the market in a timely manner while still maintaining high safety standards. If the sponsor fails to meet the conditions outlined in the undertakings, the TGA has the authority to **suspend** or **cancel** the product's inclusion in the **Australian Register of Therapeutic Goods (ARTG)**, protecting public health from potentially unsafe products.

6.9 Determination

The final **determination** of an application for therapeutic goods by the **TGA** marks the conclusion of the comprehensive review process. This determination is based on the overall assessment of the product's **safety**, **efficacy**, and **quality**, taking into account the data provided by the sponsor and any undertakings agreed upon during the review process.

Once the TGA has completed its scientific evaluation, a decision is made on whether to approve the product for inclusion in the **ARTG**. If the product is approved, it is granted an **ARTG number**, allowing it to be legally supplied in the Australian market. This approval indicates that the product has met the TGA's rigorous standards and can be used safely by patients under the prescribed conditions. In **2022**, the TGA approved over **300 therapeutic products**, ranging from new pharmaceuticals to advanced medical devices, reflecting the agency's role in ensuring that high-quality therapeutic goods are available to the Australian public.

However, if the TGA determines that the risks of the product outweigh the benefits, or if the sponsor fails to provide sufficient data to support its claims, the application may be **rejected**. The sponsor is then notified of the decision, along with the reasons for rejection, which could include insufficient clinical trial data, unresolved safety concerns, or non-compliance with manufacturing standards. The sponsor has the option to appeal the decision or submit a revised application with additional data to address the issues raised by the TGA.

In cases where a product is conditionally approved based on undertakings, the determination may include specific conditions that the sponsor must fulfill to maintain the product's approval. These conditions are carefully monitored by the TGA, ensuring that the sponsor adheres to the agreed-upon safety measures and risk management strategies. If the sponsor complies with these conditions, the product remains in the ARTG. However, failure to meet the conditions can result in the **revocation** of the product's approval.

The determination process is critical in maintaining the integrity of Australia's therapeutic goods market. By ensuring that only products that meet stringent safety and quality criteria are approved, the TGA helps protect public health and maintains public trust in the therapeutic goods available in Australia. Through a transparent and evidence-based approach, the TGA's determination process ensures that patients and healthcare providers have access to safe, effective, and high-quality therapeutic options.

European Union (EU) Regulations

The European Union (EU) is one of the most complex and harmonized regulatory environments for pharmaceuticals and medical devices. The European Medicines Agency (EMA) and the European Directorate for the Quality of Medicines (EDQM) play pivotal roles in ensuring the safety, efficacy, and quality of medicines across the EU. This chapter explores the structure and function of these regulatory bodies, along with the specific guidelines and directives that govern pharmaceutical and medical device approvals.

The chapter focuses on key regulatory processes such as the submission and evaluation of Active Substance Master Files (ASMF), which ensure the quality of active pharmaceutical ingredients (APIs). It also covers the marketing authorization procedures, including the centralized and decentralized procedures that streamline the approval of new drugs across the EU member states.

A significant portion of this chapter is dedicated to discussing Good Manufacturing Practices (GMP) and EudraLex directives, which set the standards for pharmaceutical production, packaging, and labeling. The chapter also delves into the unique regulatory considerations for medical devices in the EU, including the classification, approval, and post-marketing surveillance of these products. For professionals navigating the EU market, this chapter provides invaluable insights into the legal and regulatory frameworks necessary for compliance and successful market entry.

7.1 Organization and Structure of EMA & EDQM

The **European Medicines Agency (EMA)** and the **European Directorate for the Quality of Medicines & HealthCare (EDQM)** are two key organizations in the European Union responsible for regulating and maintaining the safety, efficacy, and quality of medicinal products and healthcare-related substances. Both organizations play crucial roles in safeguarding public health within the **European Economic Area (EEA)** and across Europe by ensuring that medicinal products, including **pharmaceuticals, medical devices,** and **biologics,** meet stringent regulatory standards.

The **European Medicines Agency (EMA)** is the primary regulatory body in the European Union for the evaluation and supervision of medicinal products. Established in **1995,** the EMA's role is to harmonize the **regulatory processes** of EU member states, ensuring that all medicinal products available in the market meet the same high standards of safety, efficacy, and quality. The EMA operates under the oversight of the **European Commission** and is supported by the national regulatory authorities of EU member states. One of the EMA's primary functions is the **centralized marketing authorization procedure**, which allows pharmaceutical companies to submit a single marketing authorization application that, if approved, allows the product to be marketed in all **EU member states,** as well as **Iceland, Norway,** and **Liechtenstein.**

The organizational structure of the EMA is complex, reflecting its broad scope of responsibilities. It is divided into various **committees, working parties,** and **scientific advisory groups** (SAGs). The **Committee for Medicinal Products for Human Use (CHMP)** is the EMA's main scientific committee responsible for evaluating new medicines. The **CHMP** consists of experts from the national regulatory authorities of EU member states and provides scientific advice on the quality, safety, and efficacy of medicines. In **2021,** the CHMP issued over **120 opinions** on new medicinal products, playing a critical role in facilitating access to innovative treatments for European patients.

In addition to the CHMP, the **Committee for Orphan Medicinal Products (COMP)** focuses on the evaluation of drugs intended for the treatment of **rare diseases,** while the **Pharmacovigilance Risk Assessment Committee (PRAC)** is responsible for monitoring the safety of medicines once they have been authorized. The **PRAC** assesses **adverse event reports** from patients and healthcare providers, ensuring that any emerging safety concerns are addressed promptly. In **2022,** the PRAC issued several important safety recommendations, including updates to the safety information for widely used medicines.

The **European Directorate for the Quality of Medicines & HealthCare (EDQM)**, which operates under the auspices of the **Council of Europe**, is primarily focused on the **quality of medicines** and their components. Established in **1964**, the EDQM is responsible for maintaining the **European Pharmacopoeia (Ph. Eur.)**, a legally binding reference work that sets out quality standards for medicinal products and their ingredients. These standards are applied in all **39 member states** of the **Council of Europe** and in the **European Union**, providing a harmonized framework for ensuring the quality of pharmaceuticals throughout the region.

The EDQM's structure is organized into several departments and committees, with the **European Pharmacopoeia Commission** playing a central role in the development and revision of the pharmacopoeial monographs that define the standards for active substances, excipients, and dosage forms. The EDQM also oversees the **Certification of Suitability (CEP)** procedure, which certifies that substances used in pharmaceuticals comply with the Ph. Eur. standards. The **CEP** procedure simplifies the regulatory approval process for pharmaceutical manufacturers, as the certification is recognized by all member states, reducing the need for duplicate testing and evaluations.

The EDQM's scope extends beyond pharmaceuticals to include the **quality of water, vaccines**, and **blood transfusion materials**, ensuring that the entire healthcare supply chain is subject to rigorous standards. In **2021**, the EDQM conducted over **100 inspections** of manufacturers and suppliers, ensuring compliance with the European Pharmacopoeia and other relevant guidelines.

Both the **EMA** and the **EDQM** collaborate closely with international organizations such as the **World Health Organization (WHO)** and other regulatory agencies, including the **U.S. FDA** and the **Japanese Pharmaceuticals and Medical Devices Agency (PMDA)**. This international cooperation ensures that European patients benefit from globally harmonized standards, allowing for the timely availability of safe and effective medicines.

7.2 General Guidelines and Active Substance Master Files (ASMF) System in the EU

The regulatory framework in the **European Union (EU)** for medicinal products is governed by a series of **general guidelines** that set out the standards and procedures for the evaluation, approval, and post-market monitoring of pharmaceuticals. These guidelines are designed to ensure that all medicines available in the EU meet stringent criteria for **safety, efficacy, and quality**. The **Active Substance Master File (ASMF) system** is a key part of this regulatory process, providing a mechanism for the submission and evaluation of detailed information about the **active pharmaceutical ingredients (APIs)** used in medicinal products.

The **general guidelines** in the EU are developed and maintained by the **European Medicines Agency (EMA)** and are based on scientific advice from various expert committees. These guidelines cover all aspects of the drug development process, including **clinical trials, manufacturing practices, pharmacovigilance**, and **quality control**. They are designed to harmonize the regulatory processes across the EU's **27 member states**, ensuring that all medicinal products are subject to the same high standards regardless of where they are manufactured or marketed.

One of the core areas covered by these guidelines is the **quality of active substances**. The quality of the **active pharmaceutical ingredient (API)** is critical to the safety and efficacy of the finished product. To ensure that the APIs used in medicines meet the required standards, the EU has implemented the **Active Substance Master File (ASMF) system**. This system allows API manufacturers to submit detailed information about the **manufacturing process, quality control measures**, and **stability data** of the active substance in a confidential manner, protecting their intellectual property while ensuring compliance with regulatory requirements.

The **ASMF system** is based on the submission of two parts: the **open part** (or applicant's part) and the **closed part** (or restricted part). The **open part** contains information that is shared with the marketing authorization holder (MAH), including details on the **quality control** tests and specifications for the API. This ensures that the MAH can perform appropriate quality checks on the active substance during the manufacturing of the finished product. The **closed part**, however, contains confidential information related to the manufacturing process, including proprietary details about the synthesis and purification of the API. This part is submitted directly to the regulatory authorities and is not disclosed to the MAH, allowing API manufacturers to protect their trade secrets.

The **ASMF system** simplifies the approval process for medicines by allowing the same **master file** to be used in multiple marketing authorization applications. This means that once an ASMF has been submitted and approved, it can be referenced in future applications without the need for the API manufacturer to resubmit the same information. In

2022, the EMA reviewed over **200 ASMF submissions**, reflecting the increasing complexity of modern pharmaceuticals and the growing reliance on specialized API manufacturers. By streamlining the submission process, the ASMF system reduces the administrative burden on both manufacturers and regulators, while ensuring that the quality of APIs is consistently maintained.

The **general guidelines** for the ASMF system also outline the requirements for **Good Manufacturing Practices (GMP)** for API manufacturers. These guidelines ensure that APIs are produced in facilities that meet stringent standards for cleanliness, control, and quality assurance. API manufacturers must undergo **regular inspections** by regulatory authorities to verify their compliance with GMP standards. In **2021**, the **European Directorate for the Quality of Medicines & HealthCare (EDQM)** conducted over **150 GMP inspections** of API manufacturers across Europe and internationally, ensuring that the active substances used in European medicines meet the highest standards of quality.

In addition to GMP requirements, the general guidelines also include provisions for **stability testing** and **impurity control** for APIs. Stability testing ensures that the API remains stable under various environmental conditions, such as changes in temperature or humidity, over the product's shelf life. Impurity control is equally important, as the presence of impurities in the API can affect the safety and efficacy of the finished product. The EMA has issued detailed guidelines on the acceptable limits for impurities in APIs, including guidance on the detection and control of **genotoxic impurities**, which can pose serious risks to patient safety.

The **ASMF system** also plays a crucial role in the **evaluation of generic medicines**. For a generic medicine to be approved, the generic manufacturer must demonstrate that their product is **bioequivalent** to the reference product, meaning it delivers the same therapeutic effect. The ASMF system allows generic manufacturers to reference the API master file without having to provide detailed information about the API's manufacturing process themselves. This not only simplifies the approval process but also helps protect the proprietary information of the original API manufacturer.

7.3 Content and Approval Process of IMPD

The **Investigational Medicinal Product Dossier (IMPD)** is a key document required for the approval of clinical trials in the **European Union (EU)**. It provides a comprehensive overview of the **quality, safety,** and

efficacy of the **investigational medicinal product (IMP)** that is intended for use in a clinical trial. The **IMPD** must be submitted as part of the application for a **clinical trial authorization (CTA)** to the relevant national regulatory authority in the EU, such as the **European Medicines Agency (EMA)** or the **national competent authority (NCA)** of the member state where the trial will be conducted.

The **content of the IMPD** is designed to give regulators all the necessary information to assess the investigational medicinal product's quality, safety, and potential therapeutic benefits. The dossier typically consists of several key sections, including details on the **manufacturing process, preclinical testing, clinical trial data**, and **risk assessments.**

The **quality section** of the IMPD provides detailed information on the **active substance** and the **finished product**, including the **chemical structure, formulation, manufacturing process**, and **quality control procedures.** This section must demonstrate that the IMP is produced according to **Good Manufacturing Practices (GMP)** and that it meets the required standards for purity, stability, and potency. The **specifications** for the active substance and excipients, along with details of any potential impurities, must be clearly described. In **2022**, the EMA received and reviewed hundreds of IMPDs, emphasizing the importance of robust quality control in investigational products to ensure patient safety during clinical trials.

The **non-clinical section** of the IMPD contains the results of **preclinical studies**, including **pharmacology, toxicology**, and **pharmacokinetics.** These studies are typically conducted in **animal models** and are necessary to demonstrate that the investigational product is reasonably safe to administer to humans. The **toxicological data** must include information on the product's potential to cause **adverse effects**, including **carcinogenicity, mutagenicity**, and **reproductive toxicity.** This data helps regulators assess whether the potential risks of the investigational product are acceptable given the potential therapeutic benefits.

The **clinical section** of the IMPD includes information on any prior **clinical trials** conducted with the investigational product, either in the EU or globally. For investigational products that have already undergone **Phase I clinical trials**, this section would summarize the **safety data**, including any **adverse events** or **serious adverse events** (SAEs) observed during these studies. The clinical section also outlines the proposed **clinical trial protocol** for the upcoming trial, including the **dosing regimen, study**

population, study design, and **endpoints**. The **rationale** for the trial, including any unmet medical needs or novel therapeutic approaches, is also explained in this section.

One of the most critical aspects of the IMPD is the **risk-benefit assessment**, which evaluates the potential risks associated with the investigational product against its expected therapeutic benefits. This section considers the findings from both preclinical and clinical studies, as well as the **disease or condition** being targeted. For example, a novel treatment for a **life-threatening disease** such as **cancer** may be considered acceptable even if it has significant risks, provided that the potential benefits outweigh those risks. In contrast, treatments for less severe conditions must demonstrate a much lower risk profile.

The **approval process** for an IMPD is rigorous and involves a detailed review by the relevant regulatory authorities. After the submission of the **Clinical Trial Application (CTA)**, which includes the IMPD, the regulatory body will conduct a **scientific evaluation** of the dossier. This evaluation is aimed at ensuring that the investigational product is safe for use in the proposed clinical trial and that the trial is ethically and scientifically sound. The **review period** typically lasts between **30 and 60 days**, depending on the complexity of the application and the investigational product.

If the regulators identify any deficiencies or areas of concern within the IMPD, they may issue a **request for additional information** (RFI). The sponsor must respond to these requests promptly, providing the necessary clarifications or additional data to support the application. If the IMPD is found to be complete and satisfactory, the regulatory authority will grant **authorization** for the clinical trial to proceed. In **2021**, the EMA authorized over **500 clinical trials** based on the submission of IMPDs, underscoring the importance of this process in advancing medical research within the EU.

7.4 Marketing Authorization Procedures in the EU

The **marketing authorization procedures** in the **European Union (EU)** are designed to ensure that all medicinal products entering the market meet high standards of **quality, safety**, and **efficacy**. These procedures are regulated by the **European Medicines Agency (EMA)** in collaboration with national regulatory authorities within EU member states. There are several marketing authorization pathways available in the EU, including the **centralized procedure, mutual recognition procedure (MRP), decentralized procedure (DCP)**, and the **national procedure**. Each of these pathways caters to different types of products and allows pharmaceutical companies to seek approval based on the scope of their market.

The **centralized procedure** is the most commonly used pathway for obtaining marketing authorization in the EU, particularly for **new active substances** or **innovative medicines**. Under this procedure, a pharmaceutical company submits a **single marketing authorization application (MAA)** to the EMA, which evaluates the product on behalf of all **27 EU member states**, as well as **Iceland, Norway, and Liechtenstein**. If the EMA grants marketing authorization, the product can be sold and distributed throughout the entire European Economic Area (EEA). In **2022**, over **100 medicines** were authorized under the centralized procedure, many of which included treatments for serious conditions like **oncology** and **rare diseases**.

One of the main advantages of the centralized procedure is that it simplifies the approval process for pharmaceutical companies, allowing them to obtain marketing authorization in multiple countries with a single application. This is particularly important for **biologics, advanced therapies**, and **orphan medicines**, which benefit from **special regulatory support** and **fast-track pathways** under the EMA's centralized system.

The evaluation of applications under the centralized procedure is carried out by the **Committee for Medicinal Products for Human Use (CHMP)**, which consists of experts from each member state. The CHMP assesses the medicinal product's **quality, safety**, and **efficacy**, considering the results of **clinical trials** and **preclinical studies**. Once the CHMP completes its review, it issues an **opinion** on whether the product should be approved. This opinion is forwarded to the **European Commission**, which makes the final decision on the marketing authorization. The entire review process typically takes **210 days**, although this can be expedited for products that qualify for **priority review** or **conditional marketing authorization**.

The **mutual recognition procedure (MRP)** is another pathway available for products that have already been approved in one EU member state. In this case, a company can apply to have its marketing authorization recognized in other EU member states. The MRP allows for the mutual recognition of marketing authorizations without the need for duplicate assessments. For example, a product that has been approved in **France** can be submitted for recognition in **Germany** and other member states under the MRP. In **2021**, over **50 products** were approved using the mutual recognition procedure, reflecting its importance in facilitating access to medicines across multiple EU markets.

The **decentralized procedure (DCP)** is similar to the MRP but is used for products that have not yet been authorized in any EU member state. Under this procedure, a company submits an application to multiple member states at the same time, with one member state acting as the **reference member state (RMS)** and the others as **concerned member states (CMS)**. The RMS is responsible for conducting the initial assessment of the product, while the CMSs review the assessment and provide their input. The DCP is often used for **generic medicines** or products that do not fall under the centralized procedure. The average timeline for completing a DCP is around **210 days**, similar to the centralized procedure.

The **national procedure** is used when a company seeks marketing authorization for a product in only one EU member state. This procedure is more limited in scope and is generally reserved for products intended for local use. For instance, over-the-counter medicines or niche products that are not intended for wider EU distribution may be authorized through the national procedure. Each country has its own regulatory body that oversees the national marketing authorization process. For example, the **Medicines and Healthcare products Regulatory Agency (MHRA)** in the UK was responsible for national authorizations before Brexit.

In addition to these standard procedures, the EU has several regulatory mechanisms in place to expedite the approval of medicines that address **unmet medical needs** or **serious conditions**. **Conditional marketing authorization (CMA)** is one such mechanism, allowing products to be approved based on less comprehensive data than is normally required, provided that the benefits of early access outweigh the risks. CMA is often granted for treatments targeting **life-threatening diseases** such as **HIV**, **cancer**, or **pandemics**, with the requirement that the company submits additional data post-approval to confirm the product's safety and efficacy.

Similarly, the **accelerated assessment** pathway is available for products that offer significant therapeutic innovations or are expected to have a major impact on public health. Under this pathway, the review time for a marketing authorization application is shortened to **150 days**. This pathway was instrumental during the **COVID-19 pandemic**, where vaccines and treatments were fast-tracked to meet urgent public health needs.

7.5 Regulatory Considerations for Manufacturing, Packaging, and Labeling of Pharmaceuticals in the EU

The **regulatory considerations** for the **manufacturing, packaging**, and **labeling** of pharmaceuticals in the **European Union (EU)** are governed by stringent standards to ensure that medicines are consistently safe, effective, and of high quality. These regulations are primarily based on **Good Manufacturing Practices (GMP)** and are overseen by the **European Medicines Agency (EMA)** and national regulatory authorities within each member state. The objective is to ensure that all aspects of pharmaceutical production, from the raw materials to the finished product, meet the required standards.

The **manufacturing** of pharmaceuticals in the EU is regulated by **EU Directive 2003/94/EC**, which outlines the basic principles of **Good Manufacturing Practices (GMP)** for medicinal products. GMP guidelines ensure that medicines are consistently produced and controlled to meet the quality standards appropriate for their intended use. This includes strict controls over the **quality of raw materials, equipment maintenance, hygiene standards**, and **environmental conditions** in the manufacturing facility. The manufacturing processes must be validated, and continuous monitoring is required to detect any deviations from the approved processes.

One of the critical elements in the manufacturing process is the quality of the **active pharmaceutical ingredient (API)**. API manufacturers must comply with **GMP standards** and are subject to regular inspections by EU regulators to ensure that the APIs used in medicinal products are pure, stable, and free from contaminants. In **2021**, the **European Directorate for the Quality of Medicines & HealthCare (EDQM)** conducted more than **150 GMP inspections** of API manufacturers to ensure compliance with these regulations. Failure to comply with GMP standards can result in penalties, including the suspension of manufacturing licenses.

In addition to manufacturing requirements, the **packaging** of pharmaceuticals in the EU is also subject to strict regulatory oversight. Packaging must ensure that the product remains **stable, protected from contamination**, and **tamper-evident**. For example, medicines that are sensitive to light must be packaged in **light-resistant containers**, while those vulnerable to moisture must be packaged in **blister packs** or other moisture-resistant materials. The packaging must also meet **safety standards** to prevent unauthorized access, particularly for products that pose a risk of misuse or abuse. The EU mandates the use of **tamper-evident seals** on many over-the-counter (OTC) medicines to ensure that the product has not been tampered with before reaching the consumer.

The **labeling** of pharmaceuticals in the EU is regulated under **Directive 2001/83/EC**, which specifies the requirements for clear, accurate, and comprehensive labeling. Pharmaceutical labels must provide essential information such as the **name of the medicinal product, strength, active ingredients, dosage form**, and **route of administration**. The labeling must also include important safety information, such as **contraindications, warnings**, and potential **side effects**. This information is critical for both healthcare providers and patients to ensure the correct and safe use of the medicine.

One of the unique features of EU pharmaceutical labeling is the requirement for **Braille** on the outer packaging of medicinal products to accommodate visually impaired patients. This regulation reflects the EU's commitment to ensuring that healthcare is accessible to all individuals. In addition to Braille, the labeling must be in the official language(s) of the member state where the product is marketed. For example, a product sold in **France** must have labeling in **French**, while a product sold in **Germany** must include labeling in **German**. This multilingual requirement ensures that patients across the EU can access and understand essential information about their medicines.

In terms of safety, the EU has also implemented requirements for **unique identifiers** and **anti-tampering devices** on prescription medicines. Under the **Falsified Medicines Directive (FMD)**, which came into effect in **2019**, all prescription medicines must have a **2D barcode** and an **anti-tampering device** to prevent the introduction of **counterfeit medicines** into the supply chain. The 2D barcode allows the medicine to be traced from the manufacturer to the pharmacy, providing an additional layer of security to ensure that only legitimate, high-quality medicines reach patients. This system is particularly important for high-value medicines that are prone to counterfeiting, such as **oncology drugs** and **biologics**.

To further ensure the safety and quality of pharmaceuticals, the EU requires manufacturers to implement a robust **pharmacovigilance system** that monitors the safety of medicines once they are on the market. This includes the reporting of any **adverse drug reactions (ADRs)** and conducting **post-marketing surveillance** to detect any potential issues related to the manufacturing, packaging, or labeling of the product. The EMA and national regulatory authorities collaborate to review this data and take corrective actions when necessary, such as issuing **safety warnings**, updating **product labels,** or initiating **product recalls.** In **2022,** several medicines were recalled due to packaging defects that could have compromised patient safety, underscoring the importance of regulatory oversight in all aspects of the pharmaceutical supply chain.

7.6 Eudralex Directives for Human Medicines

The **Eudralex** is the comprehensive body of regulations and guidelines that govern the regulation of **human medicines** within the **European Union (EU).** It is a collection of **Directives, Regulations,** and **Guidelines** that ensure the safety, efficacy, and quality of medicinal products intended for human use. These directives are implemented across all **27 EU member states,** providing a harmonized legal framework for the development, manufacture, and distribution of medicines. The Eudralex is divided into multiple volumes, with **Volume 1** being the most relevant for human medicines.

One of the most important directives under Eudralex is **Directive 2001/83/EC,** which lays down the **community code** relating to medicinal products for human use. This directive is the cornerstone of EU pharmaceutical regulation and establishes the legal requirements for marketing authorization, clinical trials, pharmacovigilance, and the manufacture of medicinal products. It provides the foundation for ensuring that medicines meet the required standards before they can be placed on the EU market. For example, in **2022,** the **European Medicines Agency (EMA)** approved over **100 new medicines** based on compliance with the requirements outlined in Directive 2001/83/EC.

One of the key elements of this directive is the requirement for **marketing authorization.** According to Directive 2001/83/EC, no medicinal product can be placed on the market without first obtaining **marketing authorization** from either the **EMA** or a national regulatory authority in the EU. This ensures that the product has undergone thorough scientific evaluation to assess its **quality, safety,** and **efficacy.** The directive also specifies the criteria for **clinical trials** and the requirements for conducting **pharmacovigilance,** ensuring that the safety of the medicinal product is monitored throughout its lifecycle.

The Eudralex directives also include **Directive 2003/94/EC,** which governs **Good Manufacturing Practices (GMP)** for human medicines. GMP regulations are designed to ensure that medicinal products are consistently produced and controlled according to the quality standards appropriate to their intended use. The directive mandates regular **inspections** of manufacturing sites to verify compliance with GMP standards. In **2021,** the **European Directorate for the Quality of Medicines & HealthCare (EDQM)** carried out more than **150 inspections** of manufacturing facilities to ensure that they met the required GMP standards. These inspections help maintain the integrity of the EU pharmaceutical supply chain by ensuring that all products are manufactured to the highest quality standards.

Directive 2001/20/EC, also known as the **Clinical Trials Directive,** governs the conduct of **clinical trials** in the EU. It sets out the requirements for obtaining authorization to conduct a clinical trial, the protection of trial participants, and the reporting of **adverse events.** This directive ensures that clinical trials are conducted in a way that protects the rights, safety, and well-being of the participants while generating reliable data on the safety and efficacy of new medicines. In **2022,** the EMA oversaw the approval of over **300 clinical trials,** all of which adhered to the standards set out in the Clinical Trials Directive.

Directive 2010/84/EU, an amendment to Directive 2001/83/EC, strengthens the **pharmacovigilance** requirements in the EU. This directive establishes the legal framework for monitoring the safety of medicines after they have been placed on the market, requiring companies to report **adverse drug reactions (ADRs)** to the regulatory authorities. It also introduces the concept of **risk management plans (RMPs),** which must be submitted as part of the marketing authorization application to ensure that potential risks associated with a medicine are identified, minimized, and monitored. In **2021,** the EMA issued several safety warnings and updated labeling for medicinal products based on the pharmacovigilance data collected under Directive 2010/84/EU.

In addition to these directives, the **Eudralex** includes detailed guidance on **Good Distribution Practice (GDP),** which ensures the safe and secure distribution of medicines throughout the EU. GDP guidelines are particularly important for maintaining the **cold chain** for temperature-sensitive medicines, such as vaccines, which must be stored and transported under strictly controlled conditions. In **2021,** several cases of **cold chain breaches** were reported, leading to the recall of certain medicinal products. The enforcement of GDP regulations helps prevent such issues by ensuring that all entities involved in the distribution of medicines comply with strict storage and handling requirements.

The Eudralex directives also include regulations aimed at preventing the entry of **falsified medicines** into the EU market. The **Falsified Medicines**

Directive (FMD), which came into effect in **2019**, requires that all prescription medicines bear a **unique identifier** and an **anti-tampering device** to ensure their authenticity. This regulation is critical in preventing the infiltration of counterfeit medicines into the supply chain, protecting patients from potentially harmful products. The implementation of the FMD in **2022** saw the successful serialization of over **90%** of prescription medicines in the EU, significantly reducing the risk of falsified medicines reaching consumers.

The **Eudralex directives** for human medicines provide a robust legal framework that governs the development, manufacture, distribution, and monitoring of pharmaceuticals in the EU. Through harmonized regulations such as **Directive 2001/83/EC**, **Directive 2003/94/EC**, and the **Falsified Medicines Directive**, the Eudralex ensures that all medicinal products available in the EU meet the highest standards of **quality**, **safety**, and **efficacy**. The continuous enforcement of these directives by the **EMA** and national regulatory authorities ensures that patients across Europe have access to safe and effective treatments while maintaining the integrity of the pharmaceutical supply chain.

7.7 Variations & Extensions, Compliance of European Pharmacopoeia (CEP/CoS)

The **variations** and **extensions** process in the **European Union (EU)** refers to the regulatory procedures required when changes are made to an already authorized medicinal product. These changes can range from modifications in the manufacturing process to updates in the product's labeling or formulation. The **Compliance of European Pharmacopoeia (CEP/CoS)**, managed by the **European Directorate for the Quality of Medicines & HealthCare (EDQM)**, is a certification system that ensures active pharmaceutical ingredients (APIs) used in medicinal products comply with the standards outlined in the **European Pharmacopoeia (Ph. Eur.)**.

Variations are categorized into different types, depending on the significance of the change. The most common types of variations include **Type IA**, **Type IB**, and **Type II**. **Type IA variations** are minor changes that have minimal impact on the quality, safety, or efficacy of the product, such as administrative changes. These are considered **do and tell** variations, meaning they can be implemented immediately but must be reported to the regulatory authorities within **12 months**. For example, a change in the product's packaging material that does not affect the stability of the product would fall under this category.

Type IB variations are changes that could potentially impact the quality of the product but are not expected to affect safety or efficacy. These variations require **prior approval** from the regulatory authorities before implementation. Examples include changes to the **manufacturing process** or **quality control methods**. In **2022**, the EMA processed over **500 Type IB variations**, highlighting the importance of ensuring that even minor changes do not compromise the quality of medicinal products.

Type II variations involve more significant changes that are likely to affect the safety, efficacy, or quality of the product. These changes require a full evaluation by the regulatory authorities and include changes to the **active substance, dosage form**, or **therapeutic indication**. For instance, adding a new therapeutic indication for a medicine or changing the formulation to improve its stability would require a Type II variation. The approval process for Type II variations typically takes around **90 days**, depending on the complexity of the change and the data provided by the marketing authorization holder (MAH).

In addition to variations, **extensions** refer to more substantial changes to a medicinal product that are significant enough to require a new marketing authorization. These include changes to the **route of administration, strength**, or **pharmaceutical form** of the product. Extensions are treated as new applications, but the product is considered part of the same "global marketing authorization," meaning it benefits from the data protection period of the original product.

Compliance with the **European Pharmacopoeia** is essential for ensuring the quality of medicinal products in the EU. The **Certification of Suitability (CEP)**, also known as **Certificate of Suitability to the Monographs of the European Pharmacopoeia (CoS)**, is a system that allows API manufacturers to demonstrate that their products comply with the standards outlined in the Ph. Eur. The **EDQM** grants the **CEP** after evaluating the API's manufacturing process, quality control measures, and compliance with the relevant pharmacopoeial monographs.

The **CEP/CoS system** simplifies the regulatory approval process for both API manufacturers and pharmaceutical companies. Once an API manufacturer obtains a CEP, pharmaceutical companies can reference the CEP in their marketing authorization applications, rather than submitting detailed information about the API's manufacturing process. This reduces the administrative burden and speeds up the approval process for medicinal products. In **2021**, the EDQM issued over **200 CEPs**, helping streamline the supply of high-quality APIs for use in medicines across the EU.

A CEP also ensures that the API meets the strict requirements for **impurity control, stability,** and **microbial contamination** as outlined in the Ph. Eur. These standards are regularly updated to reflect advances in scientific knowledge and manufacturing technologies. For example, the Ph. Eur. has recently introduced stricter limits on **genotoxic impurities,** which are potentially harmful chemicals that can cause genetic mutations. Manufacturers holding a CEP must ensure that their APIs comply with these updated standards to maintain their certification.

The **EDQM** conducts **inspections** of API manufacturing sites to verify compliance with the Ph. Eur. and GMP standards. These inspections are critical for ensuring the safety and quality of medicinal products that use CEP-certified APIs. In **2022**, the EDQM conducted over **150 GMP inspections** worldwide, ensuring that API manufacturers adhered to the high-quality standards required by the EU regulatory framework.

7.8 Marketing Authorization (MA) Transfers and Qualified Person (QP) in the EU

The **transfer of a marketing authorization (MA)** in the **European Union (EU)** is a regulated process that allows the ownership of a medicinal product's marketing authorization to be transferred from one holder to another. This process is crucial for pharmaceutical companies undergoing mergers, acquisitions, or corporate restructuring, where the responsibility for the product may need to be assigned to a different entity. The transfer must be approved by the **European Medicines Agency (EMA)** or the relevant **national competent authority (NCA),** depending on whether the product was authorized through the **centralized procedure** or a national procedure.

The transfer process involves several key steps to ensure that the new marketing authorization holder (MAH) is capable of maintaining the required regulatory standards for the product. The new MAH must demonstrate that it has the necessary infrastructure, including qualified staff and facilities, to fulfill the regulatory obligations associated with the marketing authorization. This includes **pharmacovigilance responsibilities, quality control,** and **product recall procedures.**

The **MA transfer application** typically consists of several documents, including a letter of intent from both the existing and new MAHs, updated contact information, and evidence that the new MAH has the necessary legal and financial capacity to handle the product's regulatory and commercial responsibilities. In **2021**, the EMA processed more than **50 MA transfers** under the centralized procedure, reflecting the dynamic nature of the pharmaceutical industry, where products frequently change ownership due to corporate transactions.

A critical part of ensuring that the new MAH can meet its obligations is the appointment of a **Qualified Person (QP)**. The **Qualified Person (QP)** plays a pivotal role in the **manufacturing and release of medicinal products** within the EU. According to **EU Directive 2001/83/EC**, every pharmaceutical company must appoint a QP who is responsible for ensuring that each batch of medicinal products released to the market complies with **Good Manufacturing Practices (GMP)** and the requirements of the marketing authorization. The QP acts as the final authority in releasing products, ensuring that they meet all quality standards before reaching patients.

The QP must have the necessary academic qualifications and professional experience in pharmaceutical science, as well as a deep understanding of EU GMP regulations. The **EMA** and national authorities maintain strict guidelines on the qualifications and responsibilities of QPs. In **2022**, over **1,000 QPs** across Europe were responsible for overseeing the release of medicinal products, demonstrating the critical role they play in ensuring the safety and efficacy of pharmaceuticals.

In cases where an MA is transferred, the new MAH must ensure that the appointed QP has sufficient knowledge of the product and its manufacturing processes to effectively oversee its release. The QP is required to review the manufacturing records, quality control test results, and any deviations or changes that occurred during the production process. Once the QP is satisfied that all necessary standards have been met, they can certify the batch and authorize its release onto the EU market.

The role of the QP extends beyond the manufacturing process. The QP is also involved in **pharmacovigilance** activities, ensuring that any safety issues or adverse events associated with the product are reported to the regulatory authorities in a timely manner. This is particularly important during an MA transfer, as the new MAH must ensure a seamless transition in all safety monitoring activities. The QP plays a key role in maintaining the **risk management plan (RMP)** for the product and ensuring that all post-marketing commitments are met.

Another important consideration in MA transfers is the continuity of the **supply chain**. The new MAH must ensure that there are no disruptions in the production, packaging, or distribution of the medicinal product during the transfer process. This involves close collaboration between the QP, manufacturing sites, and distribution partners to ensure that the transfer does not impact the availability of the product to patients.

In addition to these regulatory responsibilities, the new MAH must update the **product labeling** to reflect the change in ownership. This includes revising the **MAH details** on the packaging and in the product information leaflet. The new MAH must also update the **European Pharmacovigilance Database (Eudravigilance)** to reflect the change in ownership, ensuring that all pharmacovigilance data is accurately reported under the new MAH's name.

7.9 Legislation and Regulations for Import, Manufacture, Distribution, and Sale of Cosmetics in the EU

The regulation of **cosmetics** in the **European Union (EU)** is governed by **Regulation (EC) No 1223/2009**, which lays down the legal framework for the **import**, **manufacture**, **distribution**, and **sale** of cosmetic products within the EU market. This regulation ensures that cosmetics sold in the EU are safe for human use, properly labeled, and free from harmful substances. The regulation applies to all cosmetics, including **makeup, skincare products, hair care items**, and **fragrances**, and is enforced by the national authorities of each EU member state, as well as the **European Commission**.

One of the primary requirements of **Regulation 1223/2009** is that all cosmetic products must be assessed for safety before they are placed on the market. This involves conducting a thorough **safety assessment**, which includes an evaluation of the **toxicological profile** of each ingredient, the **intended use** of the product, and the **exposure level**. A qualified **safety assessor**, who must hold relevant scientific qualifications in fields such as **toxicology, pharmacology**, or **medicine**, is responsible for conducting this assessment. The safety assessment ensures that the product will not cause harm to consumers under normal or reasonably foreseeable use.

In addition to safety assessments, **Regulation 1223/2009** mandates that each cosmetic product must be assigned a **responsible person (RP)** within the EU. The **responsible person** is legally responsible for ensuring that the cosmetic product complies with all relevant requirements under EU law. This includes ensuring that the product is safe, properly labeled, and that the required **Product Information File (PIF)** is maintained. The PIF contains detailed information about the cosmetic product, including its **safety assessment, product formulation, manufacturing process**, and **labeling details**. The responsible person must also ensure that the PIF is readily available for inspection by the competent authorities at any time.

For **imported cosmetics**, the responsible person is often the importer or an authorized representative of the manufacturer. Importers must ensure that all products entering the EU comply with **Regulation 1223/2009** and that the products have undergone the necessary safety checks. In **2021**, more than **1,000 imported cosmetic products** were flagged by EU regulators for non-compliance, particularly due to incorrect labeling or the presence of **prohibited ingredients**. Importers must also register the cosmetic product in the **Cosmetic Products Notification Portal (CPNP)** before placing it on the EU market. This portal provides regulatory authorities with information about the cosmetic product, allowing for greater transparency and traceability.

Manufacturing practices for cosmetics are governed by **Good Manufacturing Practices (GMP)**, which ensure that products are consistently produced to high quality standards. GMP compliance is mandatory under **Regulation 1223/2009**, and manufacturers must follow the guidelines set out in the **ISO 22716 standard**. This standard covers all aspects of the manufacturing process, including the **procurement of raw materials, packaging, storage**, and **quality control** procedures. Regular **inspections** of manufacturing sites are conducted by regulatory authorities to verify compliance with GMP. In **2022**, several EU member states conducted over **500 inspections** of cosmetic manufacturing facilities, ensuring that the products being produced met the required safety and quality standards.

The **distribution** and **sale** of cosmetic products within the EU are also tightly regulated to prevent the sale of unsafe or counterfeit products. Distributors are responsible for verifying that the products they sell comply with all labeling and safety requirements. They must ensure that the product bears the correct **ingredient list, batch number**, and **use-by date**. Distributors are also required to report any **serious undesirable effects (SUEs)** associated with the use of cosmetic products to the responsible person and the competent authorities. SUEs may include severe allergic reactions or other adverse effects that require medical intervention.

Cosmetic products must be properly **labeled** in accordance with **Regulation 1223/2009**. The label must include key information, such as the **name and address** of the responsible person, the **country of origin** for imported products, a complete **list of ingredients**, and any specific **precautions for use**. Additionally, the product must clearly indicate its **intended use**, such as whether it is for the skin, hair, or another part of the body. The label must be provided in the official language(s) of the member state where the product is sold, ensuring that consumers can easily understand the information. The **EU Commission** regularly updates the list of **prohibited and restricted substances** that cannot be used in cosmetic formulations. In **2022**, the Commission added several new chemicals to the list of banned substances, reflecting the latest scientific research on cosmetic safety.

The **Cosmetic Regulation** also prohibits the use of animal testing for cosmetic products and ingredients in the EU. Since **2013**, a full ban on animal testing has been in place, and companies must rely on **alternative testing methods** to demonstrate the safety of their products. This requirement is part of the EU's commitment to promoting **animal welfare** while ensuring the safety of cosmetic products for consumers.

7.10 EU Directives and EudraLex Volume 3 and 9A

The **EudraLex** is the collection of rules and regulations governing medicinal products in the **European Union (EU)**. It is organized into multiple volumes, each addressing specific aspects of pharmaceutical regulation. Two critical volumes in this regulatory framework are **Volume 3**, which focuses on **guidelines on medicinal products for human use**, and **Volume 9A**, which provides guidelines for **pharmacovigilance for medicinal products** for human use. These volumes provide the necessary guidance for ensuring compliance with EU regulations, promoting public health, and maintaining safety standards for medicines throughout their lifecycle.

Volume 3 of the EudraLex contains **scientific guidelines** that provide detailed instructions on the development, evaluation, and registration of **medicinal products for human use**. These guidelines are essential for ensuring that products entering the EU market meet the highest standards of **quality, safety**, and **efficacy**. Volume 3 covers several key areas, including **clinical trials, quality control, good manufacturing practices (GMP)**, and **biosimilar product development**. It is updated regularly to reflect the latest scientific advancements and regulatory requirements.

One of the most critical sections within **Volume 3** relates to **clinical trials**, particularly the design, conduct, and reporting of clinical trials for new medicines. The guidelines outline the requirements for **good clinical practice (GCP)**, which is a set of ethical and scientific quality standards that must be followed in the conduct of trials involving human subjects. Adherence to GCP ensures that clinical trial data are reliable and that the rights, safety, and well-being of participants are protected. For example, in **2021**, several EU member states conducted over **400 clinical trials** based on the updated GCP guidelines provided in Volume 3.

Another significant area covered in Volume 3 is the **development of biosimilars.** These are biological medicinal products that are highly similar to already approved biological medicines (reference products). The guidelines specify the requirements for **comparability studies**, which demonstrate that the biosimilar has no clinically meaningful differences from its reference product in terms of **safety**, **purity**, and **potency**. In **2022**, several biosimilar products were approved in the EU based on these guidelines, providing more affordable treatment options for patients with diseases like **rheumatoid arthritis** and **cancer**.

Volume 9A of the EudraLex deals with the **pharmacovigilance** of medicinal products for human use. Pharmacovigilance refers to the science and activities related to the detection, assessment, understanding, and prevention of **adverse effects** or any other drug-related problems. The guidelines in Volume 9A provide a comprehensive framework for **monitoring the safety** of medicines once they are on the market, ensuring that any potential risks are promptly identified and managed.

The **key components** of Volume 9A include the requirements for **adverse drug reaction (ADR) reporting, risk management plans (RMPs),** and the obligations of **marketing authorization holders (MAHs)** in ensuring the ongoing safety of their products. **MAHs** are required to have a pharmacovigilance system in place to monitor the safety of their medicines and to report any **serious adverse events (SAEs)** to the regulatory authorities within **15 days** of becoming aware of the issue. In **2022**, the EMA received over **10,000 ADR reports,** many of which led to safety updates for medicines and changes to product labeling.

Risk Management Plans (RMPs) are also a central feature of Volume 9A. RMPs are required for all new medicines and for existing medicines that have undergone significant changes, such as the addition of a new indication. The RMP outlines the potential risks associated with the medicine and describes the measures that will be taken to minimize these risks. This can include **additional monitoring, post-marketing studies,** and

patient education programs. The implementation of RMPs ensures that any safety concerns are addressed proactively, rather than reactively, after a product has been on the market for a prolonged period.

Another important aspect of Volume 9A is the guidance on **Periodic Safety Update Reports (PSURs).** These reports are submitted by MAHs at regular intervals and provide a summary of the safety data collected for a medicinal product over a specified period. PSURs help regulators assess whether the **risk-benefit balance** of a medicine remains favorable and whether any changes to the product's **safety profile** are needed. The PSUR process plays a critical role in ensuring that medicines continue to be safe and effective for patients throughout their lifecycle. In **2021**, the EMA reviewed over **1,200 PSURs**, leading to several recommendations for risk minimization measures and safety labeling updates.

EudraLex Volume 3 and 9A are critical components of the EU's regulatory framework for ensuring the safety, efficacy, and quality of medicinal products for human use. **Volume 3** provides essential guidelines for the development and registration of medicines, while **Volume 9A** establishes the framework for monitoring their safety once they are on the market. Together, these volumes help protect public health by ensuring that medicines in the EU are subject to rigorous scientific evaluation and ongoing safety surveillance.

7.11 EU Annual Safety Report and EU MDD

The **EU Annual Safety Report (ASR)** is a critical component of pharmacovigilance in the **European Union (EU)**, aimed at ensuring the ongoing **safety monitoring** of medicinal products once they are on the market. The ASR is typically part of the broader **Periodic Safety Update Report (PSUR)** system, where **marketing authorization holders (MAHs)** are required to submit annual safety reports detailing any **adverse drug reactions (ADRs)**, emerging safety concerns, and **risk-benefit assessments.** These reports are essential for assessing whether the safety profile of a product remains favorable over time.

The **EU Annual Safety Report** includes detailed information on **adverse events, product recalls,** and any **safety-related changes** made to the product's labeling or usage guidelines. For instance, in **2022**, over **1,200 PSURs** were submitted to the **European Medicines Agency (EMA)**, which included annual safety reports from manufacturers of both **new** and **existing medicinal products.** The data from these reports allow regulatory authorities to identify trends or patterns in adverse events, which could indicate previously unknown risks associated with the medicine.

Risk Management Plans (RMPs) are also updated as part of the ASR, ensuring that any **risk minimization measures** are effectively implemented. For products that require additional safety monitoring, such as **new active substances** or those with a **narrow therapeutic index**, the annual safety report plays a crucial role in determining whether the product's risk profile remains acceptable. The **EMA** may recommend updates to product labeling or restrict its use based on findings in these reports.

The **Medical Devices Directive (MDD)**, previously **Council Directive 93/42/EEC**, was the EU's main regulatory framework for medical devices before it was replaced by the **Medical Device Regulation (MDR)** in **May 2021**. Under the MDD, medical devices were classified based on their **risk**, **design**, and **intended use**, with higher-risk devices subjected to more stringent regulatory controls. Although the **MDR** has superseded the MDD, certain provisions still apply during the transition period for devices that were already on the market under MDD certification.

The MDD required manufacturers to conduct **clinical evaluations** to demonstrate the safety and performance of their devices. Similar to the **Annual Safety Report** for medicinal products, the MDD mandated the continuous monitoring of medical devices through **post-market surveillance**. This system ensured that any **adverse events** related to the use of medical devices were reported to regulatory authorities, allowing for prompt corrective actions if necessary. The **MDD's role** in regulating medical devices laid the foundation for the more robust **MDR**, which now incorporates stricter post-market surveillance requirements and greater transparency in device safety data.

7.12 ISO 14155

The **ISO 14155** standard provides guidelines for the **good clinical practice (GCP)** of clinical investigations of **medical devices** in human subjects. It is the internationally recognized standard for conducting **clinical trials** on medical devices and is designed to ensure the **scientific validity** of the data generated, as well as the protection of trial participants' rights, safety, and well-being. **ISO 14155:2020**, the most recent version of this standard, aligns closely with **ICH-GCP (E6)** guidelines used for pharmaceutical trials, ensuring a harmonized approach across different types of clinical investigations.

The ISO 14155 standard emphasizes the importance of **ethical conduct** in clinical investigations, requiring that all trials be approved by an **ethics**

committee before commencing. The standard also mandates that **informed consent** must be obtained from all trial participants, ensuring they fully understand the risks and benefits associated with participating in the investigation. The focus on **participant safety** is particularly important for trials involving high-risk devices such as **implantable cardiac devices** or **neurostimulators**, where the potential for serious adverse events is higher.

A key requirement of **ISO 14155** is the establishment of a robust **risk management system** throughout the clinical investigation. This involves the continuous monitoring and assessment of risks during the trial and the implementation of measures to mitigate those risks. The standard requires that **adverse events (AEs)** and **serious adverse events (SAEs)** be reported promptly to both the **sponsor** and regulatory authorities, ensuring that any potential safety concerns are addressed in real-time.

ISO 14155 also sets out detailed requirements for the **design** and **conduct** of clinical investigations, including the selection of appropriate **clinical endpoints**, the **sample size calculation**, and the use of **statistical methods** to ensure the reliability of the results. In **2022**, the use of **ISO 14155** was critical in the approval process for several high-risk medical devices, where the clinical data generated under this standard was used to support the devices' safety and efficacy profiles.

Another important aspect of **ISO 14155** is the emphasis on **data integrity** and **documentation**. All data collected during the clinical investigation must be accurately recorded and stored in a way that ensures its integrity and traceability. This includes maintaining an **audit trail** of any changes made to the data, ensuring that the results of the investigation can be verified by regulatory authorities if necessary.

CHAPTER EIGHT

Japan Regulations

Japan's regulatory environment for pharmaceuticals and medical devices is governed by the Pharmaceuticals and Medical Devices Agency (PMDA), which ensures that all medical products meet the highest standards of safety and efficacy. This chapter provides a detailed examination of the pharmaceutical laws and regulations in Japan, offering insights into how products are reviewed, approved, and monitored post-market.

The drug regulatory approval process in Japan is highly structured, involving rigorous pre-market assessments and post-market surveillance to ensure product quality and safety. The chapter discusses the types of registration applications required for both domestically produced and imported drugs, including the use of the Drug Master Files (DMF) system to maintain confidentiality around proprietary manufacturing processes.

Furthermore, the chapter covers the regulatory requirements for biosimilars, generic drugs, and herbal medicines, reflecting Japan's comprehensive approach to drug approval. The post-marketing surveillance system in Japan is particularly robust, requiring companies to continuously monitor the safety of their products in the market. For professionals seeking to understand the regulatory framework in Japan, this chapter offers essential insights into the processes, timelines, and requirements for successful product registration and market entry.

8.1 Organization of the PMDA

The **Pharmaceuticals and Medical Devices Agency (PMDA)** is Japan's central regulatory authority responsible for the **evaluation, approval,** and **post-market surveillance** of pharmaceuticals, medical devices, and other therapeutic products. The PMDA operates under the supervision of the **Ministry of Health, Labour and Welfare (MHLW)** and plays a crucial role in ensuring that all therapeutic goods in Japan meet the required standards of **safety, efficacy,** and **quality.** The agency's organizational structure is designed to facilitate the efficient regulation of pharmaceuticals and medical devices while ensuring public health protection through rigorous assessments and monitoring systems.

The PMDA was established in **2004** through the merger of the **Pharmaceuticals and Medical Devices Evaluation Center** and the **Organization for Pharmaceutical Safety and Research (OPSR)**. The primary goal of the PMDA is to streamline the regulatory processes for pharmaceuticals and medical devices, while enhancing **drug safety** and **risk management**. Over the years, the PMDA has become one of the leading regulatory agencies globally, recognized for its proactive approach to drug and device regulation and its commitment to improving public health in Japan.

The **organizational structure** of the PMDA is composed of several divisions, each tasked with a specific function related to the regulation of pharmaceuticals and medical devices. The key divisions within the PMDA include the **Office of New Drug Review**, the **Office of Medical Devices**, the **Office of Safety**, the **Office of Compliance and Standards**, and the **Office of Relief Services**.

The **Office of New Drug Review** is responsible for evaluating the **clinical trial data**, **quality control procedures**, and **manufacturing processes** of new pharmaceutical products. This office plays a critical role in assessing whether new drugs meet the required safety and efficacy standards before they are approved for use in Japan. In **2022**, the Office of New Drug Review processed over **200 applications** for new pharmaceuticals, contributing to the timely availability of innovative treatments for Japanese patients.

The **Office of Medical Devices** focuses on the evaluation and approval of medical devices, including **in vitro diagnostics**, **implantable devices**, and **advanced therapeutic devices**. The PMDA uses a **risk-based classification system** for medical devices, with higher-risk devices undergoing more stringent reviews. The Office of Medical Devices also works closely with manufacturers to ensure that all medical devices comply with **Good Manufacturing Practices (GMP)** and other relevant standards. In **2021**, the PMDA approved over **1,000 medical devices**, many of which included cutting-edge technologies such as **robotic surgery systems** and **biomaterials**.

The **Office of Safety** within the PMDA is tasked with post-market surveillance of pharmaceuticals and medical devices. It monitors the **adverse events** reported by healthcare professionals and consumers and conducts **risk assessments** to ensure that any emerging safety issues are addressed promptly. The **Japanese Adverse Drug Event Report (JADER) database** is managed by this office, allowing for the collection and analysis of **adverse drug reactions (ADRs)**. In **2022**, the Office of Safety reviewed over **20,000 ADR reports**, leading to updates in product labeling and risk minimization measures for several drugs.

The **Office of Compliance and Standards** ensures that pharmaceutical and medical device manufacturers adhere to regulatory requirements such as **GMP, Good Clinical Practice (GCP)**, and **Good Laboratory Practice (GLP)**. This office is also responsible for conducting **inspections** of manufacturing facilities, both in Japan and internationally, to verify compliance with these standards. In **2021**, the PMDA conducted over **300 GMP inspections** globally, ensuring that manufacturers consistently produce safe and high-quality products.

The **Office of Relief Services** is a unique division within the PMDA, providing compensation to individuals who experience adverse reactions to drugs or injuries related to medical devices. The **Relief Services Scheme** ensures that patients who suffer harm from properly administered treatments are compensated, even if no fault can be attributed to the manufacturer or healthcare provider. In **2021**, the Office of Relief Services processed over **500 claims**, providing financial relief to affected patients and their families.

The PMDA also works closely with international regulatory agencies such as the **U.S. Food and Drug Administration (FDA)**, the **European Medicines Agency (EMA)**, and the **World Health Organization (WHO)**. This collaboration helps the PMDA harmonize its regulatory practices with global standards and facilitates the exchange of safety information related to pharmaceuticals and medical devices. In **2022**, the PMDA participated in over **50 international meetings** and signed several **mutual recognition agreements** with regulatory agencies worldwide, further strengthening its role in global regulatory affairs.

8.2 Pharmaceutical Laws and Regulations in Japan

The **pharmaceutical laws and regulations** in **Japan** are governed by a comprehensive legal framework that ensures the safety, efficacy, and quality of pharmaceuticals and medical devices. These regulations are primarily enforced by the **Ministry of Health, Labour and Welfare (MHLW)** and the **Pharmaceuticals and Medical Devices Agency (PMDA)**. The cornerstone of Japan's pharmaceutical regulation is the

Pharmaceuticals and Medical Devices Act (PMD Act), also known as the **Law on Securing Quality, Efficacy and Safety of Products Including Pharmaceuticals and Medical Devices**. The PMD Act serves as the primary law governing the approval, manufacturing, distribution, and post-market surveillance of pharmaceuticals and medical devices in Japan.

Originally enacted in **1960** as the **Pharmaceutical Affairs Law (PAL)**, the PMD Act has undergone multiple revisions to adapt to advancements in healthcare technologies and to align with international regulatory standards. One of the most significant amendments was made in **2014**, when the law was renamed the **Pharmaceuticals and Medical Devices Act** to reflect the growing importance of medical devices and the need for a more specialized regulatory framework. This amendment also introduced regulations for **regenerative medicine products**, highlighting Japan's proactive approach to fostering innovation in healthcare while maintaining rigorous safety standards.

The PMD Act establishes the legal requirements for the **approval of new pharmaceuticals**, which must undergo a thorough evaluation by the **PMDA** before being marketed in Japan. The process involves a review of the **safety**, **efficacy**, and **quality** data generated during **clinical trials** and **preclinical studies**. For example, in **2021**, the PMDA approved over **150 new drugs**, many of which were innovative therapies for diseases such as **oncology** and **rare diseases**. The approval process ensures that only safe and effective treatments reach Japanese patients.

A critical component of the PMD Act is the requirement for **Good Manufacturing Practices (GMP)** in the production of pharmaceuticals. GMP regulations ensure that all medicines are produced consistently and controlled according to the quality standards appropriate for their intended use. Pharmaceutical manufacturers must adhere to GMP guidelines throughout the entire production process, from the procurement of raw materials to the packaging and storage of the final product. The **PMDA** conducts regular **inspections** of manufacturing facilities to verify GMP compliance, both within Japan and internationally. In **2022**, the PMDA carried out over **200 GMP inspections**, ensuring the quality of medicinal products entering the Japanese market.

The **pharmacovigilance** system in Japan is another essential element of the pharmaceutical regulatory framework. The PMD Act mandates that **marketing authorization holders (MAHs)** implement robust pharmacovigilance systems to monitor the safety of their products post-approval. MAHs are required to report any **adverse drug reactions (ADRs)** to the PMDA, which reviews the data and determines whether additional risk mitigation measures are necessary. For instance, in **2021**, over **15,000 ADR reports** were submitted to the PMDA, leading to updates in product labeling and the issuance of safety warnings for several medicines.

In addition to the PMD Act, the **Act on Pharmaceuticals and Medical Devices Agency (Act No.192 of 2002)** establishes the roles and responsibilities of the **PMDA**. This law outlines the agency's authority to evaluate new drugs and medical devices, conduct post-market surveillance, and provide relief services for patients who suffer adverse effects from medical products. The **Relief Services Scheme**, which is unique to Japan, ensures that patients who experience harm from properly administered pharmaceuticals or medical devices receive financial compensation, even in the absence of manufacturer fault.

Japan's pharmaceutical regulations are also aligned with international standards, particularly through its participation in the **International Council for Harmonisation of Technical Requirements for Pharmaceuticals for Human Use (ICH)**. The **ICH guidelines** serve as a global standard for the development and approval of pharmaceuticals, ensuring that Japanese regulatory practices are consistent with those in other major markets, such as the **United States** and the **European Union**. This harmonization allows for faster approval of innovative therapies and facilitates Japan's involvement in global clinical trials.

Another critical law related to pharmaceuticals in Japan is the **Act on Securing Quality, Efficacy and Safety of Drugs, Medical Devices, and Other Products (Act No.145 of 1960)**. This law provides the foundation for the regulation of **over-the-counter (OTC) drugs**, **quasi-drugs**, and **cosmetics**, ensuring that all healthcare-related products meet the required safety and quality standards before being sold to the public. The law also includes provisions for **advertising** and **labeling**, mandating that pharmaceutical products must be clearly labeled with their ingredients, usage instructions, and any potential risks or side effects. Misleading or false advertising is strictly prohibited, and the **PMDA** closely monitors pharmaceutical promotions to ensure compliance.

Japan's regulatory framework for pharmaceuticals is also supported by the **National Health Insurance (NHI) System**, which provides coverage for most prescription drugs. The **pricing** of pharmaceuticals in Japan is tightly regulated by the government, and the **NHI Drug Price List** determines the reimbursement prices for all prescription drugs. The **NHI Drug Pricing Organization** reviews the price of new drugs based on factors such as **clinical benefit**, **cost-effectiveness**, and **manufacturing costs**. In **2022**, several innovative therapies, including treatments for **chronic diseases** and **rare disorders**, were added to the NHI Drug Price List, ensuring broad access to essential medications.

8.3 Types of Registration Applications and DMF System in Japan

In **Japan**, the **registration process** for pharmaceuticals and medical devices is a critical step to ensure that these products meet the required standards of **safety, efficacy**, and **quality** before they can be marketed. The **Pharmaceuticals and Medical Devices Agency (PMDA)** plays a key role in evaluating and approving various types of registration applications based on the product category. Each type of registration has specific requirements that must be met by the applicant, and the **Drug Master File (DMF) system** facilitates the registration of **active pharmaceutical ingredients (APIs)** and other key materials used in drug manufacturing.

There are several types of **registration applications** in Japan, including **New Drug Applications (NDAs)**, **Generic Drug Applications (GDAs)**, **Over-the-Counter (OTC) Drug Applications**, and **Medical Device Applications**. Each application type corresponds to a particular category of product and has distinct submission requirements.

The **New Drug Application (NDA)** is required for any **innovative drug** that contains a new **active pharmaceutical ingredient (API)** or offers a **novel therapeutic effect**. The NDA process involves a rigorous evaluation of the **clinical trial data, preclinical studies**, and **quality control** measures associated with the drug. Applicants must submit a comprehensive dossier that includes information on the **manufacturing process, pharmacokinetics, safety**, and **efficacy** of the drug. The **PMDA** evaluates this data in collaboration with the **Ministry of Health, Labour and Welfare (MHLW)** to ensure the drug meets the required safety and efficacy standards. In **2021**, the PMDA approved more than **150 new drugs**, many of which were innovative treatments for **oncology** and **rare diseases**.

Generic Drug Applications (GDAs) are required for drugs that are equivalent to a previously approved brand-name drug. The GDA process is simpler than the NDA, as generic drugs are bioequivalent to existing drugs and do not require extensive clinical trials. Instead, applicants must demonstrate **bioequivalence**, showing that the generic product provides the same **therapeutic effect** as the reference drug. In **2022**, the PMDA reviewed over **500 generic drug applications**, which helped expand access to affordable medicines for patients in Japan.

Over-the-Counter (OTC) Drug Applications are required for non-prescription drugs that can be purchased directly by consumers. These products are typically used for treating **mild conditions** such as colds, headaches, or allergies. The registration process for OTC drugs involves evaluating the safety and efficacy of the product based on its intended use and ensuring that it meets the appropriate quality standards. In **2021**, the PMDA processed over **100 OTC drug applications**, ensuring that consumers had access to safe and effective non-prescription treatments.

The **Medical Device Application** process varies depending on the **risk classification** of the device. Medical devices in Japan are classified into four categories: **Class I** (low-risk), **Class II** (medium-risk), **Class III** (high-risk), and **Class IV** (highest-risk). Devices in **Class III** and **Class IV** undergo a more stringent evaluation process that includes reviewing the **clinical trial data**, **safety profile**, and **manufacturing quality**. The PMDA evaluates these applications to ensure that medical devices meet the required safety standards and perform their intended functions effectively. In **2021**, the PMDA approved over **1,000 medical devices**, many of which included innovative technologies such as **implantable devices** and **diagnostic tools**.

The **Drug Master File (DMF) system** in Japan plays a crucial role in the registration of **active pharmaceutical ingredients (APIs), excipients**, and **packaging materials** used in the production of pharmaceuticals. The DMF system allows manufacturers of these components to submit confidential information about their products to the PMDA, ensuring that the materials used in drug production meet the required quality standards without disclosing proprietary information to the pharmaceutical companies that use them.

A **DMF registration** typically includes detailed information on the **manufacturing process, quality control procedures**, and **stability data** for the API or other material. This information is submitted directly to the PMDA, which reviews the data to ensure that the material meets the appropriate quality standards outlined in the **Japanese Pharmacopoeia**. Once the DMF is approved, the pharmaceutical companies can reference the DMF in their drug applications without having to submit the same detailed information about the API. This simplifies the registration process for both the pharmaceutical company and the API manufacturer.

The DMF system also ensures that the quality of APIs and other materials used in drug manufacturing is maintained throughout the lifecycle of the product. API manufacturers must provide regular updates to the DMF, including any changes in the manufacturing process or quality control measures. The PMDA conducts regular **inspections** of manufacturing facilities to ensure that the API continues to meet the required quality standards. In **2022**, the PMDA conducted over **150 inspections** of API manufacturing sites, ensuring that high-quality raw materials are used in the production of pharmaceuticals in Japan.

8.4 Drug Regulatory Approval Process in Japan

The **drug regulatory approval process** in **Japan** is a well-structured system that ensures pharmaceuticals meet the required standards of **safety, efficacy**, and **quality** before they can be marketed and distributed. The **Pharmaceuticals and Medical Devices Agency (PMDA)**, working under the **Ministry of Health, Labour and Welfare (MHLW)**, is the key regulatory body responsible for evaluating and approving new drugs, generic drugs, and other medicinal products.

The approval process in Japan typically begins with **preclinical studies**, where the drug is tested in **animal models** to gather preliminary data on its safety, pharmacology, and toxicology. This step is essential for identifying any potential adverse effects that may need to be addressed in later stages. Once the preclinical data is compiled, the sponsor submits an application to conduct **clinical trials** in humans.

Clinical trials in Japan are conducted in **three phases**:

- **Phase I** trials involve a small number of healthy volunteers or patients and are designed to evaluate the drug's **safety, dosage**, and **pharmacokinetics**.
- **Phase II** trials expand the patient population and focus on assessing the drug's **efficacy** while continuing to monitor its safety profile.
- **Phase III** trials are larger-scale studies conducted in patients with the target condition. These trials provide more comprehensive data on the drug's **efficacy** and **long-term safety**, which are crucial for the final evaluation of the drug.

Once clinical trials are completed, the sponsor prepares a **New Drug Application (NDA)**, which includes all data generated during preclinical and clinical studies, as well as detailed information on the drug's manufacturing process, quality control procedures, and stability data. The NDA is then submitted to the PMDA for evaluation. In 2021, the PMDA received over 150 NDAs, reflecting the robust pipeline of innovative drugs being developed in Japan.

The PMDA evaluates the NDA through a detailed review process. This involves scientific experts assessing the data to ensure that the drug meets the required standards for safety, efficacy, and quality. The review typically takes around 12 months, but this timeline can be expedited for drugs that address serious or life-threatening conditions, such as oncology drugs or rare disease therapies. In these cases, the PMDA may grant priority review status, which shortens the review time to around 6 months.

One of the key steps in the regulatory approval process is the Good Manufacturing Practices (GMP) inspection. The PMDA conducts on-site inspections of the drug's manufacturing facilities to ensure that the drug is produced consistently and under controlled conditions. In 2022, the PMDA conducted over 300 GMP inspections, both domestically and internationally, ensuring that the manufacturing process for approved drugs meets the highest quality standards.

In addition to reviewing the safety and efficacy data, the PMDA also assesses the risk management plan (RMP) submitted by the sponsor. The RMP outlines the strategies that will be implemented to monitor and mitigate any potential risks associated with the drug once it is on the market. This includes plans for post-market surveillance, adverse event reporting, and risk minimization measures. The RMP is critical for ensuring that any safety concerns that arise after the drug is approved are addressed promptly.

Once the PMDA has completed its review, it provides a recommendation to the MHLW, which makes the final decision on whether to approve the drug. If the drug is approved, it is listed on the National Health Insurance (NHI) Drug Price List, which determines the reimbursement price for the drug. The NHI system plays a critical role in ensuring that approved drugs are accessible to patients at affordable prices. In 2022, several new drugs, including therapies for chronic diseases and rare conditions, were added to the NHI Drug Price List, making them widely available to patients in Japan.

After approval, the drug enters the post-marketing phase, where its safety and efficacy continue to be monitored through pharmacovigilance activities. The Japanese Adverse Drug Event Report (JADER) database collects reports of adverse drug reactions (ADRs) from healthcare providers and patients. The PMDA analyzes these reports to identify any emerging safety issues that may require further action, such as **label updates**, **warnings**, or, in rare cases, the **withdrawal** of the drug from the market. In **2021**, over **15,000 ADR reports** were submitted to the PMDA, reflecting the agency's ongoing commitment to drug safety.

8.5 Regulatory Considerations for Manufacturing, Packaging, and Labeling of Pharmaceuticals in Japan

The **manufacturing**, **packaging**, and **labeling** of pharmaceuticals in **Japan** are strictly regulated to ensure the highest standards of **safety**, **efficacy**, and **quality**. The **Pharmaceuticals and Medical Devices Act (PMD Act)** provides the regulatory framework, and compliance with **Good Manufacturing Practices (GMP)** is mandatory for all pharmaceutical manufacturers. These regulations are enforced by the **Pharmaceuticals and Medical Devices Agency (PMDA)**, which conducts regular inspections and oversees compliance with industry standards.

Manufacturing in Japan is governed by **GMP**, which sets forth strict guidelines for the production of pharmaceuticals to ensure that they are manufactured in a consistent and controlled environment. Manufacturers must maintain detailed records of all manufacturing processes, including **raw material sourcing**, **equipment maintenance**, and **quality control procedures**. In **2022**, the **PMDA** conducted over **200 inspections** to ensure that manufacturers complied with GMP standards, identifying and addressing any deviations that could affect product safety or quality.

GMP regulations also cover the **qualification of personnel** involved in the manufacturing process. Employees must be adequately trained in the proper handling of materials and equipment, as well as in the relevant **safety protocols**. Manufacturers are required to establish **standard operating procedures (SOPs)** for every step of the manufacturing process, from **mixing** and **blending** to **filling** and **packaging**, to minimize the risk of contamination and ensure the integrity of the final product.

Packaging is another critical area regulated by the PMDA. The packaging of pharmaceuticals must ensure **product stability** and **protection** from external factors such as **light**, **moisture**, and **temperature fluctuations**. Packaging materials must be compatible with the pharmaceutical product and must not interact with the active ingredients in a way that could affect the product's safety or efficacy. For example, **moisture-sensitive drugs** are often packaged in **blister packs** or **aluminum foil** to prevent degradation. In **2021**, the PMDA reviewed packaging standards for over **100 new products**, ensuring that each met the necessary requirements for product protection.

In addition to providing physical protection, packaging must be **tamper-evident** to prevent unauthorized access or alteration of the product. This is particularly important for products with a high risk of misuse, such as **opioid medications** or **psychoactive drugs**. The PMDA requires the use of **tamper-evident seals** and other security features on packaging to ensure that consumers can identify whether a product has been tampered with before use.

The **labeling** of pharmaceuticals in Japan is governed by the **PMD Act** and must comply with strict guidelines to ensure that patients and healthcare providers have access to accurate and comprehensive information about the product. Labels must include the **name of the product**, the **active ingredients**, **dosage instructions**, and any **precautions for use**. The **expiration date** and **storage conditions** must also be clearly indicated on the packaging.

One of the unique requirements for pharmaceutical labeling in Japan is the inclusion of **Braille** on the outer packaging for products intended for human use. This is mandated to accommodate visually impaired individuals, ensuring that they can independently access information about their medications. Additionally, the label must be written in **Japanese** and must use clear and simple language to ensure that all consumers can understand the information provided. In **2021**, several labeling updates were made to ensure compliance with the latest regulations, including updates for **safety warnings** and **contraindications**.

Another important aspect of pharmaceutical labeling in Japan is the inclusion of a **barcode** or **QR code** on the packaging. This allows healthcare providers and consumers to access additional information about the product, such as detailed safety data or updates on **adverse effects**. The use of digital tools for labeling has increased in recent years as Japan continues to modernize its healthcare system. These barcodes also support the **traceability** of products, which is critical for ensuring the authenticity of pharmaceuticals and preventing the circulation of **counterfeit medicines**.

Japan's regulatory framework also includes strict requirements for the **documentation** of manufacturing and packaging processes. Manufacturers are required to maintain detailed records of **batch production**, including **test results** for each batch of the drug. These records must be made available for **PMDA inspections**, which ensure that every step of the manufacturing and packaging process complies with the approved guidelines. Failure to comply with these regulations can result in penalties, including the **suspension** or **revocation** of the manufacturer's license.

8.6 Post-Marketing Surveillance in Japan

Post-marketing surveillance (PMS) in **Japan** is a critical component of the regulatory framework for pharmaceuticals and medical devices. The **Pharmaceuticals and Medical Devices Agency (PMDA)**, in collaboration with the **Ministry of Health, Labour and Welfare (MHLW)**, oversees PMS to ensure that products remain safe and effective after they have been approved and marketed. This ongoing surveillance helps identify any **adverse events** or emerging risks that may not have been evident during clinical trials, ensuring the continued protection of public health.

The **Pharmaceuticals and Medical Devices Act (PMD Act)** mandates that all **marketing authorization holders (MAHs)** implement robust post-marketing surveillance systems. These systems are designed to collect data on the **safety, efficacy,** and **quality** of medicinal products once they are used by a broader population. In **2021,** over **15,000 adverse drug reactions (ADRs)** were reported to the PMDA, highlighting the importance of PMS in detecting potential safety issues.

One of the key elements of Japan's PMS framework is the requirement for **Risk Management Plans (RMPs)**. RMPs must be submitted as part of the approval process for new drugs and outline the strategies for monitoring and managing risks associated with the product throughout its lifecycle. The RMP specifies **risk minimization measures,** such as **additional labeling warnings, educational materials** for healthcare professionals, and **restricted distribution systems** for high-risk drugs. For example, in **2022,** several drugs used to treat **oncology** and **autoimmune diseases** were subject to RMPs that included special monitoring programs to manage known safety concerns.

The **Japanese Adverse Drug Event Report (JADER) database** is another critical tool used in post-marketing surveillance. The JADER system collects reports of **adverse drug events (ADEs)** from healthcare providers, patients, and manufacturers. These reports are then analyzed by the PMDA to identify trends or signals that may indicate new or previously unknown risks. For instance, in **2021,** several updates were made to the safety labeling of commonly used drugs based on data collected through JADER, ensuring that healthcare providers and patients were informed of any new risks.

Japan's PMS system also includes **re-examination** and **re-evaluation** processes for pharmaceuticals. **Re-examination** is required for new drugs within a specific period after marketing authorization, usually **six to ten years**. During this time, the safety and efficacy of the drug are closely monitored, and the data collected are submitted to the PMDA for review. If any significant safety concerns arise during this period, the PMDA can impose additional safety measures, update the product's labeling, or, in extreme cases, withdraw the drug from the market. In **2021**, several re-examinations led to updates in the **dosage recommendations** for drugs used to treat **cardiovascular conditions**, ensuring safer use for the broader population.

The **re-evaluation** process applies to older drugs that have been on the market for an extended period. This process ensures that these drugs continue to meet current standards for **safety, efficacy**, and **quality**. During re-evaluation, the PMDA reviews all available post-market data, including any reports of adverse events and new scientific evidence. If the drug no longer meets the required standards, the PMDA may require additional studies or restrict the drug's use. This proactive approach ensures that even well-established drugs are continuously assessed for their safety and effectiveness.

In addition to monitoring pharmaceuticals, post-marketing surveillance in Japan also extends to **medical devices**. The PMD Act requires medical device manufacturers to conduct **post-market monitoring** of their products to detect any issues related to device performance, safety, or durability. This is particularly important for high-risk devices such as **implantable devices** or **diagnostic equipment**. In **2022**, several medical devices were subject to recalls or safety updates based on PMS data, including updates for **implantable cardiac devices** that showed wear over time, affecting their performance.

Japan's PMS framework also includes provisions for **pharmacovigilance inspections**. The **PMDA** conducts regular inspections of MAHs to ensure that they are complying with post-marketing surveillance requirements, including the proper reporting of adverse events and the implementation of risk minimization measures. In **2022**, over **150 inspections** were carried out to verify compliance with PMS regulations, ensuring that all pharmaceutical and device manufacturers adhere to the highest standards of safety and quality.

8.7 Legislation and Regulations for Import, Manufacture, Distribution, and Sale of Cosmetics in Japan

In **Japan**, the regulation of **cosmetics** is governed by the **Pharmaceuticals and Medical Devices Act (PMD Act)**, which outlines the legal framework for the **import, manufacture, distribution**, and **sale** of cosmetic products. These regulations are enforced by the **Pharmaceuticals and Medical Devices Agency (PMDA)** and the **Ministry of Health, Labour and Welfare (MHLW)**. The regulatory framework aims to ensure that all cosmetic products meet stringent safety and quality standards before they are introduced into the Japanese market.

Cosmetic products in Japan are classified into two broad categories: **general cosmetics** and **quasi-drugs**. General cosmetics include products such as skincare, haircare, and makeup, while quasi-drugs refer to products that contain active ingredients with mild therapeutic effects, such as **whitening agents, anti-dandruff shampoos**, and **medicated lotions**. The regulatory requirements for quasi-drugs are more stringent than for general cosmetics, as they must undergo a **safety and efficacy review** by the PMDA before being approved for sale.

For **imported cosmetics**, the process begins with the **registration** of the product with the PMDA. Companies seeking to import cosmetics must appoint a **designated importer**, who acts as the responsible person for ensuring compliance with Japanese regulations. The importer must submit a detailed dossier to the PMDA, including information on the **ingredients, manufacturing process**, and **safety data** for the cosmetic product. In **2021**, Japan imported over **100,000 cosmetic products**, many of which required careful scrutiny to ensure they met the required safety standards.

Once the cosmetic product is approved for import, it must be **labeled** in accordance with Japanese regulations. The label must include the **product name, ingredients, usage instructions**, and **warnings**, if applicable. The label must also indicate the name and address of the **importer** and must be written in **Japanese** to ensure that consumers can easily understand the information. In **2022**, several updates were made to the labeling regulations to ensure greater transparency in the listing of ingredients, particularly for products containing **fragrances** or **preservatives** that may cause allergic reactions.

In terms of **manufacturing**, cosmetic products must be produced in compliance with **Good Manufacturing Practices (GMP)**, which ensure that products are consistently manufactured to a high standard of quality. Cosmetic manufacturers are required to implement **quality control systems** and maintain detailed records of the production process to ensure that the final product is safe for consumers. The **PMDA** conducts regular **inspections** of manufacturing facilities to verify compliance with GMP standards. In **2021**, over **200 inspections** were carried out, focusing on both domestic and international manufacturers supplying cosmetics to the Japanese market.

For **quasi-drugs**, the manufacturing process must meet even stricter standards. Manufacturers must obtain a special license to produce quasi-drugs, and the products must be approved by the PMDA based on a comprehensive review of their **active ingredients** and **therapeutic claims**. For example, whitening products that contain **active bleaching agents** must undergo rigorous testing to ensure that they do not pose a risk to consumers' health. In **2022**, several whitening products were withdrawn from the market after the PMDA found that they contained unapproved active ingredients that could cause skin irritation.

The **distribution** of cosmetics in Japan is also tightly regulated. Distributors must ensure that all products they handle comply with the PMD Act and that they are stored and transported under the appropriate conditions to prevent contamination or degradation. Cosmetics that are temperature-sensitive, for example, must be stored in climate-controlled environments to maintain their stability. Distributors are also required to report any **adverse events** related to the use of cosmetic products to the PMDA, ensuring that any emerging safety concerns are addressed promptly.

The **sale** of cosmetics in Japan is subject to specific advertising regulations. All claims made about the product's effectiveness must be supported by scientific evidence, and false or misleading advertising is prohibited. For instance, a product that claims to have **anti-aging effects** must provide data to back up these claims, ensuring that consumers are not misled by exaggerated or unsubstantiated statements. The **MHLW** regularly monitors advertisements for cosmetic products and takes action against companies that engage in deceptive marketing practices.

In conclusion, the **legislation and regulations** governing the **import**, **manufacture**, **distribution**, and **sale** of cosmetics in Japan are designed to protect consumers by ensuring that all products meet stringent **safety**, **quality**, and **labeling** standards. The PMDA and MHLW work together to enforce these regulations, conducting inspections and monitoring the market to ensure that all cosmetics sold in Japan are safe for consumer use. This comprehensive regulatory framework not only maintains the integrity of the Japanese cosmetic market but also promotes consumer confidence in the products they purchase.

Emerging Markets

Emerging markets offer significant growth opportunities for pharmaceutical companies, but they also present unique regulatory challenges. This chapter provides an in-depth analysis of the regulatory environments in emerging markets, including regions such as ASEAN, APEC, EAC, GCC, PANDRH, and SADC. These regions are increasingly important for global pharmaceutical companies looking to expand their market reach.

The chapter focuses on the regulatory harmonization efforts in these markets, particularly through initiatives like the World Health Organization's (WHO) Good Manufacturing Practices (GMP) guidelines, which aim to standardize the quality and safety of pharmaceutical products globally. Understanding the regulatory frameworks in emerging markets is essential for companies seeking to register and market their products in these regions.

In addition to outlining the general regulatory landscape, the chapter provides insights into the Certificate of Pharmaceutical Product (CoPP), a critical document for international drug registration. This section covers the general and country-specific requirements for the CoPP in countries such as South Africa, Egypt, Algeria, Nigeria, and Kenya, providing a roadmap for navigating the diverse regulatory environments in these emerging markets. By mastering these regulatory processes, professionals can tap into the immense potential of these growing pharmaceutical markets while ensuring compliance with local requirements.

9.1 Introduction to Emerging Markets

The term **emerging markets** refers to economies that are in the process of rapid industrialization and growth, transitioning from low-income to middle-income status, with expanding economic activities and rising consumer demand. These markets offer significant opportunities for growth, particularly in sectors like **pharmaceuticals**, **biotechnology**, and **medical devices**, as they develop their healthcare infrastructure and increase access to modern medical treatments. Countries such as **China, India, Brazil, Russia**, and **South Africa** are some of the most notable emerging markets, often collectively referred to as the **BRICS** nations.

Emerging markets are characterized by several key features, including **high economic growth rates, increasing foreign direct investment (FDI)**, and **growing middle-class populations**. These factors contribute to rising demand for healthcare services and products, making emerging markets attractive destinations for global pharmaceutical companies seeking to expand their operations. In **2021**, emerging markets accounted for nearly **40%** of the global pharmaceutical sales growth, driven by rapid urbanization, aging populations, and increasing prevalence of **non-communicable diseases (NCDs)** such as **diabetes, cardiovascular diseases**, and **cancer**.

One of the main drivers of growth in emerging markets is the expansion of **universal healthcare systems** and government initiatives aimed at improving access to healthcare. For example, **India's Ayushman Bharat** program, launched in **2018**, aims to provide healthcare coverage to over **500 million** low-income individuals. Similarly, **China's Healthy China 2030** initiative is designed to expand healthcare infrastructure and improve the quality of medical care across the country. These programs create a growing demand for **pharmaceuticals, vaccines**, and **medical devices**, providing opportunities for both local and multinational companies to meet this increasing need.

Another characteristic of emerging markets is the relatively lower cost of **clinical trials** and **drug development** compared to more developed economies. The availability of large, treatment-naïve populations makes these regions attractive for conducting **clinical research**. In **2020**, over **25%** of global clinical trials were conducted in emerging markets, with countries like **India, Brazil**, and **Russia** playing a key role in the development of new therapies. This trend is expected to continue, as pharmaceutical companies seek to reduce costs and accelerate time-to-market for new products.

However, entering emerging markets also presents several challenges, including **regulatory complexity, intellectual property (IP) protection issues**, and **infrastructure limitations**. Regulatory frameworks in emerging markets are often still developing, leading to variations in **approval timelines** and **compliance requirements**. For example, drug approval processes in countries like **Brazil** can take significantly longer compared to more established markets like the **United States** or **Europe**. Despite these challenges, many global pharmaceutical companies have successfully navigated these markets by forming **partnerships with local firms** and investing in **capacity-building initiatives** to ensure compliance with local regulations.

9.2 Study of Various Committees Across the Globe (ASEAN, APEC, EAC, GCC, PANDRH, SADC)

Several international committees and regional organizations play a significant role in the harmonization of pharmaceutical regulations and healthcare policies across the globe. These committees are focused on aligning regulatory frameworks, promoting trade in pharmaceuticals and medical devices, and improving public health outcomes. Each region has developed its own regulatory approach based on specific needs, economic factors, and healthcare priorities. The following sections explore the roles and objectives of key committees, including **ASEAN, APEC, EAC, GCC, PANDRH**, and **SADC**.

Association of Southeast Asian Nations (ASEAN)

The **ASEAN** committee, formed in **1967**, comprises ten Southeast Asian countries, including **Indonesia, Malaysia, Philippines, Singapore, Thailand**, and **Vietnam**. ASEAN's pharmaceutical regulatory committee aims to harmonize the region's pharmaceutical and healthcare regulations to promote trade, improve access to healthcare, and ensure the quality and safety of medicinal products. In **2009**, the ASEAN Consultative Committee for Standards and Quality (ACCSQ) developed the **ASEAN Common Technical Dossier (ACTD)** and **ASEAN Common Technical Requirements (ACTR)** to streamline the submission and approval of drug registration applications across the member states. These initiatives have led to the **faster approval of generic drugs** and improved access to affordable medicines. In **2021**, ASEAN member states approved more than **500 drugs** under the harmonized regulatory framework, enhancing healthcare outcomes in the region.

Asia-Pacific Economic Cooperation (APEC)

The **APEC** committee, established in **1989**, is a forum of **21 Pacific Rim economies**, including **Japan, China, South Korea, Australia**, and the **United States**. APEC's Life Sciences Innovation Forum (LSIF) and Regulatory Harmonization Steering Committee (RHSC) work toward harmonizing regulatory standards for pharmaceuticals and medical devices across member economies. APEC's **Regulatory Harmonization Steering Committee** focuses on aligning technical requirements for **clinical trials, Good Manufacturing Practices (GMP)**, and **post-market surveillance** of medicinal products. In **2020**, APEC members conducted over **3,000 collaborative clinical trials**, reducing duplication of efforts and ensuring that new therapies reached the market more quickly. Additionally, APEC's efforts have facilitated **pharmacovigilance** activities across the region, enhancing the safety of marketed drugs and medical devices.

East African Community (EAC)

The **EAC** consists of six member countries: **Burundi, Kenya, Rwanda, South Sudan, Tanzania**, and **Uganda**. The **EAC Medicines Regulatory Harmonization (MRH) Initiative**, launched in **2012**, seeks to harmonize regulations for pharmaceutical products to improve access to quality medicines across the region. The MRH program, supported by the **World Health Organization (WHO)** and other global health agencies, has focused on aligning guidelines for the **registration of medicines, Good Manufacturing Practices (GMP)**, and **pharmacovigilance**. In 2021, the EAC approved more than **200 new medicines** under the harmonized regulatory framework, significantly reducing approval timelines from over **24 months** to less than **12 months**. The initiative has improved healthcare access in East Africa and increased the availability of **essential medicines**.

Gulf Cooperation Council (GCC)

The GCC comprises six member states: **Saudi Arabia, Kuwait, Bahrain, Qatar, United Arab Emirates**, and **Oman**. The GCC's health committee plays a crucial role in harmonizing pharmaceutical regulations across these countries. The **GCC Health Council**, through its **Central Drug Registration (CDR) system**, ensures that medicines registered in one member state can be marketed across the region without needing separate approval processes. The CDR system has streamlined the **regulatory approval** process, reducing the time needed to bring new drugs to market. In **2021**, more than **1,000 drugs** were approved through the CDR system, improving the availability of pharmaceuticals across the Gulf region. The GCC also places a strong emphasis on **post-marketing surveillance** and **pharmacovigilance**, requiring all MAHs to report any **adverse drug reactions (ADRs)** to a centralized database.

Pan American Network for Drug Regulatory Harmonization (PANDRH)

The **PANDRH** committee was established by the **Pan American Health**

Organization (PAHO) to promote regulatory harmonization across the Americas, including North, Central, and South America. The network aims to strengthen the regulatory capacities of member countries, align technical requirements, and improve the overall quality and safety of medicines. PANDRH focuses on Good Manufacturing Practices (GMP), bioequivalence, and pharmacovigilance guidelines. In 2022, PANDRH launched new initiatives to improve the regulatory capacities of smaller countries, ensuring that they can implement efficient drug approval processes while safeguarding public health. Through collaboration with WHO and FDA, PANDRH has provided training and technical support to its members, leading to faster approval processes and improved access to essential medicines in the region.

Southern African Development Community (SADC)

The SADC is composed of 16 countries in Southern Africa, including South Africa, Botswana, Zimbabwe, Zambia, and Mozambique. The SADC Medicines Regulatory Harmonization (MRH) program, launched in 2015, aims to streamline the registration process for pharmaceuticals across the region and ensure that medicines meet international quality and safety standards. In 2020, the SADC approved guidelines for the harmonized registration of generic medicines across its member states, reducing the duplication of efforts and improving access to affordable drugs. The SADC MRH initiative has also focused on capacity-building for national regulatory authorities, providing training in pharmacovigilance, clinical trial oversight, and post-marketing surveillance. The harmonization efforts in the region have led to faster drug approvals and improved collaboration between SADC countries in addressing public health challenges.

9.3 WHO GMP and Regulatory Requirements for Registration of Drugs and Post-Approval Requirements in WHO

The World Health Organization (WHO) plays a crucial role in ensuring the global safety, efficacy, and quality of pharmaceutical products through the establishment of Good Manufacturing Practices (GMP) and regulatory guidelines for the registration and post-approval surveillance of drugs. These standards are essential for safeguarding public health and ensuring that pharmaceuticals distributed worldwide meet internationally recognized benchmarks.

Good Manufacturing Practices (GMP), as defined by the WHO, are a set of regulations and guidelines that ensure pharmaceutical products are consistently produced and controlled to quality standards appropriate for their intended use. These practices cover all aspects of drug production, from the sourcing of raw materials to the final packaging and distribution of the finished product. Compliance with WHO GMP guidelines is mandatory for pharmaceutical companies seeking to supply medicines to **low- and middle-income countries (LMICs)**, which often rely on WHO's standards to regulate the safety and efficacy of drugs.

The **WHO Prequalification of Medicines Programme (PQP)**, initiated in **2001**, is a vital mechanism for assessing the quality of medicines, particularly those used to treat **HIV/AIDS, malaria, tuberculosis**, and **other infectious diseases**. Pharmaceutical manufacturers must submit detailed dossiers to the WHO for review, which includes comprehensive information on the **manufacturing process, quality control measures**, and **clinical data** supporting the drug's safety and efficacy. In **2022**, the WHO prequalified over **150 new medicines**, improving access to essential drugs in **over 100 countries**. This program ensures that medicines purchased by **United Nations (UN)** agencies and **international procurement organizations** meet stringent safety and quality standards.

To achieve **WHO prequalification**, manufacturers must demonstrate compliance with **WHO GMP guidelines**. This involves submitting to **WHO GMP inspections**, where inspectors evaluate the manufacturing facility's adherence to guidelines related to **facility hygiene, equipment maintenance, staff qualifications**, and **quality assurance procedures**. In **2021**, WHO inspectors conducted over **200 on-site inspections** worldwide, focusing on facilities producing medicines for **priority diseases** such as malaria and tuberculosis. Facilities found to be non-compliant with WHO GMP standards must take corrective actions before they can gain or maintain prequalification status.

Another essential aspect of the WHO's regulatory framework is the requirement for **stringent testing and documentation** during the drug registration process. Manufacturers must provide extensive data on the **pharmaceutical formulation, stability, bioequivalence**, and **clinical trial outcomes**. These data are reviewed by the WHO to ensure that the drug is safe and effective for its intended use. For instance, during the approval process for **antimalarial drugs**, the WHO requires evidence that the drug has been tested in multiple regions affected by malaria to ensure its effectiveness across different strains of the disease.

In addition to GMP guidelines, the WHO has established stringent requirements for the **registration of drugs**. Pharmaceutical manufacturers must submit a **Comprehensive Dossier** to WHO, detailing the drug's **composition, pharmacodynamics, pharmacokinetics**, and clinical trial data demonstrating the drug's efficacy and safety. The WHO evaluates this data to ensure that the drug meets international standards for quality and safety before it can be prequalified and registered. In **2021**, over **120 drugs** were registered through the WHO's prequalification program, improving access to high-quality medicines in regions with limited regulatory capacity.

Post-approval requirements are also a critical component of WHO's regulatory framework. Once a drug is prequalified and registered, it must undergo continuous monitoring to ensure that it remains safe and effective over time. This is achieved through **post-marketing surveillance** and **pharmacovigilance** programs, which collect data on **adverse drug reactions (ADRs)** and other safety issues that may arise after the drug is widely used. Manufacturers are required to report any ADRs to the WHO, and the agency works with national regulatory authorities to investigate these reports and take corrective action if necessary.

In **2022**, the WHO collected over **10,000 ADR reports** related to prequalified medicines, leading to several updates in the safety labeling and, in some cases, the withdrawal of certain products from the market. The WHO's **pharmacovigilance** program ensures that medicines continue to meet the required safety standards even after they are introduced into the global market, protecting patients from potential risks.

In addition to monitoring ADRs, the WHO requires manufacturers to maintain compliance with GMP standards throughout the lifecycle of the product. Regular **GMP re-inspections** are conducted to ensure that manufacturing facilities continue to meet the high standards set by the WHO. If a facility fails to comply with GMP guidelines during a re-inspection, the WHO may suspend or revoke the drug's prequalification status until the necessary improvements are made.

9.4 Certificate of Pharmaceutical Product (CoPP) - General and Country Specific (South Africa, Egypt, Algeria, Morocco, Nigeria, Kenya, Botswana)

The **Certificate of Pharmaceutical Product (CoPP)** is an internationally recognized document issued by a national regulatory authority (NRA) that certifies the quality, safety, and efficacy of a pharmaceutical product. It is typically required when a pharmaceutical product is intended for export and serves as a confirmation that the product complies with Good Manufacturing Practices (GMP) and has been approved for marketing in the exporting country. The **World Health Organization (WHO)** established the **CoPP system** as part of its Certification Scheme on the Quality of Pharmaceutical Products moving in International Commerce. This document plays a crucial role in ensuring that medicines distributed across borders meet the necessary standards of public health protection.

The CoPP provides key information, including the **name of the product, dosage form, active ingredients, manufacturer details**, and confirmation of compliance with **GMP**. It also certifies that the product has been approved for sale in the country of origin and is subject to post-market surveillance. In **2022**, more than **30% of all pharmaceutical exports** globally required a CoPP to facilitate regulatory approval in importing countries.

Different countries have specific requirements for the CoPP, especially in emerging markets where regulatory frameworks are still evolving. The following sections provide insights into the country-specific CoPP requirements for **South Africa, Egypt, Algeria, Morocco, Nigeria, Kenya,** and **Botswana.**

South Africa

In **South Africa,** the **South African Health Products Regulatory Authority (SAHPRA)** oversees the issuance and recognition of CoPPs. Pharmaceutical companies seeking to register a product in South Africa must provide a CoPP issued by the regulatory authority in the country of origin. The CoPP must confirm that the product meets GMP standards and is approved for sale in the exporting country. South Africa places particular emphasis on post-marketing surveillance and requires that the product be subject to ongoing safety monitoring in the country of origin. In **2021**, over **70% of pharmaceutical registrations** in South Africa involved the submission of a CoPP, highlighting the importance of this certification in the country's regulatory framework.

Egypt

In **Egypt,** the **Egyptian Drug Authority (EDA)** requires a CoPP as part of the drug registration process for all imported pharmaceutical products. The CoPP must be issued by a competent authority recognized by the EDA, and it must confirm that the product is approved for sale in the country of origin and manufactured in compliance with GMP. Additionally, Egypt mandates that the CoPP be **legalized by the Egyptian embassy** in the exporting country, adding an extra layer of verification. This legal requirement ensures the authenticity of the document. In **2022**, Egypt processed over **200 new drug registrations** that involved CoPP submissions, particularly for essential medicines and generics.

Algeria

In **Algeria**, the **National Agency for Pharmaceutical Products (ANPP)** is responsible for the regulation of pharmaceuticals, including the recognition of CoPPs. A valid CoPP is required for all imported pharmaceutical products, and it must certify that the product has been manufactured in accordance with WHO GMP guidelines. Algeria also requires that the CoPP include information on **post-market surveillance** and confirm that the product is currently being sold in the country of origin. The CoPP must be submitted alongside a full registration dossier. In **2021**, the ANPP approved more than **150 new pharmaceuticals**, with the majority requiring a CoPP as part of the regulatory submission.

Morocco

In **Morocco**, the **Moroccan Ministry of Health** mandates the submission of a CoPP for all pharmaceutical products imported into the country. The CoPP must be issued by the NRA in the exporting country and confirm compliance with GMP and the product's approval for marketing in that country. Additionally, Morocco requires the CoPP to be **notarized and authenticated** by the Moroccan consulate in the exporting country. This additional step ensures that the documentation is legally valid. In **2022**, more than **100 pharmaceutical products** were registered in Morocco, with the CoPP playing a key role in the approval process for imported medicines.

Nigeria

In **Nigeria**, the **National Agency for Food and Drug Administration and Control (NAFDAC)** oversees the registration of pharmaceutical products, and a CoPP is required for all imported drugs. NAFDAC stipulates that the CoPP must certify that the product is approved for sale in the country of origin and is manufactured in accordance with GMP. Nigeria also requires a **Certificate of Analysis (CoA)** to accompany the CoPP, ensuring that the quality and potency of the product are verified through laboratory testing. In **2021**, NAFDAC processed over **300 drug applications**, many of which involved the submission of CoPPs, particularly for generics and over-the-counter medications.

Kenya

In **Kenya**, the **Pharmacy and Poisons Board (PPB)** is responsible for the registration and regulation of pharmaceutical products. A CoPP is a mandatory requirement for all pharmaceutical products being imported into Kenya. The CoPP must be issued by a recognized regulatory authority and confirm that the product is produced in accordance with GMP and is marketed in the country of origin. Kenya places a high emphasis on **pharmacovigilance**, and the CoPP must include details on the product's safety profile and any adverse events reported in the exporting country. In **2022**, over **250 pharmaceutical products** were registered in Kenya with CoPP documentation.

Botswana

In **Botswana**, the **Botswana Medicines Regulatory Authority (BoMRA)** requires the submission of a CoPP for all pharmaceutical products intended for import. The CoPP must confirm that the product is manufactured in compliance with GMP and is approved for sale in the country of origin. Botswana also requires that the CoPP be authenticated by the **Botswana embassy** in the exporting country. This step adds an additional layer of verification to ensure the document's legitimacy. In **2021**, BoMRA approved more than **80 new pharmaceutical products,** with CoPPs playing a vital role in ensuring the safety and quality of imported medicines.

In conclusion, the **Certificate of Pharmaceutical Product (CoPP)** is an essential document in the global pharmaceutical industry, ensuring that drugs meet international standards of **quality**, **safety**, and **efficacy**. While the general requirements for a CoPP are standardized by the **WHO**, different countries, including **South Africa**, **Egypt**, **Algeria**, **Morocco**, **Nigeria**, **Kenya**, and **Botswana**, have additional country-specific regulations that pharmaceutical companies must adhere to for successful drug registration. These varying requirements reflect each country's commitment to ensuring the safety and quality of pharmaceutical products in their markets, while also maintaining compliance with international health standards.

CHAPTER TEN

Brazil, ASEAN, CIS, and GCC Countries

Brazil, the ASEAN region, the Commonwealth of Independent States (CIS), and the Gulf Cooperation Council (GCC) countries represent dynamic and diverse markets with significant regulatory complexities. This chapter offers a detailed exploration of the pharmaceutical and medical device regulations in these regions, highlighting the opportunities and challenges associated with each market.

The chapter begins with an introduction to the ASEAN Common Technical Dossier (ACTD), a harmonized system designed to streamline the drug approval process in ASEAN member countries such as Vietnam, Malaysia, the Philippines, Singapore, and Thailand. The ACTD framework simplifies the submission process by providing standardized requirements, making it easier for pharmaceutical companies to gain market access in multiple ASEAN countries.

The chapter also discusses the regulatory requirements for marketing authorization in CIS countries like Russia, Kazakhstan, and Ukraine, focusing on the key legal and procedural steps needed for successful drug registration. Additionally, it provides insights into the GCC countries, including Saudi Arabia and the UAE, where the regulatory environment is rapidly evolving to meet the growing demands of the healthcare sector.

In Brazil, the chapter explores the ANVISA (Agência Nacional de Vigilância Sanitária), which regulates the approval and post-marketing surveillance of pharmaceuticals and medical devices. By providing a comparative analysis of the regulatory frameworks across these diverse regions, this chapter equips professionals with the knowledge needed to navigate the complexities of global drug registration and market entry, ensuring compliance with local regulations while maximizing opportunities for growth in these burgeoning markets.

10.1 Introduction to ACTD and Regulatory Requirements in China and South Korea

The **ASEAN Common Technical Dossier (ACTD)** is a harmonized format for submitting pharmaceutical registration applications across the **Association of Southeast Asian Nations (ASEAN)** region. It was developed to streamline the approval process for pharmaceuticals, ensuring consistency and facilitating the free trade of medicines across ASEAN member countries. Although **China** and **South Korea** are not ASEAN members, they have their own regulatory frameworks for pharmaceutical registration, which are distinct but occasionally influenced by global harmonization efforts such as the ACTD.

The **ACTD** format is divided into four main parts:

- **Part I: Administrative Data and Product Information,**
- **Part II: Quality** (covering the drug's chemistry, manufacturing, and controls),
- **Part III: Non-clinical (preclinical) Study Reports**, and
- **Part IV: Clinical Study Reports**.

The goal of the ACTD is to reduce the administrative burden on companies seeking to register pharmaceutical products in multiple ASEAN countries by providing a single, harmonized dossier format. This initiative has accelerated the **drug registration process** and improved access to essential medicines throughout the region. The implementation of the ACTD has led to faster regulatory reviews and a higher level of collaboration among ASEAN regulatory authorities. In **2021**, over **200 pharmaceutical products** were approved using the ACTD format across the ASEAN region.

Regulatory Requirements in China

China's regulatory framework for pharmaceuticals is overseen by the **National Medical Products Administration (NMPA),** formerly known as the **China Food and Drug Administration (CFDA).** China has its own set of regulatory requirements for drug registration, but it has gradually aligned with international standards to facilitate global trade and ensure the safety and efficacy of its medicines. In **2017**, China became a member of the **International Council for Harmonisation of Technical Requirements for**

Pharmaceuticals for Human Use (ICH), marking a significant step toward regulatory harmonization.

The **drug registration process** in China requires companies to submit a detailed **registration dossier**, which includes data on the **quality, safety, and efficacy** of the product. The dossier is divided into several key sections, including **chemical and manufacturing control (CMC)** data, **preclinical study reports**, and **clinical trial data**. China has also introduced a **priority review system** for drugs that address unmet medical needs, such as those treating **oncology** or **rare diseases**. In **2022**, the NMPA approved more than **300 new drugs**, many of which underwent the priority review process to meet the urgent demand for innovative therapies.

One significant regulatory advancement in China is the introduction of the **Marketing Authorization Holder (MAH) system**. This system allows the holder of a marketing authorization to contract out the manufacturing of a drug, provided that all production sites comply with **Good Manufacturing Practices (GMP)**. The MAH system has made the drug registration process more flexible and has encouraged innovation in pharmaceutical manufacturing. In **2021**, over **60% of new drug applications** in China were filed under the MAH system, reflecting its growing popularity among both domestic and international pharmaceutical companies.

Another critical component of China's regulatory system is the **preclinical and clinical trial approval process**. All **clinical trials** conducted in China must be approved by the **Center for Drug Evaluation (CDE)**, which evaluates the trial's scientific validity, ethical standards, and compliance with **Good Clinical Practice (GCP)**. China's **drug clinical trial application (IND)** system is also aligned with ICH guidelines, ensuring that the data generated from clinical trials meet international standards. In **2022**, China conducted over **2,000 clinical trials**, many of which were for innovative therapies and biologics.

Regulatory Requirements in South Korea

In **South Korea**, the **Ministry of Food and Drug Safety (MFDS)** is responsible for overseeing the regulation of pharmaceuticals and medical devices. South Korea's regulatory system is highly developed and aligned with global standards, particularly those set by the **ICH** and **WHO**. The **drug registration process** in South Korea follows a structured approach, requiring companies to submit a comprehensive **dossier** that includes data on **quality, safety,** and **efficacy.**

South Korea also uses a **Common Technical Document (CTD)** format for drug registration, similar to the ACTD, which is divided into five modules:

- **Module 1: Regional Administrative Information,**
- **Module 2: Summary of Quality, Safety, and Efficacy Data,**
- **Module 3: Quality,**
- **Module 4: Non-clinical Study Reports,** and
- **Module 5: Clinical Study Reports.**

This CTD format simplifies the submission process for companies registering drugs in multiple countries, as the data requirements are largely harmonized with international standards.

South Korea's **regulatory approval process** includes a robust **pharmacovigilance** system, which requires the continuous monitoring of drug safety after the product has been approved for marketing. The **MFDS** mandates that all pharmaceutical companies submit **periodic safety update reports (PSURs)**, which provide data on the drug's safety profile, any adverse events, and recommendations for further safety measures. In **2021**, the MFDS reviewed over **10,000 adverse event reports**, ensuring the ongoing safety of pharmaceuticals in the South Korean market.

South Korea also offers a **fast-track approval system** for drugs that address critical healthcare needs, such as treatments for **cancer, rare diseases,** and **infectious diseases.** This system shortens the approval timeline by allowing certain steps in the review process to be expedited. In **2022**, over **50 new drugs** were approved through the fast-track system, ensuring timely access to essential medicines for South Korean patients.

10.2 Regulatory Requirements for Drugs and Post-Approval Requirements in ASEAN Region (Vietnam, Malaysia, Philippines, Singapore, Thailand)

The **ASEAN region** has made significant strides in harmonizing drug regulatory requirements through the implementation of the **ASEAN Common Technical Dossier (ACTD)** and other collaborative initiatives. However, individual countries within the region, including **Vietnam, Malaysia, Philippines, Singapore,** and **Thailand,** maintain specific regulatory requirements for the approval and post-approval monitoring of pharmaceuticals. These requirements ensure that drugs meet the highest standards of **safety, efficacy**, and **quality**, while adhering to international norms set by the **World Health Organization (WHO)** and **International Council for Harmonisation (ICH)**.

Vietnam

In **Vietnam**, the drug regulatory process is overseen by the **Drug Administration of Vietnam (DAV)**, which operates under the **Ministry of Health**. Vietnam's regulatory framework aligns with the **ACTD**, ensuring a streamlined submission process for drug registration. Drug applications in Vietnam must include detailed data on the **quality, safety**, and **efficacy** of the product, as well as proof of **Good Manufacturing Practices (GMP)** compliance. Vietnam has also implemented the **ASEAN Common Technical Requirements (ACTR)**, further harmonizing its regulatory processes with other ASEAN countries.

One unique aspect of Vietnam's regulatory system is the emphasis on **local clinical trials** for innovative drugs. Vietnam often requires **Phase I clinical trials** to be conducted within the country, particularly for **new chemical entities (NCEs)**. In **2022**, over **100 clinical trials** were conducted in Vietnam, highlighting the country's growing role in pharmaceutical research and development.

In terms of **post-approval requirements**, Vietnam mandates that pharmaceutical companies submit **periodic safety update reports (PSURs)** and maintain robust **pharmacovigilance** systems. Any **adverse drug reactions (ADRs)** must be reported to the DAV promptly. In **2021**, the DAV reviewed more than **1,000 ADR reports**, leading to safety labeling updates for several drugs.

Malaysia

The **National Pharmaceutical Regulatory Agency (NPRA)** under the **Ministry of Health Malaysia** is responsible for drug registration and post-approval surveillance in **Malaysia**. The NPRA follows the **ACTD** format for drug applications and requires pharmaceutical companies to submit a comprehensive dossier covering the **quality, safety**, and **efficacy** of the drug. Additionally, Malaysia has established strict guidelines for **bioequivalence studies**, particularly for **generic drugs**. In 2021, Malaysia approved over **200 generic drugs**, most of which required bioequivalence studies to ensure therapeutic equivalence with the reference product.

Malaysia also mandates compliance with **GMP**, and the NPRA conducts regular **inspections** of manufacturing facilities to ensure adherence to these standards. Post-approval, pharmaceutical companies are required to implement **pharmacovigilance** systems and submit **PSURs** at regular intervals. The NPRA operates a robust **ADR reporting system**, and in **2022**, the agency processed over **1,500 ADR reports**, leading to several product recalls and safety updates.

Philippines

In the **Philippines**, the **Food and Drug Administration (FDA)** oversees the regulation of pharmaceuticals. The FDA Philippines follows the **ACTD** guidelines for drug registration and requires companies to submit a detailed dossier that includes **clinical trial data**, **quality control information**, and **stability studies**. The **FDA Philippines** is particularly focused on ensuring that all pharmaceutical products meet WHO and ICH standards, and it frequently collaborates with international regulatory bodies to strengthen its regulatory framework.

The Philippines also places a strong emphasis on **bioavailability and bioequivalence studies**, particularly for **generic drug applications**. In **2021**, over **300 generic drugs** were approved in the Philippines, with bioequivalence studies playing a critical role in the approval process.

In terms of **post-approval requirements**, the Philippines mandates that pharmaceutical companies maintain an active **pharmacovigilance system** and submit **PSURs**. The FDA Philippines operates an **online ADR reporting system**, allowing healthcare providers and patients to report any adverse effects associated with pharmaceuticals. In **2022**, the FDA received over **2,000 ADR reports**, leading to safety labeling changes for several high-risk drugs.

Singapore

Singapore is known for its highly developed and efficient regulatory system, overseen by the **Health Sciences Authority (HSA)**. Singapore's drug registration process is fully aligned with the **ACTD** format, and the HSA follows strict guidelines for the evaluation of **quality**, **safety**, and **efficacy** data. One of the unique features of Singapore's regulatory system is the **collaborative registration procedure (CRP)**, which allows companies to register drugs in Singapore and other ASEAN countries simultaneously, significantly reducing the time required for approval.

In **2021**, Singapore approved over **150 new drugs** through the CRP, making it a key player in the regional pharmaceutical market. The **HSA** also offers an **expedited review process** for drugs that address unmet medical needs, such as **oncology** drugs and **rare disease therapies**. This expedited process has reduced the time to market for essential medicines, ensuring faster access for patients in Singapore.

For **post-approval requirements**, Singapore mandates the submission of **PSURs** and active participation in **pharmacovigilance activities**. The HSA operates an advanced **ADR monitoring system**, and in **2022**, over **1,200 ADR reports** were submitted, leading to safety alerts and product recalls for several pharmaceuticals.

Thailand

In **Thailand**, the **Food and Drug Administration (Thai FDA)** is the regulatory authority responsible for drug registration and post-approval monitoring. Like other ASEAN countries, Thailand follows the **ACTD** for drug applications, and pharmaceutical companies must provide comprehensive data on the **quality**, **safety**, and **efficacy** of the drug. Thailand also emphasizes the need for **bioequivalence studies**, particularly for generic drugs, to ensure that they are therapeutically equivalent to the innovator product. In **2021**, Thailand approved over **250 generic drugs**, most of which required bioequivalence studies.

The **Thai FDA** mandates compliance with **GMP**, and the agency conducts regular **inspections** of both local and international manufacturing facilities. Thailand has also implemented strict **post-approval surveillance** measures, requiring companies to submit **PSURs** and actively monitor the safety of their products through **pharmacovigilance systems**. In **2022**, the Thai FDA received over **2,500 ADR reports**, leading to updates in product labeling and the recall of certain high-risk drugs.

10.3 Regulatory Requirements for Marketing Authorization in CIS Countries (Russia, Kazakhstan, Ukraine)

The **Commonwealth of Independent States (CIS)**, which includes countries like **Russia, Kazakhstan**, and **Ukraine**, has developed a regulatory framework for the approval of pharmaceuticals that reflects both regional collaboration and adherence to international standards. Each of these countries has its own **national regulatory authority** (NRA) responsible for overseeing the marketing authorization (MA) process, ensuring that drugs meet stringent **quality, safety,** and **efficacy** requirements before being marketed. These processes are closely aligned with global regulatory norms, including those established by the **World Health Organization (WHO)** and the **International Council for Harmonisation of Technical Requirements for Pharmaceuticals for Human Use (ICH).**

Russia

In **Russia**, the regulatory authority responsible for the approval of pharmaceuticals is the **Ministry of Health (MoH),** operating through its **Federal Service for Surveillance in Healthcare (Roszdravnadzor).** The regulatory requirements for marketing authorization in Russia are governed by the **Federal Law on Circulation of Medicines (No. 61-FZ),** enacted in **2010**, and updated periodically to reflect changes in the pharmaceutical landscape.

The **marketing authorization process** in Russia requires a comprehensive **dossier** submission, which follows the **Common Technical Document (CTD)** format. This dossier includes detailed information on the **quality, safety,** and **efficacy** of the drug, as well as data on the **pharmacokinetics, clinical trials,** and **stability studies.** Russia has placed particular emphasis on **Good Manufacturing Practices (GMP),** and pharmaceutical manufacturers must demonstrate that their production facilities meet GMP standards before they can receive marketing approval. In **2021**, Russia approved over **500 new drugs**, including both innovative therapies and generics, after conducting rigorous evaluations of their CTD submissions.

In addition to GMP compliance, Russia requires that **clinical trials** for new drugs be conducted within the country, particularly for **innovative drugs** and **biologics.** This local trial requirement ensures that the efficacy and safety of the drug are tested on the Russian population, which is particularly important for treatments that may interact differently due to genetic or environmental factors. In **2022**, more than **300 clinical trials** were conducted in Russia, reflecting the country's strong focus on locally generated clinical data.

For **post-marketing surveillance**, Russia mandates the submission of **Periodic Safety Update Reports (PSURs)** and requires pharmaceutical companies to maintain a robust **pharmacovigilance system** to monitor any **adverse drug reactions (ADRs)**. The **Russian Pharmacovigilance Center** actively collects and analyzes ADR data, ensuring the ongoing safety of marketed drugs. In **2021**, over **15,000 ADR reports** were filed, leading to several safety labeling changes and product recalls.

Kazakhstan

In **Kazakhstan**, the regulatory body responsible for the approval of pharmaceuticals is the **National Center for Expertise of Medicines and Medical Devices (NCEM)**, under the **Ministry of Health**. The regulatory framework for drug registration in Kazakhstan is closely aligned with the **Eurasian Economic Union (EAEU)**, which seeks to harmonize regulatory standards across member states, including Russia, Belarus, Armenia, and Kazakhstan.

The **marketing authorization process** in Kazakhstan follows the **Common Technical Document (CTD)** format, which includes detailed information on the drug's **quality**, **safety**, and **efficacy**. Kazakhstan has adopted the **Good Manufacturing Practices (GMP)** requirements of the EAEU, and all pharmaceutical manufacturers must undergo **GMP inspections** to ensure that their facilities meet the necessary standards. In **2021**, Kazakhstan approved over **200 new drugs**, including vaccines and treatments for chronic diseases, many of which were submitted under the EAEU's harmonized regulatory framework.

Kazakhstan also requires that **bioequivalence studies** be conducted for **generic drugs**, ensuring that they are therapeutically equivalent to the reference product. These studies must be conducted in compliance with **Good Clinical Practice (GCP)** guidelines, and the data must be submitted as part of the registration dossier. The NCEM plays a critical role in evaluating these studies to ensure that generic drugs meet the same safety and efficacy standards as the original.

In terms of **post-approval requirements**, Kazakhstan mandates that pharmaceutical companies submit **PSURs** at regular intervals and maintain an active **pharmacovigilance system**. The **National Pharmacovigilance Center** collects reports of **adverse drug reactions (ADRs)** and collaborates with other EAEU member states to ensure the safety of marketed drugs.

In **2021**, over **2,000 ADR reports** were filed in Kazakhstan, contributing to regional safety monitoring efforts.

Ukraine

In **Ukraine**, the regulatory authority responsible for pharmaceutical registration is the **State Expert Center (SEC)** under the **Ministry of Health of Ukraine (MoH)**. Ukraine's regulatory framework for drug registration aligns with **European Union (EU)** standards, particularly after the country signed the **EU-Ukraine Association Agreement** in **2014**, which commits Ukraine to adopting EU regulatory norms for pharmaceuticals.

The **marketing authorization process** in Ukraine also follows the **Common Technical Document (CTD)** format, requiring a detailed dossier that includes data on the **quality, safety,** and **efficacy** of the drug. Ukraine mandates that all pharmaceutical manufacturers comply with **Good Manufacturing Practices (GMP)**, and the **State Service of Ukraine on Medicines and Drugs Control** (SMDC) conducts **GMP inspections** of both domestic and international manufacturing facilities. In **2021**, Ukraine approved over **150 new drugs**, many of which were innovative therapies targeting oncology and infectious diseases.

Ukraine has implemented a **fast-track approval process** for drugs that address **urgent public health needs,** such as **vaccines** and **antivirals.** This expedited process allows pharmaceutical companies to reduce the time required for approval, ensuring faster access to essential medicines. In **2022**, over **50 drugs** were approved through the fast-track system, primarily targeting **COVID-19** and other infectious diseases.

Post-marketing surveillance in Ukraine is governed by strict regulations, with pharmaceutical companies required to submit **PSURs** and actively monitor the safety of their products through **pharmacovigilance systems.** The **Ukrainian Pharmacovigilance Center** collects data on **adverse drug reactions (ADRs),** and in **2021**, more than **3,000 ADR reports** were filed. This robust post-market monitoring system ensures that the safety of pharmaceutical products is continuously assessed, even after they have been approved for sale.

The **regulatory requirements for marketing authorization** in **Russia, Kazakhstan,** and **Ukraine** are designed to ensure the safety, efficacy, and quality of pharmaceutical products. While each country follows the **Common Technical Document (CTD)** format, their specific requirements reflect regional priorities and regulatory standards. Russia's emphasis on **local clinical trials** and **GMP compliance**, Kazakhstan's integration with the **Eurasian Economic Union (EAEU)**, and Ukraine's alignment with **European Union (EU)** standards demonstrate the diversity in regulatory approaches across the CIS region. Each country's focus on **post-marketing surveillance** and **pharmacovigilance** ensures that pharmaceuticals remain safe

10.4 Regulatory Requirements for Marketing Authorization in GCC (Saudi Arabia, UAE)

The **Gulf Cooperation Council (GCC)**, comprising countries like **Saudi Arabia** and the **United Arab Emirates (UAE)**, plays a significant role in harmonizing pharmaceutical regulations across the region. While the **GCC Health Council** provides a central framework for collaborative drug registration through the **Central Drug Registration (CDR) system**, each member state maintains specific regulatory requirements for marketing authorization, with **Saudi Arabia** and the **UAE** having well-established processes.

Saudi Arabia

In **Saudi Arabia**, the regulatory authority responsible for drug registration is the **Saudi Food and Drug Authority (SFDA)**. Established in **2003**, the SFDA is tasked with ensuring the **safety, efficacy,** and **quality** of pharmaceuticals marketed in the country. The **marketing authorization** process in Saudi Arabia is rigorous and follows the **Common Technical Document (CTD)** format, ensuring that the submission of **quality, safety,** and **efficacy** data is comprehensive.

The **application process** begins with the submission of a **dossier** that includes the drug's **clinical trial data, stability studies, Good Manufacturing Practices (GMP)** compliance, and **bioequivalence studies** for generic drugs. The SFDA requires that all pharmaceutical manufacturers, both domestic and international, comply with GMP standards as per **WHO** guidelines. In **2021**, the SFDA conducted over **300 inspections** of pharmaceutical manufacturing facilities, ensuring compliance with international quality standards.

For **biologics** and **new chemical entities (NCEs)**, Saudi Arabia mandates that **local clinical trials** be conducted to ensure that the drug is effective in the **local population**. This requirement is particularly important for biologics, where differences in **genetic factors** or **lifestyle** may affect the drug's efficacy. In **2021**, the SFDA approved more than **150 new drugs**, including several biologics and innovative therapies for **oncology** and **rare diseases**.

In terms of **post-marketing requirements**, the SFDA mandates that pharmaceutical companies submit **Periodic Safety Update Reports (PSURs)** and actively monitor **adverse drug reactions (ADRs)** through their **pharmacovigilance systems**. The SFDA operates an online **ADR reporting system**, allowing healthcare professionals and patients to report adverse events. In **2022**, the SFDA received over **10,000 ADR reports**, leading to safety labeling updates for several high-risk drugs.

United Arab Emirates (UAE)

In the **UAE**, the regulatory body responsible for drug registration is the **Ministry of Health and Prevention (MOHAP)**, specifically the **Drug Registration and Control Department**. The UAE follows a similar regulatory framework to Saudi Arabia, with the **Common Technical Document (CTD)** format being the standard for dossier submissions.

The **drug registration process** in the UAE requires pharmaceutical companies to submit detailed information on the **quality**, **safety**, and **efficacy** of their products. For **generic drugs, bioequivalence studies** are mandatory to ensure that the generic product is therapeutically equivalent to the **innovator drug**. In **2021**, the UAE approved over **200 new drugs**, many of which were generics, reflecting the country's focus on expanding access to affordable medications.

The UAE also mandates that pharmaceutical manufacturers comply with **Good Manufacturing Practices (GMP)**, and the **MOHAP** conducts regular **inspections** of both local and international manufacturing facilities to ensure compliance. In **2022**, the UAE conducted **150 GMP inspections**, ensuring that all registered drugs meet international quality standards.

A key feature of the UAE's regulatory framework is its **fast-track approval system** for drugs that address critical public health needs, such as **oncology** treatments or drugs for **rare diseases**. This fast-track process reduces the approval timeline, ensuring that patients in the UAE have rapid access to essential medicines. In **2022**, over **50 drugs** were approved under the fast-track system, many of which were cutting-edge therapies for cancer and other life-threatening conditions.

For **post-marketing surveillance**, the UAE requires pharmaceutical companies to submit **PSURs** regularly and to implement **pharmacovigilance systems** that monitor the safety of their products post-approval. The UAE operates a comprehensive **ADR reporting system**, and in **2021**, over **5,000 ADR reports** were submitted, leading to several product recalls and safety updates.

Harmonization and GCC Central Drug Registration (CDR)

The **GCC Health Council** has established the **Central Drug Registration (CDR)** system to harmonize the drug approval process across GCC countries, including Saudi Arabia and the UAE. Through this system, a pharmaceutical product registered in one GCC country can be approved for marketing in all other member states without the need for separate submissions. The **CDR** system has streamlined the approval process and reduced **duplication of efforts**, particularly for **generic drugs** and **over-the-counter (OTC) products**.

In **2021**, the CDR system approved more than **1,000 pharmaceutical products** across the GCC region, with over **300 drugs** registered through the system in Saudi Arabia and the UAE alone. This system has improved access to medicines across the Gulf region, ensuring that high-quality drugs are available to patients in all member states.

10.5 Legislation and Regulations for Import, Manufacture, Distribution, and Sale of Cosmetics in Brazil, ASEAN, CIS, and GCC Countries

The regulation of **cosmetics** varies significantly across different regions, reflecting each area's approach to ensuring the **safety, quality,** and **efficacy** of cosmetic products. Countries such as **Brazil, ASEAN member states, CIS countries,** and **GCC nations** have developed their own **legislation** and **regulatory frameworks** to control the import, manufacture, distribution, and sale of cosmetics. Each region tailors its regulatory environment to meet its unique **market needs, consumer safety** concerns, and **trade policies.**

Brazil

In **Brazil**, the **National Health Surveillance Agency (ANVISA)** regulates cosmetics under **RDC Resolution No. 7/2015**, which classifies cosmetics based on the level of **health risk** they pose. There are two primary categories of cosmetics in Brazil:

1. **Grade 1**: Products with low health risk and simple claims (e.g., shampoos, lotions).
2. **Grade 2**: Products with specific claims or ingredients that require more rigorous testing (e.g., sunscreens, hair dyes).

For **importation**, Brazil mandates that foreign manufacturers must comply with **Good Manufacturing Practices (GMP)** and register their products with ANVISA. A **Certificate of Free Sale** from the country of origin and other product-related documentation, such as ingredient listings, must be provided. In **2021**, ANVISA processed more than **3,000 cosmetic product registrations**, reflecting Brazil's large and growing market for beauty products.

The **manufacture** of cosmetics in Brazil is strictly regulated to ensure product safety. ANVISA conducts **inspections** of manufacturing facilities, both domestic and international, to verify compliance with **GMP** standards. For **distribution and sale**, cosmetic products must be properly labeled, with clear instructions for use and safety warnings in **Portuguese**. Brazil also enforces strict regulations on **advertising**, prohibiting false or misleading claims about cosmetic products.

ASEAN

The **ASEAN region** has made significant progress in harmonizing cosmetic regulations through the implementation of the **ASEAN Cosmetic Directive (ACD)**, which was adopted in **2003**. The ACD aligns the regulatory framework across all ten ASEAN member states, including **Indonesia, Malaysia, Philippines, Singapore, Thailand**, and **Vietnam**. The ACD sets out requirements for the **import, manufacture, distribution**, and **sale** of cosmetics, ensuring consistent safety standards across the region.

Under the ACD, all cosmetic products must comply with **ASEAN Common Cosmetic Ingredient Listings** and **Good Manufacturing Practices (GMP)**. Manufacturers must submit a **Product Information File (PIF)** containing details on the product's formulation, safety assessments, and labeling information. In **2021**, over **10,000 cosmetic products** were registered across the ASEAN region under the ACD framework.

For **imports**, ASEAN countries require that cosmetic products be registered with the relevant national authorities. For instance, in **Malaysia**, the **National Pharmaceutical Regulatory Agency (NPRA)** oversees the registration and regulation of cosmetics, while in **Thailand**, the **Thai FDA** plays a similar role. Proper labeling in the national language is mandatory, and products must include usage instructions, ingredient lists, and safety warnings.

Cosmetic manufacturers in ASEAN countries must comply with **GMP** to ensure that their products are manufactured to high standards of quality. For **distribution and sale**, cosmetics must meet the labeling requirements set forth by the ACD, ensuring that consumers have access to accurate and comprehensive information about the products they use.

CIS (Russia, Kazakhstan, Ukraine)

In **CIS countries**, cosmetic products are regulated under national laws and regional guidelines. In **Russia**, **Kazakhstan**, and **Ukraine**, cosmetic products must comply with the **Eurasian Economic Union (EAEU) Technical Regulation No. 009/2011**, which sets safety standards for the import, manufacture, and sale of cosmetics across the region.

In **Russia**, the **Federal Service for Surveillance in Healthcare (Roszdravnadzor)** oversees cosmetic regulations. Cosmetics must be registered and certified under **GOST-R** standards, which ensure product safety and quality. Similar procedures are followed in **Kazakhstan**, where the **Ministry of Health** oversees the regulation of cosmetics. Products must comply with the **Eurasian Customs Union** standards, which facilitate trade across the CIS region.

In **Ukraine**, the **State Service of Ukraine on Medicines and Drugs Control (SMDC)** oversees the regulation of cosmetics. The importation of cosmetics into Ukraine requires **registration**, and the product must comply with **GMP** standards. In **2021**, Ukraine imported over **$200 million worth** of cosmetics, highlighting the country's growing beauty industry.

Manufacturers in CIS countries are required to follow strict **GMP** guidelines, and the production facilities are regularly inspected to ensure compliance. For **distribution and sale**, cosmetics must be labeled according to national requirements, including the product's name, usage instructions, ingredient lists, and any necessary safety warnings. The labeling must be in the official language of the respective country, such as **Russian** or **Ukrainian**.

GCC (Saudi Arabia, UAE)

In the **Gulf Cooperation Council (GCC)** countries, including **Saudi Arabia** and the **United Arab Emirates (UAE)**, the regulation of cosmetics is governed by the **GCC Standardization Organization (GSO)**. Each member state follows the **GSO Technical Regulation on Cosmetics and Personal Care Products**, which sets out the requirements for the import, manufacture, and sale of cosmetic products across the GCC region.

In **Saudi Arabia**, the **Saudi Food and Drug Authority (SFDA)** is responsible for the regulation of cosmetics. Cosmetic products must be registered through the **SFDA's E-Cosma** portal, and manufacturers are required to submit a comprehensive dossier that includes the product's formulation, **Good Manufacturing Practices (GMP)** certification, and safety assessments. Saudi Arabia also enforces strict **import regulations**, requiring a **Certificate of Free Sale** and other relevant documentation. In **2021**, over **2,000 cosmetic products** were registered with the SFDA.

In the **UAE**, the **Ministry of Health and Prevention (MOHAP)** regulates the import and sale of cosmetics. Products must be registered with MOHAP, and the manufacturer must comply with **GMP**. UAE requires that all cosmetic products be labeled in **Arabic** and **English**, with clear instructions for use and safety warnings. Advertising of cosmetic products is closely regulated to prevent false claims.

For **manufacturing**, both Saudi Arabia and the UAE require compliance with **GMP** and conduct regular inspections to ensure that production facilities meet the necessary standards. The **distribution and sale** of cosmetics are subject to strict labeling requirements, and products must include information such as ingredients, expiry dates, and usage instructions.

CHAPTER ELEVEN

Regulatory Aspects of Drugs and Cosmetics

The regulation of drugs and cosmetics involves ensuring that products meet safety, efficacy, and labeling standards across global markets. This chapter discusses the frameworks that govern these industries, including the approval processes for **Over-the-Counter (OTC) and prescription drugs**, as well as cosmetics. By examining the requirements for marketing authorization, packaging, and post-market surveillance, this chapter offers a comprehensive view of the regulations that safeguard consumer health and product quality.

11.1 Drug Regulatory Framework in Different Countries

The **drug regulatory framework** varies significantly across countries, reflecting each nation's approach to ensuring the **safety, efficacy**, and **quality** of pharmaceutical products. These frameworks are designed to protect public health by enforcing stringent standards throughout the drug development, manufacturing, and distribution processes. Although there is global collaboration through initiatives such as the **International Council for Harmonisation of Technical Requirements for Pharmaceuticals for Human Use (ICH)** and the **World Health Organization (WHO)**, individual countries maintain unique regulatory environments based on their healthcare needs, economic conditions, and legal frameworks.

United States

In the **United States**, the regulatory authority responsible for overseeing drugs is the **U.S. Food and Drug Administration (FDA)**. The **FDA** is one of the most prominent regulatory bodies in the world, and its drug approval process is considered a global benchmark. The **drug regulatory framework** in the U.S. is governed by the **Federal Food, Drug, and Cosmetic Act (FFDCA)**, which was enacted in **1938** and has been amended multiple times to address evolving pharmaceutical needs.

The **FDA's Center for Drug Evaluation and Research (CDER)** is responsible for reviewing **New Drug Applications (NDAs)** and **Abbreviated New Drug Applications (ANDAs)** for generic drugs. Before a drug can be marketed, the **FDA** requires that the manufacturer submit comprehensive data on the drug's **preclinical** and **clinical trials, pharmacokinetics, manufacturing process**, and **quality control measures.** In **2021**, the FDA approved **53 new molecular entities (NMEs)** and **1000 generic drugs**, reflecting the country's robust pharmaceutical innovation and generics market.

The **FDA** also enforces strict **post-marketing surveillance** through its **Adverse Event Reporting System (FAERS)**, which collects data on **adverse drug reactions (ADRs)**. The FDA received over **1.2 million ADR reports** in **2022**, leading to several safety updates and recalls.

European Union

In the **European Union (EU)**, the **European Medicines Agency (EMA)** oversees drug regulation, in collaboration with national regulatory authorities of individual member states. The **regulatory framework** for pharmaceuticals in the EU is harmonized across member states, with the **EMA** coordinating the approval of drugs for the entire **EU market**. The EU follows the **Common Technical Document (CTD)** format for drug submissions, which ensures that companies provide comprehensive data on the drug's **quality, safety**, and **efficacy**.

The **centralized procedure**, managed by the EMA, allows for the simultaneous approval of drugs in all **27 EU member states**. This is particularly important for drugs addressing **rare diseases** or **innovative therapies** such as **biologics**. In **2021**, the EMA recommended approval for over **90 new medicines**, including several groundbreaking treatments for **oncology** and **gene therapies**.

The **EMA** also places a strong emphasis on **post-approval monitoring** and **pharmacovigilance** through the **EudraVigilance** system, which collects and analyzes data on ADRs across the EU. In **2021**, more than **1 million ADR reports** were filed, ensuring that emerging safety concerns are quickly identified and addressed.

India

In **India**, the regulatory framework for pharmaceuticals is governed by the **Central Drugs Standard Control Organization (CDSCO)** under the **Ministry of Health and Family Welfare**. The primary legislation is the

Drugs and Cosmetics Act of 1940, which has been amended multiple times to address the changing landscape of drug regulation. The **CDSCO** is responsible for granting marketing approvals for **new drugs**, overseeing **clinical trials**, and enforcing compliance with **Good Manufacturing Practices (GMP)**.

India is one of the world's largest producers of **generic medicines**, and the **approval process** for generics involves submitting an **Abbreviated New Drug Application (ANDA)**, which demonstrates **bioequivalence** to a reference product. In **2021**, India's pharmaceutical industry accounted for more than **$24 billion** in exports, reflecting the country's significant role in the global drug supply chain.

India also has a well-established **pharmacovigilance program** known as **PvPI (Pharmacovigilance Programme of India)**, which monitors ADRs across the country. In **2021**, the PvPI received over **50,000 ADR reports**, contributing to the global effort to improve drug safety.

Japan

In **Japan**, the regulatory authority responsible for pharmaceuticals is the **Pharmaceuticals and Medical Devices Agency (PMDA)**, working under the supervision of the **Ministry of Health, Labour and Welfare (MHLW)**. Japan follows a **well-structured regulatory process** that aligns with international standards, particularly those set by the **ICH**. The **Pharmaceutical Affairs Law** governs the regulation of drugs in Japan, and all new drugs must undergo rigorous evaluation for **safety, efficacy**, and **quality** before receiving approval.

The **New Drug Application (NDA)** process in Japan involves submitting a detailed dossier that includes clinical data generated from **local clinical trials**, especially for **biologics** and **innovative therapies**. In **2021**, the PMDA approved over **150 new drugs**, many of which were innovative treatments targeting **oncology** and **rare diseases**.

The **post-marketing surveillance** system in Japan is robust, with companies required to submit **Periodic Safety Update Reports (PSURs)** and actively monitor **adverse drug reactions (ADRs)** through the **Japanese Adverse Drug Event Report (JADER)** system. In **2021**, over **20,000 ADR reports** were submitted, ensuring continuous monitoring of drug safety.

China

China's regulatory framework is managed by the **National Medical Products Administration (NMPA)**. The **NMPA** has undergone significant reform in recent years, aligning its regulatory standards with international norms through membership in the **International Council for Harmonisation (ICH)**. The **Drug Administration Law of 2019** is the cornerstone of China's pharmaceutical regulation, covering everything from **clinical trials** to **post-marketing surveillance**.

China requires **local clinical trials** for many new drugs, particularly for biologics and innovative therapies. The **Marketing Authorization Holder (MAH) system**, introduced in **2017**, has also modernized the regulatory landscape by allowing pharmaceutical companies to hold marketing authorizations even if they do not own manufacturing facilities. In **2021**, China approved more than **300 new drugs**, reflecting its rapidly growing pharmaceutical industry.

The **post-marketing system** in China is centered on **pharmacovigilance** and **post-market surveillance**. The **NMPA** requires that companies monitor **adverse drug reactions (ADRs)** and submit regular **PSURs**. In **2022**, the NMPA processed over **30,000 ADR reports**, ensuring the safety of pharmaceuticals available in the market.

11.2 Requirements for Drug Approval and Marketing Authorization

The **requirements for drug approval** and **marketing authorization** vary across different countries, but the core principles remain the same—ensuring that pharmaceuticals meet stringent standards of **safety**, **efficacy**, and **quality** before they are made available to the public. Each country has its own regulatory authority that oversees the drug approval process, guided by national laws and international guidelines from organizations such as the **World Health Organization (WHO)** and the **International Council for Harmonisation of Technical Requirements for Pharmaceuticals for Human Use (ICH)**. The regulatory process is designed to ensure that drugs provide therapeutic benefits without posing unacceptable risks to patients.

Preclinical and Clinical Data Requirements

The drug approval process typically begins with **preclinical studies**, where the drug's safety and pharmacological profile are evaluated using **in vitro** (laboratory) studies and **in vivo** (animal) studies. These studies aim to assess the drug's **toxicity**, **pharmacokinetics**, and **pharmacodynamics**. For example, before proceeding to human trials, a drug may undergo **acute**, **subacute**, and **chronic toxicity testing** to identify any potential adverse effects at various dosage levels. Data from these studies are submitted as part of the initial **Investigational New Drug (IND)** application in countries like the **United States** or **Clinical Trial Applications (CTAs)** in countries like **India**.

Once preclinical studies demonstrate a favorable safety profile, **clinical trials** are conducted in three phases:

- **Phase I** involves a small group of healthy volunteers to determine the drug's **safety, dosage range**, and **pharmacokinetics**.
- **Phase II** expands to a larger group of patients with the target condition to assess **efficacy** and further evaluate safety.
- **Phase III** trials are large-scale studies conducted in diverse patient populations to confirm the drug's efficacy and monitor for adverse reactions over a longer period.

For instance, in the **European Union (EU)**, the **European Medicines Agency (EMA)** requires that clinical trial data be generated in compliance with **Good Clinical Practice (GCP)** guidelines, ensuring that trials are ethically conducted and scientifically sound. In **2022**, the EMA reviewed over **1,200 clinical trial applications**, ensuring that each drug met rigorous safety and efficacy standards before marketing authorization could be granted.

Common Technical Document (CTD) Format for Submission

The **Common Technical Document (CTD)** is the standard format for submitting drug approval applications to regulatory authorities in many countries, including the **United States, Europe, Japan**, and **China**. The CTD is divided into five modules:

- **Module 1**: Administrative and regional information.
- **Module 2**: Quality, non-clinical, and clinical overviews and summaries.
- **Module 3**: Quality, focusing on the **drug substance** and **drug product**.
- **Module 4**: Non-clinical study reports.
- **Module 5**: Clinical study reports.

By using the CTD format, pharmaceutical companies can streamline the submission process across multiple regions, facilitating global access to new medicines. In **2021**, the **U.S. Food and Drug Administration (FDA)** received over **5,000 new drug applications (NDAs)** and **abbreviated new drug applications (ANDAs)** in the CTD format, reflecting the international adoption of this standardized approach.

Good Manufacturing Practices (GMP) Compliance

Another critical requirement for drug approval is **Good Manufacturing Practices (GMP)** compliance. GMP ensures that drugs are consistently produced and controlled according to quality standards. Regulatory authorities such as the **FDA, EMA,** and **Japan's Pharmaceuticals and Medical Devices Agency (PMDA)** conduct **GMP inspections** to verify that manufacturing facilities meet these standards. In **2021**, the **FDA** conducted over **700 GMP inspections** worldwide to ensure the integrity of the pharmaceutical supply chain.

For generic drugs, manufacturers must submit an **Abbreviated New Drug Application (ANDA)**, which includes **bioequivalence studies** showing that the generic version is therapeutically equivalent to the brand-name product. In **India**, the **Central Drugs Standard Control Organization (CDSCO)** approved more than **300 generic drug applications** in **2021**, driven by the country's large role as a global supplier of affordable medicines.

Post-Marketing Surveillance and Pharmacovigilance

After a drug is approved, it enters the **post-marketing surveillance** phase, where its safety is continuously monitored through **pharmacovigilance** systems. Pharmaceutical companies are required to submit **Periodic Safety Update Reports (PSURs)** and report **adverse drug reactions (ADRs)**. These post-approval requirements are essential to ensuring that any emerging safety issues are identified and addressed promptly.

In **Japan**, the **PMDA** requires pharmaceutical companies to actively monitor the safety of their products through the **Japanese Adverse Drug Event Report (JADER)** system. In **2021**, over **25,000 ADR reports** were submitted, leading to updated safety information for several drugs, including changes in dosing recommendations and warnings about potential side effects.

Fast-Track and Priority Review Systems

Many countries have implemented **fast-track** or **priority review** systems to expedite the approval of drugs that address urgent medical needs, such as treatments for **cancer, rare diseases,** or **infectious diseases**. In the **United States**, the FDA's **Fast Track** designation is granted to drugs that show promise in treating serious conditions with unmet medical needs. Similarly, the **EMA** offers a **priority medicines (PRIME)** scheme for therapies that provide significant public health benefits. In **2021**, over **50 drugs** received **priority review** in the **EU**, many of which were cutting-edge treatments for oncology and **genetic disorders.**

11.3 Regulations for Over-the-Counter (OTC) Drugs and Prescription Drugs

The regulatory framework for **Over-the-Counter (OTC)** drugs and **prescription drugs** differs significantly, as these two categories serve distinct purposes in healthcare systems. OTC drugs are available without a prescription and are generally used to treat minor ailments that do not require direct supervision by a healthcare professional, while prescription drugs are intended for more complex conditions and must be prescribed by a licensed healthcare provider. Regulatory authorities across the world, such as the **U.S. Food and Drug Administration (FDA)**, **European Medicines Agency (EMA)**, and **Central Drugs Standard Control Organization (CDSCO)** in India, enforce stringent regulations to ensure the safety, efficacy, and quality of both OTC and prescription drugs.

Regulations for Over-the-Counter (OTC) Drugs

OTC drugs are designed for **self-medication**, and their safety profiles must allow for unsupervised use by consumers. These drugs typically treat common conditions such as **headaches, fever, cough, allergies**, and **digestive issues**. Regulatory frameworks for OTC drugs are built to ensure that these products are safe for use without a healthcare provider's guidance.

In the **United States**, the **FDA** regulates OTC drugs through a **monograph system**. An OTC monograph outlines the **active ingredients, dosage, labeling**, and **indications** for categories of OTC drugs. If a drug conforms to the established monograph, it does not need a separate **New Drug Application (NDA)**, simplifying the approval process. However, any OTC drug that contains new active ingredients or deviates from the monograph must undergo the **NDA** process. The **FDA's OTC Drug Review** began in **1972** to classify OTC drugs into **Category I** (safe and effective), **Category II** (unsafe or ineffective), and **Category III** (requiring further data). By **2022**, the FDA had finalized monographs for thousands of OTC products, ensuring that these drugs meet safety and efficacy standards.

In **India**, the **Central Drugs Standard Control Organization (CDSCO)** regulates OTC drugs under the **Drugs and Cosmetics Act of 1940**. While India does not have a separate monograph system like the U.S., OTC drugs must still comply with **Good Manufacturing Practices (GMP)** and meet the safety requirements outlined by the **CDSCO**. India has seen a significant rise in the sale of OTC medications in recent years, particularly for products such as **paracetamol**, **antacids**, and **cough syrups**, which accounted for over **40%** of the market in **2021**.

The **European Medicines Agency (EMA)** follows a similar approach to OTC drug regulation, with individual EU member states playing a role in the classification and regulation of these drugs. In **Germany**, for example, OTC drugs are classified into different categories based on their active ingredients and potential risks. The **Federal Institute for Drugs and Medical Devices (BfArM)** oversees the approval and safety monitoring of these products. Across the EU, OTC drugs are subject to **strict labeling requirements**, ensuring that consumers have access to clear and accurate information about the use and potential risks of these medications.

Regulations for Prescription Drugs

Prescription drugs, on the other hand, are used to treat more serious or chronic conditions that require close monitoring by a healthcare provider. These drugs often carry higher risks, including potential **adverse effects** or **drug interactions**, which is why they are dispensed only under the supervision of a physician or qualified healthcare professional.

The regulatory requirements for **prescription drugs** are more stringent than those for OTC drugs. In the **United States**, prescription drugs must undergo the full **New Drug Application (NDA)** process, which includes preclinical and clinical testing to evaluate the drug's safety and efficacy. This process is overseen by the **FDA**, and it typically involves three phases of clinical trials, followed by a thorough review of the data before the drug is approved for market. In **2021**, the FDA approved **53 new prescription drugs**, including innovative treatments for conditions such as **cancer**, **autoimmune disorders**, and **cardiovascular diseases**.

Pharmacovigilance is an essential part of the regulation of prescription drugs. Once a prescription drug is on the market, it is subject to ongoing monitoring for **adverse drug reactions (ADRs)** and other safety concerns. Pharmaceutical companies are required to submit **Periodic Safety Update Reports (PSURs)** to regulatory authorities, detailing any new safety data collected post-marketing. In **Europe**, the **EMA** requires pharmaceutical companies to actively monitor and report ADRs through its **EudraVigilance** system. In **2021**, over **1 million ADR reports** were submitted to the EMA, ensuring the continued safety of prescription medications.

In **India**, the regulation of prescription drugs is also governed by the **Drugs and Cosmetics Act of 1940**, with the CDSCO serving as the primary regulatory authority. The drug approval process in India involves the submission of an application with detailed **preclinical** and **clinical trial data**, followed by a review by the **Drugs Controller General of India (DCGI)**. In **2022**, India approved over **200 new prescription drugs**, many of which were generic formulations aimed at improving access to essential medicines.

Labeling and Advertising Regulations

Both **OTC** and **prescription drugs** are subject to strict **labeling requirements** to ensure that consumers and healthcare professionals have the information they need to use the drugs safely and effectively. For OTC drugs, labeling must include **dosage instructions**, **warnings**, **contraindications**, and **side effects**. The **FDA** requires a **Drug Facts** panel on all OTC products, providing clear guidance on the proper use of the drug. In **Europe**, labeling regulations for OTC and prescription drugs are harmonized across the EU through the **EMA**, with each product required to include key information in the **Summary of Product Characteristics (SmPC)**.

For **prescription drugs**, the labeling is more detailed and includes comprehensive information about the drug's **pharmacokinetics**, **drug interactions**, **adverse effects**, and instructions for use in special populations such as **pregnant women** or **elderly patients**. Regulatory authorities such as the **FDA, EMA**, and **CDSCO** ensure that all prescription drug labels meet the required standards before the drug is marketed.

Advertising for OTC drugs is generally permitted, but it must adhere to strict guidelines to ensure that the claims made about the product are accurate and not misleading. In the **U.S.**, the **FDA** and the **Federal Trade Commission (FTC)** regulate the advertising of OTC drugs, while the **EMA** oversees similar regulations in Europe. Prescription drug advertising, on the other hand, is more tightly controlled. In countries such as **India** and the **European Union**, direct-to-consumer (DTC) advertising for prescription drugs is prohibited, while in the **United States**, DTC advertising is allowed but subject to strict oversight by the FDA to ensure that all risks and benefits are clearly communicated.

11.4 Regulatory Requirements for Cosmetics

The **regulatory requirements for cosmetics** vary across regions, but they all share the same objective of ensuring that cosmetic products are safe for use by consumers. Cosmetics are generally defined as products that are intended for **cleansing, beautifying, promoting attractiveness**, or **altering appearance** without affecting the body's structure or functions.

This definition distinguishes cosmetics from pharmaceuticals and medical devices, which have stricter regulatory requirements due to their therapeutic effects. However, the safety, quality, and proper labeling of cosmetics are regulated through various national and international frameworks to protect consumers from potential risks.

United States

In the **United States,** the **U.S. Food and Drug Administration (FDA)** oversees the regulation of cosmetics under the **Federal Food, Drug, and Cosmetic Act (FD&C Act).** The FD&C Act defines cosmetics and establishes guidelines for their **safety, labeling,** and **manufacturing practices.** However, unlike drugs, cosmetics do not need **pre-market approval** from the FDA, except for color additives, which must be tested and approved for safety.

Cosmetic manufacturers are responsible for ensuring that their products are safe for use and properly labeled. The **FDA's Center for Food Safety and Applied Nutrition (CFSAN)** monitors cosmetics once they are on the market, focusing on compliance with **Good Manufacturing Practices (GMP),** accurate labeling, and the prevention of **misleading claims.** In **2021,** the FDA received over **5,000 reports** of adverse reactions related to cosmetics, which led to several product recalls and safety investigations.

One of the FDA's key regulatory tools is the **Voluntary Cosmetic Registration Program (VCRP),** which allows manufacturers and distributors to register their cosmetic products with the FDA. While registration is not mandatory, it helps the FDA monitor cosmetics for safety issues and ensure compliance with labeling and ingredient standards.

European Union

In the **European Union (EU),** cosmetics are regulated under **Regulation (EC) No 1223/2009,** which establishes a harmonized framework for the **safety, marketing,** and **labeling** of cosmetic products across all EU member states. The **European Medicines Agency (EMA)** and the **European Commission** oversee the enforcement of this regulation, which requires cosmetics to undergo a thorough **safety assessment** before they are marketed.

Under the EU regulation, manufacturers must ensure that each cosmetic product is evaluated by a qualified **safety assessor** who reviews the product's ingredients, formulation, and potential risks to consumers. The **Product Information File (PIF)** must contain details about the cosmetic's formulation, including data on its **toxicity, stability,** and any relevant clinical or dermatological studies. In **2022**, the EU market for cosmetics reached over **€80 billion**, with manufacturers required to comply with these stringent regulations to ensure product safety.

Cosmetics in the EU are also subject to strict **labeling requirements**, including the listing of all ingredients in descending order by weight. The **International Nomenclature of Cosmetic Ingredients (INCI)** system is used to standardize ingredient names, ensuring that consumers across the EU can understand the contents of cosmetic products. Additionally, the regulation bans the use of over **1,300 substances** in cosmetics, including certain colorants, preservatives, and fragrances that pose health risks.

India

In **India**, cosmetics are regulated under the **Drugs and Cosmetics Act of 1940** and the **Drugs and Cosmetics Rules of 1945**. The **Central Drugs Standard Control Organization (CDSCO)**, under the **Ministry of Health and Family Welfare**, is responsible for overseeing the import, manufacture, and sale of cosmetics in the country. While cosmetics in India do not require **pre-market approval**, manufacturers must comply with **Good Manufacturing Practices (GMP)**, and all cosmetic products must be **registered** with the CDSCO before they can be imported or sold in the market.

India's regulatory framework places a strong emphasis on **product safety** and **labeling**. Cosmetic products must be labeled with the **name and address of the manufacturer**, a **batch number, date of manufacture**, and **expiry date**. Additionally, **imported cosmetics** must include the name and address of the importer. In **2021**, India imported over **$2 billion worth** of cosmetics, reflecting the country's growing demand for beauty and personal care products.

India also prohibits the use of **certain harmful substances** in cosmetics, aligning its regulations with international standards. For instance, the use of **lead, mercury**, and **arsenic** in cosmetic products is strictly banned. The **CDSCO** regularly inspects manufacturing facilities to ensure compliance with safety standards and conducts market surveillance to detect any substandard or unsafe products.

Japan

In **Japan**, cosmetics are regulated by the **Pharmaceuticals and Medical Devices Agency (PMDA)**, under the **Ministry of Health, Labour and Welfare (MHLW)**. The **Pharmaceutical Affairs Law** governs the safety, manufacturing, and sale of cosmetics, with specific requirements for both

general cosmetics and **quasi-drugs. Quasi-drugs** are a category of products that have mild therapeutic effects, such as **whitening agents, anti-dandruff shampoos**, and **sunscreens**. These products are subject to more stringent regulations than general cosmetics and require approval from the **PMDA** before they can be marketed.

Japan's regulatory framework for cosmetics emphasizes **product safety** and **consumer protection**. Manufacturers are required to provide detailed information on the **ingredients, manufacturing process**, and **quality control** measures for each product. All cosmetics must be manufactured in compliance with **Good Manufacturing Practices (GMP)**, and the **PMDA** conducts regular **inspections** of manufacturing facilities to ensure adherence to these standards.

In terms of **labeling**, Japanese cosmetics must include the **product name, ingredients, directions for use**, and **warnings** about any potential side effects. Labels must be in **Japanese**, ensuring that consumers can easily understand the product information. In **2021**, Japan's cosmetics market was valued at over **¥3 trillion**, making it one of the largest markets for beauty and personal care products in the world.

Brazil

In **Brazil**, the regulation of cosmetics is overseen by the **National Health Surveillance Agency (ANVISA)**. Brazil's regulatory framework classifies cosmetics into two categories:

- **Grade 1**: Products with low risk and simple claims.
- **Grade 2**: Products with specific therapeutic claims, which require more rigorous testing.

All cosmetics sold in Brazil must be registered with ANVISA, and products in **Grade 2** must undergo a **safety evaluation** before being approved. In **2021**, Brazil's cosmetic market generated over **$30 billion** in revenue, reflecting its strong demand for beauty products. Brazilian law also mandates that cosmetic products be manufactured in compliance with **GMP** standards, and ANVISA conducts **inspections** of manufacturing facilities to ensure adherence to these standards.

11.5 Labeling and Packaging Requirements for Drugs and Cosmetics

The **labeling and packaging requirements** for **drugs** and **cosmetics** are fundamental components of regulatory frameworks worldwide, aimed at ensuring the **safety, quality**, and **effective use** of these products by consumers. Proper labeling and packaging not only provide essential information but also play a crucial role in preventing misuse, ensuring product integrity, and enhancing consumer trust. Regulatory authorities such as the U.S. **Food and Drug Administration (FDA)**, **European Medicines Agency (EMA)**, and **Central Drugs Standard Control Organization (CDSCO)** in India have established stringent guidelines that manufacturers must adhere to when designing labels and packaging for their products.

Labeling Requirements for Drugs

Drugs are subject to rigorous labeling requirements to ensure that consumers and healthcare professionals have access to accurate and comprehensive information. In the **United States**, the **FDA** mandates that drug labels include the **drug's name**, **active and inactive ingredients**, **dosage instructions**, **indications for use**, **contraindications**, **warnings and precautions**, **side effects**, and **storage conditions**. Additionally, the **FDA** requires the inclusion of a **Boxed Warning** for drugs that carry significant risks, ensuring that these warnings are prominently displayed to alert users.

In the **European Union**, the **EMA** oversees labeling requirements under the **EU Cosmetics Regulation (EC) No 1223/2009** and the **Directive 2001/83/EC** for medicinal products. Labels must include the **name of the medicinal product**, **active substances**, **manufacturer's details**, **batch number**, **expiry date**, and **storage instructions**. The **Summary of Product Characteristics (SmPC)** provides detailed information on the drug's properties and is accessible to healthcare professionals.

India'sCDSCO requires that drug labels contain the **brand name**, **generic name**, **strength**, **manufacturer's name and address**, **batch number**, **expiry date**, **dosage form**, and **usage instructions**. For prescription drugs, additional information such as **prescribing information** and **patient counseling information** must be included to guide healthcare providers and patients in the safe use of the medication.

Packaging Requirements for Drugs

Packaging plays a vital role in protecting drugs from environmental factors such as **light, moisture,** and **temperature fluctuations**, which can affect the drug's efficacy and safety. Regulatory bodies mandate that packaging materials meet specific standards to ensure product integrity. In the **U.S.**, the **FDA** requires that drug packaging undergo **Good Manufacturing Practices (GMP)** inspections to verify compliance with quality standards. **Tamper-evident packaging** is also mandated for many prescription drugs to prevent unauthorized access and ensure that the product has not been compromised before reaching the consumer.

The **EMA** enforces similar packaging standards within the **EU**, emphasizing the need for **child-resistant packaging** for certain medications to prevent accidental ingestion by children. Packaging must also facilitate easy **disposal** and **recycling**, aligning with environmental sustainability goals.

In **India**, the **CDSCO** stipulates that drug packaging must be **child-resistant** where necessary and must protect the drug from contamination and degradation. Packaging must also be designed to display all required labeling information clearly and legibly in **Hindi** and **English**, ensuring that consumers can easily understand the instructions and warnings.

Labeling Requirements for Cosmetics

Cosmetics are regulated to ensure that consumers receive accurate information about the products they use, promoting safe and informed usage. In the **U.S.**, the **FDA** requires cosmetic labels to include the **product name, net quantity of contents, ingredients** listed in descending order by weight, **manufacturer's name and address**, and **usage instructions** where applicable. For products with potential allergens, **ingredient warnings** must be clearly stated to inform sensitive individuals.

The **EU Cosmetics Regulation** mandates that all cosmetic products sold within the EU must have labels in the **official language(s)** of the member state where the product is marketed. Labels must include the **name and address of the responsible person, ingredients** following the International Nomenclature of Cosmetic Ingredients (INCI) system, **batch number, expiry date** or **period after opening (PAO)**, and **warnings** if necessary.

India'sCDSCO requires cosmetic labels to be in **Hindi** and **English**, including the **product name, manufacturer's details, net quantity, ingredients**, and any **safety warnings**. Labels must also provide clear **usage instructions** and indicate whether the product is a **general cosmetic** or a **quasi-drug**, which includes products with mild therapeutic effects.

Packaging Requirements for Cosmetics

Effective **packaging** for cosmetics ensures product protection, maintains **aesthetic appeal**, and provides a positive user experience. Packaging must prevent **contamination, theft**, and **misuse**. In the **U.S.**, the **FDA** mandates that cosmetic packaging materials are safe for their intended use and do not interact negatively with the product. **Tamper-evident packaging** is encouraged for products that require additional security, such as those containing **active ingredients** that could cause adverse effects if mishandled.

The **EU** emphasizes **environmentally friendly packaging**, encouraging the use of **recyclable materials** and minimizing **packaging waste**. Cosmetic packaging must also be designed to protect the product from **external factors** like **light** and **humidity**, which can degrade the product's quality.

In **India**, cosmetic packaging must comply with **GMP** standards, ensuring that the materials used are non-reactive and suitable for cosmetic use. Packaging must also include **clear labeling**, making it easy for consumers to identify and understand the product's purpose and usage instructions.

Global Harmonization and Challenges

While there is a push towards **global harmonization** of labeling and packaging standards through organizations like the **ICH** and **WHO**, significant challenges remain due to varying regional regulations and cultural differences. Manufacturers operating in multiple markets must navigate these diverse requirements, ensuring compliance to avoid **regulatory penalties** and maintain **market access**.

One major challenge is ensuring that labeling information is accurately translated and culturally appropriate for different regions. Misinterpretation or mistranslation can lead to **misuse** and **health risks**. Additionally, the rise of **e-commerce** has introduced new complexities in packaging, as products are often shipped internationally, necessitating adherence to multiple regulatory standards simultaneously.

11.6 Post-Marketing Surveillance and Pharmacovigilance

Post-marketing surveillance and **pharmacovigilance** are essential components of the drug and cosmetic regulatory frameworks, designed to ensure the continued safety, efficacy, and quality of products after they have been approved and are available in the market. While pre-market evaluations through clinical trials provide initial data on a product's performance, it is during the post-marketing phase that real-world use can reveal additional information about potential **adverse effects, drug interactions,** and long-term safety issues that were not fully apparent during the initial approval process. Regulatory authorities such as the **U.S. Food and Drug Administration (FDA), European Medicines Agency (EMA), Central Drugs Standard Control Organization (CDSCO)** in India, and the **Pharmaceuticals and Medical Devices Agency (PMDA)** in Japan have established robust **pharmacovigilance systems** to monitor and evaluate the safety of drugs and cosmetics continuously.

In the **United States**, the **FDA** operates the **Adverse Event Reporting System (FAERS)**, which collects data on adverse drug reactions (ADRs) from healthcare professionals, consumers, and manufacturers. In **2022**, FAERS received over **1.5 million ADR reports**, leading to several high-profile safety alerts and product recalls. The FDA also mandates that pharmaceutical companies conduct **post-marketing studies** and **risk management plans (RMPs)** to further investigate the safety profiles of their products. These studies help in identifying rare or long-term side effects and in updating **safety labeling** to inform both healthcare providers and patients.

Similarly, the **European Medicines Agency (EMA)** oversees **pharmacovigilance** through the **EudraVigilance** system, which gathers information on adverse reactions from all **27 EU member states**. In **2022**, EudraVigilance processed over **2 million ADR reports**, facilitating the swift identification of safety signals and enabling the EMA to take necessary regulatory actions such as updating product information or initiating market withdrawals when needed. The EMA also collaborates with national regulatory authorities to ensure a harmonized approach to drug safety across Europe.

In **India**, the **Pharmacovigilance Programme of India (PvPI)**, managed by the **CDSCO**, plays a pivotal role in monitoring the safety of drugs post-approval. The PvPI collects ADR reports through a network of **advisory committees** and **pharmacovigilance centers** distributed across the country. In **2022**, PvPI received over **100,000 ADR reports**, prompting regulatory actions including safety warnings and product recalls for several widely used medications. The program emphasizes the importance of **public awareness** and **healthcare professional training** to enhance the reporting and management of ADRs.

The **Pharmaceuticals and Medical Devices Agency (PMDA)** in **Japan** utilizes the **Japanese Adverse Drug Event Report (JADER)** database to collect and analyze ADR data. In **2021**, JADER recorded over **20,000 ADR reports**, leading to significant updates in safety information and the withdrawal of certain high-risk products from the market. The PMDA also requires pharmaceutical companies to implement comprehensive **pharmacovigilance systems** and submit regular **Periodic Safety Update Reports (PSURs)** to ensure ongoing monitoring of their products' safety profiles.

Post-marketing surveillance extends beyond pharmaceuticals to include **cosmetics**, where **safety** and **quality** remain paramount. In the **EU**, the **Cosmetic Products Notification Portal (CPNP)** allows manufacturers to notify authorities about cosmetic products before they enter the market, facilitating early detection of safety issues. In **Brazil, ANVISA** mandates that cosmetic products undergo continuous safety evaluations and report any adverse effects, ensuring that products remain safe for consumer use.

Despite the advancements in pharmacovigilance, challenges persist, including underreporting of ADRs, data management issues, and the need for global harmonization of safety standards. Efforts to address these challenges involve leveraging **technology** such as **big data analytics** and **artificial intelligence** to enhance the detection and analysis of safety signals. Additionally, international collaboration through organizations like the **World Health Organization (WHO)** and the **International Council for Harmonisation (ICH)** aims to unify pharmacovigilance practices, ensuring that drug safety information is shared and acted upon globally.

Regulatory Aspects of Herbals and Biologicals

Herbal medicines and biological products have unique regulatory requirements due to their complex nature and growing demand in global markets. This chapter provides a comprehensive overview of the **regulatory frameworks** governing these products, focusing on their **quality, safety, and efficacy**.

For herbal medicines, the chapter discusses the **regulatory requirements** that vary by country, addressing issues such as **standardization, adulteration**, and the **labeling** of herbal products. With the increasing global interest in natural and alternative therapies, regulatory agencies have developed stringent guidelines to ensure that these products are safe for consumption and meet quality standards. The chapter emphasizes the need for **good agricultural practices (GAP)** and **good manufacturing practices (GMP)** to ensure the integrity of herbal medicines from cultivation to distribution.

In the realm of biological products, the chapter covers the **development and approval of biosimilars**, a rapidly expanding field in pharmaceutical sciences. It delves into the complexities of **stability testing, safety assessments**, and the stringent regulatory requirements needed to ensure the safety and effectiveness of biological therapies. Professionals involved in the production and regulation of herbal and biological products will find this chapter essential for understanding the global standards and regulatory frameworks that govern these sectors.

12.1 Regulatory Requirements for Herbal Medicine

The **regulatory requirements for herbal medicine** are essential to ensure that these products are safe, effective, and of high quality before they reach consumers. Herbal medicines, derived from plants or plant extracts, are widely used for their therapeutic benefits in various cultures. However, unlike conventional pharmaceuticals, herbal medicines often lack standardized regulations, leading to variations in quality and efficacy. Regulatory authorities across different countries have established specific guidelines and frameworks to address these challenges, ensuring that herbal medicines meet the necessary standards for public health protection.

United States

In the **United States**, herbal medicines are regulated by the **U.S. Food and Drug Administration (FDA)** under the **Dietary Supplement Health and Education Act (DSHEA) of 1994**. Under DSHEA, herbal supplements are classified as **dietary supplements** rather than conventional drugs. This classification means that herbal products do not require **pre-market approval** by the FDA. However, manufacturers are responsible for ensuring that their products are **safe** and that their **labeling** is truthful and not misleading.

Herbal supplement manufacturers must comply with **Good Manufacturing Practices (GMP)** as outlined in **21 CFR Part 111**, which ensures that products are consistently produced and controlled according to quality standards. The FDA conducts **inspections** of manufacturing facilities to verify compliance with GMP. In **2022**, the FDA inspected over **200 dietary supplement facilities**, focusing on the quality control measures in place to prevent contamination and ensure product consistency.

Additionally, the FDA monitors the market for any **adverse event reports** related to herbal supplements through the **MedWatch** program. Consumers and healthcare professionals can report any negative effects, allowing the FDA to take necessary actions such as issuing **warnings** or **recalls** if a product is found to be unsafe.

European Union

In the **European Union (EU)**, herbal medicines are regulated under the **Traditional Herbal Medicinal Products Directive (THMPD) 2004/24/EC**. This directive provides a streamlined pathway for the registration of herbal medicines that have a well-established history of safe use. To qualify for registration, herbal products must demonstrate a **traditional use** of at least **30 years**, including **15 years** within the EU.

Herbal medicines in the EU must undergo a **registration process** that includes a comprehensive **benefit-risk assessment** conducted by the **European Medicines Agency (EMA)**. The **Herbal Medicinal Products Committee (HMPC)** within the EMA evaluates the safety, quality, and efficacy data provided by manufacturers. In **2021**, the EMA reviewed over **100 herbal medicinal product applications,** ensuring that only those with proven safety and traditional use were approved for the market.

Moreover, herbal products must comply with strict **labeling requirements**, including the listing of all **active ingredients, recommended dosages**, and **usage instructions** in the official language(s) of the member state where the product is sold. The EU also emphasizes the importance of **Good Manufacturing Practices (GMP)** to maintain the quality and consistency of herbal medicines.

India

In **India**, herbal medicines are regulated by the **Ministry of AYUSH (Ayurveda, Yoga & Naturopathy, Unani, Siddha, and Homoeopathy)** under the **Drugs and Cosmetics Act of 1940** and the **Drugs and Cosmetics Rules of 1945**. The Ministry of AYUSH oversees the **registration, manufacturing, import**, and **sale** of herbal medicines to ensure they meet the required standards of safety and efficacy.

Herbal product manufacturers in India must obtain a **license** from the Ministry of AYUSH, demonstrating compliance with **Good Manufacturing Practices (GMP)** as specified in **Schedule T** of the Drugs and Cosmetics Rules. Schedule T outlines the guidelines for the preparation of herbal formulations, ensuring that products are free from contaminants and accurately labeled with **ingredient information** and **dosage instructions**.

In **2022**, the Ministry of AYUSH approved over **500 new herbal formulations,** reflecting the growing demand for traditional medicine in India. The regulatory framework also mandates that manufacturers conduct **stability testing** to determine the shelf life of herbal products and ensure their **potency** over time.

Post-marketing surveillance is another critical aspect of India's regulatory requirements. The **Central Drugs Standard Control Organization (CDSCO)** monitors the safety of herbal medicines through the **Pharmacovigilance Programme of India (PvPI)**, collecting and analyzing **adverse event reports** to identify and mitigate potential risks associated with herbal products.

China

In **China**, herbal medicines are regulated by the **National Medical Products Administration (NMPA)**, formerly known as the **China Food and Drug Administration (CFDA)**. China has a long history of using herbal medicines, known as **Traditional Chinese Medicine (TCM)**, which are integrated into the national healthcare system.

The **registration process** for herbal medicines in China involves submitting a detailed **registration dossier** to the NMPA, which includes information on the **botanical identification, preclinical studies, clinical trials**, and **Good Manufacturing Practices (GMP)** compliance. Herbal products must demonstrate **safety, efficacy**, and **quality** through rigorous testing and evaluation.

In **2021**, the NMPA approved over **1,000 new TCM formulations**, emphasizing the importance of traditional knowledge combined with modern scientific validation. The NMPA also conducts regular **inspections** of manufacturing facilities to ensure adherence to GMP standards and prevent the production of adulterated or substandard herbal medicines.

Post-marketing surveillance in China is conducted through the **China Adverse Drug Reaction Monitoring System (CADRMS)**, which collects and analyzes reports of **adverse reactions** to herbal medicines. This system enables the NMPA to identify and address any safety concerns promptly, ensuring that herbal products remain safe for consumer use.

Brazil

In **Brazil**, herbal medicines are regulated by the **Agência Nacional de Vigilância Sanitária (ANVISA)** under the **Brazilian Health Regulatory Agency**. ANVISA classifies herbal medicines as **medicinal plants** and **traditional herbal medicines**, subjecting them to specific regulatory requirements to ensure their safety and efficacy.

Herbal products must undergo a **registration process** that includes the submission of a comprehensive **dossier** containing information on the **botanical sources, pharmacological properties, clinical evidence**, and **Good Manufacturing Practices (GMP)** compliance. ANVISA evaluates these dossiers through its **Technical Evaluation Committee (CTEC)**, which assesses the quality and safety data provided by manufacturers.

In **2022**, ANVISA approved over **300 new herbal medicinal products**, supporting the integration of traditional medicine into Brazil's healthcare system. The agency also enforces strict **labeling requirements**, mandating that all herbal products include detailed **ingredient lists, usage instructions, warnings**, and **manufacturer information** in **Portuguese**.

Post-marketing surveillance in Brazil is facilitated by the **National Pharmacovigilance System**, which monitors the safety of herbal medicines through the collection of **adverse event reports**. ANVISA collaborates with healthcare professionals and consumers to identify and mitigate any potential risks associated with herbal products.

Global Harmonization and Challenges

While regulatory frameworks for herbal medicines are becoming more standardized, significant challenges remain in achieving **global harmonization**. These challenges include variations in regulatory standards, differences in traditional practices, and the need for **scientific validation** of herbal therapies. Efforts by international organizations such as the **World Health Organization (WHO)** and the **International Council for Harmonisation (ICH)** aim to bridge these gaps by promoting **standardized guidelines** and **best practices** for the regulation of herbal medicines.

One of the primary challenges in regulating herbal medicines is ensuring the **quality and consistency** of herbal products, given the natural variability of plant sources. Implementing **Good Agricultural and Collection Practices (GACP)** alongside GMP can help address these issues by standardizing the cultivation and harvesting processes of medicinal plants.

Another challenge is the **integration of traditional knowledge** with modern scientific methods. Regulatory authorities must balance respect for traditional practices with the need for **rigorous scientific evidence** to support the safety and efficacy of herbal medicines. This integration is crucial for gaining consumer trust and ensuring that herbal products provide genuine therapeutic benefits.

Conclusion

The **regulatory requirements for herbal medicines** are designed to ensure that these products are safe, effective, and of high quality for consumer use. While different countries have developed their own regulatory frameworks based on their unique cultural and healthcare contexts, there is a growing trend towards **harmonization** of standards through international collaboration. By adhering to **Good Manufacturing Practices (GMP)**, conducting thorough **safety and efficacy evaluations**, and implementing robust **post-marketing surveillance**, regulatory authorities worldwide are working to protect public health and promote the safe use of herbal medicines. As the global market for herbal products continues to expand, ongoing efforts to standardize regulations and integrate traditional knowledge with modern science will be essential in addressing the challenges and ensuring the continued growth and acceptance of herbal medicines.

12.2 Quality, Safety, and Efficacy of Herbal Products

Ensuring the **quality, safety,** and **efficacy** of **herbal products** is paramount for regulatory authorities and manufacturers alike. Herbal medicines, derived from natural sources such as plants, herbs, and botanicals, offer therapeutic benefits that have been utilized for centuries in various traditional medicine systems. However, the inherent variability in plant materials and the complexity of their active constituents present unique challenges in maintaining consistent quality and ensuring safety and efficacy. Regulatory frameworks across different countries have been established to address these challenges, implementing stringent standards and guidelines to protect consumers and promote the effective use of herbal medicines.

Quality Assurance in Herbal Products

Quality assurance of herbal products begins with the **standardization of raw materials**. This process involves the identification and authentication of plant species to prevent adulteration and ensure that the correct botanical ingredients are used. Techniques such as **DNA barcoding** and **chromatographic profiling** are employed to verify the authenticity of herbal ingredients. In **India**, the **Central Drugs Standard Control Organization (CDSCO)** mandates that herbal manufacturers adhere to **Good Manufacturing Practices (GMP)**, which include stringent controls over the sourcing, harvesting, and processing of herbal materials. Similarly, in the **European Union (EU)**, the **European Medicines Agency (EMA)** requires herbal products to comply with the **Traditional Herbal Medicinal Products Directive (THMPD) 2004/24/EC**, which emphasizes the importance of standardized extraction methods and quality control measures.

Consistency in **active ingredient concentration** is another critical aspect of quality assurance. Herbal products must contain a defined amount of active constituents to ensure their therapeutic efficacy. **High-Performance Liquid Chromatography (HPLC)** and **Mass Spectrometry (MS)** are commonly used analytical techniques to quantify active compounds and monitor batch-to-batch variability. For instance, in **China**, the **National Medical Products Administration (NMPA)** requires detailed analytical data in the drug registration dossier, ensuring that each batch of herbal medicine meets the specified quality standards.

Safety Evaluation of Herbal Products

The **safety** of herbal products is assessed through comprehensive evaluations that include both preclinical and clinical studies. **Preclinical**

studies involve **in vitro** and **in vivo** testing to identify potential toxicities, pharmacokinetic profiles, and interactions with other substances. These studies are essential for detecting any harmful effects that could arise from the use of herbal medicines. In **Brazil**, the **National Health Surveillance Agency (ANVISA)** mandates that herbal products undergo rigorous safety assessments before they are approved for market release. This includes testing for **heavy metals, pesticide residues**, and **microbial contamination** to ensure that the products are free from harmful substances.

Clinical trials are conducted to evaluate the **efficacy** and **safety** of herbal medicines in human populations. These trials are designed to provide evidence of the therapeutic benefits of herbal products while monitoring for any adverse effects. In **Japan**, the **Pharmaceuticals and Medical Devices Agency (PMDA)** requires that clinical trials for herbal medicines adhere to the **Good Clinical Practice (GCP)** guidelines, ensuring that the trials are ethically conducted and scientifically valid. The results of these trials are crucial for supporting the claims made about the herbal product's benefits and for obtaining **marketing authorization**.

Efficacy of Herbal Products

The **efficacy** of herbal products is demonstrated through well-designed **clinical studies** that assess their therapeutic effects on specific health conditions. **Randomized Controlled Trials (RCTs)** are considered the gold standard for evaluating the efficacy of herbal medicines, providing robust data on their effectiveness compared to placebos or standard treatments. For example, in **India**, numerous studies have been conducted to validate the efficacy of **Ashwagandha** in reducing stress and anxiety, showing significant improvements in patient outcomes compared to control groups.

In the **European Union**, the **EMA's HMPC** conducts scientific assessments of traditional herbal medicinal products, evaluating the evidence supporting their efficacy based on traditional use and available clinical data. This dual approach ensures that herbal products not only have a long history of use but also meet modern scientific standards for efficacy. In **2022**, the HMPC approved several herbal medicines for the treatment of **digestive disorders** and **respiratory conditions**, based on strong evidence from clinical studies and traditional usage data.

Regulatory Challenges and Global Harmonization

Despite advancements in regulatory frameworks, several **challenges** persist in ensuring the quality, safety, and efficacy of herbal products. One major challenge is the **standardization of herbal extracts**, as natural variability in plant materials can lead to inconsistencies in active ingredient concentrations. Additionally, the **lack of comprehensive clinical data** for many traditional herbal medicines poses difficulties in demonstrating their efficacy to meet regulatory standards.

Global harmonization efforts, spearheaded by organizations such as the **World Health Organization (WHO)** and the **International Council for Harmonisation (ICH)**, aim to bridge these gaps by developing standardized guidelines for the regulation of herbal medicines. The **WHO's Guidelines on Good Agricultural and Collection Practices (GACP)** and the **ICH's Q3D Guideline on Elemental Impurities** provide valuable frameworks for ensuring the quality and safety of herbal products. These initiatives promote the adoption of consistent standards across different regions, facilitating international trade and enhancing consumer trust in herbal medicines.

Conclusion

The **quality**, **safety**, and **efficacy** of herbal products are critical factors that determine their acceptance and success in the global market. Regulatory authorities around the world have established comprehensive frameworks to address the unique challenges posed by herbal medicines, ensuring that these products are safe, effective, and of high quality. Through the implementation of **Good Manufacturing Practices (GMP)**, rigorous **safety evaluations**, and robust **clinical studies**, the pharmaceutical industry can uphold the standards necessary to protect public health and promote the beneficial use of herbal medicines. Continued efforts towards **global harmonization** and the integration of traditional knowledge with modern scientific methodologies will further enhance the regulatory landscape for herbal products, fostering their safe and effective use worldwide.

12.3 Regulatory Framework for Biological Products

The **regulatory framework for biological products** is a critical component in ensuring that these advanced therapies are safe, effective, and of high quality before they reach patients. Biological products, which include **biologics, vaccines, gene therapies**, and **cell therapies**, are derived from living organisms and often involve complex manufacturing processes. Due to their intricate nature and the potential for significant therapeutic benefits, regulatory authorities around the world have established stringent guidelines and procedures to oversee their development, approval, and post-marketing surveillance.

United States

In the **United States**, the **U.S. Food and Drug Administration (FDA)** is the primary regulatory authority responsible for the oversight of biological products. The FDA regulates biologics under the **Public Health Service Act** and the **Federal Food, Drug, and Cosmetic Act (FD&C Act)**. The **Center for Biologics Evaluation and Research (CBER)** within the FDA specifically handles the regulation of biologics, including vaccines, blood products, and gene therapies.

The **approval process** for biological products in the U.S. involves submitting a **Biologics License Application (BLA)**, which includes comprehensive data from **preclinical studies** and **clinical trials** demonstrating the product's **safety, efficacy,** and **quality**. In **2022**, the FDA approved over **50 new biologics**, reflecting the rapid advancements in biotechnology and the increasing demand for innovative therapies. The FDA also enforces **Good Manufacturing Practices (GMP)** for biologics to ensure consistent production quality and prevent contamination. Post-approval, biological products are subject to **post-marketing surveillance** through programs like the **Biologics Effectiveness and Safety (BEST)** system, which monitors adverse events and long-term safety outcomes.

European Union

In the **European Union (EU)**, the **European Medicines Agency (EMA)** oversees the regulation of biological products through its **Committee for Medicinal Products for Human Use (CHMP)**. The EMA employs a **centralized procedure** for the approval of biologics, allowing manufacturers to submit a single application for approval across all **27 EU member states**. This centralized approach streamlines the approval process and facilitates faster access to innovative therapies for patients across Europe.

Biological products in the EU must undergo a rigorous evaluation process, which includes the submission of a **Marketing Authorization Application (MAA)** containing detailed information on the product's **quality, preclinical** and **clinical** data, and **manufacturing processes**. In **2022**, the EMA approved over **40 new biologics**, including several breakthrough gene therapies and monoclonal antibodies for cancer treatment. The EMA also mandates **Good Manufacturing Practices (GMP)** compliance and conducts regular inspections of manufacturing facilities to ensure adherence to quality standards. Post-marketing, the EMA utilizes the **EudraVigilance** system to monitor the safety of biologics, collecting and analyzing data on adverse drug reactions to promptly address any emerging safety concerns.

Japan

In **Japan**, the **Pharmaceuticals and Medical Devices Agency (PMDA)** is the regulatory body responsible for the oversight of biological products. The PMDA operates under the **Ministry of Health, Labour and Welfare (MHLW)** and follows the **Pharmaceuticals and Medical Devices Act**. The approval process for biologics in Japan involves submitting a **New Drug Application (NDA)** for biologics, which includes extensive data from **clinical trials** demonstrating the product's **safety, efficacy**, and **quality**.

Japan has been at the forefront of **gene therapy** regulation, with the PMDA approving several advanced therapies in **2022**, including CAR-T cell therapies for cancer treatment. The PMDA enforces **Good Manufacturing Practices (GMP)** and conducts thorough **facility inspections** to ensure the integrity of the manufacturing process. Additionally, Japan has implemented **post-marketing surveillance** programs to continuously monitor the safety and effectiveness of biological products through the **Pharmacovigilance** system, collecting data on adverse events and long-term outcomes to inform regulatory decisions.

India

In **India**, the **Central Drugs Standard Control Organization (CDSCO)** under the **Ministry of Health and Family Welfare** regulates biological products. The regulatory framework for biologics in India is governed by the **Drugs and Cosmetics Act of 1940** and the **Drugs and Cosmetics Rules of 1945**, which have been updated to accommodate the complexities of biological products. The **Biologics and Genetic Medicines Authority (BGMA)**, a part of CDSCO, oversees the approval and regulation of biologics, including vaccines, blood products, and gene therapies.

The **approval process** in India requires the submission of a **Biologics License Application (BLA)**, which includes detailed **clinical trial data** and **manufacturing information** to demonstrate the product's **safety, efficacy, and quality**. In **2022**, CDSCO approved over **30 new biologics**, including vaccines for emerging infectious diseases and innovative gene therapies for genetic disorders. The CDSCO enforces **Good Manufacturing Practices (GMP)** for biologics, conducting regular **inspections** of manufacturing facilities to ensure compliance with quality standards. Post-approval, biological products in India are subject to **pharmacovigilance** through the **Pharmacovigilance Programme of India (PvPI)**, which monitors adverse events and ensures ongoing product safety.

China

In **China**, the **National Medical Products Administration (NMPA)** is the regulatory authority responsible for biological products. The NMPA, formerly known as the **China Food and Drug Administration (CFDA)**, oversees the regulation of biologics through the **Pharmaceutical Affairs Law**. The approval process for biological products in China involves submitting a **Biologics License Application (BLA)**, which includes comprehensive data from **preclinical** and **clinical trials**.

China has made significant strides in the regulation of **biologics**, particularly in areas such as **monoclonal antibodies** and **gene therapies**. In **2022**, the NMPA approved over **100 new biologics**, reflecting the country's growing emphasis on biopharmaceutical innovation. The NMPA enforces **Good Manufacturing Practices (GMP)** and conducts regular **facility inspections** to ensure that manufacturing processes meet stringent quality standards. Post-marketing, the NMPA utilizes the **China Adverse Drug Reaction Monitoring System (CADRMS)** to track the safety of biological products, collecting and analyzing data on adverse events to maintain ongoing product safety.

Global Harmonization and Challenges

Despite the advancements in regulatory frameworks for biological products, several **challenges** persist globally. The **complexity** of biologics, coupled with their intricate manufacturing processes, poses significant hurdles in ensuring consistent **quality** and **safety**. Additionally, the rapid pace of **biotechnological innovation** necessitates continuous updates to regulatory guidelines to keep pace with new developments.

Global harmonization efforts, spearheaded by organizations such as the **International Council for Harmonisation (ICH)** and the **World Health Organization (WHO)**, aim to unify regulatory standards across different regions. These efforts facilitate the **international approval** and **trade** of biological products, reducing duplication of regulatory efforts and accelerating access to innovative therapies worldwide. However, achieving harmonization remains challenging due to differences in **regulatory priorities, economic conditions**, and **healthcare infrastructure** among countries.

Conclusion

The **regulatory framework for biological products** is essential in ensuring that these advanced therapies are safe, effective, and of high quality for patient use. Regulatory authorities in the **United States**,

European Union, Japan, India, and **China** have established comprehensive guidelines and approval processes to oversee the development, manufacturing, and post-marketing surveillance of biologics. Despite ongoing challenges, global harmonization efforts continue to enhance the consistency and efficiency of biologics regulation, facilitating the widespread availability of life-saving therapies. As the field of biotechnology advances, regulatory frameworks will need to evolve accordingly, ensuring that biological products can meet the growing healthcare needs of populations worldwide while maintaining the highest standards of **safety, efficacy**, and **quality**.

12.4 Development and Approval of Biosimilars

The **development and approval of biosimilars** represent a significant advancement in the pharmaceutical industry, offering more affordable alternatives to original biologic therapies. **Biosimilars** are highly similar to an already approved **reference biologic product** in terms of **quality, safety**, and **efficacy**, with no clinically meaningful differences in their **molecular structure** or **biological activity**. The introduction of biosimilars into the market enhances patient access to essential biologic treatments while promoting competition and reducing healthcare costs. However, the development and approval process for biosimilars is inherently complex due to the intricate nature of biologic products and the stringent regulatory standards required to ensure their equivalence to reference products.

Development Process of Biosimilars

The **development of biosimilars** involves a comprehensive series of steps to demonstrate that the biosimilar product matches the reference biologic in terms of **structural characteristics, functional properties**, and **clinical performance**. The process begins with an extensive **comparative analytical assessment**, where the biosimilar is rigorously compared to the reference product using advanced **analytical techniques** such as **mass spectrometry, chromatography**, and **bioassays**. These analyses ensure that the biosimilar exhibits the same **molecular structure, post-translational modifications**, and **biological activity** as the reference biologic.

Following the analytical characterization, **preclinical studies** are conducted to evaluate the **toxicology** and **pharmacokinetics** of the biosimilar. These studies are essential for identifying any potential **immunogenicity** issues and ensuring that the biosimilar behaves similarly to the reference product in **animal models**. Successful preclinical results provide the foundation for proceeding to **clinical trials**.

Regulatory Requirements for Biosimilars

Regulatory authorities around the world have established specific **guidelines** and **requirements** for the approval of biosimilars to ensure their **safety, efficacy**, and **quality**. Key regulatory bodies, including the **U.S. Food and Drug Administration (FDA)**, the **European Medicines Agency (EMA)**, and the **Central Drugs Standard Control Organization (CDSCO)** in India, have developed comprehensive frameworks to evaluate biosimilar applications.

In the **United States**, the FDA regulates biosimilars under the **Biologics Price Competition and Innovation Act (BPCIA)** of 2009. The FDA requires that biosimilars demonstrate **biosimilarity** to the reference product through a combination of **analytical studies, preclinical studies**, and **clinical studies**. The approval pathway typically involves the submission of a **Biosimilar License Application (BLA)**, which includes detailed data supporting the biosimilar's similarity in terms of **structural and functional characteristics, clinical efficacy**, and **safety** profiles.

The **European Medicines Agency (EMA)** was the first major regulatory body to establish a comprehensive pathway for biosimilar approval in 2005. The EMA's guidelines emphasize the importance of **total comparability studies**, including **analytical characterization, non-clinical studies**, and **clinical trials** to demonstrate biosimilarity. The EMA also requires extensive **pharmacovigilance** plans to monitor the long-term safety and efficacy of approved biosimilars.

In **India**, the **CDSCO** regulates biosimilars under the **Drugs and Cosmetics Act of 1940** and the **Drugs and Cosmetics Rules of 1945**. The CDSCO requires that biosimilars undergo a series of **comparative studies** with the reference biologic, including **analytical, non-clinical, and clinical evaluations**. The approval process also mandates adherence to **Good Manufacturing Practices (GMP)** to ensure consistent quality and safety of the biosimilar product.

Approval Pathways and Clinical Trials

The **approval pathways** for biosimilars are designed to be **exhaustive yet efficient**, ensuring that biosimilars meet the same high standards as reference biologics while facilitating faster market entry compared to original biologic development. **Clinical trials** for biosimilars focus on demonstrating **equivalence** in **efficacy** and **safety** rather than establishing **novel therapeutic effects**.

In the **United States**, the FDA employs a **totality of the evidence** approach, integrating data from analytical, preclinical, and clinical studies to assess biosimilarity. **Phase I clinical trials** typically involve healthy volunteers to evaluate **pharmacokinetics** and **pharmacodynamics**, while **Phase III trials** assess **clinical efficacy** and **safety** in patients with the target condition. The FDA also requires a **comparability exercise** to evaluate any minor differences that may arise during the manufacturing process.

The **EMA** follows a similar approach, requiring **interchangeability** and **extrapolation** of indications to ensure that biosimilars can be used interchangeably with reference products across multiple therapeutic areas. The EMA's **extrapolation** principle allows biosimilars approved for one indication to be approved for other indications held by the reference product, provided that the biosimilarity has been demonstrated convincingly.

In **India**, biosimilar approval involves conducting **bioequivalence studies** and **clinical trials** to establish similarity in **efficacy** and **safety**. The CDSCO also emphasizes the importance of **post-marketing surveillance** to monitor the long-term safety of biosimilars and to gather real-world data on their performance.

Manufacturing and Quality Control

The **manufacturing process** for biosimilars is highly complex and must adhere to stringent **quality control** measures to ensure consistency and reproducibility. **Good Manufacturing Practices (GMP)** are critical in the production of biosimilars, as any variations in the manufacturing process can lead to differences in the final product's **molecular structure** and **biological activity**. Regulatory authorities mandate that biosimilar manufacturers implement robust **quality management systems** and conduct regular **inspections** to verify compliance with GMP standards.

Advanced **biotechnology techniques**, such as **recombinant DNA technology**, **cell culture processes**, and **bioreactor systems**, are employed to produce biosimilars. These technologies enable the precise control of **biological processes** and **production conditions**, ensuring that the biosimilar mirrors the reference product's characteristics as closely as possible.

Post-Approval Monitoring and Pharmacovigilance

Post-approval, biosimilars undergo continuous **monitoring** to ensure their **ongoing safety** and **efficacy** in the general population. **Pharmacovigilance** systems are established to collect and analyze data on

adverse drug reactions (ADRs) and other **safety concerns** that may emerge after the biosimilar is marketed. Regulatory authorities require manufacturers to submit **Periodic Safety Update Reports (PSURs)** and engage in **active surveillance** to promptly identify and address any potential risks associated with the biosimilar.

In the **United States**, the FDA's **Biologics Effectiveness and Safety (BEST)** system plays a pivotal role in monitoring biosimilars post-approval. Similarly, the **EMA's EudraVigilance** system collects ADR data across the EU, enabling the EMA to take swift regulatory actions if necessary. In **India**, the **Pharmacovigilance Programme of India (PvPI)** monitors the safety of biosimilars through the collection and analysis of ADR reports, ensuring that any emerging safety issues are promptly addressed.

Market and Economic Considerations

The **market introduction** of biosimilars has significant **economic implications** for the healthcare system. Biosimilars offer a more **cost-effective** alternative to expensive biologic therapies, potentially reducing healthcare costs and increasing **access** to essential treatments for patients. The **global biosimilars market** was valued at approximately **$10 billion** in **2021** and is projected to grow rapidly, driven by increasing demand for biologic therapies and the expiration of patents for several high-cost biologics.

In regions such as the **European Union** and **United States**, the entry of biosimilars has led to **price reductions** and **increased competition** among manufacturers, encouraging innovation and improving market dynamics. In **India**, the approval and widespread use of biosimilars have positioned the country as a significant player in the global biosimilars market, with a robust domestic production capacity and a growing export market.

Challenges and Future Directions

Despite the promising prospects of biosimilars, several **challenges** persist in their development and approval. These include the **high cost** of development, the complexity of manufacturing processes, and the need for extensive **clinical data** to demonstrate biosimilarity. Additionally, **intellectual property** issues and **market exclusivity** periods for reference biologics can impact the entry and competitiveness of biosimilars.

Looking ahead, advancements in **biotechnology** and **manufacturing technologies** are expected to streamline the development process for biosimilars, reducing costs and accelerating time-to-market. Regulatory bodies are also working towards further **harmonization** of biosimilar guidelines globally, facilitating easier market access and fostering international collaboration. As the biosimilars market continues to expand, ongoing efforts to address regulatory, economic, and scientific challenges will be crucial in realizing the full potential of biosimilars in improving global healthcare outcomes.

Conclusion

The **development and approval of biosimilars** are integral to the advancement of modern medicine, offering affordable alternatives to high-cost biologic therapies and enhancing patient access to essential treatments. Through rigorous **development processes**, adherence to **regulatory requirements**, and robust **post-marketing surveillance**, biosimilars ensure that patients receive safe, effective, and high-quality therapies. As the global biosimilars market continues to grow, ongoing efforts towards **regulatory harmonization**, **technological innovation**, and **economic optimization** will be essential in maximizing the benefits of biosimilars for patients worldwide.

12.5 Stability and Safety Testing of Biologicals

Ensuring the **stability** and **safety** of **biological products** is paramount in the pharmaceutical industry, as these products are derived from living organisms and are inherently more complex than traditional chemical drugs. **Stability testing** assesses how the quality of a biological product varies with time under the influence of various environmental factors such as **temperature, humidity,** and **light exposure.** This testing is crucial to determine the **shelf life** of the product and to ensure that it maintains its **efficacy** and **safety** throughout its intended storage period.

In the **United States,** the **FDA's Center for Biologics Evaluation and Research (CBER)** mandates rigorous stability testing protocols for all biological products. Manufacturers must conduct **accelerated stability studies** under elevated temperature and humidity conditions to predict the product's behavior over time. Additionally, **real-time stability studies** are performed under recommended storage conditions to validate the product's **expiry date.** In **2022,** the FDA updated its **guidelines** to include more comprehensive testing for **biosimilars,** ensuring that these products meet the same stability standards as their reference biologics.

Safety testing involves evaluating the biological product for any potential **adverse effects** that could arise from its use. This includes **toxicity studies, immunogenicity assessments,** and **pharmacovigilance** activities post-approval. In **India,** the **Central Drugs Standard Control Organization**

(CDSCO) requires that all biological products undergo extensive safety evaluations during both the **preclinical** and **clinical** phases. In **2021**, over **500 biological products** were subjected to comprehensive safety testing, ensuring that they meet the stringent standards set by regulatory authorities.

Advanced **analytical techniques** such as **High-Performance Liquid Chromatography (HPLC)**, **Mass Spectrometry (MS)**, and **Enzyme-Linked Immunosorbent Assay (ELISA)** are employed to monitor the stability and safety of biologicals. These techniques enable precise measurement of **active ingredient concentrations**, **degradation products**, and **immune responses**, providing detailed insights into the product's performance over time. For instance, in **Japan**, the **Pharmaceuticals and Medical Devices Agency (PMDA)** utilizes **biophysical characterization** methods to assess the structural integrity of biologics, ensuring that any **degradation** does not compromise the product's therapeutic effects.

Furthermore, **post-marketing surveillance** plays a crucial role in continuously monitoring the **safety** of biological products once they are available to the public. Systems such as the **FDA's Biologics Effectiveness and Safety (BEST)** program and **India's Pharmacovigilance Programme of India (PvPI)** collect and analyze data on **adverse drug reactions (ADRs)**, enabling regulatory bodies to take prompt action if any safety concerns arise. In **2022**, the BEST program received over **50,000 ADR reports**, leading to several **safety alerts** and **product recalls** to protect public health.

In conclusion, the **stability and safety testing** of **biologicals** is a multifaceted process that involves rigorous **preclinical** and **clinical** evaluations, advanced **analytical methods**, and continuous **post-marketing surveillance**. These measures ensure that biological products remain **safe**, **effective**, and of high **quality** throughout their lifecycle, thereby safeguarding consumer health and maintaining the integrity of the pharmaceutical market.

12.6 Labeling and Packaging Requirements for Herbal and Biological Products

The **labeling and packaging requirements** for **herbal** and **biological products** are critical components of their regulatory frameworks, designed to ensure that consumers receive accurate information and that the products are protected from contamination and degradation. Proper labeling and packaging not only facilitate the correct usage of these products but also play a vital role in maintaining their **quality** and **safety**.

Labeling Requirements for Herbal Products

Herbal products must adhere to specific **labeling regulations** to provide clear and comprehensive information to consumers. In the **United States,** the **FDA** mandates that herbal supplements include a **Supplement Facts panel** that lists all **active and inactive ingredients, dosage instructions, usage recommendations,** and **warnings** where applicable. Labels must also display the **manufacturer's name and address,** ensuring transparency and accountability. In **2021,** the FDA implemented stricter labeling guidelines to prevent **misleading claims** and to ensure that consumers are fully informed about the products they are using.

In the **European Union (EU),** the **EMA** requires that herbal products follow the **Traditional Herbal Medicinal Products Directive (THMPD) 2004/24/EC,** which stipulates that labels must include the **product name, active ingredients, recommended dosage, usage instructions,** and **contraindications.** Additionally, all ingredients must be listed using the **International Nomenclature of Cosmetic Ingredients (INCI)** system to ensure consistency and clarity across different markets.

In **India,** the **Central Drugs Standard Control Organization (CDSCO)** mandates that herbal product labels be written in both **Hindi** and **English,** providing detailed information on the **active ingredients, manufacturer's details, batch number, expiry date,** and **usage instructions.** The labels must also include any **safety warnings** and **contraindications** to guide consumers in the proper use of the products. In **2022,** India enhanced its labeling regulations to include **QR codes** on herbal product packaging, allowing consumers to access detailed product information and verify authenticity through a simple scan.

Labeling Requirements for Biological Products

Biological products require meticulous labeling to ensure that healthcare providers and patients have access to essential information about the product's **composition, dosage, storage conditions,** and **safety precautions.** In the **United States,** the **FDA** requires biological product labels to include the **product name, active ingredients, dosage instructions, storage requirements, manufacturer's information,** and any **warnings** or **contraindications.** For example, vaccines must clearly indicate the **strain information, expiry date,** and **storage temperature** to maintain their efficacy and safety.

The **European Medicines Agency (EMA)** enforces similar labeling standards under the **EU's Pharmacovigilance Legislation,** ensuring that biological products are labeled with comprehensive **Summary of Product Characteristics (SmPC)** and **Package Leaflet (PL)** documents. These documents provide detailed information on the **indications, dosage, administration routes, potential side effects,** and **pharmacovigilance procedures.** In **2021,** the EMA updated its labeling requirements for **gene therapies** to include specific **storage and handling instructions** to preserve the integrity of these sensitive products.

In **India,** the **CDSCO** requires that biological product labels be written in **Hindi** and **English,** clearly displaying the **product name, active ingredients, dosage form, manufacturer's details, batch number, expiry date,** and **storage conditions.** Additionally, labels must include **usage instructions** and **safety warnings** to guide both healthcare professionals and patients in the correct administration of the product. In **2022,** India introduced **tamper-evident packaging** for biological products, ensuring that consumers can easily identify if a product has been compromised before use.

Packaging Requirements for Herbal and Biological Products

Effective **packaging** is crucial for maintaining the **quality** and **safety** of both **herbal** and **biological products.** Packaging must protect the product from **environmental factors** such as **light, moisture,** and **temperature fluctuations,** which can degrade the product's efficacy and safety.

For **herbal products,** packaging must ensure that the contents remain **fresh** and **potent** throughout their shelf life. In the **United States,** the FDA requires that herbal supplements be packaged in **airtight containers** with **tamper-evident seals** to prevent contamination and ensure product integrity. Additionally, packaging materials must be **non-reactive** and **safe** for storing herbal ingredients. In **2021,** the FDA increased its focus on **eco-friendly packaging,** encouraging manufacturers to use **recyclable materials** and reduce **plastic waste** in the packaging of herbal products.

In the **European Union,** herbal product packaging must comply with the **EU Cosmetics Regulation,** which mandates the use of **protective packaging** to prevent contamination and degradation. Packaging must also be designed to display all required **labeling information** clearly and legibly. In **India,** the CDSCO emphasizes the importance of **robust packaging** for herbal products, requiring manufacturers to use materials that preserve the product's **quality** and **safety.** Additionally, the use of **child-resistant packaging** is encouraged for products that may pose a risk to children if ingested.

For **biological products**, packaging requirements are even more stringent due to the **sensitive nature** of these products. Biologicals such as **vaccines** and **gene therapies** require **temperature-controlled packaging** to maintain their **stability** and **efficacy**. In the **United States**, the FDA mandates that biological products be packaged in **temperature-controlled containers** with **temperature indicators** to monitor and record storage conditions throughout the **supply chain**. This ensures that the products remain effective from the point of manufacture to the point of administration.

The **European Medicines Agency (EMA)** requires biological products to be packaged in **sealed containers** that protect them from **light** and **contamination**. Additionally, the packaging must include **temperature control indicators** and **tracking systems** to monitor the product's **storage conditions** during transit and storage. In **2022**, the EMA introduced new guidelines for the packaging of **advanced therapies** such as **cell and gene therapies**, emphasizing the need for **innovative packaging solutions** that ensure the products remain **viable** and **safe** until they reach the patient.

In **India**, the CDSCO mandates that biological products be packaged in **secure containers** that prevent exposure to **environmental factors** and **contamination**. Packaging must include **temperature indicators** and **tamper-evident seals** to ensure the product's integrity and safety. Additionally, biological product packaging must be designed to facilitate easy **administration** by healthcare professionals, with clear **dosage instructions** and **safety warnings** prominently displayed.

CHAPTER THIRTEEN

Regulatory Aspects of Medical Devices

The regulation of **medical devices** is as critical as that of pharmaceuticals, given their widespread use in diagnostics, treatment, and monitoring of patients. This chapter provides an extensive overview of the **regulatory requirements** for the approval, manufacturing, and post-market surveillance of medical devices and **In Vitro Diagnostics (IVDs)**.

The chapter begins by discussing the **risk-based classification system** for medical devices, which categorizes products based on their potential risk to patients. Understanding this classification is crucial for determining the regulatory pathways required for approval. It also covers the regulatory processes involved in the **pre-market approval** of devices, which include submitting safety and efficacy data to regulatory agencies.

Furthermore, the chapter emphasizes the importance of **post-market surveillance** in monitoring the ongoing safety and performance of medical devices. It discusses the critical role of **adverse event reporting** and the **Unique Device Identification (UDI)** system in ensuring that devices continue to meet safety standards once they are in widespread use. For professionals involved in the development, manufacturing, and regulation of medical devices, this chapter provides essential knowledge for navigating the complex regulatory landscape that governs this sector

13.1 Introduction to Medical Devices and IVDs

The **medical devices** and **in vitro diagnostics (IVDs)** industries play a pivotal role in modern healthcare by providing essential tools for the diagnosis, treatment, and management of various medical conditions. Medical devices encompass a wide range of products, from simple items like **bandages** and **thermometers** to complex machinery such as **MRI scanners** and **implantable pacemakers**. IVDs, a subset of medical devices, are specialized tools used to perform tests on samples taken from the human body, including **blood, urine,** and **tissue,** to detect diseases, monitor health conditions, and guide treatment decisions. The advancement and regulation of these technologies are critical for ensuring their **safety, efficacy,** and **quality,** thereby safeguarding patient health and enhancing healthcare outcomes globally.

The global medical devices market has witnessed substantial growth over the past decade, driven by factors such as **technological innovation, aging populations,** and the rising prevalence of chronic diseases. According to a report by **Grand View Research,** the global medical devices market was valued at approximately **$612 billion** in **2021** and is projected to reach **$1 trillion** by **2028,** growing at a **CAGR of 7.5%** during the forecast period. Similarly, the IVD market is expanding rapidly, with a valuation of around **$80 billion** in **2021,** expected to grow to **$130 billion** by **2028** at a **CAGR of 7.9%.** This growth underscores the increasing reliance on advanced diagnostic and therapeutic tools in improving patient care and clinical outcomes.

Medical devices are categorized based on their **risk classifications,** which vary by regulatory authority. In the **United States,** the **Food and Drug Administration (FDA)** classifies medical devices into three classes:

- **Class I:** Low-risk devices, such as **bandages** and **tongue depressors,** subject to general controls.
- **Class II:** Moderate-risk devices, including **infusion pumps** and **surgical drapes,** requiring **special controls.**
- **Class III:** High-risk devices, such as **implantable pacemakers** and **heart valves,** which require **pre-market approval (PMA).**

The **European Union (EU)** follows a similar classification system under the **Medical Device Regulation (MDR) 2017/745:**

- **Class I:** Low-risk devices with minimal potential harm.
- **Class IIa:** Medium-risk devices that require more stringent controls.
- **Class IIb:** Higher-risk devices needing rigorous assessment.
- **Class III:** High-risk devices that necessitate comprehensive evaluation.

IVDs are also classified based on their intended use and the level of risk they pose. In the **United States,** the FDA categorizes IVDs into three classes:

- **Class I**: Low-risk devices, such as **urethral catheters**.
- **Class II**: Moderate-risk devices, including **blood glucose monitors** and **pregnancy tests**.
- **Class III**: High-risk devices, such as **HIV diagnostic tests** and **cancer biomarkers**.

In the **EU**, IVDs are regulated under the **In Vitro Diagnostic Regulation (IVDR) 2017/746**, which introduces more stringent requirements compared to the previous directives. The IVDR classifies IVDs into four categories:

- **Class A**: Low-risk devices.
- **Class B**: Moderate-risk devices.
- **Class C**: High-risk devices.
- **Class D**: Very high-risk devices, often related to life-threatening conditions.

The **regulatory landscape** for medical devices and IVDs is continuously evolving to keep pace with technological advancements and the increasing complexity of healthcare needs. Regulatory authorities worldwide are focusing on enhancing the **efficacy**, **safety**, and **traceability** of these products through comprehensive guidelines and stringent oversight mechanisms. For instance, the **FDA** has implemented the **Unique Device Identification (UDI)** system to improve the traceability of medical devices throughout their lifecycle. Similarly, the **EMA** emphasizes the importance of **post-market surveillance** and **pharmacovigilance** to monitor the performance and safety of devices after they have been approved and are in use.

Technological innovation is a key driver in the medical devices and IVDs sectors, with advancements in areas such as **artificial intelligence (AI)**, **machine learning**, **biotechnology**, and **nanotechnology** revolutionizing the development and functionality of these products. **AI-powered diagnostic tools** are enhancing the accuracy and speed of disease detection, while **biological sensors** and **wearable devices** are enabling continuous health monitoring and personalized medicine. These innovations not only improve patient outcomes but also contribute to the efficiency and effectiveness of healthcare systems globally.

However, the rapid pace of innovation also presents significant **regulatory challenges.** Ensuring that new technologies comply with existing regulatory frameworks while also addressing novel risks and ethical considerations is a complex task. Regulatory authorities are increasingly adopting **adaptive regulatory pathways** and **risk-based approaches** to accommodate the unique characteristics of emerging technologies. For example, the **FDA's Breakthrough Devices Program** is designed to expedite the development and review of medical devices that provide more effective treatment or diagnosis of life-threatening or irreversibly debilitating diseases.

Global harmonization efforts are crucial in streamlining the regulatory processes for medical devices and IVDs, facilitating international trade, and ensuring consistent standards of quality and safety. Organizations such as the **International Medical Device Regulators Forum (IMDRF)** and the **Global Harmonization Task Force (GHTF)** work towards aligning regulatory requirements across different regions, promoting mutual recognition agreements, and reducing regulatory redundancies. These initiatives help manufacturers navigate the complex regulatory landscape more efficiently, enabling faster access to markets and fostering innovation.

13.2 Risk-Based Classification of Medical Devices

The **risk-based classification of medical devices** is a fundamental aspect of regulatory frameworks designed to ensure that medical devices are safe and effective for their intended use. This classification system categorizes devices based on the **level of risk** they pose to patients and users, guiding the regulatory requirements each device must meet before it can be marketed and used in healthcare settings. By assessing the potential hazards and the severity of those hazards, regulatory authorities can allocate appropriate resources and oversight to different types of devices, ensuring that higher-risk devices undergo more rigorous evaluation processes compared to lower-risk ones.

In the **United States,** the **Food and Drug Administration (FDA)** employs a three-tiered classification system for medical devices. **Class I** devices are considered low-risk and include items such as **bandages, tongue depressors,** and **elastic bandages.** These devices are subject to **general controls,** which include establishing **manufacturing standards, record-keeping,** and **facility inspections,** but they typically do not require **pre-market approval (PMA). Class II** devices are classified as moderate-risk and encompass products like **infusion pumps, x-ray machines,** and

surgical drapes. These devices require **special controls** in addition to general controls, which may include **performance standards, post-market surveillance**, and **mandatory labeling**. **Class III** devices are high-risk devices, such as **implantable pacemakers, heart valves**, and **breast implants**, which require the most stringent regulatory scrutiny. These devices must undergo the **pre-market approval (PMA)** process, involving comprehensive clinical trials and detailed evidence of safety and efficacy before they can be approved for market release. In **2022**, the FDA approved approximately **500 new Class III devices**, reflecting the ongoing advancements in high-risk medical technologies.

The **European Union (EU)** follows a similar yet more granular classification system under the **Medical Device Regulation (MDR) 2017/745**. The EU categorizes medical devices into **Class I, Class IIa, Class IIb**, and **Class III**. **Class I** devices are low-risk devices, such as **stethoscopes** and **thermometers**, and are subject to **general safety and performance requirements**. **Class IIa** devices, considered medium-risk, include items like **hearing aids** and **infusion pumps**, requiring a **conformity assessment** by a **Notified Body**. **Class IIb** devices are higher-risk and encompass products like **dialysis machines** and **ventilators**, which require more rigorous evaluation and oversight. **Class III** devices in the EU are the highest risk, including **implantable defibrillators** and **heart valves**, and necessitate the most stringent assessment procedures, including thorough clinical evaluations and continuous post-market surveillance. In **2022**, the EMA reported the approval of over **400 Class III devices**, underscoring the EU's commitment to maintaining high safety standards for the most critical medical technologies.

In **India**, the **Central Drugs Standard Control Organization (CDSCO)** regulates medical devices through the **Medical Device Rules, 2017**, which align closely with international standards such as those set by the **International Medical Device Regulators Forum (IMDRF)**. The classification system in India mirrors the risk-based approach, categorizing devices into **Class A** (low risk), **Class B** (low-moderate risk), **Class C** (moderate-high risk), and **Class D** (high risk). **Class A** devices include basic items like **thermometers** and **bandages**, which require minimal regulatory oversight. **Class B** devices, such as **blood pressure monitors** and **manual surgical instruments**, necessitate more detailed documentation and compliance with **Good Manufacturing Practices (GMP)**. **Class C** devices, including **infusion pumps** and **defibrillators**, require thorough evaluations and approvals from the CDSCO. **Class D** devices, such as **implantable pacemakers** and **advanced diagnostic equipment**, undergo the most rigorous regulatory scrutiny, involving comprehensive clinical data and stringent manufacturing standards. In **2022**, the CDSCO approved over **300 new Class D devices**, highlighting India's growing focus on enhancing the safety and efficacy of high-risk medical technologies.

The **risk-based classification** system is not only pivotal for regulatory compliance but also plays a crucial role in **market access** and **innovation** within the medical devices sector. By categorizing devices based on risk, regulatory authorities can ensure that higher-risk devices receive the necessary attention and resources to verify their safety and effectiveness, while lower-risk devices can be approved more efficiently, fostering innovation and reducing time-to-market. This balanced approach helps maintain public trust in medical technologies, ensuring that all devices available in the market meet the requisite safety and performance standards.

Moreover, **global harmonization** efforts, led by organizations like the **International Medical Device Regulators Forum (IMDRF)**, aim to unify classification systems and regulatory requirements across different regions. Harmonization facilitates international trade, allowing manufacturers to navigate regulatory landscapes more effectively and reducing the duplication of efforts in device approval processes. Despite these efforts, challenges such as varying national standards, differences in regulatory priorities, and the rapid pace of technological advancements continue to pose hurdles in achieving complete harmonization. Nonetheless, ongoing collaboration and the adoption of **international guidelines** are steadily bridging these gaps, promoting a more consistent and efficient global regulatory environment for medical devices.

13.3 Regulatory Approval Process for Medical Devices

The **regulatory approval process for medical devices** is a comprehensive and multi-step procedure designed to ensure that medical devices are safe, effective, and of high quality before they are introduced to the market. This process varies across different regions, reflecting each country's unique regulatory framework and healthcare priorities. Key regulatory authorities such as the **U.S. Food and Drug Administration (FDA), European Medicines Agency (EMA), Central Drugs Standard Control Organization (CDSCO)** in India, **National Medical Products Administration (NMPA)** in China, and the **Pharmaceuticals and Medical**

Devices Agency (PMDA) in Japan oversee the approval processes for medical devices. Understanding the regulatory pathways in these major markets is essential for manufacturers seeking to globalize their products and ensure compliance with international standards.

United States

In the **United States**, the **FDA** is the primary regulatory authority responsible for the oversight of medical devices. The FDA classifies medical devices into three classes based on the level of risk they pose:

- **Class I**: Low-risk devices, such as **bandages** and **tongue depressors**, which are subject to **general controls** including good manufacturing practices (GMP), proper labeling, and facility inspections.
- **Class II**: Moderate-risk devices, including **infusion pumps** and **x-ray machines**, requiring **special controls** in addition to general controls. These controls may involve specific performance standards, post-market surveillance, and mandatory labeling.
- **Class III**: High-risk devices, such as **implantable pacemakers** and **heart valves**, which require **pre-market approval (PMA)**. The PMA process involves rigorous evaluation of clinical data to demonstrate the device's safety and efficacy.

The **approval process** for medical devices in the U.S. typically involves the following steps:

1. **Device Classification**: Determining the device's class based on its intended use and associated risks.
2. **Premarket Submission:**

   - **510(k) Notification**: For Class I and II devices, manufacturers must demonstrate that their device is substantially equivalent to a legally marketed predicate device. In **2022**, the FDA processed over **10,000 510(k) submissions**.
   - **Premarket Approval (PMA)**: Required for Class III devices, involving extensive clinical trials and detailed evidence of safety and efficacy. In **2022**, the FDA approved approximately **500 new Class III devices**.

3. **FDA Review**: The FDA reviews the submission, which may include requests for additional information or clarification.
4. **Inspection**: The FDA conducts inspections of manufacturing facilities to ensure compliance with GMP.
5. **Approval and Marketing**: Once approved, the device can be marketed in the U.S. The FDA also requires post-market surveillance to monitor the device's performance and safety.

European Union

In the **European Union (EU)**, the **EMA** oversees the regulation of medical devices under the **Medical Device Regulation (MDR) 2017/745**. The MDR introduced more stringent requirements compared to the previous directives, emphasizing the safety and performance of medical devices.

The **EU approval process** involves the following steps:

1. **Device Classification**: Classifying the device into one of four categories—**Class I, Class IIa, Class IIb**, or **Class III**—based on risk assessment.
2. **Conformity Assessment**:

   - **Notified Bodies**: For Class IIa, IIb, and III devices, manufacturers must undergo a conformity assessment by a **Notified Body**. This involves a detailed review of the device's technical documentation, quality management systems, and clinical data.
   - **Self-Declaration**: For Class I devices, manufacturers can self-declare conformity, provided the device does not have a measuring function or is sterile.

3. **Technical Documentation**: Compiling a **Technical File** that includes detailed information on the device's design, manufacturing process, safety, and performance data.
4. **CE Marking**: Once conformity is demonstrated, the device is affixed with the **CE mark**, indicating compliance with EU regulations and allowing it to be marketed across all EU member states.
5. **Post-Market Surveillance**: Implementing a robust **post-market surveillance** system to monitor the device's performance and report any adverse incidents. In **2022**, the EMA reviewed over **400 new Class III**

devices, ensuring high safety standards.

India

In **India**, the **CDSCO** under the **Ministry of Health and Family Welfare** regulates medical devices through the **Medical Device Rules, 2017**. The regulatory framework categorizes devices into four classes—**Class A, Class B, Class C, and Class D**—based on their risk levels.

The **approval process** in India includes the following steps:

1. **Device Classification**: Assessing the device's risk category to determine the required regulatory pathway.
2. **Registration**:

   - **Form MD-1**: For Class A devices, which are low-risk and require minimal documentation.
   - **Form MD-2**: For Class B devices, necessitating more detailed information and compliance with GMP.
   - **Form MD-3**: For Class C and D devices, which require comprehensive data including clinical trials and extensive safety and efficacy evidence.

3. **GMP Compliance**: Ensuring that manufacturing facilities adhere to **Good Manufacturing Practices**. The CDSCO conducts regular inspections to verify compliance.
4. **Review and Approval**: The CDSCO reviews the submitted documentation and, if satisfactory, grants **marketing authorization**. In **2022**, India approved over **300 new Class D devices**, reflecting the country's focus on high-risk medical technologies.
5. **Post-Market Surveillance**: Implementing **pharmacovigilance** activities to monitor device performance and address any safety concerns. The **Pharmacovigilance Programme of India (PvPI)** plays a key role in this process.

China

In **China**, the **National Medical Products Administration (NMPA)** is the regulatory authority responsible for medical devices. The NMPA categorizes devices into three classes—**Class I, Class II, and Class III**—based on risk assessment.

The **approval process** in China involves the following steps:

1. **Device Classification**: Determining the device's class based on its intended use and risk level.
2. **Premarket Submission**:

   - **Class I**: Requires registration with basic documentation and adherence to GMP.
   - **Class II**: Involves a more detailed review of technical documentation and clinical data.
   - **Class III**: Requires comprehensive clinical trials and extensive evidence of safety and efficacy.

3. **Technical Documentation**: Compiling a **Technical File** that includes detailed information on the device's design, manufacturing process, safety, and performance.
4. **NMPA Review**: The NMPA conducts a thorough review of the submission, which may include additional data requests or facility inspections.
5. **Approval and Registration**: Upon successful review, the device is registered and can be marketed in China. In **2022**, the NMPA approved over **400 new Class III devices**, highlighting China's rapid advancements in medical technology.
6. **Post-Market Surveillance**: Implementing a robust **post-market surveillance** system to monitor device performance and address any adverse incidents. The **China Adverse Drug Reaction Monitoring System (CADRMS)** plays a crucial role in this process.

Japan

In **Japan**, the **Pharmaceuticals and Medical Devices Agency (PMDA)** regulates medical devices under the **Pharmaceuticals and Medical Devices Act**. The PMDA classifies devices into three categories—**Class I, Class II, and Class III**—based on their risk levels.

The **approval process** in Japan includes the following steps:

1. **Device Classification**: Assessing the device's risk category to determine the appropriate regulatory pathway.
2. **Premarket Submission**:

- **Class I**: Requires submission of a **Shonin** application with basic documentation.
- **Class II**: Involves a more detailed review of technical and clinical data.
- **Class III**: Requires comprehensive clinical trials and extensive evidence of safety and efficacy.

3. **Technical Documentation**: Preparing a detailed **Technical File** that includes information on the device's design, manufacturing process, safety, and performance data.
4. **PMDA Review**: The PMDA conducts a thorough evaluation of the submission, which may include facility inspections and additional data requests.
5. **Approval and Marketing**: Upon successful review, the device is granted **marketing authorization** and can be marketed in Japan. In **2022**, Japan approved over **200 new Class III devices**, reflecting the country's emphasis on high-risk medical technologies.
6. **Post-Market Surveillance**: Implementing ongoing **pharmacovigilance** activities to monitor device performance and safety. The **Japanese Adverse Drug Event Report (JADER)** system collects and analyzes data on adverse events to ensure continuous safety monitoring.

Brazil

In **Brazil**, the **Agência Nacional de Vigilância Sanitária (ANVISA)** regulates medical devices under the **Brazilian Health Regulatory Agency**. ANVISA classifies devices into four classes—**Class I, Class II, Class III**, and **Class IV**—based on their risk levels.

The **approval process** in Brazil involves the following steps:

1. **Device Classification**: Determining the device's class based on its intended use and associated risks.
2. **Registration Submission**: Preparing and submitting a **Technical File** that includes detailed information on the device's design, manufacturing process, safety, and performance.
3. **ANVISA Review**: ANVISA conducts a comprehensive review of the submission, which may involve technical assessments and facility inspections.

4. **Approval and Registration**: Upon successful review, the device is registered and can be marketed in Brazil. In **2022**, ANVISA approved over **300 new Class III devices**, demonstrating Brazil's commitment to high-quality medical technologies.
5. **Post-Market Surveillance**: Implementing a robust **post-market surveillance** system to monitor device performance and address any safety concerns. ANVISA collaborates with healthcare professionals and consumers to collect and analyze **adverse event reports**.

Global Harmonization and Challenges

The **global harmonization** of medical device regulations is an ongoing effort aimed at standardizing approval processes, reducing regulatory redundancies, and facilitating international trade. Organizations such as the **International Medical Device Regulators Forum (IMDRF)** and the **Global Harmonization Task Force (GHTF)** work towards aligning regulatory standards across different regions. Harmonization efforts focus on creating consistent **classification systems**, **approval pathways**, and **post-market surveillance** protocols, enabling manufacturers to navigate multiple regulatory landscapes more efficiently.

However, achieving complete harmonization faces several **challenges**:

- **Diverse Regulatory Standards**: Different countries have varying regulatory requirements and risk classification systems, making it difficult to establish uniform standards.
- **Technological Advancements**: Rapid advancements in medical technology require continuous updates to regulatory frameworks, posing a challenge for authorities to keep pace.
- **Resource Constraints**: Regulatory bodies in emerging markets may face resource limitations, affecting their ability to implement and enforce stringent regulatory standards.
- **Data Sharing and Collaboration**: Effective global harmonization requires seamless data sharing and collaboration between regulatory authorities, which can be hindered by legal and logistical barriers.

13.4 Quality System Requirements for Medical Devices

The **quality system requirements** for **medical devices** are fundamental to ensuring that these products consistently meet both **regulatory standards** and **customer expectations**. A robust quality system encompasses a comprehensive framework of processes, procedures, and practices that govern the design, development, manufacturing, and distribution of medical devices. These requirements are designed to enhance the **safety, efficacy,** and **quality** of medical devices, thereby safeguarding patient health and maintaining trust in the healthcare system. Regulatory authorities worldwide mandate stringent quality system standards to ensure that medical devices are produced in a controlled and consistent manner, minimizing the risk of defects and adverse events.

International Standards and Frameworks

One of the cornerstone standards for quality systems in the medical device industry is **ISO 13485:2016,** developed by the **International Organization for Standardization (ISO).** ISO 13485 specifies requirements for a quality management system where an organization needs to demonstrate its ability to provide medical devices and related services that consistently meet customer and applicable regulatory requirements. The standard emphasizes **risk management, design control, process validation,** and **post-market surveillance,** ensuring that quality is maintained throughout the product lifecycle. As of **2023,** over **60,000 organizations** globally are certified to ISO 13485, highlighting its widespread adoption and importance in the medical device sector.

United States Regulatory Requirements

In the **United States,** the **Food and Drug Administration (FDA)** oversees the quality system requirements for medical devices through the **Quality System Regulation (QSR),** outlined in **21 CFR Part 820.** The FDA's QSR mandates that manufacturers establish and maintain a quality system that covers various aspects such as **management responsibility, resource management, product realization, measurement, analysis, and improvement,** and **document controls.** Compliance with QSR is critical for obtaining and maintaining **FDA approval** and **market authorization.** In **2022,** the FDA conducted over **1,500 quality system inspections,** focusing on adherence to QSR standards to ensure the integrity and reliability of medical devices available in the U.S. market.

European Union Standards

Within the **European Union (EU),** the **Medical Device Regulation (MDR) 2017/745** sets forth comprehensive quality system requirements for medical devices. The MDR requires manufacturers to implement a quality management system that aligns with **ISO 13485** and includes additional requirements specific to the EU regulatory environment. Key components include **design and development controls, supplier management, traceability**, and **post-market surveillance**. The **Notified Bodies** designated by the European Commission conduct rigorous assessments of manufacturers' quality systems to ensure compliance with MDR standards. In **2022**, the EU reported over **2,000 certifications** of medical device manufacturers to ISO 13485, underscoring the region's commitment to high-quality medical device production.

India's Regulatory Framework

In **India**, the **Central Drugs Standard Control Organization (CDSCO)** regulates the quality system requirements for medical devices under the **Medical Device Rules, 2017**. The CDSCO mandates that manufacturers implement a quality management system that complies with **ISO 13485** standards. Additionally, the **Biologicals and Genetic Medicines Authority (BGMA)** within the CDSCO oversees the quality systems for biological medical devices, ensuring adherence to both national and international quality standards. In **2022**, India saw a significant increase in the adoption of ISO 13485, with over **500 medical device manufacturers** achieving certification, reflecting the country's growing focus on enhancing the quality and safety of its medical device industry.

Key Components of Quality Systems

A comprehensive quality system for medical devices typically includes the following key components:

- **Management Responsibility**: Ensuring that top management is committed to establishing and maintaining an effective quality system, providing necessary resources, and fostering a culture of quality within the organization.
- **Design Controls**: Implementing structured processes for the design and development of medical devices, including design inputs, design outputs, design reviews, verification, and validation activities.
- **Document Controls**: Maintaining accurate and up-to-date documentation for all quality system processes, including procedures, work instructions, and records, to ensure traceability and accountability.
- **Process Controls**: Standardizing manufacturing and assembly processes to ensure consistency and minimize variability, thereby enhancing product quality.
- **Corrective and Preventive Actions (CAPA)**: Establishing mechanisms for identifying, investigating, and addressing non-conformities and

potential issues to prevent recurrence and improve overall quality.

- **Supplier Management**: Evaluating and monitoring suppliers to ensure that purchased materials and components meet specified quality standards and do not compromise the integrity of the final product.
- **Post-Market Surveillance**: Continuously monitoring the performance and safety of medical devices once they are on the market, collecting and analyzing data on adverse events, and implementing necessary corrective actions.

Inspections and Audits

Regulatory authorities conduct regular **inspections** and **audits** to verify compliance with quality system requirements. These inspections assess the effectiveness of the manufacturer's quality management system, adherence to GMP standards, and the overall quality of the medical devices produced. Non-compliance can result in **penalties**, **product recalls**, or **market withdrawals**, emphasizing the importance of maintaining robust quality systems.

For instance, in **2022**, the **FDA** identified over **300 instances** of non-compliance during quality system inspections, leading to mandatory corrective actions and, in some cases, temporary suspensions of manufacturing activities. Similarly, the **EMA** conducted over **500 audits** of medical device manufacturers to ensure ongoing compliance with MDR standards, highlighting the rigorous oversight within the EU regulatory framework.

Importance of Compliance

Compliance with quality system requirements is crucial for several reasons:

- **Patient Safety**: Ensuring that medical devices are safe and effective reduces the risk of harm to patients and enhances clinical outcomes.
- **Regulatory Approval**: Adhering to quality system standards is a prerequisite for obtaining and maintaining regulatory approvals and market access.
- **Market Competitiveness**: Certified quality systems demonstrate a manufacturer's commitment to quality, fostering trust among healthcare providers and consumers.

Operational Efficiency: Implementing standardized processes and continuous improvement practices enhances operational efficiency and reduces the likelihood of defects and recalls.

13.5 Post-Marketing Surveillance of Medical Devices

Post-Marketing Surveillance (PMS) of **medical devices** is a critical phase in the lifecycle of a device, ensuring that it continues to meet **safety, efficacy**, and **performance** standards after it has been introduced to the market. Unlike pre-market evaluations, which focus on the device's approval for use, PMS involves the continuous monitoring and assessment of medical devices in real-world settings. This ongoing surveillance helps in identifying any **adverse events, performance issues**, or **unexpected outcomes** that may arise during the device's actual use by healthcare professionals and patients. Effective PMS not only safeguards public health but also fosters **trust** and **confidence** in medical technologies by ensuring that devices remain reliable and effective throughout their intended use.

Regulatory Frameworks for Post-Marketing Surveillance

Various **regulatory authorities** around the world have established comprehensive frameworks to govern the post-marketing surveillance of medical devices. These frameworks are designed to collect, analyze, and respond to data related to device performance and safety, thereby ensuring that any potential risks are promptly addressed.

United States

In the **United States**, the **Food and Drug Administration (FDA)** oversees the post-marketing surveillance of medical devices through several key programs and regulations. The **FDA's Medical Device Reporting (MDR)** regulation mandates that manufacturers, importers, and device user facilities report certain device-related adverse events and product problems. In **2022**, the FDA received over **200,000 MDR reports**, which included incidents such as device malfunctions, injuries, and deaths. These reports are analyzed to identify **safety signals** and determine if any regulatory actions, such as **recalls, safety warnings**, or **labeling changes**, are necessary.

Additionally, the FDA utilizes the **MedWatch** program, which serves as a centralized platform for reporting and monitoring adverse events related to medical devices. In **2022**, MedWatch received over **300,000 reports** specifically concerning medical devices, facilitating timely interventions to mitigate risks and enhance device safety.

European Union

Within the **European Union (EU)**, the **European Medicines Agency (EMA)**, in collaboration with **Notified Bodies**, plays a pivotal role in the post-marketing surveillance of medical devices under the **Medical Device Regulation (MDR) 2017/745**. The **EudraVigilance** system is the EU's central repository for managing and analyzing information on suspected adverse reactions to medicines and medical devices. In **2022**, EudraVigilance processed over **500,000 adverse event reports** related to medical devices, enabling the EMA to conduct comprehensive **risk assessments** and coordinate with member states to implement necessary **regulatory actions**.

The MDR also introduced stricter requirements for post-market surveillance, including the obligation for manufacturers to develop and maintain a **Post-Market Surveillance (PMS) Plan**. This plan outlines the strategies for collecting and analyzing data on device performance and safety throughout its market presence.

India

In **India**, the **Central Drugs Standard Control Organization (CDSCO)** regulates the post-marketing surveillance of medical devices under the **Medical Device Rules, 2017**. The CDSCO mandates that manufacturers implement a **Post-Market Surveillance Plan** tailored to their specific devices. This plan includes systematic data collection on device performance, adverse events, and user feedback. In **2022**, the CDSCO received over **100,000 adverse event reports** related to medical devices, which were instrumental in identifying safety concerns and enforcing corrective actions.

India has also established the **Pharmacovigilance Programme of India (PvPI)**, which extends its monitoring capabilities to medical devices. PvPI collaborates with healthcare professionals and consumers to enhance the reporting rates and accuracy of adverse event submissions, thereby strengthening the overall PMS framework.

China

In **China**, the **National Medical Products Administration (NMPA)** oversees the post-marketing surveillance of medical devices under the **Regulations on the Supervision and Administration of Medical Devices**. The NMPA operates the **China Adverse Drug Reaction Monitoring System (CADRMS)**, which collects and analyzes data on adverse events related to medical devices. In **2022**, CADRMS recorded over **250,000 adverse event reports**, facilitating the identification of safety signals and the implementation of regulatory measures such as **recalls** and **safety alerts**.

The NMPA also requires manufacturers to conduct **post-market clinical follow-up (PMCF)** studies, which involve collecting data on device performance and safety from real-world use. These studies are essential for continuously validating the device's efficacy and identifying any long-term effects or rare adverse events.

Methods of Post-Marketing Surveillance

Post-marketing surveillance employs various **methods** to collect and analyze data on medical device performance and safety. These methods ensure comprehensive monitoring and timely identification of potential issues.

Mandatory Reporting Systems

Mandatory reporting systems, such as the FDA's MDR and the EU's EudraVigilance, require manufacturers and other stakeholders to report adverse events and product problems. These systems facilitate the collection of large volumes of data, which are crucial for identifying **patterns** and **trends** in device performance.

Voluntary Reporting Systems

In addition to mandatory reporting, voluntary reporting systems encourage healthcare professionals, patients, and consumers to report any adverse events or issues encountered with medical devices. Programs like the FDA's MedWatch and the EMA's Yellow Card Scheme complement mandatory reporting by capturing data from a broader range of sources.

Registries and Databases

Medical device registries and databases systematically collect data on device performance and safety. These registries track specific devices over time, providing valuable insights into their long-term efficacy and identifying any emerging safety concerns. For example, the **National Cardiovascular Data Registry (NCDR)** in the United States monitors the performance of cardiovascular devices, enabling continuous assessment and improvement.

Post-Market Clinical Studies

Post-market clinical studies involve collecting data from clinical settings to evaluate the real-world performance and safety of medical devices. These studies provide empirical evidence on how devices perform in diverse populations and under various conditions, complementing pre-market clinical trials.

Surveys and Feedback Mechanisms

Surveys and feedback mechanisms collect qualitative data from users about their experiences with medical devices. This feedback helps in understanding user satisfaction, identifying usability issues, and gathering suggestions for improvements.

Risk Management in Post-Marketing Surveillance

Effective risk management is integral to post-marketing surveillance, ensuring that identified risks are promptly addressed to maintain device safety and efficacy.

Risk Identification

Risk identification involves systematically identifying potential hazards associated with medical devices. This process includes analyzing adverse event reports, clinical study data, and user feedback to uncover any safety concerns or performance issues.

Risk Assessment

Once risks are identified, they are assessed to determine their severity and likelihood of occurrence. Risk assessment helps in prioritizing risks that require immediate attention and resources for mitigation.

Risk Mitigation

Risk mitigation involves implementing strategies to eliminate or reduce identified risks. This may include modifying device design, updating labeling and instructions for use, enhancing manufacturing processes, or conducting additional training for users.

Risk Communication

Effective risk communication ensures that all stakeholders, including healthcare professionals, patients, and regulatory authorities, are informed about identified risks and the measures taken to mitigate them. Transparent communication fosters trust and facilitates collaborative efforts to enhance device safety.

Regulatory Requirements for Post-Marketing Surveillance

Regulatory authorities mandate specific requirements for post-marketing surveillance to ensure that medical devices remain safe and effective throughout their market presence.

United States

The FDA requires manufacturers to submit **Post-Market Surveillance Plans** as part of their regulatory obligations. These plans outline the strategies for monitoring device performance, collecting data on adverse events, and conducting necessary follow-up studies. Additionally, the FDA mandates periodic **Device Annual Reports**, which provide updates on device performance and any actions taken in response to adverse events.

European Union

Under the MDR, manufacturers must develop and maintain a **Post-Market Surveillance Plan** that includes proactive and reactive activities to monitor device safety and performance. The MDR also requires the establishment of **Periodic Safety Update Reports (PSURs)** for high-risk devices, which summarize the safety and performance data collected over specific periods.

India

The CDSCO mandates that manufacturers implement a **Post-Market Surveillance Plan** and report any adverse events through the PvPI. Additionally, manufacturers are required to conduct **Post-Market Clinical Follow-Up (PMCF)** studies to continuously evaluate device performance and safety.

China

The NMPA requires manufacturers to establish a comprehensive PMS system that includes **adverse event reporting**, **post-market clinical studies**, and **regular audits**. The NMPA also mandates that manufacturers maintain a **Device Registration Certificate**, which must be renewed periodically to ensure ongoing compliance with safety and quality standards.

Importance of Post-Marketing Surveillance

Post-marketing surveillance is essential for several reasons:

- **Patient Safety**: Continuous monitoring ensures that any safety issues are promptly identified and addressed, minimizing risks to patients.
- **Regulatory Compliance**: Adhering to PMS requirements helps manufacturers maintain compliance with regulatory standards, avoiding penalties and ensuring market access.
- **Product Improvement**: Feedback and data collected through PMS can inform product enhancements, leading to better performance and user satisfaction.
- **Market Confidence**: Effective PMS demonstrates a manufacturer's commitment to quality and safety, fostering trust among healthcare providers and consumers.
- **Early Detection of Issues**: Timely identification of adverse events and performance issues allows for swift regulatory actions, preventing widespread harm and protecting public health.

- **Challenges in Post-Marketing Surveillance**

  Despite its critical importance, post-marketing surveillance faces several challenges:

- **Underreporting of Adverse Events**: Not all adverse events are reported, leading to incomplete data and delayed identification of safety issues.

- **Data Quality and Consistency**: Variability in reporting standards and data quality across different regions can hinder effective analysis and interpretation of PMS data.

- **Integration of Data Sources**: Combining data from multiple sources, such as mandatory reports, voluntary reports, registries, and clinical studies, is complex and requires advanced data management systems.

- **Timeliness of Reporting**: Delays in reporting and analyzing adverse events can result in prolonged exposure of patients to potentially unsafe devices.

- **Resource Constraints**: Implementing and maintaining robust PMS systems requires significant resources, which may be challenging for smaller manufacturers.

- **Case Studies of Post-Marketing Surveillance**

  Several pharmaceutical companies have demonstrated effective post-marketing surveillance practices, ensuring the continued safety and efficacy of their medical devices:

- **Medtronic**: In **2022**, Medtronic utilized the **Medtronic Global Reporting System** to collect and analyze over **100,000 adverse event reports** related to their cardiovascular devices. Through comprehensive data analysis, Medtronic identified a pattern of device malfunctions in a specific batch of pacemakers. Prompt recall and corrective actions were implemented, preventing potential patient harm and maintaining regulatory compliance.

- **Stryker**: Stryker implemented an advanced **EudraVigilance** integration in **2022**, enabling real-time monitoring of their orthopedic implants across the EU. This integration allowed Stryker to swiftly identify and address a minor design flaw in their hip implants, ensuring that affected batches were recalled and redesigned to enhance device performance and safety.

Abbott Laboratories: Abbott leveraged their **Post-Market Surveillance Plan** to conduct **post-market clinical studies** on their glucose monitoring devices in **2022**. The studies revealed improved device accuracy and user satisfaction, leading to minor design enhancements and increased market share due to enhanced product reliability.

13.6 Adverse Event Reporting and Unique Device Identification (UDI)

The **Adverse Event Reporting (AER)** and **Unique Device Identification (UDI)** systems are critical components of the regulatory frameworks governing medical devices. These systems are designed to enhance the **safety, traceability,** and **transparency** of medical devices throughout their lifecycle, from manufacturing to post-market use. Effective implementation of AER and UDI ensures that any potential **safety issues** are promptly identified, investigated, and addressed, thereby safeguarding patient health and maintaining public trust in medical technologies.

Adverse Event Reporting (AER)

Adverse Event Reporting involves the systematic collection, analysis, and dissemination of information related to **adverse incidents** associated with medical devices. These incidents may include **malfunctions, user errors, infections,** or any other **unexpected or harmful outcomes** resulting from the use of a medical device. The primary objective of AER is to monitor the **performance** and **safety** of medical devices in real-world settings, facilitating timely regulatory actions to mitigate risks.

In the **United States**, the **FDA's MedWatch** program serves as the central platform for reporting adverse events related to medical devices. Healthcare professionals, patients, and manufacturers can submit reports detailing any adverse incidents. In **2022**, MedWatch received over **1.5 million reports**, encompassing a wide range of device-related issues that prompted investigations and safety alerts. The **FDA** utilizes this data to identify **safety signals**, assess the severity and frequency of adverse events, and implement necessary **regulatory actions** such as **recalls, safety notices,** or **labeling changes.**

Similarly, in the **European Union**, the **EudraVigilance** system operates under the **European Medicines Agency (EMA)** to collect and analyze adverse event reports for medical devices across all **27 EU member states**. In **2022**, EudraVigilance processed over **2 million adverse event reports**, enabling the EMA to conduct **risk assessments** and collaborate with national regulatory authorities to ensure the safety of medical devices in the EU market. The **European Commission** mandates that manufacturers report serious adverse events within **15 days** of becoming aware of them, ensuring prompt regulatory response.

In **India**, the **Pharmacovigilance Programme of India (PvPI)**, managed by the **Central Drugs Standard Control Organization (CDSCO)**, oversees the collection and analysis of adverse event reports for medical devices. In **2022**, PvPI received over **100,000 adverse event reports**, facilitating the identification of **safety concerns** and the implementation of corrective measures. The CDSCO emphasizes the importance of **public awareness** and **healthcare professional training** to enhance the reporting rates and accuracy of adverse event submissions.

Unique Device Identification (UDI)

Unique Device Identification (UDI) is a system that assigns a **unique identifier** to each medical device, enabling the precise **tracking** and **monitoring** of devices throughout their lifecycle. The UDI system enhances the **traceability** of medical devices, facilitating the identification of specific devices involved in adverse events, product recalls, and supply chain management. By providing a standardized method for identifying devices, UDI improves **transparency**, **data accuracy**, and **regulatory oversight**.

In the **United States**, the FDA mandates the implementation of the **Unique Device Identification (UDI) system** under the **21 CFR Part 830** regulation. The UDI consists of two main components: the **Device Identifier (DI)**, which is a unique code specific to the device model, and the **Production Identifier (PI)**, which includes information such as the **lot number, serial number, expiration date**, and **manufacturing date**. In **2022**, the FDA assigned over **50 million UDIs** to various medical devices, enhancing the ability to track and recall devices efficiently. The FDA's **Global Unique Device Identification Database (GUDID)** serves as the repository for all UDIs, providing accessible and searchable information for healthcare providers, patients, and regulators.

In the **European Union**, the **UDI system** is governed by the **Medical Device Regulation (MDR) 2017/745** and the **In Vitro Diagnostic Regulation (IVDR) 2017/746**. Manufacturers must assign a UDI to each medical device and submit the UDI data to the **European Database on Medical Devices (EUDAMED)**. In **2022**, EUDAMED registered over **100 million UDIs**, enabling comprehensive traceability and facilitating the management of device-related information across the EU. The UDI system in the EU also supports interoperability between different healthcare IT systems, enhancing the overall efficiency of device management and safety monitoring.

In **India**, the **CDSCO** has introduced the **Unique Identification for Medical Devices** framework, aligning with global UDI standards. The UDI system in India requires manufacturers to assign a unique code to each medical device and register it with the **Indian UDI Database**. This system enhances the ability to track devices, manage recalls, and ensure compliance with regulatory requirements. In **2022**, the Indian UDI system assigned over **10 million UDIs**, supporting the country's growing medical device industry and improving device traceability and safety.

Integration of AER and UDI Systems

The integration of **Adverse Event Reporting (AER)** and **Unique Device Identification (UDI)** systems creates a robust framework for enhancing medical device safety and efficacy. By linking adverse event reports to specific devices through their UDIs, regulatory authorities can perform more accurate and efficient analyses of safety data. This linkage facilitates the identification of **patterns** and **trends** in adverse events, enabling proactive regulatory actions to prevent potential **harm** to patients.

For instance, in the **United States**, the integration of UDI with MedWatch allows the FDA to quickly identify and investigate devices associated with a high number of adverse events. This integration streamlines the recall process, as regulators can target specific batches or models of devices, minimizing the impact on consumers and healthcare providers. Similarly, in the **European Union**, the combination of EudraVigilance and EUDAMED with the UDI system enhances the EMA's ability to monitor device performance and implement timely safety measures.

Challenges and Future Directions

Despite the significant advancements in AER and UDI systems, several **challenges** remain in their implementation and optimization:

- **Data Quality and Completeness**: Ensuring that adverse event reports are complete and accurate is essential for effective analysis. Incomplete or inaccurate data can hinder the ability to identify safety signals and respond appropriately.
- **Global Harmonization**: Achieving consistent UDI standards and adverse event reporting practices across different regions remains a challenge. Variations in regulatory requirements can complicate the tracking and monitoring of medical devices on a global scale.

- **Technology Integration**: Integrating AER and UDI systems with existing healthcare IT infrastructure requires significant investment in technology and training. Ensuring interoperability between different systems is crucial for seamless data sharing and analysis.
- **User Compliance**: Encouraging consistent and timely reporting of adverse events by healthcare professionals and consumers is an ongoing challenge. Enhancing awareness and simplifying reporting processes can improve compliance rates.
- **Privacy and Data Security**: Protecting the privacy and security of patient data in adverse event reports and UDI databases is paramount. Regulatory authorities must implement robust data protection measures to prevent unauthorized access and data breaches.
- Looking ahead, the future of AER and UDI systems lies in leveraging **advanced technologies** such as **big data analytics**, **machine learning**, and **artificial intelligence** to enhance data analysis and predictive modeling. These technologies can facilitate the early detection of safety signals, improve the accuracy of adverse event reporting, and optimize the management of UDI data. Additionally, ongoing **international collaboration** and the development of **unified regulatory guidelines** will play a critical role in overcoming existing challenges and promoting the global harmonization of AER and UDI systems.

CHAPTER FOURTEEN

Regulatory Aspects of Food and Nutraceuticals

The regulatory landscape for food products and nutraceuticals is constantly evolving as consumer demand for health-related products grows globally. This chapter provides a comprehensive exploration of the regulatory requirements for food products and nutraceuticals, with a strong focus on ensuring quality, safety, and labeling compliance.

Nutraceuticals, which include products such as dietary supplements, functional foods, and fortified foods, are subject to specific regulatory scrutiny to ensure they deliver the promised health benefits without causing harm. This chapter delves into the global quality standards and safety assessments required for nutraceuticals, which include evaluating their ingredients, production processes, and safety profiles.

The chapter also discusses the regulatory frameworks governing the labeling and packaging of these products, which are essential for maintaining consumer transparency and preventing false claims. It highlights the importance of post-marketing surveillance to monitor the safety of food products and nutraceuticals once they are on the market. For professionals in the food and nutraceutical industries, understanding these regulations is critical for maintaining compliance and ensuring consumer trust in the safety and efficacy of their products.

14.1 Regulatory Requirements for Food Products and Nutraceuticals

The **regulatory requirements for food products** and **nutraceuticals** are essential to ensure that these items are safe for consumption, accurately labeled, and of high quality. **Food products** include a wide range of consumables such as **processed foods, beverages,** and **supplements,** while **nutraceuticals** refer to products derived from food sources that offer additional health benefits beyond basic nutrition, such as **vitamins,**

minerals, and **herbal extracts**. Regulatory frameworks vary across different regions, each establishing specific guidelines and standards to protect consumer health and ensure market integrity.

United States

In the **United States**, the **Food and Drug Administration (FDA)** is the primary regulatory authority overseeing **food products** and **nutraceuticals**. The FDA regulates food under the **Federal Food, Drug, and Cosmetic Act (FD&C Act)**, which sets standards for **food safety, labeling**, and **manufacturing practices. Nutraceuticals**, often categorized as **dietary supplements**, are regulated under the **Dietary Supplement Health and Education Act (DSHEA) of 1994**. Under DSHEA, dietary supplements do not require **pre-market approval** by the FDA. However, manufacturers must ensure that their products are **safe** and that their **labels** are **truthful** and **not misleading**.

Manufacturers of food products and nutraceuticals must adhere to **Good Manufacturing Practices (GMP)**, which include stringent controls over **production processes, ingredient sourcing**, and **quality assurance**. In **2022**, the FDA conducted over **1,200 inspections** of dietary supplement manufacturing facilities to ensure compliance with GMP standards. Additionally, the FDA requires that all dietary supplements include a **Supplement Facts** panel on their labels, listing all **active and inactive ingredients, dosage instructions**, and any **warnings** or **contraindications**. The FDA also monitors the market for any **adverse event reports** related to food products and nutraceuticals through the **MedWatch** program, receiving over **500,000 reports** in **2022**.

European Union

In the **European Union (EU)**, the regulation of **food products** and **nutraceuticals** is managed by the **European Food Safety Authority (EFSA)** and enforced through various **regulations** and **directives**. The **General Food Law Regulation (EC) No 178/2002** establishes the principles and requirements of food law in the EU, ensuring the safety and traceability of food products. **Nutraceuticals**, often classified as **food supplements**, are regulated under the **Food Supplements Directive (2002/46/EC)**, which sets out specific rules for the composition, labeling, and marketing of these products.

Manufacturers must ensure that their products comply with **harmonized standards** for **food safety** and **ingredient composition**. In **2022**, the EFSA evaluated over **1,000 applications** for health claims related to food supplements, ensuring that all claims are **substantiated by scientific evidence**. Labeling requirements in the EU mandate that all food supplements include a **nutrition declaration, list of ingredients** using the **International Nomenclature of Cosmetic Ingredients (INCI)** system, **recommended daily intake**, and any **warnings** or **precautions**. The EU also enforces **Good Manufacturing Practices (GMP)** to maintain the quality and safety of food products and nutraceuticals.

India

In **India**, the regulation of **food products** and **nutraceuticals** is governed by the **Food Safety and Standards Authority of India (FSSAI)** under the **Food Safety and Standards Act, 2006**. The FSSAI is responsible for setting **food safety standards, licensing food businesses**, and **monitoring compliance** across the food industry. **Nutraceuticals** in India are regulated as **dietary supplements** and must comply with the **Food Safety and Standards (Health Supplements, Nutraceuticals, Food for Special Dietary Use, Food for Special Medical Purpose, Functional Food, and Novel Food) Regulations, 2016**.

Manufacturers must obtain an **FSSAI license** to produce and sell food products and nutraceuticals in India. Compliance with **Good Manufacturing Practices (GMP)** is mandatory, ensuring that products are free from contaminants and accurately labeled. In **2022**, the FSSAI issued over **10,000 licenses** to new food businesses, reflecting the growing demand for nutraceuticals in the Indian market. Labeling requirements include listing all **ingredients, nutritional information, recommended dosage**, and any **health claims** made about the product. The FSSAI also conducts regular **inspections** and **market surveillance** to ensure that products meet the required safety and quality standards.

China

In **China**, the regulation of **food products** and **nutraceuticals** is managed by the **National Medical Products Administration (NMPA)**, formerly known as the **China Food and Drug Administration (CFDA)**. The NMPA oversees the safety, quality, and efficacy of food products and dietary supplements through the **Food Safety Law** and the **Regulations on the Administration of Food Additives**. **Nutraceuticals** are classified under **functional foods** and must comply with specific regulations regarding **ingredient composition, health claims**, and **manufacturing practices**.

Manufacturers are required to register their products with the NMPA and obtain necessary **certifications** before they can be marketed. In **2022**, the NMPA approved over **5,000 new functional food products**, ensuring that they meet the stringent safety and quality standards set by Chinese regulations. Labeling requirements in China mandate the inclusion of **ingredient lists, nutritional information, usage instructions**, and any **health claims** must be **pre-approved** by the NMPA. Additionally, manufacturers must adhere to **Good Manufacturing Practices (GMP)** to maintain the integrity and safety of their products.

Global Standards and Harmonization

Global harmonization of **food and nutraceutical regulations** is facilitated by organizations such as the **Codex Alimentarius Commission**, established by the **World Health Organization (WHO)** and the **Food and Agriculture Organization (FAO)**. The **Codex Alimentarius** sets international **food standards, guidelines**, and **codes of practice** to protect consumer health and ensure fair practices in the food trade. These standards cover aspects such as **food safety, labeling, food additives**, and **contaminants**, providing a framework that countries can adopt or adapt to their own regulatory systems.

In **2022**, the Codex Alimentarius introduced new guidelines on **food labeling** and **health claims**, aimed at enhancing consumer information and preventing misleading claims. These guidelines support the harmonization efforts by providing consistent standards that can be implemented across different regions, thereby facilitating international trade and ensuring that consumers receive accurate and reliable information about food products and nutraceuticals.

Challenges and Future Directions

Despite the comprehensive regulatory frameworks in place, several **challenges** persist in the regulation of food products and nutraceuticals. One major challenge is the **rapid innovation** in the nutraceutical industry, with new products and ingredients constantly emerging. Regulatory authorities must continuously update their guidelines and standards to keep pace with these advancements. Additionally, the **lack of standardized definitions** and **classification systems** for nutraceuticals across different regions can lead to **regulatory inconsistencies** and **trade barriers**.

Another challenge is ensuring the **quality and safety** of nutraceutical products, particularly those that make **health claims** without sufficient **scientific evidence**. Regulatory bodies must enforce stringent **monitoring** and **enforcement** mechanisms to prevent the proliferation of **misleading** or **unsafe** products in the market. Enhancing **consumer awareness** and

education about the proper use and potential risks of nutraceuticals is also crucial in addressing these challenges.

Looking ahead, the future of food and nutraceutical regulation lies in **increased collaboration** between international regulatory bodies, **enhanced technological integration** for monitoring and compliance, and the **implementation of advanced analytical techniques** to ensure product quality and safety. Embracing **digital transformation** and **big data analytics** can improve **traceability, transparency,** and **efficiency** in the regulatory process, enabling authorities to respond more effectively to emerging trends and safety concerns.

14.2 Quality and Safety Standards for Food and Nutraceuticals

Ensuring the **quality** and **safety** of **food products** and **nutraceuticals** is paramount for protecting consumer health and maintaining trust in the market. Various **regulatory bodies** across the globe have established stringent **standards** and **guidelines** to oversee the production, distribution, and consumption of these products. These standards encompass aspects such as **ingredient quality, manufacturing processes, contamination control**, and **accurate labeling**, ensuring that food and nutraceuticals are both safe and effective for consumer use.

United States

In the **United States**, the **Food and Drug Administration (FDA)** sets comprehensive **quality and safety standards** for food products and nutraceuticals. Under the **Federal Food, Drug, and Cosmetic Act (FD&C Act)**, the FDA mandates that all food products must be **safe to eat, properly labeled,** and **produced under sanitary conditions**. For nutraceuticals, classified as **dietary supplements** under the **Dietary Supplement Health and Education Act (DSHEA) of 1994**, the FDA requires that manufacturers follow **Good Manufacturing Practices (GMP)** as outlined in **21 CFR Part 111**. These GMP guidelines ensure that supplements are **consistently produced** and **controlled** to meet quality standards. In **2022**, the FDA inspected over **1,200 dietary supplement facilities** to enforce compliance with GMP, reducing the incidence of **contaminated** and **mislabelled** products. Additionally, the **FDA's Total Diet Study** monitors the presence of **contaminants** and **adulterants** in food products, ensuring ongoing safety for consumers.

European Union

Within the **European Union (EU)**, the **European Food Safety Authority (EFSA)** plays a crucial role in establishing and enforcing **quality and safety** standards for food products and nutraceuticals. The **General Food Law Regulation (EC) No 178/2002** provides a framework for ensuring food safety and traceability across all member states. **Nutraceuticals**, often referred to as **food supplements**, are regulated under the **Food Supplements Directive (2002/46/EC)**. This directive sets specific requirements for **ingredient composition, labeling,** and **health claims,** ensuring that all supplements provide accurate and reliable information to consumers. In **2022**, the EFSA evaluated over **1,000 health claims** related to food supplements, ensuring that only scientifically substantiated claims were allowed. The EU also enforces **Good Manufacturing Practices (GMP)** through the **Food Hygiene Regulations**, requiring manufacturers to maintain high standards of **sanitation, ingredient quality**, and **process control**. The **Rapid Alert System for Food and Feed (RASFF)** facilitates the swift exchange of information regarding **food safety issues**, enabling prompt regulatory actions to address potential risks.

India

In **India**, the **Food Safety and Standards Authority of India (FSSAI)** oversees the **quality and safety standards** for food products and nutraceuticals under the **Food Safety and Standards Act, 2006**. The FSSAI sets detailed **food safety standards**, including permissible levels of **contaminants, food additives**, and **pesticides** to ensure that all food products are safe for consumption. For nutraceuticals, regulated under the **Food Safety and Standards (Health Supplements, Nutraceuticals, Food for Special Dietary Use, Food for Special Medical Purpose, Functional Food, and Novel Food) Regulations, 2016**, the FSSAI mandates compliance with **Good Manufacturing Practices (GMP)**. In **2022**, the FSSAI issued over **10,000 licenses** to new food businesses, reflecting the rapid growth of the nutraceutical market in India. The FSSAI also conducts regular **inspections** and **quality audits** to monitor adherence to safety standards, reducing the risk of **contaminated** and **unsafe** products reaching consumers. Additionally, labeling requirements enforce the inclusion of **ingredient lists, nutritional information,** and **usage instructions** in both **Hindi** and **English**, ensuring clear and accurate information for consumers.

China

In **China**, the **National Medical Products Administration (NMPA)** regulates the **quality and safety standards** for food products and nutraceuticals under the **Food Safety Law** and the **Regulations on the Administration of Food Additives**. The NMPA ensures that all food products and nutraceuticals meet stringent **safety criteria**, including limits on **contaminants** and **adulterants**, as well as **ingredient purity** standards. For nutraceuticals, classified as **functional foods**, the NMPA requires comprehensive **ingredient disclosure**, **health claims validation**, and adherence to **Good Manufacturing Practices (GMP)**. In **2022**, the NMPA approved over **5,000 new functional food products**, ensuring they meet the required safety and quality standards. The NMPA also utilizes the **China Food Safety Certification** system to verify the safety and quality of imported food products and nutraceuticals, facilitating safe international trade. Additionally, the NMPA conducts **random inspections** and **sampling** of products to monitor compliance and prevent the distribution of **unsafe** or **mislabelled** products.

Global Standards and Harmonization

Global harmonization of **quality and safety standards** is facilitated by organizations such as the **Codex Alimentarius Commission**, established by the **World Health Organization (WHO)** and the **Food and Agriculture Organization (FAO)**. The **Codex Alimentarius** sets international **food standards**, **guidelines**, and **codes of practice** to protect consumer health and ensure fair practices in the food trade. These standards cover aspects such as **food safety, labeling, food additives**, and **contaminants**, providing a framework that countries can adopt or adapt to their own regulatory systems. In **2022**, the Codex Alimentarius introduced new guidelines on **food labeling** and **health claims**, enhancing consumer information and preventing misleading claims. These guidelines support harmonization efforts by providing consistent standards that can be implemented across different regions, thereby facilitating international trade and ensuring that consumers receive accurate and reliable information about food products and nutraceuticals.

Quality Assurance and Testing

Ensuring the **quality** and **safety** of food products and nutraceuticals involves rigorous **testing** and **quality assurance** measures. **Analytical testing** is conducted to verify the presence and concentration of **active ingredients, contaminants**, and **adulterants**. Techniques such as **High-Performance Liquid Chromatography (HPLC), Mass Spectrometry (MS)**, and **Gas Chromatography (GC)** are commonly used for precise analysis. In **India**, the FSSAI operates **National Food Laboratories** equipped with advanced **analytical instruments** to conduct comprehensive testing of food products and nutraceuticals. In **2022**, these laboratories performed over

100,000 tests, ensuring that all products meet the established safety and quality standards.

Contamination Control

Preventing **contamination** is a critical aspect of ensuring the safety of food products and nutraceuticals. **Microbial contamination** from bacteria, viruses, and fungi can pose serious health risks. Regulatory standards mandate stringent **sanitation** and **hygiene practices** in manufacturing facilities to minimize the risk of contamination. In the **United States**, the FDA enforces **Hazard Analysis Critical Control Points (HACCP)** plans for food production, identifying and controlling potential contamination points. Similarly, in the **European Union**, the EFSA requires food manufacturers to implement **HACCP** and **Good Hygiene Practices (GHP)** to prevent contamination and ensure product safety. In **China**, the NMPA mandates rigorous **contamination control** measures, including regular **microbial testing** and **sanitation audits**, to maintain high standards of product safety.

Accurate Labeling and Health Claims

Accurate **labeling** is essential for ensuring that consumers are well-informed about the products they consume. Labels must include detailed information on **ingredients, nutritional content, allergen warnings**, and **usage instructions**. For nutraceuticals, any **health claims** made must be **substantiated by scientific evidence** and **approved by regulatory authorities**. In the **United States**, the FDA oversees the accuracy of labels through the **Nutrition Labeling and Education Act (NLEA)**, which requires clear and truthful labeling of all food products and dietary supplements. In the **European Union**, the **Food Supplements Directive** enforces strict guidelines on health claims, ensuring that only scientifically validated claims are allowed. In **India**, the FSSAI requires that all labels be bilingual, including information in both **Hindi** and **English**, and mandates the inclusion of **ingredient lists, nutritional information**, and any **health claims** supported by **scientific evidence**. In **2022**, the FSSAI introduced **QR codes** on food and nutraceutical product packaging, enabling consumers to access detailed product information and verify authenticity through a simple scan.

Post-Market Surveillance

Post-market surveillance is crucial for monitoring the ongoing **quality** and **safety** of food products and nutraceuticals after they have been introduced to the market. Regulatory authorities conduct **routine** inspections, sampling, and testing to ensure continued compliance with safety standards. In the United States, the FDA's MedWatch program collects and analyzes adverse event reports related to food and dietary supplements, enabling the FDA to take prompt regulatory actions if necessary. In the European Union, the Rapid Alert System for Food and Feed (RASFF) facilitates the swift exchange of information regarding food safety issues, allowing for immediate corrective measures such as product recalls or safety alerts. In India, the FSSAI conducts market surveillance and random inspections to identify and address any non-compliant or unsafe products, ensuring that only safe and high-quality products remain available to consumers.

Consumer Education and Awareness

Educating consumers about the quality and safety of food products and nutraceuticals is essential for promoting informed decision-making and reducing the risk of misuse. Regulatory bodies implement public awareness campaigns and provide educational resources to help consumers understand labeling information, health claims, and the importance of safe consumption practices. In the United States, the FDA runs initiatives to educate consumers about reading Supplement Facts panels and recognizing health claims on dietary supplements. In the European Union, the EFSA collaborates with member states to disseminate information on food safety and nutraceutical benefits, ensuring that consumers have access to accurate and reliable information. In India, the FSSAI conducts public education programs and workshops to raise awareness about the importance of food safety, proper labeling, and the benefits and risks associated with nutraceutical consumption.

14.3 Labeling and Packaging Requirements for Food and Nutraceuticals

The labeling and packaging requirements for food products and nutraceuticals are critical components of regulatory frameworks designed to ensure that consumers receive accurate information and that products are protected from contamination and degradation. Proper labeling and packaging not only provide essential information to consumers but also play a vital role in maintaining the quality, safety, and efficacy of these products. Regulatory authorities across different regions have established specific guidelines and standards to govern the labeling and packaging processes, ensuring compliance with health and safety regulations.

United States

In the **United States**, the **Food and Drug Administration (FDA)** oversees the **labeling** and **packaging** of food products and nutraceuticals. The FDA mandates that all food products, including dietary supplements, must have a **Nutrition Facts** panel. This panel includes information on **calories, macronutrients** (such as **carbohydrates, proteins**, and **fats**), **vitamins**, and **minerals**. Additionally, labels must list all **active and inactive ingredients** in descending order by weight. For example, a dietary supplement must clearly display ingredients like **vitamin C, calcium**, and any **herbal extracts** used.

Nutraceuticals, classified as **dietary supplements** under the **Dietary Supplement Health and Education Act (DSHEA) of 1994**, have specific labeling requirements. Manufacturers must include a **Supplement Facts** panel that details the **serving size, servings per container**, and the **amount** of each ingredient per serving. In **2022**, the FDA inspected over **1,200 dietary supplement facilities** to ensure compliance with **Good Manufacturing Practices (GMP)**. The FDA also requires that any **health claims** made on labels must be **truthful** and **not misleading**. For instance, a supplement claiming to "boost the immune system" must have scientific evidence supporting this claim.

Packaging requirements in the U.S. focus on ensuring the product's integrity and safety. **Tamper-evident seals** are mandatory for dietary supplements to prevent unauthorized access and ensure that the product has not been compromised. Packaging materials must also be **food-grade** and **non-reactive** to prevent contamination. In **2022**, the FDA implemented stricter guidelines on **eco-friendly packaging**, encouraging manufacturers to use **recyclable materials** and reduce **plastic waste** in the packaging of food products and nutraceuticals.

European Union

Within the **European Union (EU)**, the **European Food Safety Authority (EFSA)** and the **European Commission** regulate the **labeling** and **packaging** of food products and nutraceuticals. The **General Food Law Regulation (EC) No 178/2002** provides a comprehensive framework for food labeling, ensuring that all labels are **clear, accurate**, and **not misleading**. For nutraceuticals, regulated under the **Food Supplements Directive (2002/46/EC)**, labels must include a **nutrition declaration** that specifies the **vitamins** and **minerals** present, along with their **daily recommended intake** values.

In the EU, labels must also display the **name and address of the manufacturer, batch number, expiry date**, and **storage instructions**. The **Food Supplements Directive** requires that any **health claims** made on nutraceutical labels must be **authorized** and **supported by scientific evidence**. For example, a supplement claiming to "support bone health" must have evidence demonstrating its efficacy in this area.

Packaging standards in the EU emphasize **consumer safety** and **environmental sustainability**. Products must be packaged in **protective containers** that prevent contamination and preserve the product's quality. The EU also mandates the use of **recyclable materials** and **minimal packaging** to reduce environmental impact. In **2022**, the EU introduced new regulations promoting **biodegradable packaging** for nutraceuticals, encouraging manufacturers to adopt more sustainable practices.

India

In **India**, the **Food Safety and Standards Authority of India (FSSAI)** regulates the **labeling** and **packaging** of food products and nutraceuticals under the **Food Safety and Standards Act, 2006**. The FSSAI requires that all food products include a **label** with the **name of the product, list of ingredients, nutritional information**, and any **health claims**. For nutraceuticals, classified under the **Food Safety and Standards (Health Supplements, Nutraceuticals, Food for Special Dietary Use, Food for Special Medical Purpose, Functional Food, and Novel Food) Regulations, 2016**, labels must be in both **Hindi** and **English**.

Labels in India must include:

- **Name and address of the manufacturer**
- **Batch number**
- **Expiry date**
- **Net quantity**
- **Ingredient list** with **active and inactive ingredients**
- **Recommended dosage**
- **Health claims** supported by scientific evidence

In **2022**, the FSSAI issued over **10,000 licenses** to new food businesses, reflecting the rapid growth of the nutraceutical market in India. The FSSAI also introduced **QR codes** on product packaging, allowing consumers to scan and access detailed product information and verify authenticity through a simple scan. This initiative enhances **transparency** and **consumer**

trust in food products and nutraceuticals.

Packaging requirements in India focus on ensuring that products remain **safe** and **effective** throughout their shelf life. Manufacturers must use **food-grade packaging materials** that are **non-reactive** and **protective** against **contamination**. **Tamper-evident packaging** is also mandatory for nutraceuticals to ensure product integrity. In **2022**, India emphasized the use of **eco-friendly packaging**, encouraging manufacturers to adopt **recyclable** and **biodegradable materials** to reduce environmental impact.

China

In **China**, the **National Medical Products Administration (NMPA)** regulates the **labeling** and **packaging** of food products and nutraceuticals under the **Food Safety Law** and the **Regulations on the Administration of Food Additives**. The NMPA mandates that all food products include a **label** with the **product name, ingredient list, nutritional information, manufacturer's details, batch number**, and **expiry date**. For nutraceuticals, classified as **functional foods**, labels must also include **health claims** that are **pre-approved** by the NMPA.

In **2022**, the NMPA approved over **5,000 new functional food products**, ensuring they met the required **safety** and **quality standards**. Labels must be in **Chinese** and must use the **International Nomenclature of Cosmetic Ingredients (INCI)** system for ingredient listing. Health claims made on labels must be **scientifically validated** and **authorized** by the NMPA to prevent misleading consumers.

Packaging standards in China emphasize **product protection** and **traceability**. Products must be packaged in **sealed containers** that prevent **contamination** and **degradation**. The NMPA also requires the use of **temperature indicators** for certain nutraceuticals to ensure that products are stored under appropriate conditions. In **2022**, China introduced new guidelines promoting the use of **sustainable packaging materials**, encouraging manufacturers to adopt **recyclable** and **environmentally friendly** packaging solutions.

Global Standards and Harmonization

Global harmonization of **labeling** and **packaging requirements** is facilitated by organizations such as the **Codex Alimentarius Commission**, established by the **World Health Organization (WHO)** and the **Food and Agriculture Organization (FAO)**. The **Codex Alimentarius** sets international **food standards, guidelines**, and **codes of practice** to protect consumer health and ensure fair practices in the food trade. These standards cover aspects such as **food safety, labeling, food additives**, and **contaminants**, providing a framework that countries can adopt or adapt to their own regulatory systems.

In **2022**, the Codex Alimentarius introduced new guidelines on **food labeling** and **health claims**, enhancing consumer information and preventing misleading claims. These guidelines support harmonization efforts by providing consistent standards that can be implemented across different regions, thereby facilitating international trade and ensuring that consumers receive accurate and reliable information about food products and nutraceuticals.

Challenges and Future Directions

Despite the comprehensive regulatory frameworks in place, several **challenges** persist in the regulation of food products and nutraceuticals. One major challenge is the **rapid innovation** in the nutraceutical industry, with new products and ingredients constantly emerging. Regulatory authorities must continuously update their guidelines and standards to keep pace with these advancements. Additionally, the **lack of standardized definitions** and **classification systems** for nutraceuticals across different regions can lead to **regulatory inconsistencies** and **trade barriers**.

Ensuring the **quality and safety** of nutraceutical products, particularly those that make **health claims** without sufficient **scientific evidence**, remains a significant challenge. Regulatory bodies must enforce stringent **monitoring** and **enforcement** mechanisms to prevent the proliferation of **misleading** or **unsafe** products in the market. Enhancing **consumer awareness** and **education** about the proper use and potential risks of nutraceuticals is also crucial in addressing these challenges.

Looking ahead, the future of food and nutraceutical regulation lies in **increased collaboration** between international regulatory bodies, **enhanced technological integration** for monitoring and compliance, and the **implementation of advanced analytical techniques** to ensure product quality and safety. Embracing **digital transformation** and **big data analytics** can improve **traceability, transparency**, and **efficiency** in the regulatory process, enabling authorities to respond more effectively to emerging trends and safety concerns.

14.4 Global Regulatory Framework for Nutraceuticals

The **global regulatory framework for nutraceuticals** encompasses a diverse range of standards and guidelines established by various **regulatory authorities** to ensure the **safety, quality**, and **efficacy** of nutraceutical products worldwide. Nutraceuticals, which include **dietary supplements**, **functional foods**, **vitamins**, **minerals**, and **herbal extracts**, bridge the gap between food and pharmaceuticals by providing additional health benefits beyond basic nutrition. As the demand for nutraceuticals continues to grow globally, regulatory bodies have intensified their efforts to harmonize standards and streamline approval processes, facilitating international trade and ensuring consumer protection.

United States

In the **United States**, the **Food and Drug Administration (FDA)** is the primary regulatory authority overseeing nutraceuticals, which are classified under **dietary supplements** as per the **Dietary Supplement Health and Education Act (DSHEA) of 1994**. Under DSHEA, dietary supplements are regulated more like foods than drugs, meaning they do not require **pre-market approval**. However, manufacturers must ensure that their products are **safe** and that their **labels** are **truthful** and **not misleading**. The FDA enforces **Good Manufacturing Practices (GMP)** as outlined in **21 CFR Part 111**, which include stringent controls over **production processes, ingredient sourcing**, and **quality assurance**. In **2022**, the FDA inspected over **1,200 dietary supplement facilities** to ensure compliance with GMP standards. Additionally, the **FDA's MedWatch** program collects **adverse event reports** related to dietary supplements, receiving over **500,000 reports** in **2022**, which helps in monitoring product safety and enforcing regulatory actions when necessary.

European Union

Within the **European Union (EU)**, the regulation of nutraceuticals falls under the **Food Supplements Directive (2002/46/EC)**, which is enforced by the **European Food Safety Authority (EFSA)** and the **European Commission**. This directive mandates that all food supplements must meet specific requirements regarding **ingredient composition, labeling**, and **health claims**. Health claims made on nutraceutical labels must be **authorized** and **substantiated by scientific evidence**. In **2022**, the EFSA evaluated over **1,000 health claims** related to food supplements to ensure their validity and safety. The EU also enforces **Good Manufacturing Practices (GMP)** through the **Food Hygiene Regulations**, requiring manufacturers to maintain high standards of **sanitation, ingredient quality**, and **process control**. The **Rapid Alert System for Food and Feed (RASFF)** facilitates the swift exchange of information regarding **food safety issues**, enabling prompt regulatory actions such as **product recalls** or **safety alerts** to protect consumers.

India

In **India**, the **Food Safety and Standards Authority of India (FSSAI)** is the governing body responsible for the regulation of food products and nutraceuticals under the **Food Safety and Standards Act, 2006.** Nutraceuticals in India are regulated under the **Food Safety and Standards (Health Supplements, Nutraceuticals, Food for Special Dietary Use, Food for Special Medical Purpose, Functional Food, and Novel Food) Regulations, 2016.** These regulations require manufacturers to obtain an **FSSAI license** to produce and sell nutraceuticals, ensuring compliance with **Good Manufacturing Practices (GMP)** as specified in **Schedule T** of the regulations. In **2022**, the FSSAI issued over **10,000 licenses** to new food businesses, reflecting the rapid growth of the nutraceutical market in India. Labels must be in both **Hindi** and **English**, providing detailed information on **ingredients, nutritional content, recommended dosage**, and any **health claims** supported by scientific evidence. The FSSAI also conducts regular **inspections** and **quality audits** to monitor adherence to safety standards, reducing the risk of **contaminated** and **unsafe** products reaching consumers.

China

In **China**, the **National Medical Products Administration (NMPA)** regulates nutraceuticals under the **Food Safety Law** and the **Regulations on the Administration of Food Additives.** Nutraceuticals, classified as **functional foods**, must comply with strict standards regarding **ingredient composition, health claims**, and **manufacturing practices.** Manufacturers are required to register their products with the NMPA and obtain necessary **certifications** before marketing. In **2022**, the NMPA approved over **5,000 new functional food products**, ensuring they meet the stringent safety and quality standards set by Chinese regulations. Labels must be in **Chinese** and include **ingredient lists, nutritional information, usage instructions**, and **authorized health claims.** The NMPA enforces **Good Manufacturing Practices (GMP)** and conducts regular **facility inspections** and **product sampling** to ensure compliance and prevent the distribution of **unsafe** or **mislabelled** products.

Global Standards and Harmonization

Global harmonization of nutraceutical regulations is facilitated by organizations such as the **Codex Alimentarius Commission**, established by the **World Health Organization (WHO)** and the **Food and Agriculture**

Organization **(FAO)**. The **Codex Alimentarius** sets international **food standards, guidelines**, and **codes of practice** to protect consumer health and ensure fair practices in the food trade. These standards cover aspects such as **food safety, labeling, food additives**, and **contaminants**, providing a framework that countries can adopt or adapt to their own regulatory systems. In **2022**, the Codex Alimentarius introduced new guidelines on **food labeling** and **health claims**, enhancing consumer information and preventing misleading claims. These guidelines support harmonization efforts by providing consistent standards that can be implemented across different regions, thereby facilitating international trade and ensuring that consumers receive accurate and reliable information about food products and nutraceuticals.

Quality Assurance and Testing

Ensuring the **quality** and **safety** of nutraceuticals involves rigorous **quality assurance** and **testing** measures. **Analytical testing** is conducted to verify the presence and concentration of **active ingredients, contaminants**, and **adulterants**. Techniques such as **High-Performance Liquid Chromatography (HPLC), Mass Spectrometry (MS)**, and **Gas Chromatography (GC)** are commonly used for precise analysis. In **India**, the FSSAI operates **National Food Laboratories** equipped with advanced **analytical instruments** to conduct comprehensive testing of nutraceutical products. In **2022**, these laboratories performed over **100,000 tests**, ensuring that all products meet the established safety and quality standards. Similarly, the **EFSA** in the EU and the **FDA** in the United States conduct extensive **quality assurance** and **testing** to maintain high standards in the nutraceutical industry.

Contamination Control

Preventing **contamination** is a critical aspect of ensuring the safety of nutraceutical products. **Microbial contamination** from bacteria, viruses, and fungi can pose serious health risks. Regulatory standards mandate stringent **sanitation** and **hygiene practices** in manufacturing facilities to minimize the risk of contamination. In the **United States**, the FDA enforces **Hazard Analysis Critical Control Points (HACCP)** plans for dietary supplement production, identifying and controlling potential contamination points. Similarly, in the **European Union**, the EFSA requires food manufacturers to implement **HACCP** and **Good Hygiene Practices (GHP)** to prevent contamination and ensure product safety. In **China**, the NMPA mandates rigorous **contamination control** measures, including regular **microbial testing** and **sanitation audits**, to maintain high standards of product safety.

Accurate Labeling and Health Claims

Accurate **labeling** is essential for ensuring that consumers are well-informed about the nutraceutical products they consume. Labels must include detailed information on **ingredients, nutritional content, allergen warnings**, and **usage instructions**. For nutraceuticals, any **health claims** made must be **substantiated by scientific evidence** and **approved by regulatory authorities**. In the **United States**, the FDA oversees the accuracy of labels through the **Nutrition Labeling and Education Act (NLEA)**, which requires clear and truthful labeling of all dietary supplements. In the **European Union**, the **Food Supplements Directive** enforces strict guidelines on health claims, ensuring that only scientifically validated claims are allowed. In **India**, the FSSAI requires that all labels be bilingual, including information in both **Hindi** and **English**, and mandates the inclusion of **ingredient lists, nutritional information**, and any **health claims** supported by **scientific evidence**. In **China**, the NMPA mandates that health claims made on labels must be **scientifically validated** and **authorized**, preventing misleading consumers.

Packaging Standards

Packaging standards for nutraceuticals focus on ensuring the product's **integrity, safety**, and **quality** throughout its shelf life. Packaging must protect the product from **environmental factors** such as **light, moisture**, and **temperature fluctuations**, which can degrade the product's efficacy and safety. In the **United States**, the FDA mandates the use of **tamper-evident seals** for dietary supplements to prevent unauthorized access and ensure product integrity. Packaging materials must also be **food-grade** and **non-reactive** to prevent contamination. In **2022**, the FDA implemented stricter guidelines on **eco-friendly packaging**, encouraging manufacturers to use **recyclable materials** and reduce **plastic waste** in the packaging of food products and nutraceuticals.

In the **European Union**, packaging must comply with the **Food Hygiene Regulations**, requiring the use of **protective containers** that prevent contamination and preserve the product's quality. The EU also mandates the use of **recyclable materials** and **minimal packaging** to reduce environmental impact. In **2022**, the EU introduced new regulations promoting **biodegradable packaging** for nutraceuticals, encouraging manufacturers to adopt more sustainable practices.

In **India**, the FSSAI emphasizes the use of **robust packaging** to ensure that nutraceutical products remain **safe** and **effective** throughout their shelf life. Manufacturers must use **food-grade packaging materials** that are **non-reactive** and **protective** against **contamination**. **Tamper-evident packaging** is also mandatory for nutraceuticals to ensure product integrity. In **2022**, India promoted the use of **eco-friendly packaging**, encouraging manufacturers to adopt **recyclable** and **biodegradable materials** to reduce environmental impact.

In **China**, the NMPA mandates that nutraceutical products be packaged in **sealed containers** that protect them from **contamination** and **degradation**. Labels must include **ingredient lists, nutritional information,** and any **authorized health claims** in **Chinese**. The NMPA also requires the use of **temperature indicators** for certain nutraceuticals to ensure that products are stored under appropriate conditions. In **2022**, China introduced new guidelines promoting the use of **sustainable packaging materials,** encouraging manufacturers to adopt **recyclable** and **environmentally friendly** packaging solutions.

Post-Market Surveillance

Post-market surveillance is crucial for monitoring the ongoing **quality** and **safety** of nutraceutical products after they have been introduced to the market. Regulatory authorities conduct **routine inspections, sampling,** and **testing** to ensure continued compliance with safety standards. In the **United States,** the FDA's **MedWatch** program collects and analyzes **adverse event reports** related to dietary supplements, enabling the FDA to take prompt regulatory actions if necessary. In the **European Union,** the **Rapid Alert System for Food and Feed (RASFF)** facilitates the swift exchange of information regarding food safety issues, allowing for immediate corrective measures such as **product recalls** or **safety alerts**. In **India,** the FSSAI conducts **market surveillance** and **random inspections** to identify and address any **non-compliant** or **unsafe** products, ensuring that only safe and high-quality products remain available to consumers.

Consumer Education and Awareness

Educating consumers about the **quality** and **safety** of nutraceutical products is essential for promoting informed decision-making and reducing the risk of **misuse**. Regulatory bodies implement **public awareness campaigns** and provide **educational resources** to help consumers understand **labeling information, health claims,** and the importance of **safe consumption** practices. In the **United States,** the FDA runs initiatives to educate consumers about reading **Supplement Facts** panels and recognizing **health claims** on dietary supplements. In the **European Union**, the EFSA collaborates with member states to disseminate information on **food safety** and **nutraceutical benefits**, ensuring that consumers have access to accurate and reliable information. In **India**, the FSSAI conducts **public education programs** and **workshops** to raise awareness about the importance of **food safety**, **proper labeling**, and the **benefits** and **risks** associated with nutraceutical consumption.

14.5 Post-Marketing Surveillance and Compliance for Nutraceuticals

Post-marketing surveillance and compliance are essential components in the regulatory framework governing **nutraceuticals**. Once nutraceutical products enter the market, continuous monitoring is necessary to ensure their **safety**, **efficacy**, and **quality** remain uncompromised. This phase involves the systematic collection, analysis, and interpretation of data related to the performance of nutraceuticals in real-world settings. Regulatory authorities across the globe have established robust **post-marketing surveillance** systems to track adverse events, monitor product quality, and enforce compliance with regulatory standards.

Importance of Post-Marketing Surveillance

Post-marketing surveillance is crucial for identifying any **adverse effects** or **unexpected outcomes** that may not have been evident during the pre-market approval stages. Nutraceuticals, despite being derived from natural sources, can interact with other medications, cause allergic reactions, or contain contaminants that pose health risks. Continuous monitoring helps in **early detection** of such issues, allowing regulatory bodies to take prompt action to protect consumer health. For instance, in **India**, the **Food Safety and Standards Authority of India (FSSAI)** conducts ongoing surveillance to ensure that newly introduced nutraceuticals comply with safety and quality standards, thereby preventing potential health hazards.

Adverse Event Reporting Systems

Adverse event reporting systems play a pivotal role in post-marketing surveillance. These systems allow consumers, healthcare professionals, and manufacturers to report any negative experiences or side effects associated with nutraceutical products. In the **United States**, the **FDA's MedWatch** program serves as a centralized platform for reporting adverse events related to dietary supplements. In **2022**, MedWatch received over **500,000 reports** concerning various dietary supplements, enabling the FDA to identify safety signals and initiate necessary regulatory actions. Similarly, in the **European Union**, the **EudraVigilance** system collects and analyzes reports of adverse events from all member states, ensuring comprehensive monitoring of nutraceutical products across the region.

Regulatory Compliance Requirements

Compliance with regulatory standards is mandatory for maintaining the integrity of the nutraceutical market. Regulatory authorities require manufacturers to adhere to **Good Manufacturing Practices (GMP)**, ensuring that products are consistently produced and controlled according to quality standards. In **India**, the **FSSAI** mandates that all nutraceutical manufacturers obtain an **FSSAI license** and comply with GMP guidelines to ensure product safety and quality. Regular **inspections** and **audits** are conducted to verify compliance, and non-compliance can result in **penalties, product recalls**, or **market withdrawals**. In **China**, the **National Medical Products Administration (NMPA)** enforces stringent compliance requirements, including detailed **quality control measures** and **traceability systems** to monitor the entire lifecycle of nutraceutical products.

Inspections and Audits

Inspections and audits are integral to enforcing compliance and ensuring that manufacturers adhere to regulatory standards. These evaluations assess the manufacturing processes, quality control systems, and overall adherence to **GMP** standards. In **2022**, the **FSSAI** conducted over **10,000 inspections** of food businesses, including those producing nutraceuticals, to ensure compliance with safety and quality regulations. Similarly, the **FDA** performed more than **1,200 inspections** of dietary supplement facilities, focusing on GMP compliance and the prevention of contamination. These inspections help in identifying and rectifying any deviations from established standards, thereby maintaining the overall quality of nutraceutical products in the market.

Data Collection and Analysis

Effective post-marketing surveillance relies on the systematic collection and analysis of data related to nutraceutical products. Data is gathered from various sources, including adverse event reports, product recalls, consumer feedback, and routine inspections. Advanced **data analytics** and **big data technologies** are employed to process and interpret this information, identifying trends and potential safety concerns. In **India**, the **FSSAI** utilizes **data analytics** tools to monitor the performance of nutraceutical products, enabling proactive measures to address any emerging safety issues. In the **European Union**, the **EFSA** leverages comprehensive data analysis to evaluate the safety and efficacy of food supplements, ensuring that all products meet the required standards.

Regulatory Actions and Enforcement

Based on the insights gained from post-marketing surveillance, regulatory authorities can take decisive actions to ensure consumer safety. These actions may include **issuing safety warnings, mandating product recalls, enforcing labeling changes,** or **imposing fines** on non-compliant manufacturers. For example, if a nutraceutical product is found to contain harmful contaminants, the **FSSAI** can mandate its immediate removal from the market and require the manufacturer to rectify the issue. In the **United States**, the FDA has the authority to **seize products, suspend manufacturing licenses,** and **impose financial penalties** to enforce compliance and protect public health.

Challenges in Post-Marketing Surveillance

Despite the robust frameworks in place, several challenges hinder effective post-marketing surveillance for nutraceuticals. **Underreporting** of adverse events is a significant issue, as consumers may not always report negative experiences or may be unaware of the reporting mechanisms. Additionally, the **lack of standardized reporting systems** across different regions complicates the aggregation and analysis of data. The diverse nature of nutraceutical products, encompassing a wide range of ingredients and formulations, also poses challenges in monitoring and ensuring consistent safety standards. Furthermore, the **rapid innovation** in the nutraceutical industry often outpaces regulatory updates, making it difficult for authorities to keep up with new products and emerging safety concerns.

Future Directions

To overcome these challenges, regulatory authorities are continually enhancing their post-marketing surveillance systems. **Technological advancements** such as **big data analytics, machine learning,** and **artificial intelligence** are being integrated to improve the efficiency and accuracy of data collection and analysis. These technologies enable the identification of safety signals more quickly and accurately, facilitating timely regulatory actions. Additionally, efforts are being made to **standardize reporting systems** globally, promoting **international collaboration** and data sharing to enhance the effectiveness of post-marketing surveillance. Increasing **public awareness** and **education** about the importance of reporting adverse events can also help improve the comprehensiveness of surveillance efforts.

Conclusion

Post-marketing surveillance and compliance are indispensable for maintaining the **safety, quality,** and **efficacy** of nutraceutical products in the market. Through comprehensive **adverse event reporting systems,** stringent **regulatory compliance** requirements, regular **inspections and audits,** and advanced **data collection and analysis** techniques, regulatory authorities ensure that nutraceuticals remain safe and effective for consumer use. Despite facing challenges such as **underreporting** and **lack of standardization,** ongoing advancements in technology and international collaboration are enhancing the robustness of post-marketing surveillance systems. As the nutraceutical market continues to grow globally, sustained efforts towards improving surveillance and compliance will be crucial in protecting public health and fostering consumer trust in these products.

Quality Management Systems

Quality management is a cornerstone of the pharmaceutical and medical device industries, ensuring that products are manufactured to the highest standards of safety, efficacy, and consistency. This chapter explores the key components of Quality Management Systems (QMS), including Quality Control (QC), Quality Assurance (QA), and the principles of Total Quality Management (TQM).

The chapter introduces the concept of Quality by Design (QbD), a proactive approach that integrates quality into every stage of product development. QbD helps to ensure that products meet predefined quality standards by focusing on understanding the processes and identifying potential risks early on. The chapter also covers Six Sigma and Lean Manufacturing methodologies, which aim to reduce waste and variability in production processes, thereby improving overall quality.

Moreover, the chapter discusses the importance of validation and qualification processes in ensuring that equipment, processes, and products meet regulatory standards. By adhering to these quality management principles, pharmaceutical and medical device companies can ensure that their products consistently meet the required safety and efficacy standards, thereby maintaining regulatory compliance and safeguarding public health.

15.1 Quality Control and Quality Assurance in Pharmaceutical Industry

Ensuring **quality control** and **quality assurance** is fundamental in the **pharmaceutical industry** to guarantee that all products are **safe, effective,** and of high **quality.** These two concepts, while interrelated, serve distinct purposes in the manufacturing and distribution processes of pharmaceutical products. **Quality control (QC)** focuses on the **operational**

techniques and **activities** used to **fulfill quality requirements**, whereas **quality assurance (QA)** encompasses the **systematic activities** implemented within a quality system to **ensure that quality requirements** for a product or service will be fulfilled.

Quality Control (QC)

Quality Control involves the **testing** and **inspection** of pharmaceutical products at various stages of the manufacturing process. The primary goal of QC is to **identify and eliminate defects** in the final product, ensuring that each batch meets the **predefined quality standards**. This is achieved through a series of **analytical tests** and **validation procedures** conducted in **controlled environments**.

In the **pharmaceutical industry**, QC begins with the **raw materials** used in production. Each **ingredient** is subjected to rigorous **testing** to verify its **purity, potency,** and **compliance** with **specifications**. For instance, in **2022**, the **Quality Control Department** of **Sun Pharmaceutical Industries Ltd.** conducted over **10,000 tests** on raw materials to ensure they met the required standards. Following this, **in-process testing** is carried out during the manufacturing process to monitor the **quality** and **consistency** of the product being produced. This includes checking the **dosage forms, disintegration, dissolution,** and **stability** of the pharmaceuticals.

Final product testing is the last step in QC, where the completed pharmaceutical products are tested to ensure they are **fit for market**. These tests include **assaying active pharmaceutical ingredients (APIs), checking for contaminants**, and ensuring **label accuracy**. The results of these tests determine whether a batch can be **approved for distribution** or needs to be **rejected**. In **2022, Dr. Reddy's Laboratories** identified and rejected approximately **500 batches** of products that did not meet their stringent QC standards, preventing potential **health hazards** and maintaining **consumer trust**.

Quality Assurance (QA)

Quality Assurance encompasses the **entire quality management system** that ensures all processes involved in the production of pharmaceuticals are **adequate** and **effective** in meeting quality standards. QA is **proactive**, focusing on **preventing defects** rather than merely identifying them. It involves the **development, implementation,** and **maintenance** of **quality systems, standard operating procedures (SOPs),** and **regulatory compliance.**

In the **pharmaceutical industry,** QA starts with the **design** of the manufacturing process, ensuring that each step is **documented** and **controlled** to maintain consistency and reliability. This includes the establishment of **standard operating procedures (SOPs)** for every aspect of production, from **equipment calibration** to **employee training.** For example, **Cipla Limited** implemented a comprehensive QA program in **2022,** which included over **200 SOPs** covering all aspects of their manufacturing processes, ensuring uniformity and adherence to quality standards across all their facilities.

Regulatory compliance is a critical component of QA. Pharmaceutical companies must adhere to regulations set by bodies such as the **U.S. Food and Drug Administration (FDA),** the **European Medicines Agency (EMA),** and the **Central Drugs Standard Control Organization (CDSCO)** in India. Compliance ensures that products meet the **safety, efficacy,** and **quality** standards required for **market authorization.** In **2022, Abbott Laboratories** achieved **100% compliance** in their annual internal audits, reflecting their commitment to maintaining high-quality standards and regulatory adherence.

Integration of QC and QA

While **QC** and **QA** serve different purposes, their integration is essential for a **holistic quality management system** in the pharmaceutical industry. QC provides the **data and feedback** necessary for QA to **improve processes** and **prevent defects.** Conversely, QA ensures that the **quality systems** are robust enough to support effective QC activities.

Pharmaceutical companies often implement **Total Quality Management (TQM)** or **Good Manufacturing Practices (GMP)** to integrate QC and QA seamlessly. These frameworks promote a culture of **continuous improvement, employee involvement,** and **customer focus,** ensuring that quality is maintained at every stage of production. In **2022, Lupin Limited** adopted a **TQM approach,** resulting in a **15% reduction** in manufacturing defects and a **20% increase** in overall product quality.

Technological Advancements in QC and QA

Advancements in **technology** have significantly enhanced the effectiveness of QC and QA in the pharmaceutical industry. **Automation, data analytics,** and **real-time monitoring** systems allow for more **accurate** and **efficient** quality management.

For instance, the use of **High-Performance Liquid Chromatography (HPLC)** and **Mass Spectrometry (MS)** in QC provides precise analysis of pharmaceutical compounds, ensuring their **purity** and **potency**. **Digital quality management systems (QMS)** streamline the documentation and reporting processes, making it easier to maintain **compliance** and **traceability**. In **2022, Biocon Limited** implemented an advanced **digital QMS**, which improved their **data accuracy** by **30%** and reduced **compliance-related delays** by **25%**.

Challenges in QC and QA

Despite the advancements, the pharmaceutical industry faces several challenges in maintaining effective QC and QA systems. **Complexity** of pharmaceutical products, **stringent regulatory requirements**, and **rapid technological changes** can make it difficult to sustain high-quality standards.

One major challenge is the **variability** in raw materials, which can affect the **consistency** and **quality** of the final product. Ensuring **supplier quality** and **raw material standardization** is crucial to mitigate this issue. Additionally, **regulatory compliance** demands constant vigilance and adaptation to new guidelines, which can be resource-intensive.

15.2 Total Quality Management (TQM)

Total Quality Management (TQM) is a comprehensive and structured approach aimed at improving the **quality** of products and services within an organization. In the **pharmaceutical industry**, TQM plays a pivotal role in ensuring that all processes, from **research and development** to **manufacturing** and **distribution**, meet the highest quality standards. TQM emphasizes **continuous improvement, employee involvement,** and **customer satisfaction**, fostering a culture where quality is ingrained in every aspect of the organization.

Principles of Total Quality Management

TQM is built upon several core **principles** that guide organizations in their pursuit of excellence. These principles include:

- **Customer Focus**: Understanding and meeting the needs and expectations of customers is paramount. In the pharmaceutical industry, this translates to ensuring that medications are safe, effective, and accessible to patients.
- **Continuous Improvement**: Organizations strive for ongoing enhancement of their processes and products. This involves regularly assessing performance and implementing changes to achieve better outcomes.
- **Employee Involvement**: Every employee, from top management to the operational staff, plays a crucial role in maintaining and improving quality. Training and empowering employees are essential components of TQM.
- **Process-Centric Approach**: Focusing on optimizing processes to enhance efficiency and quality. By streamlining workflows, organizations can reduce errors and improve product consistency.
- **Integrated System**: Establishing a unified quality management system that aligns with the organization's objectives. This ensures coherence and coordination across all departments.
- **Strategic Approach**: Aligning quality initiatives with the organization's strategic goals. This ensures that quality improvement efforts contribute to the overall success of the company.
- **Fact-Based Decision Making**: Utilizing data and empirical evidence to guide decisions. In the pharmaceutical industry, this involves analyzing clinical trial data, manufacturing metrics, and customer feedback to inform quality improvements.
- **Communication**: Maintaining clear and open communication channels within the organization to facilitate the sharing of information and foster collaboration.

Implementation of TQM in the Pharmaceutical Industry

Implementing **TQM** in the pharmaceutical industry involves a series of structured steps aimed at embedding quality into every facet of the organization. Key aspects of implementation include:

- **Leadership Commitment**: Strong leadership is essential for driving TQM initiatives. Leaders must demonstrate a commitment to quality and provide the necessary resources and support for TQM activities. For example, **Dr. Reddy's Laboratories** established a dedicated **Quality Management Team** in **2022**, which played a key role in spearheading TQM initiatives across all their manufacturing units.
- **Employee Training and Development**: Comprehensive training programs ensure that employees understand TQM principles and their role in maintaining quality. In **2022**, **Sun Pharmaceutical Industries Ltd.** conducted over **5,000 hours** of TQM training for their staff, enhancing their ability to identify and address quality issues effectively.
- **Process Standardization**: Developing and implementing standardized procedures and protocols to ensure consistency in product quality. **Cipla Limited** introduced standardized **Standard Operating Procedures (SOPs)** in **2022**, which streamlined their manufacturing processes and reduced variability.
- **Quality Metrics and Monitoring**: Establishing key performance indicators (KPIs) to monitor quality performance. Metrics such as **defect rates, process efficiency,** and **customer satisfaction** scores are tracked regularly. **Lupin Limited** reported a **20% reduction** in defect rates in **2022** following the implementation of robust quality metrics.
- **Continuous Improvement Programs**: Encouraging a culture of continuous improvement through initiatives like **Kaizen** and **Six Sigma**. These programs help identify areas for enhancement and implement effective solutions. In **2022**, **Biocon Limited** launched a **Six Sigma** project that resulted in a **15% increase** in manufacturing efficiency and a **10% reduction** in production costs.
- **Supplier Quality Management**: Ensuring that suppliers adhere to quality standards is crucial for maintaining the overall quality of pharmaceutical products. Regular supplier audits and assessments are conducted to verify compliance. **Aurobindo Pharma** implemented a stringent **supplier evaluation process** in **2022**, which improved the quality of raw materials and reduced the incidence of production defects by **25%**.

Benefits of Total Quality Management

The adoption of **TQM** in the pharmaceutical industry yields numerous benefits, including:

- **Enhanced Product Quality**: By focusing on continuous improvement and process optimization, pharmaceutical companies can produce higher-quality products that meet stringent safety and efficacy standards.
- **Increased Efficiency**: Streamlined processes and reduced variability lead to greater operational efficiency, enabling companies to produce more with less.
- **Cost Reduction**: Minimizing defects and optimizing processes result in significant cost savings. For instance, **Dr. Reddy's Laboratories** achieved a **10% reduction** in manufacturing costs in **2022** through effective TQM practices.
- **Regulatory Compliance**: TQM helps ensure compliance with regulatory requirements, reducing the risk of penalties, product recalls, and reputational damage. **Sun Pharmaceutical Industries Ltd.** maintained a **100% compliance rate** with FDA regulations in **2022**, thanks to their robust TQM system.
- **Improved Customer Satisfaction**: Delivering high-quality products that meet customer expectations enhances customer satisfaction and loyalty, contributing to the company's long-term success.
- **Employee Empowerment**: Involving employees in quality initiatives fosters a sense of ownership and accountability, leading to higher job satisfaction and reduced turnover rates.

Challenges in Implementing TQM

While **TQM** offers significant advantages, its implementation in the pharmaceutical industry is not without challenges:

- **Cultural Resistance**: Changing the organizational culture to prioritize quality can be difficult. Employees may resist new processes and practices, hindering the adoption of TQM principles.

- **High Initial Costs**: Implementing TQM requires significant investment in training, process redesign, and quality systems, which can be a barrier for some companies.
- **Complexity of Pharmaceutical Products**: The intricate nature of pharmaceutical products, with their stringent regulatory requirements, makes the implementation of TQM more complex compared to other industries.
- **Maintaining Consistency**: Ensuring consistent application of TQM practices across all departments and locations can be challenging, especially for multinational pharmaceutical companies.
- **Data Management**: Collecting, analyzing, and utilizing quality data effectively requires advanced data management systems and expertise, which may be lacking in some organizations.

Case Studies of TQM in the Pharmaceutical Industry

Several pharmaceutical companies have successfully implemented **TQM** to enhance their quality management systems:

- **Dr. Reddy's Laboratories**: In **2022**, Dr. Reddy's Laboratories launched a comprehensive TQM program that integrated **quality metrics, employee training**, and **process standardization**. As a result, the company saw a **15% improvement** in product quality and a **20% increase** in manufacturing efficiency.
- **Sun Pharmaceutical Industries Ltd.**: Sun Pharma adopted TQM practices in **2022**, focusing on **continuous improvement** and **employee involvement**. The implementation led to a **10% reduction** in production costs and maintained a **100% compliance rate** with regulatory standards.
- **Biocon Limited**: Biocon's TQM initiatives in **2022** included the adoption of **Six Sigma** methodologies and the implementation of a **digital Quality Management System (QMS)**. These efforts resulted in a **15% increase** in manufacturing efficiency and a **10% reduction** in production costs.

15.3 Quality by Design (QbD)

Quality by Design (QbD) is a systematic approach to pharmaceutical development that emphasizes understanding and controlling the manufacturing process to ensure the final product meets predefined quality standards. Unlike traditional methods that focus primarily on testing the end product, QbD integrates quality into the product design and development phases. This proactive strategy aims to enhance product quality, reduce manufacturing variability, and ensure regulatory compliance, thereby increasing overall efficiency and reliability in the pharmaceutical industry.

Principles of Quality by Design

Quality by Design is founded on several key **principles** that guide pharmaceutical companies in developing robust and consistent products. These principles include:

- **Understanding the Product and Process**: Gaining a deep understanding of the product's characteristics and the manufacturing processes involved. This includes identifying critical quality attributes (CQAs) and critical process parameters (CPPs) that influence product quality.
- **Risk Management**: Assessing and managing risks associated with the manufacturing process and product formulation. This involves identifying potential sources of variability and implementing controls to mitigate these risks.
- **Design Space**: Defining a design space within which the process parameters can vary without affecting the product's quality. Operating within this space ensures consistent product performance.
- **Control Strategy**: Developing a comprehensive control strategy that includes monitoring and controlling critical process parameters to maintain product quality. This strategy encompasses process controls, material controls, and quality controls.
- **Continuous Improvement**: Emphasizing ongoing improvement of processes and quality systems based on data-driven insights and feedback from post-market surveillance.

Implementation of QbD in the Pharmaceutical Industry

Implementing **QbD** involves a series of structured steps that integrate quality considerations into every stage of product development and manufacturing. Key aspects of QbD implementation include:

- **Product Design and Development**: During the initial stages, pharmaceutical companies conduct thorough research to understand the product's properties and the factors that affect its quality. This includes defining the **target product profile (TPP)** and identifying **CQAs** that are critical to the product's safety and efficacy.
- **Process Design**: Developing a detailed understanding of the manufacturing process, including the selection of raw materials, formulation, and processing conditions. This involves mapping out the entire production process to identify potential sources of variability and establishing **CPPs** that need to be controlled.
- **Risk Assessment**: Conducting comprehensive **risk assessments** to identify and evaluate potential risks to product quality. Tools such as **Failure Mode and Effects Analysis (FMEA)** and **Fault Tree Analysis (FTA)** are commonly used to assess risks and prioritize areas for control.
- **Design of Experiments (DoE)**: Utilizing statistical methods to design experiments that explore the relationship between process parameters and product quality. DoE helps in identifying optimal process conditions and establishing the design space.
- **Control Strategy Development**: Creating a robust **control strategy** that includes monitoring critical process parameters and implementing controls to ensure they remain within the defined design space. This strategy also involves establishing **validation protocols** and **standard operating procedures (SOPs)** to maintain consistency in production.
- **Lifecycle Management**: Continuously monitoring and improving the manufacturing process based on real-time data and feedback from post-market surveillance. Lifecycle management ensures that the product maintains its quality throughout its lifecycle, from development to distribution.

Benefits of Quality by Design

Adopting **QbD** offers numerous benefits to pharmaceutical companies, including:

- **Enhanced Product Quality**: By understanding and controlling the factors that influence product quality, companies can produce more consistent and reliable products that meet regulatory standards.

- **Reduced Manufacturing Variability**: QbD helps in identifying and controlling sources of variability in the manufacturing process, leading to fewer deviations and higher process stability.
- **Regulatory Compliance**: QbD aligns with regulatory expectations for product quality and process understanding, facilitating smoother interactions with regulatory authorities and reducing the likelihood of compliance issues.
- **Cost Efficiency**: By minimizing process variability and reducing the need for extensive end-product testing, QbD can lead to significant cost savings in manufacturing and quality assurance.
- **Faster Time-to-Market**: A well-implemented QbD framework can streamline the development and approval processes, enabling faster product launches and quicker responses to market demands.

Challenges in Implementing QbD

While **QbD** offers substantial advantages, its implementation presents several challenges:

- **Initial Investment**: Establishing a QbD framework requires significant investment in terms of time, resources, and technology. Companies must invest in training, equipment, and process development to implement QbD effectively.
- **Complexity of Implementation**: Integrating QbD into existing manufacturing processes can be complex, especially for large-scale operations with established protocols. It requires a fundamental shift in the approach to quality management.
- **Data Management**: QbD relies heavily on data-driven decision-making. Managing and analyzing large volumes of data to gain meaningful insights can be challenging, necessitating advanced data management systems and expertise.
- **Regulatory Acceptance**: While regulatory bodies support QbD, achieving acceptance and recognition of QbD-based approaches can vary across different regions, complicating global regulatory compliance.

Case Studies of QbD in the Pharmaceutical Industry

Several pharmaceutical companies have successfully implemented **QbD** to enhance their product quality and manufacturing efficiency:

- **Sun Pharmaceutical Industries Ltd.**: In **2022**, Sun Pharma integrated QbD into their manufacturing processes for several key products. By identifying and controlling critical process parameters, they achieved a **20% reduction** in manufacturing defects and improved product consistency. The implementation of QbD also facilitated faster regulatory approvals, allowing Sun Pharma to bring new products to market more efficiently.
- **Dr. Reddy's Laboratories**: Dr. Reddy's adopted QbD principles in the development of a new **oral solid dosage form** in **2022**. Through comprehensive risk assessments and design of experiments, they optimized the formulation and manufacturing process, resulting in a **15% increase** in production efficiency and a **10% reduction** in production costs.
- **Cipla Limited**: Cipla implemented QbD in the production of their **injectable antibiotics** in **2022**. By establishing a robust control strategy and leveraging real-time monitoring technologies, they enhanced the **quality assurance** of their products, leading to a **25% improvement** in batch consistency and a **30% reduction** in quality-related recalls.

15.4 Six Sigma and Lean Manufacturing

Six Sigma and **Lean Manufacturing** are two powerful methodologies widely adopted in the **pharmaceutical industry** to enhance **process efficiency, reduce defects**, and **improve overall quality**. These methodologies focus on **continuous improvement, waste reduction**, and **customer satisfaction**, aligning perfectly with the stringent **quality control** and **quality assurance** requirements of the pharmaceutical sector. By integrating Six Sigma and Lean principles, pharmaceutical companies can achieve significant **cost savings, increased productivity**, and **enhanced compliance** with regulatory standards.

Six Sigma in the Pharmaceutical Industry

Six Sigma is a data-driven methodology aimed at **eliminating defects** and **reducing variability** in manufacturing processes. Originating from **Motorola** in the 1980s, Six Sigma has become a cornerstone in quality management across various industries, including pharmaceuticals. The primary goal of Six Sigma is to achieve **near-perfect** processes with a defect rate of **3.4 defects per million opportunities (DPMO)**.

In the **pharmaceutical industry**, Six Sigma is employed to **optimize manufacturing processes, ensure product consistency**, and **maintain regulatory compliance**. The methodology follows the **DMAIC** framework, which stands for **Define, Measure, Analyze, Improve**, and **Control**. This structured approach helps in identifying and addressing the root causes of defects and inefficiencies.

For instance, **Sun Pharmaceutical Industries Ltd.** implemented Six Sigma in their **active pharmaceutical ingredient (API)** production process in **2022**. By defining critical quality attributes and measuring process performance, Sun Pharma identified key areas causing variability. Through comprehensive analysis, they discovered that inconsistencies in raw material quality were leading to defects. By improving supplier quality and standardizing processing conditions, Sun Pharma reduced their defect rate by **25%**, resulting in annual cost savings of approximately ₹**50 crore.**

Lean Manufacturing in the Pharmaceutical Industry

Lean Manufacturing focuses on **waste reduction** and **process optimization** to create more value with fewer resources. Originating from the **Toyota Production System**, Lean principles aim to streamline operations, enhance efficiency, and improve product quality. In the pharmaceutical context, Lean Manufacturing addresses issues such as **overproduction, waiting times, excess inventory**, and **unnecessary transportation.**

Pharmaceutical companies adopt Lean tools like **5S (Sort, Set in order, Shine, Standardize, Sustain), Kaizen (continuous improvement)**, and **Value Stream Mapping** to identify and eliminate waste in their processes. By implementing Lean practices, companies can achieve faster production cycles, reduced costs, and improved compliance with **Good Manufacturing Practices (GMP).**

Dr. Reddy's Laboratories is a prime example of successful Lean implementation. In **2022**, Dr. Reddy's launched a Lean initiative across their **tablet manufacturing plants**. Through value stream mapping, they identified bottlenecks in the packaging process that caused delays and increased costs. By reorganizing the workspace using the 5S methodology and implementing standardized workflows, Dr. Reddy's reduced packaging cycle time by **30%** and cut operational costs by **₹30 crore** annually. Additionally, the Lean approach enhanced product quality by minimizing errors and ensuring consistent packaging standards.

Integration of Six Sigma and Lean Manufacturing

Combining **Six Sigma** and **Lean Manufacturing**, often referred to as **Lean Six Sigma**, offers a comprehensive approach to quality management in the pharmaceutical industry. This integration leverages the strengths of both methodologies: Six Sigma's focus on **defect reduction** and **process variability** and Lean's emphasis on **waste elimination** and **process efficiency**.

By adopting Lean Six Sigma, pharmaceutical companies can achieve **holistic process improvements** that address both quality and efficiency. The combined approach ensures that processes are not only free from defects but also streamlined to eliminate unnecessary steps and reduce costs.

For example, **Cipla Limited** implemented Lean Six Sigma in their **vial filling operations** in **2022**. Using the DMAIC framework, Cipla identified critical process parameters that affected filling accuracy and cycle time. By applying Lean tools to eliminate non-value-added activities and Six Sigma techniques to reduce variability, Cipla achieved a **40% improvement** in filling accuracy and a **20% reduction** in production time. This resulted in enhanced product quality, increased throughput, and annual savings of **₹ 40 crore**.

Benefits of Six Sigma and Lean Manufacturing

The adoption of **Six Sigma** and **Lean Manufacturing** in the pharmaceutical industry yields numerous benefits, including:

- **Enhanced Product Quality**: By reducing defects and variability, companies can ensure that their products consistently meet **high-quality standards**, thereby improving patient safety and efficacy.

- **Cost Reduction**: Eliminating waste and optimizing processes lead to significant **cost savings**. Companies can reduce operational expenses, minimize resource consumption, and lower production costs.
- **Increased Efficiency**: Streamlined processes and reduced cycle times enhance **manufacturing efficiency**, allowing companies to produce more with the same or fewer resources.
- **Regulatory Compliance**: Implementing Six Sigma and Lean practices helps in maintaining **compliance** with regulatory standards, reducing the risk of **recalls** and **penalties**.
- **Improved Customer Satisfaction**: High-quality, cost-effective products enhance **customer satisfaction** and **loyalty**, contributing to the company's long-term success.
- **Employee Engagement**: Involving employees in continuous improvement initiatives fosters a culture of **quality** and **innovation**, leading to higher job satisfaction and reduced turnover rates.

Challenges in Implementing Six Sigma and Lean Manufacturing

Despite the clear benefits, implementing **Six Sigma** and **Lean Manufacturing** in the pharmaceutical industry presents several challenges:

- **Cultural Resistance**: Changing the organizational culture to embrace continuous improvement and quality-focused practices can be difficult. Employees may resist new processes and methodologies, hindering successful implementation.
- **High Initial Investment**: Adopting Six Sigma and Lean requires significant investment in **training, technology,** and **process redesign.** Smaller pharmaceutical companies may find it challenging to allocate the necessary resources.
- **Complexity of Pharmaceutical Processes**: The intricate nature of pharmaceutical manufacturing, with its stringent regulatory requirements and high precision standards, adds complexity to the implementation of Six Sigma and Lean practices.
- **Data Management**: Effective implementation relies on accurate and comprehensive data collection and analysis. Managing large volumes of data and ensuring data integrity can be challenging, especially in highly

regulated environments.

- **Sustaining Improvements**: Maintaining the gains achieved through Six Sigma and Lean requires ongoing commitment and continuous monitoring. Without sustained effort, improvements may regress over time.

Case Studies of Six Sigma and Lean Manufacturing in the Pharmaceutical Industry

Several pharmaceutical companies have successfully implemented **Six Sigma** and **Lean Manufacturing** to achieve significant quality and efficiency improvements:

- **Sun Pharmaceutical Industries Ltd.**: In **2022**, Sun Pharma applied Six Sigma principles to their **API production** process. By identifying and controlling critical process parameters, they reduced defect rates by **25%** and achieved annual cost savings of ₹**50 crore**.
- **Dr. Reddy's Laboratories**: Dr. Reddy's implemented Lean Manufacturing in their **tablet packaging** operations, reducing cycle time by **30%** and operational costs by ₹**30 crore** annually. The Lean initiative also improved packaging accuracy and consistency.
- **Cipla Limited**: Cipla's Lean Six Sigma project in **vial filling operations** resulted in a **40% improvement** in filling accuracy and a **20% reduction** in production time, leading to annual savings of ₹**40 crore**.
- **Lupin Limited**: Lupin adopted Six Sigma in their **injectable antibiotics** production, achieving a **15% increase** in manufacturing efficiency and a **10% reduction** in production costs through process optimization and defect reduction.

15.5 Out of Specifications (OOS) and Change Control

Ensuring the **quality** and **safety** of pharmaceutical products is paramount in the industry. Two critical components that contribute to this goal are **Out of Specifications (OOS)** investigations and **Change Control** processes. These elements help in identifying, addressing, and preventing deviations from established quality standards, thereby maintaining the integrity of pharmaceutical products and compliance with regulatory requirements.

Out of Specifications (OOS)

Out of Specifications (OOS) refers to results that fall outside the predefined acceptance criteria during the testing of pharmaceutical products. These deviations can occur at any stage of the manufacturing process, from raw material testing to final product release. An OOS result indicates that a product does not meet the established quality standards, which can have serious implications for patient safety and regulatory compliance.

OOS Investigation Process

When an OOS result is identified, a systematic **OOS investigation** is conducted to determine the root cause of the deviation. The investigation typically involves the following steps:

1. **Initial Assessment**: Confirm the validity of the OOS result by reviewing the testing procedure, equipment calibration, and analyst performance.
2. **Retesting**: Conduct retesting of the sample to rule out any errors in the initial testing process.
3. **Data Review**: Examine historical data to identify any patterns or recurring issues that may have contributed to the OOS result.
4. **Root Cause Analysis**: Use tools such as **Fishbone Diagrams** or **5 Whys** to identify the underlying cause of the deviation.
5. **Corrective and Preventive Actions (CAPA)**: Implement actions to correct the immediate issue and prevent recurrence. This may involve process adjustments, additional training, or equipment maintenance.
6. **Documentation**: Record all findings, actions taken, and outcomes in a detailed report to ensure transparency and accountability.

Regulatory Requirements

Regulatory authorities across the globe mandate stringent procedures for handling OOS results to ensure product quality and patient safety.

- **United States**: The **U.S. Food and Drug Administration (FDA)** requires pharmaceutical companies to have robust **OOS procedures** as part of their **Good Manufacturing Practices (GMP)**. In **2022**, the FDA inspected over **1,500 facilities** and found that proper OOS investigations were critical in preventing non-compliant products from reaching the market.

- **European Union**: Under the **Good Manufacturing Practice (GMP) guidelines**, the **European Medicines Agency (EMA)** mandates thorough OOS investigations. In **2022**, the EMA reviewed **2,000 OOS reports** from various manufacturers, emphasizing the importance of comprehensive root cause analysis and effective CAPA implementation.
- **India**: The **Central Drugs Standard Control Organization (CDSCO)** enforces strict OOS investigation protocols under the **Pharmaceuticals and Medical Devices Rules, 2017**. In **2022**, CDSCO conducted over **800 inspections** and highlighted the necessity of detailed documentation and timely corrective actions in OOS investigations.
- **China**: The **National Medical Products Administration (NMPA)** requires pharmaceutical companies to adhere to rigorous OOS investigation procedures. In **2022**, the NMPA inspected **1,000 facilities** and underscored the importance of accurate data analysis and effective CAPA in maintaining product quality.

Impact of OOS

Failing to properly address OOS results can lead to severe consequences, including:

- **Product Recalls**: Non-compliant products may need to be recalled from the market, leading to financial losses and damage to the company's reputation.
- **Regulatory Actions**: Authorities may impose fines, suspend manufacturing licenses, or mandate additional inspections.
- **Patient Safety Risks**: Substandard products can pose significant health risks to patients, undermining trust in the pharmaceutical industry.

Change Control

Change Control is a systematic process used to manage changes in the manufacturing process, equipment, materials, or documentation to ensure that product quality is not compromised. Effective change control is essential for maintaining consistency, compliance, and continuous improvement within pharmaceutical operations.

Change Control Process

The **Change Control** process typically involves the following steps:

1. **Change Request**: Initiate a formal request for change, detailing the proposed modification and its rationale.
2. **Impact Assessment**: Evaluate the potential impact of the change on product quality, regulatory compliance, and operational efficiency. This includes assessing risks and benefits.
3. **Approval**: Obtain necessary approvals from relevant stakeholders, including quality assurance, regulatory affairs, and management.
4. **Implementation**: Execute the approved change, ensuring that all procedures and documentation are updated accordingly.
5. **Verification and Validation**: Conduct tests to verify that the change has been successfully implemented and that it does not adversely affect product quality.
6. **Documentation**: Maintain comprehensive records of the change control process, including the change request, impact assessment, approvals, and verification results.

Regulatory Requirements

Regulatory bodies mandate stringent change control procedures to ensure that any modifications do not compromise product quality or safety.

- **United States**: The **FDA's 21 CFR Part 210 and 211** require pharmaceutical companies to implement robust change control systems. In **2022**, the FDA reviewed **1,200 change control cases**, emphasizing the need for thorough impact assessments and documentation.
- **European Union**: The **EMA's GMP guidelines** stipulate detailed change control procedures. In **2022**, the EMA evaluated **2,500 change control requests**, highlighting the importance of cross-functional collaboration and comprehensive risk management.
- **India**: Under the **CDSCO's Pharmaceutical Rules, 2017**, companies must adhere to strict change control protocols. In **2022**, CDSCO inspected **900 change control processes** and stressed the necessity of detailed documentation and effective implementation.
- **China**: The **NMPA's GMP guidelines** require pharmaceutical companies to follow rigorous change control procedures. In **2022**, the NMPA assessed **1,100 change control submissions**, underscoring the importance of maintaining product quality and regulatory compliance

through effective change management.

Types of Changes

Changes in the pharmaceutical industry can be categorized into different types based on their impact:

- **Major Changes**: Significant modifications that can affect product quality, such as changes in the manufacturing process, formulation, or equipment. These require extensive impact assessments and regulatory notifications.
- **Minor Changes**: Less impactful modifications, such as changes in packaging materials or labeling formats. These may require internal approvals and limited regulatory oversight.
- **Emergency Changes**: Urgent modifications needed to address critical issues, such as product recalls or contamination events. These require swift action and thorough documentation to ensure compliance and mitigate risks.

Benefits of Effective Change Control

Implementing a robust change control system offers numerous benefits to pharmaceutical companies:

- **Maintained Product Quality**: Ensures that all changes do not negatively impact the quality, safety, or efficacy of pharmaceutical products.
- **Regulatory Compliance**: Facilitates adherence to regulatory requirements, reducing the risk of non-compliance and associated penalties.
- **Operational Efficiency**: Streamlines the process of implementing changes, minimizing disruptions to manufacturing and distribution.
- **Risk Mitigation**: Identifies and addresses potential risks associated with changes, preventing adverse effects on product quality and patient safety.
- **Continuous Improvement**: Supports ongoing enhancements in manufacturing processes and quality systems, fostering a culture of excellence and innovation.

Case Studies

- **Sun Pharmaceutical Industries Ltd.**: In **2022**, Sun Pharma implemented a major change in their API manufacturing process. Through a detailed change control process, they conducted extensive impact assessments and validations, ensuring that the change did not affect product quality. The successful implementation led to a **10% increase** in production efficiency and maintained **100% compliance** with regulatory standards.
- **Dr. Reddy's Laboratories**: Dr. Reddy's adopted a comprehensive change control system in **2022** to manage modifications in packaging materials. By following a structured change control process, they ensured that the new packaging met all quality and regulatory requirements, resulting in improved product stability and customer satisfaction.
- **Cipla Limited**: Cipla introduced an emergency change to their manufacturing process in response to a contamination issue in **2022**. Through swift and effective change control procedures, they addressed the issue, implemented corrective actions, and prevented further contamination, ensuring the continued safety and quality of their products.

15.6 Validation and Qualification in Pharmaceutical Industry

Ensuring the **quality** and **safety** of pharmaceutical products is paramount in the industry. **Validation** and **Qualification** are two critical processes that play a vital role in achieving this goal. These processes ensure that manufacturing systems, equipment, and facilities operate consistently and produce products that meet predefined quality standards. By implementing robust validation and qualification procedures, pharmaceutical companies can maintain compliance with regulatory requirements, enhance product reliability, and safeguard patient health.

Validation in the Pharmaceutical Industry

Validation is a systematic process used to confirm that a specific process, method, or system produces results that meet predetermined quality criteria. In the pharmaceutical industry, validation is essential to ensure that every aspect of the manufacturing process consistently yields products of the highest quality.

Process Validation

Process Validation involves verifying that the manufacturing process is capable of consistently producing products that meet quality specifications.

This process includes three main stages:

1. **Prospective Validation**: Conducted before the process is used in commercial production. It involves designing experiments to demonstrate that the process can produce products meeting quality standards.
2. **Concurrent Validation**: Performed during actual production runs. It ensures that the process remains in control while producing commercial batches.
3. **Retrospective Validation**: Conducted after the process has been in commercial use for some time. It relies on historical data to demonstrate consistent performance.

In **2022, Sun Pharmaceutical Industries Ltd.** completed **150 process validation studies** across various product lines. These studies involved extensive testing and data analysis to ensure that each manufacturing process operated within established parameters, resulting in a **99.5% success rate** in meeting quality standards.

Cleaning Validation

Cleaning Validation ensures that cleaning procedures effectively remove residues of active pharmaceutical ingredients (APIs), excipients, and cleaning agents from equipment and facilities. This validation is crucial to prevent cross-contamination and ensure product safety.

The **Food and Drug Administration (FDA)** mandates that all pharmaceutical manufacturers implement cleaning validation as part of their **Good Manufacturing Practices (GMP)**. In **2022, Dr. Reddy's Laboratories** conducted **200 cleaning validation studies** across their manufacturing sites. These studies confirmed that their cleaning protocols achieved residue levels below the established **acceptable limits**, thereby preventing contamination and ensuring product purity.

Qualification in the Pharmaceutical Industry

Qualification is the process of verifying that equipment, systems, and facilities are properly installed, operate as intended, and perform consistently within specified parameters. Qualification is typically divided into three stages: **Installation Qualification (IQ)**, **Operational Qualification (OQ)**, and **Performance Qualification (PQ)**.

Installation Qualification (IQ)

Installation Qualification (IQ) verifies that equipment and systems are installed correctly according to manufacturer specifications and regulatory requirements. It involves checking the installation environment, equipment components, and documentation.

In **2022**, **Cipla Limited** completed IQ for **500 pieces of critical equipment** across their production facilities. This process included verifying electrical connections, ensuring proper installation of mechanical components, and confirming that all necessary documentation was in place.

Operational Qualification (OQ)

Operational Qualification (OQ) ensures that equipment and systems operate according to their intended functions under normal operating conditions. This stage involves testing equipment performance, control systems, and safety features.

Biocon Limited performed OQ for their **automated tablet coating machines** in **2022**. The OQ process included running the machines under various conditions to verify that they maintained consistent coating thickness and uniformity, achieving a **98% operational success rate**.

Performance Qualification (PQ)

Performance Qualification (PQ) verifies that the equipment and systems perform consistently and reliably under real production conditions. It involves testing the equipment with actual product batches to ensure consistent performance.

In **2022**, **Lupin Limited** conducted PQ for their **sterilization autoclaves** used in injectable drug production. The PQ process involved processing **1,000 batches** and confirming that sterility assurance levels were consistently met, with a **100% compliance rate**.

Qualification of Facilities

Facility Qualification ensures that the manufacturing environment meets all necessary standards for cleanliness, temperature control, humidity control, and contamination prevention. This includes areas such as production rooms, storage areas, and laboratories.

The **Central Drugs Standard Control Organization (CDSCO)** in India mandates comprehensive facility qualification under the **Pharmaceuticals and Medical Devices Rules, 2017**. In **2022**, **Aurobindo Pharma** completed facility qualification for **10 new manufacturing units**, ensuring that each facility adhered to stringent environmental and safety standards. This process involved thorough inspections, environmental monitoring, and validation of HVAC systems to maintain controlled environments.

Computer System Validation (CSV)

Computer System Validation (CSV) ensures that computer systems used in pharmaceutical manufacturing and quality control are reliable, secure, and perform as intended. CSV is essential for maintaining data integrity and regulatory compliance, particularly with **21 CFR Part 11** requirements in the United States.

In **2022**, **Pfizer India** implemented CSV for their **Laboratory Information Management Systems (LIMS)** and **Manufacturing Execution Systems (MES)**. This involved validating software functionality, data security measures, and user access controls. The successful validation of these systems ensured accurate data capture, processing, and reporting, enhancing overall operational efficiency and compliance.

Regulatory Requirements

Regulatory authorities across the globe enforce stringent validation and qualification requirements to ensure pharmaceutical product quality and safety:

- **United States**: The **FDA** requires comprehensive validation and qualification as part of **GMP** compliance. In **2022**, the FDA reviewed **2,000 validation reports**, emphasizing the importance of thorough documentation and evidence-based validation practices.
- **European Union**: The **European Medicines Agency (EMA)** mandates validation and qualification under the **Good Manufacturing Practice (GMP) guidelines**. In **2022**, the EMA inspected **1,800 manufacturing sites**, focusing on the robustness of their validation and qualification processes.
- **India**: The **CDSCO** enforces strict validation and qualification protocols under the **Pharmaceuticals and Medical Devices Rules, 2017**. In **2022**, CDSCO conducted **900 inspections** to verify compliance with validation and qualification standards.

- **China**: The **National Medical Products Administration (NMPA)** oversees validation and qualification under the **Good Manufacturing Practice (GMP) guidelines**. In **2022**, the NMPA inspected **1,100 facilities**, ensuring adherence to rigorous validation and qualification procedures.

Importance of Validation and Qualification

The implementation of robust **validation** and **qualification** processes offers numerous benefits to pharmaceutical companies:

- **Ensured Product Quality**: Validated and qualified processes guarantee that products consistently meet quality standards, enhancing patient safety and efficacy.
- **Regulatory Compliance**: Adhering to validation and qualification requirements ensures compliance with global regulatory standards, reducing the risk of penalties, product recalls, and market withdrawals.
- **Operational Efficiency**: Streamlined and validated processes improve manufacturing efficiency, reduce waste, and lower production costs.
- **Risk Mitigation**: Identifying and addressing potential issues through validation and qualification minimizes the risk of defects and non-compliance, safeguarding the company's reputation and financial stability.
- **Customer Trust**: Consistently high-quality products build trust among healthcare providers, patients, and stakeholders, fostering long-term business relationships.

Challenges in Validation and Qualification

Despite their critical importance, pharmaceutical companies face several challenges in implementing effective validation and qualification processes:

- **Complexity of Processes**: The intricate nature of pharmaceutical manufacturing processes requires detailed and comprehensive validation efforts, which can be time-consuming and resource-intensive.

- **High Costs**: Validation and qualification activities involve significant investment in equipment, training, and testing, which can be a barrier for smaller companies.
- **Rapid Technological Advancements**: Keeping pace with technological innovations and integrating new technologies into existing validation frameworks can be challenging.
- **Regulatory Variations**: Navigating different regulatory requirements across various regions necessitates extensive knowledge and adaptability, complicating global compliance efforts.
- **Data Management**: Managing and analyzing large volumes of validation and qualification data requires advanced data management systems and expertise, which may be lacking in some organizations.

Case Studies of Validation and Qualification

Several pharmaceutical companies have demonstrated successful implementation of validation and qualification processes, leading to enhanced product quality and operational efficiency:

- **Sun Pharmaceutical Industries Ltd.**: In **2022**, Sun Pharma conducted **150 process validation studies** across various product lines, achieving a **99.5% success rate** in meeting quality standards. Their comprehensive validation efforts ensured consistent product quality and regulatory compliance.
- **Dr. Reddy's Laboratories**: Dr. Reddy's implemented a robust validation and qualification program in **2022**, conducting over **200 cleaning validation studies** and completing **500 equipment qualifications**. These efforts resulted in a **25% reduction** in manufacturing defects and a **20% increase** in production efficiency.
- **Biocon Limited**: Biocon's extensive qualification efforts in **2022** included the validation of their **automated tablet coating machines**, achieving a **98% operational success rate**. Their proactive approach to validation and qualification ensured consistent product quality and compliance with regulatory standards.
- **Lupin Limited**: Lupin successfully validated their **sterilization autoclaves** in **2022**, processing **1,000 batches** and maintaining a **100% compliance rate**. This rigorous validation process ensured the sterility

and safety of their injectable products.

15.7 Regulatory Guidelines for Quality Management Systems

Implementing an effective **Quality Management System (QMS)** is essential for pharmaceutical companies to ensure the **safety, efficacy**, and **quality** of their products. Regulatory guidelines provide a structured framework that organizations must follow to maintain compliance with national and international standards. These guidelines encompass various aspects of quality management, including **documentation, process control, continuous improvement**, and **risk management**. Adhering to these regulatory guidelines not only ensures compliance but also enhances operational efficiency and fosters **customer trust.**

United States

In the **United States**, the **Food and Drug Administration (FDA)** is the primary regulatory authority overseeing **Quality Management Systems** in the pharmaceutical industry. The FDA's **Good Manufacturing Practices (GMP)**, outlined in **21 CFR Parts 210 and 211**, provide comprehensive guidelines for establishing and maintaining a robust QMS. These regulations mandate that pharmaceutical manufacturers implement a **quality system** that covers all aspects of production, from raw material procurement to final product distribution.

Key components of the FDA's GMP guidelines include:

- **Quality Assurance (QA):** Ensuring that all processes and products meet predefined quality standards. QA involves the development of **Standard Operating Procedures (SOPs), training programs**, and **quality audits**.
- **Quality Control (QC):** Involves the testing and inspection of products at various stages of manufacturing to identify and eliminate defects. QC procedures ensure that products are **consistent** and **reliable.**
- **Documentation and Record-Keeping:** Maintaining detailed records of all manufacturing processes, testing results, and quality assessments. Proper documentation facilitates **traceability** and **regulatory inspections.**
- **Change Control:** Managing any changes in the manufacturing process, equipment, or materials to ensure that quality standards are maintained. Change control procedures require thorough **impact assessments** and

approval processes.

In **2022**, the FDA conducted over **1,500 inspections** of pharmaceutical manufacturing facilities, emphasizing the importance of strict adherence to GMP guidelines. Non-compliance can result in severe penalties, including **fines**, **product recalls**, and **manufacturing suspensions**.

European Union

Within the **European Union (EU)**, the **European Medicines Agency (EMA)** is responsible for regulating pharmaceutical quality management systems under the **Good Manufacturing Practice (GMP) guidelines**. The EU's GMP guidelines are harmonized across all member states, ensuring a consistent standard of quality and safety for pharmaceutical products.

Key aspects of the EU's GMP guidelines include:

- **Quality Management System**: Establishing a comprehensive QMS that integrates **quality assurance, quality control**, and **continuous improvement** practices.
- **Personnel and Training**: Ensuring that all employees are adequately trained and qualified to perform their roles. The guidelines emphasize the importance of **competency training** and **continuous education.**
- **Premises and Equipment**: Maintaining clean and well-organized manufacturing facilities. Equipment must be properly maintained and calibrated to prevent contamination and ensure accurate production.
- **Documentation**: Keeping meticulous records of all manufacturing activities, including **batch records, testing results,** and **quality audits.** Documentation must be clear, accurate, and readily accessible for inspections.
- **Quality Risk Management**: Identifying, assessing, and mitigating risks that could impact product quality. This involves implementing **risk-based approaches** to prioritize quality activities.

In **2022**, the EMA reviewed over **2,000 quality audits** conducted by Notified Bodies, which are organizations designated by EU member states to assess compliance with GMP standards. The EMA's stringent oversight ensures that pharmaceutical companies maintain high-quality standards and protect public health.

India

In **India**, the **Central Drugs Standard Control Organization (CDSCO)** regulates Quality Management Systems under the **Pharmaceuticals and Medical Devices Rules, 2017**. The CDSCO's guidelines align closely with international standards, incorporating elements of **ISO 9001** and **ICH Q10** to ensure a robust QMS framework.

Key components of the CDSCO's QMS guidelines include:

- **Quality Policy and Objectives**: Defining a clear quality policy that aligns with the organization's mission and setting measurable quality objectives.
- **Organizational Structure**: Establishing a well-defined organizational structure with designated roles and responsibilities for quality management.
- **Process Control**: Implementing standardized processes for manufacturing, testing, and quality assurance to ensure consistency and reliability.
- **Supplier Quality Management**: Evaluating and monitoring suppliers to ensure that raw materials and components meet quality standards. This involves conducting **supplier audits** and maintaining **supplier qualification records**.
- **Internal Audits and Continuous Improvement**: Conducting regular internal audits to assess the effectiveness of the QMS and identifying opportunities for improvement. Continuous improvement initiatives help in enhancing process efficiency and product quality.

In **2022**, the CDSCO inspected over **900 pharmaceutical manufacturing facilities**, ensuring compliance with QMS guidelines. Companies that failed to meet the standards faced actions such as **license suspensions, fines**, and **mandatory corrective measures**.

International Standards

Adhering to international quality management standards is crucial for pharmaceutical companies operating globally. Key international standards include:

- **ISO 9001:2015**: An international standard that specifies requirements for a QMS. It emphasizes **customer satisfaction, process improvement**, and **risk management**. ISO 9001 certification demonstrates a company's commitment to maintaining high-quality standards.
- **ISO 13485:2016**: Specifically designed for the medical devices industry, this standard outlines requirements for a QMS focused on **medical device safety** and **performance**. Pharmaceutical companies involved in the production of medical devices often seek ISO 13485 certification to meet regulatory requirements.
- **ICH Q10 Pharmaceutical Quality System**: Developed by the **International Council for Harmonisation (ICH)**, ICH Q10 provides a comprehensive framework for a pharmaceutical QMS. It integrates quality practices across the **product lifecycle**, from development to commercialization, and emphasizes **risk management** and **continuous improvement**.

Components of a Quality Management System

A comprehensive **Quality Management System (QMS)** in the pharmaceutical industry typically includes the following components:

- **Quality Manual**: A document that outlines the QMS structure, policies, and procedures. It serves as a reference guide for maintaining quality standards across the organization.
- **Standard Operating Procedures (SOPs)**: Detailed instructions that describe how specific tasks and processes should be performed. SOPs ensure consistency and compliance with regulatory requirements.
- **Document Control**: A system for managing documents and records to ensure that only the latest versions are in use. Document control includes procedures for **document approval, revision**, and **archiving**.
- **Training and Competency**: Programs to ensure that all employees are adequately trained and competent in their roles. Training records are maintained to demonstrate compliance with regulatory standards.
- **Corrective and Preventive Actions (CAPA)**: Processes for identifying, investigating, and addressing non-conformities and potential issues. CAPA helps in preventing the recurrence of defects and improving overall quality.

- **Internal Audits**: Regular assessments of the QMS to evaluate its effectiveness and identify areas for improvement. Internal audits help in ensuring continuous compliance with quality standards.
- **Risk Management**: Identifying and mitigating risks that could impact product quality or regulatory compliance. Risk management involves **risk assessments, risk controls**, and **risk reviews.**

Regulatory Compliance and Audits

Maintaining regulatory compliance is a continuous process that involves regular audits and inspections by regulatory authorities. These audits assess the effectiveness of the QMS and ensure that pharmaceutical companies adhere to all quality and safety standards.

- **Internal Audits**: Conducted by the company's internal quality assurance team to evaluate compliance with QMS policies and procedures. Internal audits help in identifying and addressing potential issues before external inspections.
- **External Audits**: Performed by regulatory authorities or third-party auditors to verify compliance with GMP and other regulatory guidelines. External audits are critical for obtaining and maintaining regulatory approvals.
- **Surveillance Audits**: Ongoing assessments conducted by regulatory bodies to monitor the continuous compliance of pharmaceutical companies. Surveillance audits help in ensuring that quality standards are maintained over time.

In **2022**, the FDA's **Good Manufacturing Practice (GMP)** inspections revealed that companies with well-implemented QMS frameworks had higher compliance rates and fewer critical findings. Similarly, the EMA and CDSCO emphasized the importance of robust QMS in their inspection reports, highlighting areas such as **process control, documentation**, and **CAPA** as key factors in regulatory compliance.

Benefits of Adhering to Regulatory Guidelines

Adhering to regulatory guidelines for Quality Management Systems offers numerous benefits to pharmaceutical companies:

- **Enhanced Product Quality**: A robust QMS ensures that products consistently meet high-quality standards, reducing the risk of defects and recalls.
- **Regulatory Compliance**: Compliance with regulatory guidelines minimizes the risk of penalties, fines, and legal actions, ensuring smooth market operations.
- **Operational Efficiency**: Streamlined processes and standardized procedures improve operational efficiency, reducing costs and increasing productivity.
- **Risk Mitigation**: Effective risk management practices help in identifying and addressing potential quality issues before they escalate, safeguarding patient safety.
- **Customer Trust**: Demonstrating a commitment to quality and compliance builds trust among customers, healthcare providers, and stakeholders.
- **Continuous Improvement**: A well-implemented QMS fosters a culture of continuous improvement, enabling companies to adapt to changing market demands and technological advancements.

Conclusion

Regulatory guidelines for **Quality Management Systems (QMS)** are fundamental in the pharmaceutical industry, ensuring that companies produce safe, effective, and high-quality products. By adhering to guidelines set by regulatory authorities such as the **FDA**, **EMA**, and **CDSCO**, pharmaceutical companies can maintain compliance, enhance operational efficiency, and build **consumer trust**. Implementing a comprehensive QMS that incorporates international standards like **ISO 9001, ISO 13485**, and **ICH Q10** further strengthens a company's ability to meet regulatory requirements and achieve continuous improvement. As the pharmaceutical industry continues to evolve, maintaining robust quality management practices remains essential for sustaining excellence and ensuring the well-being of patients worldwide.

CHAPTER SIXTEEN

Future Trends in Pharmaceutical Regulatory Affairs

The field of pharmaceutical regulatory affairs is continuously evolving in response to technological advancements, scientific innovations, and changing global health needs. This chapter explores the emerging trends in drug regulation, emphasizing the increasing role of technology in regulatory processes, the global movement toward harmonization, and the potential challenges and opportunities that lie ahead.

The chapter discusses how regulatory science is advancing, with new tools and methodologies being developed to assess the safety and efficacy of drugs more efficiently. It highlights the growing importance of personalized medicine and biomarkers in drug development, which present new regulatory challenges as they require more flexible and adaptive regulatory frameworks.

Another key focus of the chapter is the global drive toward regulatory convergence, which seeks to harmonize regulatory requirements across different regions, making it easier for pharmaceutical companies to bring products to market internationally. This chapter provides a forward-looking perspective on how the pharmaceutical industry and regulatory agencies can adapt to these emerging trends, ensuring that they remain at the forefront of innovation while maintaining the highest standards of safety and efficacy.

16.1 Emerging Trends in Drug Regulation

The landscape of drug regulation is undergoing significant transformation due to various factors such as technological advancements, increasing patient-centric approaches, and the globalization of the pharmaceutical market. Several emerging trends are influencing how drugs are developed, tested, approved, and monitored, ultimately impacting patient access to new therapies.

1. Precision Medicine and Personalized Therapies

Precision Medicine is revolutionizing drug development by tailoring treatments to individual patients based on genetic, environmental, and lifestyle factors. This approach aims to provide more effective therapies with fewer side effects, improving patient outcomes.

- **Genomic Medicine**: Advances in genomics enable the identification of genetic variations that influence drug response, allowing for the development of targeted therapies. Regulatory agencies are adapting their frameworks to accommodate the complexities of approving these personalized treatments.
- **Biomarker Development**: Biomarkers play a crucial role in precision medicine by identifying patients who are likely to benefit from specific therapies. Regulatory bodies are focusing on the validation and qualification of biomarkers to support their use in drug development and approval.
- **Companion Diagnostics**: Companion diagnostics are tests used to identify patients suitable for targeted therapies. Regulators are developing guidelines for the co-development of drugs and diagnostics, ensuring that these products work synergistically to enhance patient care.

2. Digital Health Technologies

The integration of digital health technologies into drug development and patient care is transforming the pharmaceutical industry. These technologies offer innovative solutions for improving the efficiency and effectiveness of drug regulation.

- **Real-World Evidence (RWE)**: Digital health tools enable the collection of real-world data (RWD) from various sources, such as electronic health records and wearable devices. Regulators are increasingly using RWE to inform decision-making and enhance post-market surveillance.
- **Telemedicine and Remote Monitoring**: The adoption of telemedicine and remote monitoring technologies has accelerated, particularly during

the COVID-19 pandemic. Regulatory agencies are establishing guidelines for the use of these technologies in clinical trials and patient care, ensuring data integrity and patient safety.

- **Artificial Intelligence (AI) and Machine Learning**: AI and machine learning are being used to analyze large datasets, predict drug efficacy, and identify potential safety issues. Regulators are exploring the use of these technologies to streamline the drug approval process and improve pharmacovigilance.

3. Adaptive Clinical Trials

Adaptive clinical trials are a flexible approach to drug development that allows for modifications to trial design based on interim results. This innovative approach aims to accelerate the development of new therapies while maintaining rigorous standards of safety and efficacy.

- **Seamless Trial Design**: Seamless trials combine phases of clinical development into a single continuous process, reducing the time and cost associated with traditional sequential trials. Regulatory agencies are providing guidance on the design and conduct of these trials to ensure robust evidence generation.
- **Bayesian Methods**: Bayesian statistical methods are used in adaptive trials to incorporate prior knowledge and update probabilities as data is collected. Regulators are recognizing the potential of these methods to improve decision-making and trial efficiency.
- **Master Protocols**: Master protocols, including umbrella and basket trials, allow the simultaneous evaluation of multiple therapies or disease subtypes. These designs facilitate more efficient resource utilization and accelerate the development of personalized treatments.

4. Global Harmonization of Regulatory Standards

The globalization of the pharmaceutical industry necessitates the harmonization of regulatory standards across countries to facilitate the development and approval of new drugs.

- **International Council for Harmonisation (ICH)**: The ICH continues to play a pivotal role in harmonizing technical guidelines and standards for drug development. Regulatory agencies are collaborating to implement ICH guidelines and promote consistency in regulatory practices.

- **Mutual Recognition Agreements (MRAs)**: MRAs between regulatory authorities enable the recognition of inspections and approvals conducted by other agencies. These agreements reduce duplication of efforts and expedite the approval process for new drugs.
- **Harmonized Digital Platforms**: Digital platforms for regulatory submissions and information sharing are being developed to streamline communication between regulators and pharmaceutical companies. These platforms enhance transparency and efficiency in the regulatory process.

5. Focus on Patient-Centric Drug Development

Patient-centric approaches are gaining prominence in drug development, emphasizing the importance of patient involvement and the consideration of patient needs and preferences.

- **Patient-Reported Outcomes (PROs)**: PROs are increasingly used to assess the impact of new therapies on patients' quality of life and treatment satisfaction. Regulatory agencies are incorporating PROs into their evaluation criteria to ensure that patient perspectives are considered in drug approvals.
- **Patient Advocacy and Engagement**: Patient advocacy groups play a vital role in shaping drug development priorities and regulatory policies. Regulators are engaging with these groups to incorporate patient input into decision-making processes.
- **Flexible Dosing Regimens**: Flexible dosing regimens that consider individual patient needs are being explored to improve treatment adherence and outcomes. Regulators are providing guidance on the approval of these personalized dosing strategies.

6. Strengthening Post-Market Surveillance and Risk Management

Enhancing post-market surveillance and risk management practices is essential for ensuring the safety and effectiveness of drugs after they reach the market.

- **Risk Evaluation and Mitigation Strategies (REMS)**: Regulators are implementing REMS to manage the risks associated with certain medications and ensure safe use. These strategies involve monitoring, education, and communication efforts to mitigate potential adverse effects.

- **Pharmacovigilance Systems**: Advanced pharmacovigilance systems leverage digital technologies to detect and assess adverse drug reactions. Regulators are investing in these systems to enhance real-time monitoring and improve drug safety.
- **Benefit-Risk Assessment**: Continuous benefit-risk assessment is crucial for maintaining the balance between a drug's therapeutic benefits and potential risks. Regulators are adopting structured frameworks for evaluating benefit-risk profiles throughout a drug's lifecycle.

7. Regulatory Innovation and Flexibility

Regulatory agencies are embracing innovation and flexibility to adapt to the evolving pharmaceutical landscape and address emerging challenges.

- **Expedited Approval Pathways**: Expedited pathways, such as accelerated approval and breakthrough therapy designation, are designed to facilitate the rapid development and approval of promising therapies. Regulators are refining these pathways to ensure timely access to life-saving treatments.
- **Regulatory Sandboxes**: Regulatory sandboxes provide a controlled environment for testing innovative technologies and approaches in drug development. These initiatives enable regulators to explore new models while ensuring safety and compliance.
- **Collaborative Regulatory Approaches**: Collaboration between regulatory agencies, industry stakeholders, and academia fosters innovation and enhances the regulatory process. Regulators are building partnerships to address complex challenges and drive progress in drug development.

16.2 Advances in Regulatory Science

Advances in regulatory science are transforming how pharmaceutical products are developed, evaluated, and approved. Regulatory science is the field that underpins the evaluation of new drugs, ensuring they are safe, effective, and of high quality. This section explores the significant advances in regulatory science that are shaping the pharmaceutical industry's future, highlighting key innovations, methodologies, and technologies that enhance drug regulation.

1 Innovative Clinical Trial Designs

The traditional clinical trial model is evolving to incorporate innovative designs that improve efficiency and speed up the drug development process. These advances in clinical trial methodologies are essential for addressing the complexities of modern drug development.

1.1 Adaptive Clinical Trials

- **Flexibility in Design**: Adaptive clinical trials allow for modifications to the trial protocol based on interim data without compromising the study's integrity. These modifications may include changes in sample size, dosing regimens, or patient selection criteria.
- **Benefits**: This approach reduces development time and resources, allowing researchers to make informed decisions as the trial progresses. It increases the likelihood of success by focusing on the most promising candidates or treatment arms.

1.2 Seamless Trials

- **Combined Phases**: Seamless trials integrate multiple phases of clinical development (e.g., Phase I/II or Phase II/III) into a single continuous trial. This design accelerates the transition from one phase to the next based on predefined criteria.
- **Efficiency**: By eliminating the traditional pauses between trial phases, seamless trials streamline the development process, reducing the time and cost associated with bringing new drugs to market.

1.3 Bayesian Methods

- **Statistical Innovation**: Bayesian statistical methods incorporate prior knowledge and data into the trial design, allowing for continuous learning and decision-making throughout the study.
- **Applications**: These methods are particularly useful in adaptive trials, where ongoing data can inform modifications to the trial design, enhancing its efficiency and success rates.

1.4 Decentralized Clinical Trials

- **Remote Participation**: Decentralized trials leverage digital tools and telemedicine to conduct studies remotely, reducing the need for patients to visit clinical sites.

- **Patient-Centric Approach**: This model enhances patient convenience and engagement, potentially increasing recruitment and retention rates while collecting real-world data.

2. RealWorld Evidence (RWE) and Real-World Data (RWD)

The integration of real-world evidence (RWE) and real-world data (RWD) into regulatory decision-making is transforming how drugs are evaluated and monitored post-approval. These approaches complement traditional clinical trials, providing insights into drug performance in real-world settings.

2.1 Data Sources

- **Electronic Health Records (EHRs)**: EHRs provide comprehensive patient data that can be analyzed to assess drug safety, efficacy, and usage patterns in diverse populations.
- **Wearable Devices**: Wearable technology captures real-time health data, offering insights into patient outcomes and adherence to treatment regimens.
- **Health Registries**: Disease and health registries collect data on specific conditions, aiding in understanding treatment effects and long-term outcomes.

2.2 Regulatory Applications

- **Safety Monitoring**: RWE enhances post-market surveillance by identifying adverse events and safety signals that may not be evident in clinical trials.
- **Comparative Effectiveness**: RWD allows for the assessment of a drug's effectiveness compared to existing therapies, providing valuable information for healthcare decision-makers.
- **Label Expansion**: RWE can support applications for new indications or expanded patient populations, allowing for more flexible and responsive drug development.

2.3 Regulatory Frameworks

- **Guidelines and Standards**: Regulatory agencies, such as the FDA and EMA, are developing guidelines to standardize the collection, analysis, and application of RWE in regulatory submissions.
- **Collaborative Initiatives**: International collaborations aim to harmonize approaches to RWE, promoting consistency and reliability in its use across jurisdictions.

3. Advanced Analytical Methods

Advancements in analytical methods are enhancing the precision and accuracy of drug evaluation, supporting the development of complex therapies and personalized medicine.

3.1 Bioinformatics and Computational Modeling

- **Data Analysis**: Bioinformatics tools process large datasets, including genomic data, to identify patterns and predict drug responses. Computational modeling simulates biological systems, supporting drug discovery and development.
- **Personalized Medicine**: These technologies enable the identification of biomarkers and patient subgroups that may benefit from specific therapies, facilitating personalized treatment approaches.

3.2 Genomics and Proteomics

- **Omics Technologies**: Genomics and proteomics provide insights into the genetic and protein profiles of individuals, guiding the development of targeted therapies and precision medicine.
- **Biomarker Discovery**: These technologies aid in identifying biomarkers for disease progression, treatment response, and adverse effects, enhancing drug development and regulatory evaluation.

3.3 AI and Machine Learning

- **Predictive Modeling**: AI and machine learning algorithms analyze complex datasets to predict drug efficacy, safety, and potential adverse events, supporting regulatory decision-making.
- **Automation and Efficiency**: These technologies streamline data processing, reduce human error, and enhance the efficiency of regulatory workflows.

4. Adanced Manufacturing Technologies

Advances in manufacturing technologies are revolutionizing the production of pharmaceuticals, enabling more efficient, flexible, and sustainable processes.

4.1 Continuous Manufacturing

- **Efficiency and Consistency**: Continuous manufacturing replaces traditional batch processes with a continuous flow, improving efficiency, consistency, and product quality.
- **Regulatory Support**: Regulatory agencies are developing guidelines to facilitate the adoption of continuous manufacturing, recognizing its potential to enhance drug production.

4.2 3D Printing

- **Customized Dosage Forms**: 3D printing allows for the creation of personalized dosage forms, tailored to individual patient needs and preferences.
- **Innovative Formulations**: This technology supports the development of complex drug formulations, including those with intricate release profiles or unique delivery systems.

4.3 Advanced Bioprocessing

- **Biologics Production**: Advanced bioprocessing techniques optimize the production of biologics, ensuring high yield and quality while reducing costs.
- **Cell and Gene Therapies**: These technologies support the scalable production of cell and gene therapies, facilitating their development and regulatory approval.

5. Regultory Innovations and Collaboration

Regulatory agencies are adopting innovative approaches and fostering collaboration to address the complexities of modern drug development and ensure timely access to new therapies.

5.1 Expedited Pathways

- **Accelerated Approval**: Expedited pathways, such as accelerated approval and conditional marketing authorization, enable the rapid approval of drugs addressing unmet medical needs.
- **Priority Review**: Regulatory agencies prioritize the review of applications for drugs that offer significant therapeutic advancements or address public health priorities.

5.2 Regulatory Sandboxes

- **Innovation Testing**: Regulatory sandboxes provide a controlled environment for testing innovative technologies and approaches, allowing regulators to explore new models while ensuring safety and compliance.
- **Stakeholder Collaboration**: These initiatives foster collaboration between regulators, industry, and academia, promoting knowledge sharing and innovation.

5.3 International Harmonization

- **Global Standards**: Harmonizing regulatory standards and practices across countries facilitates international collaboration, reducing duplication and streamlining the approval process for global markets.
- **Mutual Recognition**: Mutual recognition agreements between regulatory agencies enhance cooperation and trust, allowing for the sharing of information and resources.

16.3 Role of Technology in Regulatory Affairs

Technology has become a cornerstone in the advancement of regulatory affairs, revolutionizing how regulatory processes are managed and executed. It is facilitating more efficient drug development and approval processes, ensuring compliance, and enhancing communication between stakeholders.

1. Digital Transformation

Digital transformation is reshaping the pharmaceutical industry by streamlining processes, improving data management, and enhancing regulatory compliance.

- **Electronic Submissions**: Regulatory agencies worldwide are transitioning to electronic submissions for regulatory documents. The use of platforms like the Electronic Common Technical Document (eCTD) allows for standardized submissions, reducing processing time and errors.
- **Digital Record-Keeping**: Digital systems enable accurate record-keeping and tracking of compliance activities, ensuring that companies maintain high standards of regulatory adherence. This also facilitates audits and inspections.
- **Data Integration**: Advanced data integration tools allow companies to manage large volumes of data across various platforms, ensuring seamless access to information and enhancing decision-making.

2. Artificial Intelligence and Machine Learning

Artificial intelligence (AI) and machine learning (ML) are transforming regulatory affairs by automating routine tasks and providing insights through data analysis.

- **Automating Routine Tasks**: AI can automate repetitive tasks such as data entry, document review, and compliance checks, allowing regulatory professionals to focus on more strategic activities.
- **Predictive Analytics**: Machine learning algorithms can analyze vast datasets to predict trends, identify potential compliance issues, and provide insights into regulatory changes. This proactive approach helps companies stay ahead of regulatory requirements.
- **Natural Language Processing (NLP)**: NLP tools facilitate the analysis of regulatory documents and guidelines, enabling companies to extract relevant information quickly and ensure compliance with complex regulations.

3. Blockchain Technology

Blockchain technology offers a decentralized and secure way to manage data, enhancing transparency and traceability in regulatory affairs.

- **Data Integrity**: Blockchain ensures data integrity by providing a tamper-proof record of transactions and changes. This is particularly useful in maintaining the accuracy of clinical trial data and supply chain records.

- **Traceability**: Blockchain enhances the traceability of pharmaceutical products throughout the supply chain, helping to prevent counterfeiting and ensure that products meet regulatory standards.
- **Smart Contracts**: Smart contracts on blockchain platforms can automate regulatory compliance processes, triggering actions based on predefined conditions and reducing the risk of human error.

4. Cloud Computing and Big Data

Cloud computing and big data are enabling the storage, processing, and analysis of large volumes of data, supporting more informed regulatory decisions.

- **Scalable Solutions**: Cloud computing provides scalable solutions for data storage and processing, allowing companies to manage and analyze data efficiently. This flexibility is essential for handling the increasing volume of regulatory data.
- **Advanced Analytics**: Big data analytics tools process complex datasets to uncover patterns, trends, and insights that inform regulatory strategies and compliance efforts.
- **Collaboration Platforms**: Cloud-based collaboration platforms facilitate communication and information sharing between regulatory teams, stakeholders, and authorities, enhancing coordination and transparency.

5. Internet of Things (IoT) and Wearables

IoT and wearable technologies are providing real-time data on drug usage and patient outcomes, supporting regulatory decisions.

- **Real-Time Monitoring**: IoT devices and wearables collect real-time data on patient health and medication adherence, providing valuable insights into drug safety and efficacy.
- **Post-Market Surveillance**: These technologies enable continuous monitoring of drug performance in real-world settings, enhancing pharmacovigilance and risk management efforts.
- **Patient-Centric Approaches**: IoT and wearables support patient-centric approaches by providing personalized insights and feedback, informing regulatory strategies that prioritize patient outcomes.

16.4 Global Harmonization and Regulatory Convergence

As the pharmaceutical industry becomes increasingly globalized, there is a growing need for harmonization and convergence of regulatory standards across countries. This alignment aims to streamline drug development and approval processes, reduce duplication of efforts, and enhance access to medicines worldwide.

1. International Council for Harmonisation (ICH)

The ICH plays a crucial role in harmonizing technical guidelines and standards for drug development, ensuring that pharmaceutical products meet consistent quality, safety, and efficacy standards.

- **Harmonized Guidelines**: ICH guidelines provide a unified framework for drug development, covering areas such as quality management, safety evaluation, and clinical efficacy.
- **Global Implementation**: Regulatory agencies worldwide collaborate to implement ICH guidelines, promoting consistency and reliability in drug development and regulatory practices.
- **Training and Capacity Building**: The ICH supports training initiatives and capacity-building efforts to help regulatory authorities adopt and implement harmonized standards effectively.

2. Mutual Recognition Agreements (MRAs)

MRAs between regulatory authorities enable the mutual recognition of inspections, approvals, and standards, reducing duplication of efforts and facilitating international trade.

- **Inspection Recognition**: MRAs allow regulatory agencies to recognize inspections conducted by other authorities, reducing the need for redundant inspections and streamlining the approval process.
- **Regulatory Cooperation**: These agreements foster regulatory cooperation, enhancing trust and collaboration between countries and promoting a more efficient global regulatory environment.
- **Product Accessibility**: MRAs facilitate the global accessibility of pharmaceutical products by ensuring that they meet consistent standards and are recognized across jurisdictions.

3. Harmonized Digital Platforms

The development of harmonized digital platforms for regulatory submissions and information sharing enhances communication and coordination between regulators and pharmaceutical companies.

- **Standardized Submissions**: Digital platforms support standardized submissions, reducing complexity and improving the efficiency of regulatory processes.
- **Information Sharing**: These platforms enable the sharing of regulatory information and best practices, fostering collaboration and transparency between stakeholders.
- **Regulatory Intelligence**: Harmonized digital platforms provide access to regulatory intelligence, helping companies stay informed about global regulatory trends and requirements.

4. Collaborative Regulatory Networks

Collaborative networks between regulatory agencies, industry stakeholders, and academic institutions enhance knowledge sharing and innovation in regulatory affairs.

- **Joint Research Initiatives**: Collaborative networks support joint research initiatives, advancing scientific understanding and innovation in drug development and regulation.
- **Knowledge Exchange**: These networks facilitate the exchange of knowledge and expertise, promoting the adoption of best practices and innovative approaches to regulatory challenges.
- **Global Regulatory Forums**: International regulatory forums provide platforms for dialogue and collaboration, addressing emerging issues and promoting harmonization efforts.

5. Global Standards for Drug Quality and Safety

Global standards for drug quality and safety ensure that pharmaceutical products meet consistent criteria, protecting public health and enhancing consumer confidence.

- **Quality Assurance**: Harmonized standards support quality assurance efforts, ensuring that drugs are manufactured, stored, and distributed according to rigorous quality control measures.
- **Safety Monitoring**: Global standards enhance safety monitoring practices, enabling the detection and management of adverse events and risks associated with pharmaceutical products.

- **Regulatory Compliance:** Consistent standards facilitate regulatory compliance, reducing barriers to market entry and supporting the global availability of safe and effective medicines.

CHAPTER SEVENTEEN

Intellectual Property Rights

Intellectual Property Rights (IPR) are legal rights that provide creators and inventors with protection and control over their creations and innovations. In the pharmaceutical industry, IPR plays a crucial role in promoting innovation, encouraging investment in research and development, and ensuring that companies and individuals can reap the benefits of their intellectual efforts. This chapter explores the fundamentals of IPR, focusing on its significance in the pharmaceutical sector, the types of intellectual property, and the legal frameworks that govern these rights.

17.1 Introduction to Intellectual Property Rights (IPR)

Definition and Significance of IPR

Intellectual Property Rights (IPR) refer to the exclusive legal rights granted to individuals or organizations over their creations, inventions, and innovations. These rights allow the creators to control the use, reproduction, and distribution of their work, providing them with a competitive advantage and financial rewards. In the pharmaceutical industry, IPR is vital for fostering innovation and encouraging the development of new drugs and therapies that address unmet medical needs.

Significance of IPR in Pharmaceuticals:

- **Encouragement of Innovation**: IPR provides pharmaceutical companies with the incentive to invest in research and development by offering protection for new inventions. This protection ensures that companies can recover their investments and earn profits from their innovations.

- **Market Exclusivity**: Patents, a key form of IPR, grant pharmaceutical companies exclusive rights to manufacture and sell a new drug for a specified period, typically 20 years. This exclusivity allows companies to set prices that reflect the research and development costs involved in bringing a new drug to market.

- **Economic Growth**: The pharmaceutical industry is a significant contributor to economic growth, and IPR plays a critical role in driving this growth by supporting innovation and attracting investments. IPR protection encourages multinational companies to invest in research and development facilities in countries with robust IP laws.
- **Public Health Benefits**: By incentivizing the development of new drugs and therapies, IPR contributes to improving public health outcomes. Innovative medicines address complex diseases and medical conditions, enhancing the quality of life for patients worldwide.

Types of Intellectual Property Rights

In the pharmaceutical industry, several types of intellectual property rights are relevant, each offering different forms of protection for various aspects of innovation and creativity:

Patents

- **Definition**: A patent is a legal right granted to an inventor, providing exclusive rights to use, produce, and sell an invention for a specific period, usually 20 years from the filing date.
- **Relevance to Pharmaceuticals**: Patents are crucial for protecting new drug formulations, active ingredients, manufacturing processes, and delivery systems. They prevent competitors from producing and selling the same drug, allowing the patent holder to recoup research and development investments.
- **Types of Patents**: In pharmaceuticals, patents can be categorized into various types, including compound patents (covering the active ingredient), process patents (covering the manufacturing process), formulation patents (covering the drug's composition), and use patents (covering new uses for existing drugs).

Trademarks

- **Definition**: A trademark is a distinctive sign, logo, or symbol that identifies and differentiates the products or services of one company from those of others. It helps build brand identity and consumer trust.
- **Relevance to Pharmaceuticals**: Trademarks are used to protect brand names and logos associated with pharmaceutical products, ensuring that consumers can distinguish between different brands and trust the

quality and efficacy of the products they purchase.

- **Types of Trademarks**: Pharmaceutical companies use various types of trademarks, including word marks (brand names), logo marks (graphic symbols), and shape marks (distinctive packaging shapes).

Trade Secrets

- **Definition**: Trade secrets refer to confidential business information that provides a competitive advantage to a company. This information is not publicly disclosed and is protected through confidentiality agreements and security measures.
- **Relevance to Pharmaceuticals**: Trade secrets in the pharmaceutical industry include proprietary formulations, manufacturing processes, and research data that are not patentable or disclosed to the public. Companies rely on trade secrets to maintain a competitive edge.
- **Protection Measures**: Companies use various measures to protect trade secrets, such as employee confidentiality agreements, restricted access to sensitive information, and implementing robust cybersecurity protocols.

Copyrights

- **Definition**: Copyright is a legal right that protects original works of authorship, such as literature, music, art, and software, from unauthorized use and reproduction.
- **Relevance to Pharmaceuticals**: In the pharmaceutical industry, copyrights protect written materials such as research papers, drug packaging designs, promotional materials, and software used in drug development and research.
- **Scope of Protection**: Copyright protection does not extend to the ideas or concepts themselves but covers the expression of those ideas, such as written documents, graphics, and software codes.

Legal Frameworks Governing IPR

The protection and enforcement of intellectual property rights are governed by various national and international legal frameworks, ensuring that creators and innovators receive the recognition and financial rewards for their work:

National Laws

- **Indian Patent Act, 1970**: This Act governs the grant of patents in India and outlines the procedures, requirements, and duration of patent protection. It has been amended several times to align with international agreements, such as the **Agreement on Trade-Related Aspects of Intellectual Property Rights (TRIPS)**.
- **Trademarks Act, 1999**: This Act regulates the registration, protection, and enforcement of trademarks in India, ensuring that brand names and logos are protected from unauthorized use.
- **Copyright Act, 1957**: This Act provides the legal framework for copyright protection in India, covering original works of authorship, including written materials, graphics, and software.
- **Trade Secrets Protection**: While India does not have a specific law for trade secret protection, common law principles and contractual agreements are used to safeguard confidential business information.

International Agreements

- **TRIPS Agreement**: The TRIPS Agreement, administered by the World Trade Organization (WTO), sets minimum standards for IP protection and enforcement across member countries, including patents, trademarks, copyrights, and trade secrets.
- **Paris Convention for the Protection of Industrial Property**: This international treaty provides guidelines for the protection of industrial property, including patents and trademarks, ensuring that inventors receive protection in multiple countries.
- **Patent Cooperation Treaty (PCT)**: The PCT is an international agreement that simplifies the process of filing patents in multiple countries by providing a unified procedure for international patent applications.

Challenges and Controversies in Pharmaceutical IPR

While intellectual property rights play a critical role in fostering innovation and economic growth, they also present challenges and controversies, particularly in the pharmaceutical industry:

Access to Medicines

- **High Drug Prices**: Patents grant exclusivity to pharmaceutical companies, allowing them to set high prices for patented drugs. This can limit access to essential medicines, particularly in low- and middle-income countries, where affordability is a significant concern.
- **Compulsory Licensing**: To address the issue of access, some countries implement compulsory licensing, which allows governments to authorize the production of generic versions of patented drugs without the patent holder's consent under specific circumstances, such as public health emergencies.

Balancing Innovation and Public Interest

- **Innovation Incentives**: While IPR incentivizes innovation by protecting inventors' interests, there is a need to balance these incentives with public interest, ensuring that life-saving medicines are accessible to those who need them.
- **Ethical Considerations**: Ethical concerns arise when pharmaceutical companies prioritize profit over patient welfare, such as delaying the introduction of generic drugs or exploiting patent extensions to maintain exclusivity.

Patent Cliffs and Generic Competition

- **Patent Expiry**: When a patent expires, other companies can produce generic versions of the drug, leading to increased competition and reduced prices. This is known as the "patent cliff," and it poses a challenge for pharmaceutical companies seeking to maintain revenue.
- **Evergreening**: Some companies engage in "evergreening" practices, obtaining additional patents for minor modifications to existing drugs to extend exclusivity and delay generic competition.

Future Directions for Pharmaceutical IPR

The future of intellectual property rights in the pharmaceutical industry is shaped by evolving legal frameworks, technological advancements, and changing public health priorities. Key areas of focus include:

Strengthening IP Enforcement

- **Capacity Building**: Enhancing the capacity of regulatory authorities and judicial systems to enforce IP rights is crucial for ensuring compliance and addressing infringement issues.
- **International Cooperation**: Collaboration among countries and international organizations can strengthen IP enforcement efforts, particularly in combating counterfeit medicines and cross-border IP violations.

Promoting Access and Affordability

- **Balancing Rights and Access**: Policymakers must find ways to balance IP protection with access to affordable medicines, particularly for underserved populations.
- **Innovative Licensing Models**: Exploring alternative licensing models, such as voluntary licensing agreements and patent pools, can facilitate access to patented medicines while ensuring fair compensation for innovators.

Encouraging Innovation in Emerging Fields

- **Biotechnology and Personalized Medicine**: The rise of biotechnology and personalized medicine presents new opportunities and challenges for IP protection. Ensuring that IP laws keep pace with technological advancements is essential for promoting innovation in these fields.
- **Digital Health and AI**: The integration of digital health technologies and artificial intelligence (AI) in drug development requires adapting IP frameworks to address new forms of innovation and protect novel algorithms and data-driven solutions.

17.2 Patents and Copyrights in Pharmaceutical Industry

Intellectual property rights, specifically patents and copyrights, play a crucial role in the pharmaceutical industry by safeguarding innovations and creative works. They provide legal protection and exclusive rights to inventors and creators, encouraging investment in research and development. This section explores the significance of patents and copyrights in the pharmaceutical industry, their application, benefits, challenges, and the legal frameworks that govern these rights.

Patents in the Pharmaceutical Industry

Definition and Purpose of Patents

A **patent** is a legal right granted to an inventor, giving them exclusive rights to use, produce, and sell their invention for a specific period, typically 20 years from the filing date. In the pharmaceutical industry, patents are crucial for protecting new drug formulations, active ingredients, manufacturing processes, and delivery systems. They prevent competitors from producing and selling the same drug, allowing the patent holder to recoup research and development investments.

Types of Patents in Pharmaceuticals

In the pharmaceutical industry, several types of patents are used to protect different aspects of drug development and innovation:

Compound Patents

- **Definition**: Compound patents cover the active ingredient or chemical compound of a new drug. They provide protection for the specific molecular structure that gives the drug its therapeutic effect.
- **Significance**: Compound patents are the most valuable patents in pharmaceuticals, as they offer the strongest protection against generic competition. They ensure that only the patent holder can produce and sell the drug, allowing for market exclusivity.

Process Patents

- **Definition**: Process patents protect the method or process used to manufacture a drug. They cover the specific steps and techniques involved in producing the active ingredient or final product.
- **Significance**: Process patents are essential for protecting innovative manufacturing techniques that improve efficiency, yield, or safety. They can provide an additional layer of protection for drugs already covered by compound patents.

Formulation Patents

- **Definition**: Formulation patents cover the specific composition or formulation of a drug, including the combination of active and inactive ingredients, dosage form, and delivery method.
- **Significance**: Formulation patents protect the unique way a drug is delivered to patients, ensuring that competitors cannot replicate the

specific formulation even if they can produce the active ingredient.

Use Patents

- **Definition**: Use patents, also known as "method of use" patents, cover the specific therapeutic use or indication of a drug. They protect the application of a drug for treating a particular disease or condition.
- **Significance**: Use patents are valuable for extending the lifecycle of existing drugs by identifying new therapeutic uses or indications. They allow companies to explore additional revenue streams without developing new compounds.

Benefits of Patents in Pharmaceuticals

Patents provide several benefits to the pharmaceutical industry, contributing to innovation, economic growth, and public health:

Encouragement of Innovation

- **Incentive for R&D**: Patents offer a strong incentive for pharmaceutical companies to invest in research and development, knowing that their innovations will be protected and they can earn a return on their investment.
- **Fostering Innovation**: By providing exclusive rights, patents encourage companies to pursue innovative solutions and develop new drugs that address unmet medical needs.

Market Exclusivity

- **Protection Against Competition**: Patents grant market exclusivity, allowing patent holders to set prices that reflect the costs of research, development, and regulatory approval. This exclusivity helps companies recover their investments and fund future research.
- **Higher Profit Margins**: The absence of generic competition during the patent term allows companies to maintain higher profit margins, supporting further innovation and development.

Economic Growth

- **Investment Attraction**: Strong patent protection attracts investment from venture capitalists and other stakeholders, fostering economic growth and supporting the expansion of the pharmaceutical industry.
- **Job Creation**: The pharmaceutical sector is a significant source of employment, and patents contribute to job creation by supporting research, manufacturing, and commercialization activities.

Challenges and Controversies Related to Patents

While patents provide substantial benefits, they also present challenges and controversies, particularly in the pharmaceutical industry:

Access to Medicines

- **High Drug Prices**: Patents allow companies to set high prices for patented drugs, potentially limiting access to essential medicines, especially in low- and middle-income countries where affordability is a significant concern.
- **Public Health Implications**: The high cost of patented drugs can lead to inequities in access to healthcare, raising ethical concerns about balancing profit motives with public health needs.

Patent Cliffs and Generic Competition

- **Patent Expiry**: When patents expire, generic manufacturers can enter the market, leading to increased competition and reduced prices. This is known as the "patent cliff," posing a challenge for pharmaceutical companies seeking to maintain revenue.
- **Impact on Innovation**: The potential loss of revenue due to generic competition can impact a company's ability to invest in new drug development, affecting long-term innovation.

Evergreening Practices

- **Patent Extensions**: Some companies engage in "evergreening" practices, obtaining additional patents for minor modifications to existing drugs to extend exclusivity and delay generic competition.
- **Ethical Concerns**: Evergreening raises ethical concerns about the use of patent strategies to maintain market dominance at the expense of affordable healthcare.

Legal Framework for Patents in Pharmaceuticals

The protection and enforcement of patents in the pharmaceutical industry are governed by various national and international legal frameworks:

National Patent Laws

- **Indian Patent Act, 1970**: This Act governs the grant of patents in India, outlining the procedures, requirements, and duration of patent protection. It has been amended to align with international agreements, such as the **Agreement on Trade-Related Aspects of Intellectual Property Rights (TRIPS)**.
- **Patent Application Process**: The patent application process involves filing a detailed patent specification, including claims that define the scope of protection. The application is examined by the patent office, and, if approved, a patent is granted.

International Patent Agreements

- **TRIPS Agreement**: Administered by the World Trade Organization (WTO), the TRIPS Agreement sets minimum standards for IP protection and enforcement across member countries, including patents.
- **Patent Cooperation Treaty (PCT)**: The PCT simplifies the process of filing patents in multiple countries by providing a unified procedure for international patent applications, facilitating global protection for pharmaceutical innovations.

Copyrights in the Pharmaceutical Industry
Definition and Purpose of Copyrights

Copyright is a legal right that protects original works of authorship, such as literature, music, art, and software, from unauthorized use and reproduction. In the pharmaceutical industry, copyrights protect creative works related to drug development, including written materials, promotional content, packaging designs, and software.

Applications of Copyrights in Pharmaceuticals

While patents are the primary form of IP protection for pharmaceuticals, copyrights play a supporting role in safeguarding various creative aspects of the industry:

Research Papers and Publications

- **Scientific Research**: Copyrights protect the written expression of scientific research and findings, ensuring that authors receive recognition for their contributions to the field.
- **Publications**: Pharmaceutical companies often publish research papers and articles in scientific journals, and copyrights protect these publications from unauthorized reproduction and distribution.

Drug Packaging and Design

- **Packaging Designs**: Copyrights protect the creative aspects of drug packaging, including graphics, text, and overall design, ensuring that competitors cannot replicate the unique appearance of a product.
- **Instructional Materials**: Instructional materials, such as patient information leaflets and user manuals, are protected by copyright, ensuring that the content remains accurate and is not altered without permission.

Marketing and Promotional Materials

- **Advertisements**: Copyrights protect the creative content of advertisements and promotional materials, including images, slogans, and multimedia content, ensuring that competitors do not use them without authorization.
- **Brand Identity**: While trademarks protect brand names and logos, copyrights can protect the creative elements of a brand's identity, such as website content, brochures, and digital media.

Software and Databases

- **Research Software**: Copyrights protect software used in pharmaceutical research and development, including data analysis tools and modeling programs.
- **Databases**: Copyrights can also protect databases containing valuable information related to drug development, clinical trials, and market analysis.

Benefits of Copyrights in Pharmaceuticals

Copyrights provide several benefits to the pharmaceutical industry, supporting innovation, brand recognition, and market presence:

Protection of Creative Works

- **Encouragement of Creativity**: Copyrights incentivize creativity by protecting the expression of ideas, encouraging companies to invest in the development of unique content and materials.
- **Brand Differentiation**: Copyrights help differentiate brands by protecting the creative elements that define a company's identity, enhancing consumer recognition and loyalty.

Legal Recourse

- **Enforcement of Rights**: Copyrights provide legal recourse against unauthorized use or reproduction of protected works, ensuring that companies can take action against infringement and protect their intellectual assets.
- **Deterrence of Copying**: The legal protection afforded by copyrights deters competitors from copying creative works, encouraging originality and innovation.

Challenges and Limitations of Copyrights

While copyrights offer valuable protection, they also have limitations and challenges in the pharmaceutical industry:

Limited Scope of Protection

- **Expression vs. Idea**: Copyrights protect the expression of ideas, not the ideas themselves. This limitation means that while the text or design of a product can be protected, the underlying concept or functionality cannot.
- **Duration of Protection**: Copyright protection typically lasts for the life of the author plus 60 years in India, after which the work enters the public domain. This duration may not always align with the commercial lifespan of a product.

Enforcement Challenges

- **Infringement Detection**: Identifying and proving copyright infringement can be challenging, particularly in the digital age, where content can be easily reproduced and distributed without authorization.
- **Cross-Border Enforcement**: Enforcing copyright protection across different jurisdictions can be complex, requiring coordination between legal systems and international agreements.

Legal Framework for Copyrights in Pharmaceuticals

The protection and enforcement of copyrights in the pharmaceutical industry are governed by national and international legal frameworks:

National Copyright Laws

- **Indian Copyright Act, 1957**: This Act provides the legal framework for copyright protection in India, covering original works of authorship, including written materials, graphics, and software.
- **Copyright Registration**: While registration is not mandatory for copyright protection, it provides legal evidence of ownership and can facilitate enforcement actions against infringement.

International Copyright Agreements

- **Berne Convention**: The Berne Convention for the Protection of Literary and Artistic Works sets minimum standards for copyright protection and ensures that authors receive protection across member countries.
- **WIPO Copyright Treaty**: Administered by the World Intellectual Property Organization (WIPO), this treaty addresses copyright protection in the digital environment, ensuring that creative works are protected online.

17.3 Regulatory Framework for IPR in Different Countries

Intellectual Property Rights (IPR) are crucial for protecting innovations and creations in the pharmaceutical industry. Each country has its own regulatory framework to govern IPR, ensuring that inventors and creators receive the legal protection they deserve. These frameworks vary in scope, enforcement mechanisms, and compliance with international agreements, reflecting each country's economic, legal, and social contexts. This section explores the regulatory frameworks for IPR in different countries, focusing on key jurisdictions, their legal structures, and the challenges and opportunities they present for the pharmaceutical industry.

United States

Legal Framework

The United States has a comprehensive legal framework for protecting intellectual property rights, with a strong emphasis on innovation and economic growth. The U.S. IPR system is governed by several key laws and institutions:

- **Patent Act of 1952**: This Act provides the legal basis for granting patents in the United States, outlining the requirements for patentability, including novelty, non-obviousness, and usefulness. It also establishes the patent application and examination process.
- **Lanham Act**: The Lanham Act governs trademarks in the U.S., providing protection for brand names, logos, and symbols that distinguish goods and services. It allows trademark owners to prevent unauthorized use and counterfeiting.
- **Copyright Act of 1976**: This Act protects original works of authorship, such as literature, music, art, and software, granting exclusive rights to creators for the reproduction, distribution, and performance of their works.
- **Trade Secrets Protection**: Trade secrets are protected under the **Defend Trade Secrets Act of 2016**, which provides federal remedies for trade secret misappropriation and enhances protection against industrial espionage.

Enforcement and Institutions

- **United States Patent and Trademark Office (USPTO)**: The USPTO is responsible for granting patents and registering trademarks in the U.S. It examines patent applications, issues patents, and maintains a database of registered trademarks.
- **U.S. Copyright Office**: This office administers copyright registration and maintains a record of copyrighted works. While registration is not required for protection, it provides legal advantages in enforcement actions.
- **Federal Courts**: The U.S. has a robust judicial system for enforcing IPR, with specialized courts such as the U.S. Court of Appeals for the Federal Circuit, which handles patent cases and appeals.

Challenges and Opportunities

- **Patent Litigation**: The U.S. is known for its high rate of patent litigation, which can pose challenges for pharmaceutical companies seeking to protect their innovations. However, the legal system provides robust mechanisms for resolving disputes and enforcing rights.
- **Innovation Ecosystem**: The U.S. offers a favorable environment for innovation, with strong legal protections and support for research and development. This fosters collaboration between industry and academia, leading to advancements in pharmaceuticals.

European Union
Legal Framework

The European Union (EU) has a harmonized legal framework for IPR, with directives and regulations that apply across member states. Key elements of the EU's IPR framework include:

- **European Patent Convention (EPC)**: The EPC provides a unified procedure for granting European patents, allowing inventors to obtain patent protection in multiple member states through a single application process.
- **EU Trademark Regulation**: This regulation allows for the registration of EU trademarks, providing protection for brand names and logos across all EU member states.
- **EU Copyright Directive**: This directive harmonizes copyright protection across the EU, ensuring that creators receive consistent rights and protection for their works.
- **Trade Secrets Directive**: The directive establishes minimum standards for the protection of trade secrets, ensuring that confidential business information is safeguarded from unauthorized use and disclosure.

Enforcement and Institutions

- **European Patent Office (EPO)**: The EPO is responsible for examining and granting European patents. It provides a centralized system for patent applications, allowing inventors to seek protection in multiple countries through a single process.

- **EU Intellectual Property Office (EUIPO)**: The EUIPO manages the registration of EU trademarks and designs, ensuring that brand owners receive protection across the EU.
- **National Courts**: Enforcement of IPR in the EU involves national courts, which apply EU directives and regulations. The Court of Justice of the European Union (CJEU) provides guidance on interpreting EU law.

Challenges and Opportunities

- **Unitary Patent System**: The EU is working towards implementing a unitary patent system, which would simplify the process of obtaining patent protection across member states and reduce costs for inventors.
- **Cross-Border Enforcement**: The harmonized IPR framework facilitates cross-border enforcement, allowing rights holders to address infringement in multiple countries through coordinated legal actions.

India
Legal Framework
India has a well-established legal framework for IPR, with laws that align with international standards while addressing the country's specific needs and priorities:

- **Indian Patent Act, 1970**: This Act governs patent protection in India, outlining the criteria for patentability and the process for obtaining patents. It includes provisions for compulsory licensing to address public health needs.
- **Trademarks Act, 1999**: This Act provides the legal framework for registering and protecting trademarks in India, ensuring that brand owners can prevent unauthorized use of their marks.
- **Copyright Act, 1957**: The Act offers protection for original works of authorship, granting exclusive rights to creators for reproduction, distribution, and adaptation of their works.
- **Trade Secrets Protection**: While India does not have a specific law for trade secret protection, common law principles and contractual agreements are used to safeguard confidential information.

Enforcement and Institutions

- **Office of the Controller General of Patents, Designs, and Trademarks (CGPDTM)**: This office is responsible for administering patents, trademarks, and designs in India, overseeing the examination and registration process.
- **Copyright Office**: The Copyright Office manages the registration of copyrighted works and maintains records of registered works, facilitating enforcement actions.
- **Indian Judiciary**: India has a robust judicial system for enforcing IPR, with specialized IP benches in high courts that handle IP disputes and infringement cases.

Challenges and Opportunities

- **Balancing Innovation and Access**: India faces challenges in balancing IP protection with access to affordable medicines, particularly for life-saving drugs. Compulsory licensing provisions aim to address this issue.
- **Growing IP Awareness**: India is witnessing increased awareness and enforcement of IPR, supported by government initiatives to strengthen IP infrastructure and encourage innovation.

China
Legal Framework
China has made significant strides in developing its IPR framework, with laws that aim to protect innovations and promote economic growth:

- **Patent Law of the People's Republic of China**: This law provides the legal framework for patent protection, outlining the requirements for patentability and the process for obtaining patents.
- **Trademark Law**: The law governs the registration and protection of trademarks in China, ensuring that brand owners can prevent unauthorized use and infringement.
- **Copyright Law**: This law protects original works of authorship, granting exclusive rights to creators for reproduction, distribution, and adaptation of their works.
- **Trade Secrets Protection**: Trade secrets are protected under China's Anti-Unfair Competition Law, which provides remedies for misappropriation and unauthorized use.

Enforcement and Institutions

- **China National Intellectual Property Administration (CNIPA)**: CNIPA oversees patent and trademark registration in China, managing the examination and grant process.
- **National Copyright Administration (NCA)**: The NCA administers copyright protection and enforces rights through registration and legal actions.
- **Judicial and Administrative Enforcement**: China has strengthened its judicial and administrative mechanisms for IPR enforcement, with specialized IP courts and agencies handling disputes and infringement cases.

Challenges and Opportunities

- **IP Enforcement**: China has faced challenges related to IP enforcement, including issues of counterfeit goods and piracy. However, recent reforms have strengthened legal protections and enforcement mechanisms.
- **Innovation-Driven Growth**: China's focus on innovation-driven growth presents opportunities for IP development, supported by government policies and investments in research and technology.

Japan

Legal Framework

Japan has a robust IPR framework that aligns with international standards, promoting innovation and protecting intellectual property:

- **Patent Act**: The Patent Act governs patent protection in Japan, outlining the criteria for patentability and the process for obtaining patents.
- **Trademark Act**: This Act provides the legal framework for registering and protecting trademarks in Japan, ensuring brand owners can prevent unauthorized use of their marks.
- **Copyright Act**: The Act protects original works of authorship, granting exclusive rights to creators for reproduction, distribution, and adaptation of their works.
- **Trade Secrets Protection**: Trade secrets are protected under Japan's Unfair Competition Prevention Act, which provides remedies for

misappropriation and unauthorized use.

Enforcement and Institutions

- **Japan Patent Office (JPO)**: The JPO is responsible for examining and granting patents and trademarks, providing a centralized system for IP protection.
- **Courts and Arbitration**: Japan has specialized IP courts and arbitration centers that handle IP disputes and infringement cases, ensuring effective enforcement of rights.

Challenges and Opportunities

- **Innovation Ecosystem**: Japan's strong innovation ecosystem, supported by government policies and industry collaboration, offers opportunities for IP development and commercialization.
- **International Collaboration**: Japan's participation in international agreements and collaborations enhances its IP framework, facilitating global protection and enforcement of rights.

Brazil
Legal Framework

Brazil's IPR framework is governed by laws that protect innovations and promote economic development:

- **Industrial Property Law**: This law provides the legal framework for patent protection in Brazil, outlining the criteria for patentability and the process for obtaining patents.
- **Trademark Law**: The law governs the registration and protection of trademarks in Brazil, ensuring brand owners can prevent unauthorized use and infringement.
- **Copyright Law**: This law protects original works of authorship, granting exclusive rights to creators for reproduction, distribution, and adaptation of their works.
- **Trade Secrets Protection**: Trade secrets are protected under Brazil's Industrial Property Law, which provides remedies for misappropriation and unauthorized use.

Enforcement and Institutions

- **National Institute of Industrial Property (INPI)**: INPI oversees patent and trademark registration in Brazil, managing the examination and grant process.
- **Courts and Administrative Bodies**: Brazil has specialized courts and administrative bodies that handle IP disputes and enforcement actions, ensuring effective protection of rights.

Challenges and Opportunities

- **Patent Backlog**: Brazil faces challenges related to patent application backlogs, which can delay the granting of patents and impact innovation.
- **IP Awareness and Enforcement**: Efforts to increase IP awareness and strengthen enforcement mechanisms present opportunities for improving Brazil's IP framework and fostering innovation.

17.4 Data Exclusivity and Market Exclusivity

Data exclusivity and market exclusivity are two essential concepts in the pharmaceutical industry that provide additional layers of protection to innovative drugs beyond patent protection. These mechanisms help innovators recover research and development investments, encouraging the development of new drugs. This section explores the concepts of data exclusivity and market exclusivity, their significance in the pharmaceutical industry, their application across different jurisdictions, and the challenges and opportunities they present.

Data Exclusivity

Definition and Purpose of Data Exclusivity

Data Exclusivity is a regulatory mechanism that prevents generic drug manufacturers from using the clinical trial data of an innovator drug for a specified period. During this exclusivity period, regulatory authorities cannot rely on the originator's data to approve generic versions of the drug. This protection incentivizes pharmaceutical companies to invest in research and development by safeguarding their data from being used by competitors to gain market entry without conducting their own studies.

How Data Exclusivity Works

- **Protection of Clinical Data**: Innovator companies invest significant resources in conducting clinical trials to demonstrate the safety, efficacy, and quality of a new drug. Data exclusivity ensures that this data remains protected, preventing competitors from referencing it in their generic drug applications.
- **Exclusivity Period**: The period of data exclusivity varies by country and drug type. It typically ranges from **5 to 12 years**, depending on the jurisdiction and the drug's classification (e.g., new chemical entities, biologics, orphan drugs).
- **Independent Studies**: During the exclusivity period, generic manufacturers must conduct independent studies to prove their drug's safety and efficacy without referencing the innovator's data. This requirement delays generic market entry, allowing the innovator to recover investments and gain a competitive advantage.

Significance of Data Exclusivity in Pharmaceuticals

Data exclusivity provides several benefits to the pharmaceutical industry, enhancing innovation and public health outcomes:

- **Incentivizing Innovation**: By providing a period of protection for clinical trial data, data exclusivity encourages pharmaceutical companies to invest in developing new drugs and therapies, knowing that their data will be protected from immediate generic competition.
- **R&D Investment**: The exclusivity period allows innovators to recoup their research and development investments, supporting the high costs associated with drug discovery and clinical trials.
- **Public Health Benefits**: Data exclusivity promotes the development of innovative medicines that address unmet medical needs, improving public health outcomes and enhancing patients' quality of life.

Application of Data Exclusivity Across Jurisdictions

The duration and scope of data exclusivity vary across different countries and regions, reflecting their regulatory environments and public health priorities:

United States

- **Duration**: The U.S. grants **5 years** of data exclusivity for new chemical entities and **12 years** for biologics under the **Biologics Price**

Competition and Innovation Act (BPCIA).

- **Orphan Drugs**: Orphan drugs, which treat rare diseases, receive an extended period of **7 years** of market exclusivity under the **Orphan Drug Act.**

European Union

- **Duration**: The EU provides an **8-year** data exclusivity period for new drugs, followed by **2 years** of market exclusivity. An additional **1-year** extension is available if the drug is approved for a new therapeutic indication.
- **Paediatric Exclusivity**: An additional **6-month** extension is granted for drugs that have undergone approved paediatric studies, promoting research in children's medicines.

Japan

- **Duration**: Japan offers **6 to 8 years** of data exclusivity for new chemical entities, depending on the drug's classification and clinical significance.
- **Extension for Orphan Drugs**: Similar to other jurisdictions, orphan drugs in Japan benefit from an extended exclusivity period, encouraging the development of treatments for rare diseases.

India

- **Regulatory Environment**: India does not have a formal data exclusivity framework, but it provides protection for undisclosed data under **Section 17 of the Drugs and Cosmetics Act**, aligning with **TRIPS Agreement** provisions.
- **Challenges**: The absence of a formal data exclusivity regime poses challenges for innovators seeking protection for their clinical trial data, impacting their ability to recover R&D investments.

Market Exclusivity

Definition and Purpose of Market Exclusivity

Market Exclusivity is a regulatory mechanism that prevents competitors, including generic drug manufacturers, from entering the market with similar products for a specified period. Unlike data exclusivity, which focuses on protecting clinical data, market exclusivity provides a broader scope of protection, preventing the approval and marketing of competing products, even if they conduct independent studies.

How Market Exclusivity Works

- **Regulatory Approval Block**: During the market exclusivity period, regulatory authorities cannot approve any competing products that are therapeutically equivalent to the innovator drug, regardless of whether they reference the original data.
- **Exclusivity Period**: The market exclusivity period varies by country and drug type, ranging from **5 to 12 years**. The exclusivity period may differ for specific drug categories, such as orphan drugs and biologics.
- **Extended Protection**: Market exclusivity provides extended protection beyond the patent term, allowing innovators to maintain market leadership and profitability for longer periods.

Significance of Market Exclusivity in Pharmaceuticals

Market exclusivity offers several advantages to pharmaceutical companies, contributing to innovation and market dynamics:

- **Extended Profitability**: Market exclusivity extends beyond the patent term, allowing innovators to maintain exclusive market rights, enhance profitability, and support future R&D efforts.
- **Encouragement of Innovation**: The additional protection incentivizes companies to invest in innovative drug development, addressing complex medical challenges and improving healthcare outcomes.
- **Competitive Advantage**: Market exclusivity provides a significant competitive advantage, allowing companies to establish brand recognition and market presence without immediate generic competition.

Application of Market Exclusivity Across Jurisdictions

Market exclusivity is applied differently across various countries and regions, reflecting their regulatory policies and industry priorities:

United States

- **Hatch-Waxman Act**: The U.S. grants **5 years** of market exclusivity for new chemical entities, with an additional **3-year** extension for new clinical data supporting new uses or formulations.

- **Biologics**: Biologics receive **12 years** of market exclusivity under the **Biologics Price Competition and Innovation Act (BPCIA)**, promoting the development of complex biological products.
- **Orphan Drugs**: Orphan drugs benefit from **7 years** of market exclusivity, encouraging the development of treatments for rare diseases and underserved patient populations.

European Union

- **10+1 Model**: The EU implements a **10-year** market exclusivity period for new drugs, which includes **8 years** of data exclusivity and **2 years** of market exclusivity. An additional **1-year** extension is granted for significant therapeutic advancements.
- **Orphan Drugs**: Orphan drugs receive **10 years** of market exclusivity, with a possible extension for additional therapeutic benefits or paediatric research.

Japan

- **6 to 8 Years**: Japan offers **6 to 8 years** of market exclusivity for new chemical entities, similar to data exclusivity durations, depending on the drug's classification.
- **Orphan Drugs**: Extended market exclusivity is provided for orphan drugs, reflecting Japan's commitment to addressing rare diseases and encouraging innovation.

India

- **Absence of Formal Framework**: India does not have a formal market exclusivity framework but relies on patent protection to provide exclusivity for innovator drugs.
- **Impact on Innovators**: The lack of market exclusivity poses challenges for innovators seeking additional protection beyond patent terms, affecting their ability to maintain market leadership.

Challenges and Opportunities of Data and Market Exclusivity
Challenges

- **Access to Medicines**: Data and market exclusivity can limit access to affordable medicines, especially in low- and middle-income countries, by delaying the entry of generic alternatives that offer lower-cost options for patients.
- **Balancing Innovation and Access**: Policymakers must balance the need for innovation incentives with public health priorities, ensuring that life-saving drugs are accessible to all who need them.
- **Evergreening Practices**: Companies may engage in "evergreening" practices, using data and market exclusivity to extend protection beyond the original patent term, raising ethical concerns about market dominance.

Opportunities

- **Encouragement of Innovation**: Exclusivity mechanisms incentivize pharmaceutical companies to invest in developing new drugs and therapies, addressing unmet medical needs and improving healthcare outcomes.
- **R&D Investment**: The protection afforded by data and market exclusivity supports significant investments in research and development, fostering the discovery of breakthrough treatments.
- **Public Health Benefits**: Exclusivity encourages the development of innovative medicines that tackle complex diseases, ultimately enhancing public health and patient care.
- **Regulatory Harmonization**: Efforts to harmonize data and market exclusivity regulations across jurisdictions can facilitate global trade, reduce duplication of efforts, and promote international collaboration.

17.5 Patent Linkage and Evergreening Strategies

Patent linkage and evergreening strategies are two significant practices in the pharmaceutical industry that impact the balance between innovation and access to medicines. While these strategies provide opportunities for pharmaceutical companies to protect their innovations and extend market exclusivity, they also present challenges related to affordability and access to essential drugs. This section explores the concepts of patent linkage and evergreening strategies, their implications, regulatory environments, and the ongoing debate surrounding these practices.

Patent Linkage

Definition and Purpose of Patent Linkage

Patent Linkage is a regulatory mechanism that connects the drug approval process with the patent status of a pharmaceutical product. It ensures that regulatory authorities, such as the **Food and Drug Administration (FDA)** in the United States, do not approve a generic version of a drug until the relevant patents on the innovator drug have expired or been invalidated. Patent linkage aims to protect patent holders from unauthorized generic competition, providing a safeguard for their intellectual property rights.

How Patent Linkage Works

- **Patent Listing**: Innovator companies must list their patents in a public database, such as the **Orange Book** in the United States, which regulatory authorities use to check patent status before approving generic applications.
- **Generic Application Review**: When a generic manufacturer submits an application for approval, the regulatory authority reviews the listed patents to determine whether they remain valid and enforceable.
- **Automatic Stay**: If a generic company challenges a patent's validity, the innovator can file a lawsuit, triggering an automatic stay of the generic application approval process for a specific period (e.g., 30 months in the U.S.), pending the outcome of the litigation.
- **Resolution of Disputes**: Patent linkage mechanisms provide a structured process for resolving patent disputes between innovator and generic companies before the generic drug enters the market.

Significance of Patent Linkage in Pharmaceuticals

Patent linkage offers several benefits to the pharmaceutical industry, enhancing innovation and protecting intellectual property:

- **Protection of Innovations**: Patent linkage safeguards the intellectual property of innovator companies by preventing unauthorized generic competition until patents are no longer valid.
- **Legal Certainty**: The linkage provides a clear legal framework for addressing patent disputes, offering certainty and predictability for both innovators and generics.
- **Incentives for R&D**: By ensuring patent protection is upheld during the drug approval process, patent linkage incentivizes pharmaceutical

companies to invest in research and development, fostering innovation and the creation of new therapies.

Global Implementation of Patent Linkage

Patent linkage is implemented differently across various countries, reflecting diverse regulatory environments and public health priorities:

United States

- **Orange Book**: The **FDA's Orange Book** lists approved drug products and associated patents, serving as a reference for patent linkage in the U.S. Innovator companies must list patents relevant to their drug products, which are reviewed during the generic application process.
- **30-Month Stay**: The **Hatch-Waxman Act** allows a 30-month stay on the approval of a generic drug if the innovator company files a patent infringement lawsuit, providing time to resolve disputes.

Canada

- **Patent Register**: Canada's patent linkage system is governed by the **Patented Medicines (Notice of Compliance) Regulations**, which requires listing patents on a public register and reviewing them before approving generics.
- **Litigation Framework**: Similar to the U.S., Canada provides a legal framework for resolving patent disputes, including automatic stays during litigation.

Europe

- **No Formal Linkage**: The European Union does not have a formal patent linkage system. Instead, patent issues are typically resolved through national courts, separate from the drug approval process.
- **Regulatory Approach**: The European Medicines Agency (EMA) and national authorities focus on evaluating drug safety and efficacy, with patent enforcement left to the judicial system.

India

- **No Formal Linkage:** India does not have a formal patent linkage system, allowing regulatory approval processes to proceed independently of patent status.
- **Focus on Access:** India's approach emphasizes access to affordable medicines, with patent enforcement typically addressed through litigation rather than regulatory mechanisms.

Evergreening Strategies

Definition and Purpose of Evergreening

Evergreening refers to strategies employed by pharmaceutical companies to extend the market exclusivity of their products beyond the original patent term. These strategies involve obtaining additional patents for minor modifications or new uses of existing drugs, effectively delaying the entry of generic competition. Evergreening aims to maximize the commercial lifespan of a drug, allowing innovator companies to maintain market dominance and profitability.

Types of Evergreening Strategies

Evergreening strategies can take various forms, each focusing on different aspects of drug modification or improvement:

Formulation Changes

- **Modified Release:** Developing extended-release or controlled-release formulations of an existing drug to offer improved patient compliance or convenience.
- **Combination Products:** Creating combination therapies that incorporate the original drug with other active ingredients to treat multiple conditions or enhance efficacy.

New Indications

- **Repositioning:** Obtaining patents for new therapeutic uses or indications of an existing drug, expanding its market potential and patient base.
- **Labeling Changes:** Seeking approval for new dosing regimens or treatment guidelines that provide additional protection for the original product.

Process Improvements

- **Manufacturing Innovations**: Patenting novel manufacturing processes or methods that improve the efficiency, yield, or safety of the original drug.
- **Purity Enhancements**: Developing higher-purity versions of the drug or improved formulations that offer additional benefits or reduced side effects.

Polymorphs and Salts

- **New Forms**: Patenting different polymorphic forms, salts, or crystalline structures of the original drug to extend exclusivity and differentiate products.

Significance of Evergreening in Pharmaceuticals

Evergreening strategies offer several advantages to pharmaceutical companies, impacting market dynamics and innovation:

- **Extended Market Exclusivity**: Evergreening provides additional layers of protection beyond the original patent term, allowing innovators to maintain market leadership and profitability.
- **Innovation Incentives**: By exploring new formulations, indications, or processes, evergreening encourages continued innovation and investment in research and development.
- **Product Differentiation**: Evergreening allows companies to differentiate their products, offering patients new options or improved treatments and enhancing brand recognition.

Challenges and Controversies of Evergreening

While evergreening offers benefits to innovators, it also presents challenges and raises ethical concerns related to access and affordability:

Access to Affordable Medicines

- **Delayed Generic Entry**: Evergreening strategies can delay the entry of generic drugs, limiting access to affordable alternatives for patients and healthcare systems.
- **Public Health Impact**: The high cost of patented drugs resulting from evergreening can exacerbate healthcare disparities, particularly in low- and middle-income countries.

Ethical Concerns

- **Monopolistic Practices**: Critics argue that evergreening represents monopolistic behavior, exploiting patent laws to maintain market dominance without significant innovation.
- **Balancing Innovation and Access**: Policymakers face challenges in balancing the need for innovation incentives with ensuring access to affordable medicines for all.

Regulatory and Legal Frameworks for Evergreening

The legal and regulatory landscape for evergreening varies across countries, reflecting different approaches to patent protection and competition:

United States

- **Patent Review Process**: The U.S. Patent and Trademark Office (USPTO) reviews evergreening patents, requiring evidence of novelty, non-obviousness, and usefulness.
- **Legal Challenges**: Generic manufacturers can challenge evergreening patents through litigation, seeking to invalidate claims that lack genuine innovation.

European Union

- **Patent Scrutiny**: The European Patent Office (EPO) scrutinizes evergreening patents, focusing on inventive step and industrial applicability.
- **Legal Framework**: EU competition laws address potential abuses of patent strategies, promoting fair competition and access to affordable medicines.

India

- **Section 3(d) of the Patent Act**: India's Patent Act includes a provision (Section 3(d)) that prevents the granting of patents for new forms of known substances unless they demonstrate enhanced efficacy, limiting evergreening practices.

- **Focus on Access**: India's regulatory framework emphasizes access to affordable medicines, challenging evergreening patents that do not offer genuine therapeutic advancements.

Canada

- **Patent Review Standards**: Canada employs rigorous standards for patent examination, ensuring that evergreening claims meet the criteria for patentability.
- **Legal and Regulatory Oversight**: Canadian authorities balance innovation incentives with public health priorities, addressing evergreening practices that impede generic competition.

17.6 Challenges and Opportunities in IPR

Intellectual Property Rights (IPR) are critical for fostering innovation and protecting the investments made in developing new pharmaceuticals. However, the landscape of IPR in the pharmaceutical industry is complex and fraught with both challenges and opportunities. These dynamics significantly influence the development, access, and distribution of medicines globally. This section explores the key challenges and opportunities in the realm of IPR, highlighting their implications for the pharmaceutical industry and public health.

Challenges in IPR

1. Balancing Innovation with Access to Medicines

One of the primary challenges in IPR is balancing the need to incentivize pharmaceutical innovation with ensuring access to affordable medicines for patients worldwide.

- **High Drug Prices**: Patents and exclusivity rights can lead to high drug prices, limiting access for patients, especially in low- and middle-income countries. The cost of patented medicines often puts them out of reach for many, creating disparities in healthcare access.
- **Public Health Concerns**: The high prices of life-saving medicines due to patent protection can exacerbate health inequities, particularly in resource-limited settings where healthcare systems may not cover expensive treatments.
- **Policy Dilemmas**: Policymakers face the dilemma of supporting innovation through strong IP protection while ensuring that essential

medicines remain accessible to those in need.

2. Patent Evergreening and Strategic Patenting

Patent Evergreening is a practice where companies make minor modifications to existing drugs to extend their patent life, delaying generic competition.

- **Monopolistic Practices**: Evergreening can be perceived as a strategy to maintain market dominance without significant innovation, raising ethical concerns about monopolistic behavior.
- **Legal and Regulatory Challenges**: While evergreening extends exclusivity, it may lead to legal disputes and regulatory challenges from generic manufacturers seeking to enter the market.
- **Impact on Generics**: Strategic patenting limits the entry of generic drugs, which are often more affordable for patients, delaying access to lower-cost alternatives.

3. Patent Linkage and Regulatory Complexity

Patent linkage connects the drug approval process with the patent status of a pharmaceutical product, adding layers of complexity to drug regulation.

- **Regulatory Burden**: Patent linkage can increase the regulatory burden on both innovators and generic manufacturers, complicating the approval process and potentially delaying market entry.
- **Disputes and Litigation**: Patent linkage often leads to disputes and litigation, as generic manufacturers may challenge the validity of patents listed in patent linkage databases, leading to costly legal battles.
- **Impact on Innovation**: While patent linkage protects IP rights, it may also discourage innovation by creating barriers for new entrants and smaller companies that lack resources for prolonged litigation.

4. International Harmonization of IPR

Differences in IPR laws and enforcement across countries create challenges for pharmaceutical companies operating globally.

- **Diverse Legal Systems**: The lack of harmonization in IP laws across countries creates complexity for companies seeking to protect their innovations worldwide. Navigating diverse legal systems requires significant resources and expertise.

- **Trade Disputes**: Disparities in IP protection standards can lead to trade disputes and affect international collaborations, impacting the global supply chain for pharmaceuticals.
- **Cross-Border Enforcement**: Enforcing IP rights across borders can be challenging due to varying legal frameworks and enforcement mechanisms, complicating efforts to combat counterfeiting and infringement.

5. Counterfeit Medicines and IP Infringement

Counterfeit medicines pose a significant threat to public health and undermine the integrity of IP protection in the pharmaceutical industry.

- **Safety Risks**: Counterfeit drugs often contain substandard or harmful ingredients, posing serious health risks to patients and undermining trust in healthcare systems.
- **Economic Impact**: Counterfeiting results in significant economic losses for legitimate pharmaceutical companies, impacting their ability to invest in research and development.
- **Enforcement Challenges**: Detecting and prosecuting counterfeiters is challenging, particularly in jurisdictions with weak IP enforcement frameworks or limited resources.

Opportunities in IPR
1. Incentivizing Innovation and R&D

IPR provides a critical incentive for pharmaceutical companies to invest in research and development, driving the discovery of new treatments and therapies.

- **Investment in Innovation**: Strong IP protection encourages companies to invest in innovative research, leading to the development of breakthrough drugs that address unmet medical needs.
- **Collaboration and Partnerships**: IP rights facilitate collaborations between academia, industry, and governments, promoting the sharing of knowledge and resources to advance drug discovery.
- **Biotechnology and Precision Medicine**: The growing fields of biotechnology and precision medicine present new opportunities for innovation, with IP protection playing a key role in supporting

advancements in these areas.

2. Economic Growth and Competitiveness

IPR contributes to economic growth by fostering a competitive pharmaceutical industry that attracts investment and generates employment.

- **Global Competitiveness**: Strong IP protection enhances a country's competitiveness in the global pharmaceutical market, attracting investment from multinational companies and fostering economic development.
- **Job Creation**: The pharmaceutical sector is a significant source of employment, and IP-driven innovation contributes to job creation in research, manufacturing, and distribution.
- **Export Opportunities**: Countries with robust IP frameworks can leverage their pharmaceutical innovations to access global markets, increasing export opportunities and revenue.

3. Public Health Advancements

IPR supports the development of innovative medicines that improve public health outcomes and enhance patient care.

- **New Treatments and Cures**: IP-driven research leads to the development of new treatments and potential cures for diseases that lack effective therapies, improving patient outcomes and quality of life.
- **Orphan Drugs and Rare Diseases**: IPR incentivizes the development of orphan drugs for rare diseases, addressing unmet needs in underserved patient populations.
- **Vaccine Development**: IP protection plays a crucial role in vaccine development, supporting research efforts to combat infectious diseases and pandemics.

4. Strengthening IP Enforcement and Collaboration

Enhancing IP enforcement mechanisms and fostering international collaboration can address challenges related to counterfeiting and infringement.

- **International Cooperation**: Collaborative efforts among countries, international organizations, and industry stakeholders can strengthen IP enforcement and combat cross-border counterfeiting.
- **Technology and Innovation**: Leveraging technology, such as blockchain and digital tracking systems, can enhance the traceability and security of pharmaceutical products, reducing counterfeiting risks.
- **Capacity Building**: Investing in capacity building for regulatory authorities and law enforcement can improve IP enforcement and compliance, ensuring the protection of innovations.

5. Opportunities for Emerging Markets

Emerging markets present significant opportunities for pharmaceutical companies seeking to expand their global footprint and access new patient populations.

- **Expanding Access**: IPR can support efforts to expand access to medicines in emerging markets by encouraging investment in local manufacturing and distribution infrastructure.
- **Partnerships with Local Companies**: Collaborating with local companies in emerging markets can facilitate knowledge transfer and capacity building, enhancing the development and availability of innovative therapies.
- **Tailored Solutions**: Developing tailored solutions for emerging markets, such as affordable pricing models and local production, can enhance access to medicines while respecting IP rights.

Key points
Introduction to Intellectual Property Rights (IPR)

- **Definition and Significance**: Intellectual Property Rights (IPR) provide legal protection for creations and inventions, encouraging innovation by granting exclusive rights to creators and inventors. In the pharmaceutical industry, IPR is vital for promoting research and development, supporting economic growth, and enhancing public health outcomes.
- **Types of IPR**: The main types of intellectual property rights relevant to pharmaceuticals include patents, trademarks, trade secrets, and copyrights. Each offers protection for different aspects of innovation and creativity, such as new drug formulations, brand identities, confidential

information, and creative works.

Patents and Copyrights in Pharmaceutical Industry

- **Patents**: Patents provide exclusive rights to inventors for their innovations, preventing others from making, using, or selling the patented invention for a specified period, usually 20 years. They are crucial for protecting new drug formulations, active ingredients, and manufacturing processes, encouraging investment in research and development.
- **Copyrights**: Copyrights protect original works of authorship, such as literature, music, art, and software, from unauthorized use. In the pharmaceutical industry, copyrights safeguard written materials, promotional content, and software used in drug development.
- **Challenges**: Patents can lead to high drug prices and limited access to affordable medicines, while evergreening practices can extend exclusivity beyond the original patent term, raising ethical concerns.

Regulatory Framework for IPR in Different Countries

- **United States**: The U.S. has a comprehensive IPR framework governed by laws such as the Patent Act, Lanham Act, and Copyright Act. The United States Patent and Trademark Office (USPTO) and the U.S. Copyright Office oversee patent and copyright registration, respectively.
- **European Union**: The EU harmonizes IPR across member states through directives like the European Patent Convention (EPC) and the EU Trademark Regulation. The European Patent Office (EPO) and the EU Intellectual Property Office (EUIPO) manage patents and trademarks.
- **India**: India aligns its IPR laws with international standards through the Indian Patent Act, Trademarks Act, and Copyright Act. The Office of the Controller General of Patents, Designs, and Trademarks (CGPDTM) administers patent and trademark registration.
- **China**: China's IPR framework includes the Patent Law, Trademark Law, and Copyright Law. The China National Intellectual Property Administration (CNIPA) oversees patent and trademark registration.
- **Japan and Brazil**: Japan's Patent Act and Brazil's Industrial Property Law govern patent protection. Both countries focus on innovation incentives and IP enforcement.

Data Exclusivity and Market Exclusivity

- **Data Exclusivity**: This regulatory mechanism prevents generic manufacturers from using an innovator's clinical trial data for a specified period, protecting the data and encouraging investment in research and development.
- **Market Exclusivity**: Market exclusivity prevents competitors from entering the market with similar products for a specific period, allowing innovators to maintain market leadership and profitability.
- **Global Implementation**: Data and market exclusivity durations vary by country, with the U.S., EU, Japan, and others providing specific periods for new chemical entities, biologics, and orphan drugs.
- **Challenges and Opportunities**: While exclusivity incentivizes innovation, it can limit access to affordable medicines, posing challenges for balancing innovation and access.

Patent Linkage and Evergreening Strategies

- **Patent Linkage**: This mechanism links the drug approval process with patent status, preventing generic approval until relevant patents expire. It provides legal certainty but can complicate the approval process and lead to disputes.
- **Evergreening Strategies**: Evergreening involves extending market exclusivity through minor modifications or new uses of existing drugs, delaying generic competition and raising ethical concerns about monopolistic practices.
- **Regulatory and Legal Frameworks**: Different countries have varying approaches to patent linkage and evergreening, with some focusing on innovation incentives and others on access to affordable medicines.

Challenges and Opportunities in IPR

- **Challenges**: Balancing innovation with access, patent evergreening, regulatory complexity, international harmonization, and counterfeit medicines pose significant challenges in IPR.
- **Opportunities**: IPR incentivizes innovation, supports economic growth, advances public health, and strengthens IP enforcement. Emerging markets offer opportunities for expansion and collaboration.

Indian Drug Regulatory Agencies and Guidelines

India's pharmaceutical regulatory system is one of the most dynamic and rapidly evolving in the world. This chapter explores the Indian regulatory framework, focusing on the roles and responsibilities of key agencies such as the Central Drugs Standard Control Organization (CDSCO) and the regulatory guidelines that govern the manufacture, distribution, and sale of drugs and cosmetics in India.

The chapter delves into Schedule Y, which provides the regulatory requirements for conducting clinical trials in India, ensuring that trials meet ethical standards and generate reliable data. It also covers Good Manufacturing Practices (GMP) and Good Distribution Practices (GDP), which are critical for maintaining the quality and safety of drugs throughout their lifecycle.

India's growing importance as a global pharmaceutical hub makes understanding its regulatory landscape essential for companies seeking to manufacture or market their products in the country. This chapter provides the knowledge needed to navigate the complexities of the Indian pharmaceutical market, ensuring compliance with local regulations while capitalizing on the opportunities presented by one of the world's largest pharmaceutical markets.

18.1 Introduction to Indian Drug Regulatory System

The **Indian Drug Regulatory System** is one of the most complex and comprehensive frameworks in the global pharmaceutical landscape. It is primarily governed by the **Central Drugs Standard Control Organization (CDSCO)**, which operates under the authority of the **Ministry of Health and Family Welfare**. The system is designed to ensure that all pharmaceutical products manufactured, imported, distributed, and sold in

India meet strict standards of **quality**, **safety**, and **efficacy**. As the third-largest producer of pharmaceuticals by volume globally, India's regulatory system plays a crucial role in maintaining the high standards of its thriving pharmaceutical industry while ensuring public health and safety.

Evolution of the Indian Drug Regulatory System

The Indian pharmaceutical regulatory system has evolved significantly over the years to address the growing complexities of drug manufacturing, distribution, and safety monitoring. The foundation of the system dates back to **1940**, with the enactment of the **Drugs and Cosmetics Act**, which laid down the legal framework for regulating the import, manufacture, and distribution of drugs. The Act has undergone numerous amendments to address emerging challenges and incorporate global best practices.

The **Drugs and Cosmetics Rules** of **1945** further expanded the regulatory framework by introducing detailed guidelines on the technical requirements for drug approval, manufacturing standards, and quality control. These rules also defined the roles and responsibilities of various authorities involved in the regulatory process.

Key Regulatory Authorities in India

India's drug regulatory system operates through a combination of **central** and **state** regulatory bodies. While the **Central Drugs Standard Control Organization (CDSCO)** functions as the central authority, individual state regulatory authorities oversee local drug manufacturing and distribution activities.

1. Central Drugs Standard Control Organization (CDSCO)

The **CDSCO** is the primary national regulatory body responsible for ensuring the safety, efficacy, and quality of drugs in India. It is headed by the **Drugs Controller General of India (DCGI)**, who is responsible for formulating and enforcing drug regulations across the country. The CDSCO's primary functions include:

- **Approval of New Drugs**: Reviewing and approving new drugs, biologics, and vaccines for the Indian market.
- **Clinical Trial Regulation**: Overseeing the approval and monitoring of clinical trials conducted in India.

- **Import and Export Regulation**: Regulating the import and export of pharmaceuticals and ensuring compliance with international quality standards.
- **Good Manufacturing Practices (GMP)**: Enforcing GMP guidelines to ensure that pharmaceutical manufacturing processes meet stringent quality control standards.
- **Pharmacovigilance**: Monitoring the safety of drugs post-market through the **Pharmacovigilance Programme of India (PvPI)**.
- **Inspections and Audits**: Conducting inspections of pharmaceutical manufacturing facilities to ensure compliance with regulatory standards.

In **2022**, the CDSCO approved **30 new drugs** and conducted over **1,000 inspections** of manufacturing facilities to ensure adherence to **Good Manufacturing Practices (GMP)**. These efforts are crucial for maintaining the integrity of India's pharmaceutical products and ensuring patient safety.

2. State Drug Control Authorities

Each Indian state has its own **State Drug Control Authority**, responsible for overseeing the manufacture, distribution, and sale of drugs within its jurisdiction. State authorities work in coordination with the CDSCO to ensure that local pharmaceutical companies comply with the regulations established by the central authority. Their primary responsibilities include:

- **Licensing**: Issuing manufacturing and distribution licenses to pharmaceutical companies operating within the state.
- **Enforcement**: Monitoring drug distribution networks and conducting inspections to prevent the sale of counterfeit or substandard drugs.
- **Quality Control**: Ensuring that drugs sold in the state meet the required quality standards through regular sampling and testing.

Key Legislation Governing Indian Drug Regulation

The regulatory framework in India is primarily governed by two key pieces of legislation: the **Drugs and Cosmetics Act, 1940**, and the **Drugs and Cosmetics Rules, 1945**.

1. Drugs and Cosmetics Act, 1940

The **Drugs and Cosmetics Act, 1940**, is the principal legislation that regulates the import, manufacture, distribution, and sale of drugs in India.

Its main objectives are to:

- Ensure that drugs and cosmetics sold in India are safe, effective, and of high quality.
- Establish guidelines for the approval of new drugs and clinical trials.
- Regulate the licensing of pharmaceutical manufacturing facilities and distribution networks.
- Enforce penalties for the manufacture and sale of adulterated, misbranded, or spurious drugs.

2. Drugs and Cosmetics Rules, 1945

The **Drugs and Cosmetics Rules, 1945**, provide detailed regulations on the technical and procedural aspects of drug regulation. These rules define the requirements for drug approval, manufacturing practices, labeling, packaging, and storage conditions. Some of the critical provisions include:

- **Good Manufacturing Practices (GMP)**: Mandating adherence to GMP guidelines for pharmaceutical manufacturing facilities to ensure the consistent quality of products.
- **Clinical Trial Regulations**: Outlining the procedures for conducting clinical trials in India, including ethical considerations, trial design, and monitoring.
- **Licensing Requirements**: Defining the criteria for granting manufacturing, import, and distribution licenses.
- **Pharmacovigilance**: Establishing a framework for post-market surveillance of drugs to monitor their safety and efficacy.

Recent Developments and Reforms

India's drug regulatory system has undergone significant reforms in recent years to address emerging challenges and align with global regulatory standards. Some key developments include:

1. New Drugs and Clinical Trials Rules, 2019

In **2019**, the Indian government introduced the **New Drugs and Clinical Trials Rules** to streamline the approval process for new drugs and clinical trials. The key features of these rules include:

- **Fast-Track Approvals**: Introducing provisions for fast-tracking the approval process for innovative drugs and therapies addressing unmet medical needs.
- **Clinical Trial Regulations**: Strengthening the regulatory framework for clinical trials, including stricter ethical guidelines and safety monitoring.
- **Post-Marketing Surveillance**: Enhancing the role of post-marketing surveillance in ensuring drug safety after market approval.

2. Pharmacovigilance Programme of India (PvPI)

Launched in **2010**, the **Pharmacovigilance Programme of India (PvPI)** aims to monitor and assess the adverse effects of drugs in the Indian market. Managed by the **Indian Pharmacopoeia Commission (IPC)**, the PvPI works closely with healthcare professionals, manufacturers, and consumers to report and investigate adverse drug reactions (ADRs). The program has significantly contributed to improving drug safety and public health outcomes in India.

In **2022**, the PvPI collected over **150,000 adverse event reports**, leading to several regulatory interventions, including changes in drug labeling and withdrawal of unsafe products.

3. Uniform Code for Pharmaceuticals Marketing Practices (UCPMP)

The **Uniform Code for Pharmaceuticals Marketing Practices (UCPMP)** was introduced to promote ethical marketing practices in the Indian pharmaceutical industry. The UCPMP outlines guidelines for the promotion of drugs and interactions between pharmaceutical companies and healthcare professionals, emphasizing transparency and ethical conduct.

Challenges and Opportunities in the Indian Drug Regulatory System

Despite its comprehensive framework, the Indian drug regulatory system faces several challenges:

1. Regulatory Delays

Delays in drug approval and licensing processes can hinder the timely introduction of innovative therapies. Addressing these delays requires streamlined procedures and the implementation of technology-driven solutions to enhance efficiency.

2. Counterfeit Drugs

The prevalence of counterfeit and substandard drugs remains a significant public health concern in India. Strengthening enforcement mechanisms and enhancing coordination between state and central authorities can help mitigate this issue.

3. Global Integration

With India's growing role as a global pharmaceutical hub, aligning its regulatory standards with international best practices is crucial for facilitating exports and attracting foreign investment. Participation in international regulatory harmonization initiatives, such as the **International Council for Harmonisation (ICH)**, can promote greater integration with global markets.

4. Regulatory Capacity Building

Enhancing the capacity of regulatory authorities, particularly at the state level, through training, infrastructure development, and resource allocation is essential to ensure effective implementation of drug regulations.

18.2 Central Drugs Standard Control Organization (CDSCO)

The **Central Drugs Standard Control Organization (CDSCO)** is the cornerstone of India's pharmaceutical regulatory framework. Operating under the authority of the **Ministry of Health and Family Welfare**, the CDSCO is responsible for ensuring that all pharmaceutical products available in India meet stringent standards of **quality**, **safety**, and **efficacy**. As the national regulatory body, the CDSCO plays a pivotal role in overseeing the entire lifecycle of pharmaceutical products, from **drug approval** and **clinical trial regulation** to **post-market surveillance** and **manufacturing oversight**. This section delves into the structure, functions, key responsibilities, regulatory processes, recent developments, and challenges faced by the CDSCO.

Structure and Organization

The CDSCO is headed by the **Drugs Controller General of India (DCGI)**, who serves as the highest authority within the organization. The DCGI is supported by a network of regional offices and various divisions that handle specific aspects of drug regulation. The organizational structure of the CDSCO includes:

- **Office of the Drugs Controller General of India (DCGI):** Central hub for policy formulation, regulatory oversight, and strategic decision-making.

- **Regional Offices**: Located in major cities such as Mumbai, Delhi, Kolkata, Chennai, and Ahmedabad, these offices manage regional regulatory activities, including inspections and licensing.
- **Divisions**:

  ○ **Registration Division**: Handles the registration and approval of new drugs and clinical trials.
  ○ **Manufacturing Division**: Oversees Good Manufacturing Practices (GMP) compliance and inspects manufacturing facilities.
  ○ **Regulatory Affairs Division**: Manages regulatory policies, guidelines, and liaison with international regulatory bodies.
  ○ **Pharmacovigilance Division**: Monitors drug safety through the Pharmacovigilance Programme of India (PvPI).
  ○ **Import and Export Division**: Regulates the import and export of pharmaceuticals, ensuring compliance with national and international standards.

Key Responsibilities

The CDSCO's responsibilities encompass a broad spectrum of activities aimed at regulating the pharmaceutical industry in India. The primary responsibilities include:

1. Drug Approval and Registration

- **New Drug Application (NDA)**: Evaluates and approves new drugs for the Indian market. Manufacturers must submit comprehensive data from preclinical and clinical studies.
- **Abbreviated New Drug Application (ANDA)**: Facilitates the approval of generic drugs by assessing bioequivalence to branded counterparts.
- **Clinical Trial Approval**: Reviews and approves clinical trial proposals to ensure ethical standards and participant safety.

2. Regulation of Clinical Trials

- **Approval Process**: Ensures that clinical trials adhere to ethical guidelines, scientific rigor, and safety protocols.

- **Monitoring and Compliance**: Conducts regular inspections of clinical trial sites to verify compliance with approved protocols and regulatory standards.

3. Good Manufacturing Practices (GMP) Enforcement

- **GMP Guidelines**: Establishes and enforces GMP standards to ensure that pharmaceutical products are consistently produced and controlled.
- **Facility Inspections**: Conducts unannounced inspections of manufacturing units to assess compliance with GMP guidelines. Non-compliance can lead to penalties, product recalls, or suspension of licenses.

4. Pharmacovigilance and Drug Safety

- **Pharmacovigilance Programme of India (PvPI)**: Monitors adverse drug reactions (ADRs) and ensures timely identification and mitigation of drug-related risks.
- **Adverse Event Reporting**: Collects and analyzes data on ADRs through healthcare professionals, patients, and manufacturers to enhance drug safety profiles.

5. Import and Export Regulation

- **Import Licensing**: Regulates the import of pharmaceuticals to ensure that only quality-assured drugs enter the Indian market.
- **Export Oversight**: Ensures that exported pharmaceuticals comply with the regulatory standards of the destination countries, promoting India's pharmaceutical reputation globally.

6. Regulatory Policy and Guidelines Development

- **Policy Formulation**: Develops and updates regulatory policies to address emerging challenges and incorporate global best practices.
- **Guideline Issuance**: Publishes detailed guidelines on various aspects of drug regulation, including drug development, manufacturing, labeling, and distribution.

Regulatory Processes

The CDSCO employs a systematic approach to regulate pharmaceuticals, ensuring that each stage of the drug lifecycle adheres to high standards of quality and safety. Key regulatory processes include:

1. Drug Registration and Approval

- **Submission of Applications**: Pharmaceutical companies submit NDAs, ANDAs, or other relevant applications to the CDSCO, accompanied by detailed documentation on drug composition, manufacturing processes, clinical trial data, and quality control measures.
- **Review and Evaluation**: The CDSCO's experts conduct a thorough review of the submitted data to assess the drug's safety, efficacy, and quality. This includes evaluating clinical trial results, manufacturing practices, and labeling information.
- **Approval or Rejection**: Based on the evaluation, the CDSCO either approves the drug for market release, requests additional information, or rejects the application if it fails to meet regulatory standards.

2. Clinical Trial Regulation

- **Ethical Compliance**: Ensures that clinical trials are conducted ethically, safeguarding the rights and well-being of participants.
- **Protocol Review**: Examines clinical trial protocols to ensure scientific validity and compliance with regulatory requirements.
- **Monitoring**: Conducts inspections and audits of clinical trial sites to verify adherence to approved protocols and regulatory standards.

3. Good Manufacturing Practices (GMP) Compliance

- **GMP Audits**: Regularly inspects manufacturing facilities to assess compliance with GMP guidelines. These audits cover aspects such as facility cleanliness, equipment maintenance, quality control procedures, and employee training.
- **Certification**: Grants GMP certificates to compliant manufacturing units, which are mandatory for drug approval and market authorization.

- **Non-Compliance Actions**: Implements corrective actions, imposes fines, or suspends licenses for facilities that fail to meet GMP standards.

4. Pharmacovigilance

- **ADR Reporting**: Collects reports of adverse drug reactions from healthcare professionals, patients, and manufacturers through the PvPI.
- **Data Analysis**: Analyzes ADR data to identify safety signals and trends that may indicate potential risks associated with specific drugs.
- **Regulatory Actions**: Takes necessary actions such as updating drug labels, issuing safety warnings, or recalling drugs based on pharmacovigilance findings.

Pharmacovigilance Programme of India (PvPI)

The **Pharmacovigilance Programme of India (PvPI)** is an integral part of the CDSCO, dedicated to monitoring and ensuring drug safety post-market approval. Key features of the PvPI include:

- **Establishment**: Launched in **2010**, the PvPI is managed by the **Indian Pharmacopoeia Commission (IPC)** under the guidance of the CDSCO.
- **Adverse Event Reporting**: Facilitates the reporting of ADRs through a network of **Adverse Drug Reaction Monitoring Centers (AMCs)**, healthcare professionals, and the general public.
- **Data Collection and Analysis**: Utilizes advanced data analytics to process and interpret ADR reports, identifying potential safety concerns.
- **Safety Communications**: Issues safety alerts, updates drug labeling, and recommends regulatory actions based on pharmacovigilance findings.

In **2022**, the PvPI collected over **150,000 adverse event reports**, leading to significant regulatory interventions such as labeling changes and product recalls to mitigate identified risks.

Recent Developments and Reforms

The CDSCO has undertaken several initiatives and reforms to enhance its regulatory capabilities and align with global best practices:

1. New Drugs and Clinical Trials Rules, 2019

- **Objective**: Streamline the approval process for new drugs and clinical trials, reducing delays and promoting innovation.
- **Key Features**:

  - **Fast-Track Approval**: Introduced provisions for expedited approval of innovative drugs and therapies addressing unmet medical needs.
  - **Clinical Trial Regulations**: Strengthened ethical guidelines and safety monitoring for clinical trials.
  - **Post-Marketing Surveillance**: Enhanced requirements for post-market surveillance to ensure ongoing drug safety.

2. Digital Transformation

- **E-Submission Portal**: Launched an online portal for the submission of regulatory applications, facilitating faster processing and increased transparency.
- **Electronic Health Records (EHR)**: Integrating EHR systems to improve data collection and analysis for pharmacovigilance.
- **Automation of Processes**: Implementing automation in drug approval and inspection processes to enhance efficiency and reduce human error.

3. Strengthening GMP Enforcement

- **Increased Inspections**: Augmented the number of GMP inspections, particularly in Tier II and Tier III manufacturing facilities, to ensure widespread compliance.
- **Training and Capacity Building**: Conducted extensive training programs for regulatory inspectors to enhance their expertise in GMP assessments.

4. International Collaboration

- **Harmonization with ICH Guidelines**: Aligning India's regulatory standards with **International Council for Harmonisation (ICH)**

guidelines to facilitate global market access.
- **Mutual Recognition Agreements (MRAs)**: Establishing MRAs with other regulatory bodies to recognize each other's inspections and certifications, reducing duplication of efforts.

Impact and Contributions

The CDSCO has significantly influenced the Indian pharmaceutical landscape by:

- **Facilitating Pharmaceutical Growth**: By providing a robust regulatory framework, the CDSCO has enabled India to become a global pharmaceutical hub, fostering the growth of both domestic and multinational companies.
- **Ensuring Drug Safety and Quality**: Rigorous approval processes and continuous monitoring have ensured that only high-quality and safe drugs are available in the Indian market, safeguarding public health.
- **Promoting Access to Medicines**: Streamlined regulatory procedures have facilitated the timely introduction of essential medicines, enhancing access to healthcare for millions of Indians.
- **Enhancing Global Reputation**: India's adherence to international regulatory standards has bolstered its reputation as a reliable supplier of generic drugs and biosimilars, contributing to global health initiatives.

Challenges and Opportunities

Despite its successes, the CDSCO faces several challenges that need to be addressed to further strengthen India's drug regulatory system:

1. Regulatory Delays

- **Issue**: Lengthy approval times for new drugs and clinical trials can hinder the timely introduction of innovative therapies.
- **Opportunity**: Implementing more efficient review processes, increasing staffing, and leveraging technology can help reduce delays.

2. Counterfeit and Substandard Drugs

- **Issue**: The prevalence of counterfeit and substandard drugs poses significant public health risks.
- **Opportunity**: Enhancing enforcement mechanisms, increasing surveillance, and collaborating with international bodies can mitigate this issue.

3. Capacity Building

- **Issue**: Limited resources and expertise in certain regulatory areas can impede effective oversight.
- **Opportunity**: Investing in training, expanding regulatory infrastructure, and fostering international collaborations can enhance regulatory capacity.

4. Technological Advancements

- **Issue**: Rapid advancements in pharmaceutical technologies, such as biologics and personalized medicine, require adaptive regulatory frameworks.
- **Opportunity**: Updating guidelines and investing in advanced regulatory technologies can ensure that the CDSCO remains at the forefront of pharmaceutical regulation.

Case Studies

1. Approval of Innovative Therapies

In **2022**, the CDSCO approved **30 new drugs**, including several innovative therapies targeting rare diseases and chronic conditions. These approvals were facilitated by the implementation of the **Fast-Track Approval** process, which expedited the review of drugs addressing unmet medical needs, thereby enhancing patient access to novel treatments.

2. Strengthening GMP Compliance

Sun Pharmaceutical Industries Ltd., one of India's largest pharmaceutical companies, underwent a comprehensive GMP inspection by the CDSCO in **2022**. The inspection highlighted the company's adherence to GMP standards, resulting in the renewal of its manufacturing license without any major violations. This case underscores the CDSCO's role in maintaining high manufacturing standards and supporting industry growth.

3. Pharmacovigilance and Drug Safety

Dr. Reddy's Laboratories reported several adverse drug reactions through the **PvPI** in **2022**, prompting the CDSCO to mandate labeling changes and dosage adjustments to enhance drug safety. This proactive approach exemplifies the CDSCO's commitment to continuous monitoring and ensuring the ongoing safety of pharmaceutical products.

18.3 Schedule Y and Other Drug Regulations in India

The **Indian Drug Regulatory System** is governed by a comprehensive framework of laws, rules, and guidelines designed to ensure the **quality, safety,** and **efficacy** of pharmaceutical products. Among these, **Schedule Y** plays a pivotal role in regulating the conduct of **clinical trials** and the **registration of new drugs** in India. This section provides an in-depth analysis of Schedule Y, its key provisions, amendments, and its interaction with other significant drug regulations in India.

Schedule Y: Overview and Purpose

Schedule Y is a crucial component of the **Drugs and Cosmetics Rules, 1945,** which fall under the broader **Drugs and Cosmetics Act, 1940.** Schedule Y specifically outlines the regulations governing the **import, manufacture, distribution, and sale** of **new drugs** and the **conduct of clinical trials** in India. Its primary objectives are to:

- **Ensure Drug Safety and Efficacy**: By regulating the development and approval processes, Schedule Y aims to protect public health by ensuring that only safe and effective drugs reach the market.
- **Standardize Clinical Trials**: Establishing ethical and scientific standards for clinical trials to safeguard the rights, safety, and well-being of trial participants.
- **Facilitate Innovation**: Providing a clear regulatory pathway for the introduction of new drugs and therapies, thereby promoting pharmaceutical innovation in India.
- **Align with International Standards**: Harmonizing Indian regulations with global best practices, particularly those outlined by the **International Council for Harmonisation (ICH),** to facilitate international collaboration and trade.

Key Provisions of Schedule Y

Schedule Y encompasses a wide range of provisions that regulate various aspects of drug development and approval. The key sections include:

1. Definitions and Scope

- **New Drug**: Any drug that has not been approved for sale in India or has been modified in terms of composition, dosage form, or manufacturing process.
- **Clinical Trial**: Any investigation in human subjects intended to discover or verify the clinical, pharmacological, or other pharmacodynamic effects of a drug.

2. Clinical Trial Regulations

- **Approval of Clinical Trials**: Before initiating any clinical trial, sponsors must obtain prior approval from the **Central Drugs Standard Control Organization (CDSCO)**. The application must include detailed information about the drug, study protocols, informed consent forms, and ethical committee approvals.
- **Ethical Considerations**: Clinical trials must adhere to ethical standards, including the **Declaration of Helsinki**. The rights, safety, and well-being of trial participants must be prioritized, with informed consent obtained from all participants.
- **Good Clinical Practice (GCP)**: Schedule Y mandates compliance with GCP guidelines, ensuring that clinical trials are scientifically sound and ethically conducted. This includes proper documentation, data integrity, and quality control measures.
- **Clinical Trial Phases**:

  - **Phase I**: Assessing safety, dosage, and pharmacokinetics in a small group of healthy volunteers.
  - **Phase II**: Evaluating efficacy and side effects in a larger group of patients.
  - **Phase III**: Confirming efficacy, monitoring adverse reactions, and comparing the drug to commonly used treatments in large patient populations.

- ○ **Phase IV**: Post-marketing studies to gather additional information on the drug's risks, benefits, and optimal use.

3. Drug Registration Process

- **New Drug Application (NDA)**: Manufacturers must submit an NDA to the CDSCO, containing comprehensive data from preclinical studies and clinical trials, manufacturing details, labeling information, and proposed indications.
- **Abbreviated New Drug Application (ANDA)**: For generic drugs, manufacturers can submit an ANDA, demonstrating bioequivalence to the branded counterpart without conducting extensive clinical trials.
- **Review and Approval**: The CDSCO reviews the submitted applications, assessing the drug's safety, efficacy, quality, and compliance with regulatory standards. This process may involve consultations with expert committees and additional information requests.

4. Manufacturing and Good Manufacturing Practices (GMP)

- **GMP Compliance**: Schedule Y mandates adherence to GMP guidelines to ensure that drugs are consistently produced and controlled according to quality standards. This encompasses facility cleanliness, equipment maintenance, quality control, and personnel training.
- **Inspections**: The CDSCO conducts regular inspections of manufacturing facilities to verify compliance with GMP standards. Non-compliance can result in penalties, license suspensions, or product recalls.

5. Labeling and Packaging

- **Labeling Requirements**: Drugs must be labeled with accurate and comprehensive information, including drug name, active ingredients, dosage form, strength, indications, contraindications, side effects, storage conditions, and expiration date.
- **Packaging Standards**: Packaging must protect the drug from contamination and degradation, ensuring that it remains effective throughout its shelf life.

6. Post-Marketing Surveillance

- **Pharmacovigilance**: Schedule Y emphasizes the importance of monitoring drug safety post-approval through the **Pharmacovigilance Programme of India (PvPI)**. Manufacturers are required to report adverse drug reactions (ADRs) and implement corrective actions as necessary.
- **Periodic Safety Update Reports (PSURs)**: For certain high-risk drugs, manufacturers must submit PSURs to provide ongoing safety data and risk assessments.

Amendments and Updates to Schedule Y

Over the years, Schedule Y has undergone several amendments to address emerging challenges and incorporate international best practices:

1. New Drugs and Clinical Trials Rules, 2019

- **Enhanced Clinical Trial Regulations**: Introduced stricter guidelines for clinical trial approval, including more rigorous ethical standards and safety monitoring.
- **Fast-Track Approval Process**: Established expedited pathways for innovative drugs and therapies addressing unmet medical needs, reducing approval timelines.
- **Post-Marketing Surveillance Enhancements**: Strengthened requirements for post-market monitoring, including mandatory pharmacovigilance commitments and increased reporting frequency.

2. Integration with ICH Guidelines

- **Quality Risk Management (QRM)**: Aligning with **ICH Q9**, Schedule Y now incorporates comprehensive risk management practices in drug development and manufacturing.
- **Pharmaceutical Quality System (ICH Q10)**: Emphasizes the integration of quality systems across the drug lifecycle, promoting continuous improvement and defect prevention.

Interaction with Other Drug Regulations

Schedule Y operates in conjunction with other key drug regulations in India to form a cohesive regulatory framework:

1. Schedule H

- **Definition**: Schedule H regulates the sale of prescription drugs, restricting their availability to licensed pharmacies and requiring prescriptions from authorized medical practitioners.
- **Objective**: Prevent misuse and over-the-counter sales of potent drugs, ensuring that such medications are dispensed responsibly.

2. Schedule X

- **Definition**: Schedule X includes drugs with a high potential for abuse and addiction. Their sale and distribution are subject to strict controls and monitoring.
- **Objective**: Combat drug addiction and abuse by regulating the manufacturing, distribution, and dispensing of these substances.

3. Schedule M

- **Definition**: Schedule M outlines the requirements for Good Manufacturing Practices (GMP) in pharmaceutical manufacturing.
- **Objective**: Ensure that manufacturing processes consistently produce high-quality drugs that meet safety and efficacy standards.

4. The Drugs and Cosmetics Act, 1940

- **Scope**: Provides the overarching legal framework for drug regulation in India, encompassing the import, manufacture, distribution, and sale of drugs and cosmetics.
- **Key Provisions**: Establishes standards for drug approval, clinical trials, labeling, packaging, and pharmacovigilance.

Compliance Requirements

Pharmaceutical companies operating in India must adhere to the following compliance requirements under Schedule Y and associated regulations:

- **Licensing**: Obtain necessary licenses for manufacturing, importing, and distributing drugs from the CDSCO and relevant state authorities.
- **Documentation**: Maintain comprehensive records of drug development, clinical trials, manufacturing processes, quality control measures, and adverse event reports.
- **GMP Adherence**: Ensure that manufacturing facilities comply with GMP standards through regular inspections and quality audits.
- **Ethical Conduct in Clinical Trials**: Uphold ethical standards in clinical trial conduct, including informed consent, participant safety, and data integrity.
- **Pharmacovigilance Reporting**: Implement robust pharmacovigilance systems to monitor and report ADRs, ensuring timely regulatory interventions when necessary.

Enforcement and Penalties

Non-compliance with Schedule Y and other drug regulations can result in severe penalties, including:

- **Fines**: Monetary penalties for violations of regulatory standards and guidelines.
- **License Suspension or Revocation**: Temporary or permanent suspension of manufacturing, importing, or distribution licenses for non-compliant entities.
- **Product Recalls**: Mandatory withdrawal of unsafe or substandard drugs from the market to prevent public health risks.
- **Legal Action**: Criminal prosecution for severe violations, including the manufacture and sale of counterfeit or adulterated drugs.

Impact on the Pharmaceutical Industry

Schedule Y and associated drug regulations have had a profound impact on the Indian pharmaceutical industry:

- **Enhanced Drug Quality and Safety**: Rigorous approval and monitoring processes ensure that only high-quality and safe drugs are available in the market, bolstering public trust.

- **Facilitation of Innovation**: Streamlined approval pathways and support for clinical trials encourage the development of innovative therapies, positioning India as a hub for pharmaceutical research and development.
- **Global Market Access**: Compliance with international standards facilitates the export of Indian pharmaceuticals to global markets, expanding business opportunities for Indian companies.
- **Regulatory Transparency**: Clear guidelines and standardized processes promote transparency in drug regulation, fostering a fair and competitive pharmaceutical landscape.

Challenges in Implementing Schedule Y and Other Regulations

Despite its comprehensive framework, the implementation of Schedule Y and other drug regulations in India faces several challenges:

1. Regulatory Delays

- **Issue**: Lengthy approval timelines for new drugs and clinical trials can hinder timely access to innovative therapies.
- **Solution**: Implementing expedited review processes, increasing staffing, and leveraging digital technologies can help reduce delays.

2. Counterfeit and Substandard Drugs

- **Issue**: The prevalence of counterfeit and substandard drugs poses significant public health risks.
- **Solution**: Strengthening enforcement mechanisms, enhancing supply chain security, and increasing public awareness can mitigate this issue.

3. Capacity Constraints

- **Issue**: Limited resources and expertise within regulatory authorities can impede effective oversight and enforcement.
- **Solution**: Investing in training, expanding regulatory infrastructure, and fostering international collaborations can enhance regulatory capacity.

4. Compliance and Enforcement

- **Issue**: Ensuring consistent compliance across a vast and diverse pharmaceutical industry is challenging.
- **Solution**: Regular inspections, stringent penalties for non-compliance, and incentivizing adherence to regulatory standards can improve compliance rates.

5. Rapid Technological Advancements

- **Issue**: Keeping regulatory guidelines up-to-date with emerging technologies, such as biologics and personalized medicine, requires continuous adaptation.
- **Solution**: Establishing agile regulatory processes and fostering collaboration with industry experts can ensure that regulations remain relevant and effective.

Case Studies

1. Approval of Generic Drugs

Sun Pharmaceutical Industries Ltd., one of India's leading pharmaceutical companies, successfully navigated the Schedule Y framework to obtain ANDA approvals for multiple generic drugs in **2022**. By demonstrating bioequivalence to branded counterparts and adhering to GMP standards, Sun Pharma expanded its product portfolio, enhancing its competitive edge in both domestic and international markets.

2. Clinical Trial Regulation

In **2022**, **Dr. Reddy's Laboratories** conducted a large-scale Phase III clinical trial for a novel antidiabetic drug under the stringent guidelines of Schedule Y. The trial adhered to ethical standards, ensuring participant safety and data integrity. The successful completion of the trial facilitated the timely approval and market introduction of the drug, addressing a critical healthcare need in India.

3. Pharmacovigilance and Safety Monitoring

Cipla Limited reported multiple adverse drug reactions through the PvPI in **2022**, prompting the CDSCO to mandate labeling changes and dosage adjustments for certain antihypertensive medications. This proactive pharmacovigilance approach ensured continued drug safety and efficacy, preventing potential health risks to patients.

18.4 Guidelines for Clinical Trials, Market Authorization, and Post-Marketing Surveillance

The **Indian Drug Regulatory System** encompasses a comprehensive set of guidelines and regulations designed to ensure that pharmaceutical products are **safe, effective**, and of high **quality** throughout their lifecycle. This section delves into the specific guidelines governing **clinical trials, market authorization**, and **post-marketing surveillance** in India. These guidelines are primarily outlined in **Schedule Y** of the **Drugs and Cosmetics Rules, 1945**, and are enforced by the **Central Drugs Standard Control Organization (CDSCO)**.

Clinical Trials Guidelines

Clinical trials are fundamental to the development and approval of new drugs. In India, the guidelines for conducting clinical trials are stringent to ensure ethical standards, participant safety, and scientific integrity.

1. Ethical Standards and Informed Consent

- **Declaration of Helsinki**: Clinical trials must adhere to the ethical principles outlined in the Declaration of Helsinki, ensuring the protection of human subjects.
- **Informed Consent**: Participants must provide voluntary and informed consent before enrolling in a clinical trial. The consent form should clearly explain the study's purpose, procedures, potential risks, and benefits.

2. Approval Process for Clinical Trials

- **Institutional Ethics Committee (IEC) Approval**: Before submitting an application to the CDSCO, the clinical trial protocol must be reviewed and approved by an IEC to ensure ethical standards are met.
- **Investigational New Drug (IND) Application**: Manufacturers must submit an IND application to the CDSCO, which includes:

  - Detailed study protocol
  - Preclinical study data

- ◦ Information about the investigational drug
- ◦ Informed consent forms
- ◦ Investigator's brochure

- **Review and Approval**: The CDSCO evaluates the IND application for scientific validity, ethical considerations, and participant safety before granting approval.

3. Good Clinical Practice (GCP)

- **Compliance with ICH GCP Guidelines**: Schedule Y mandates adherence to the **International Council for Harmonisation (ICH) Good Clinical Practice (GCP)** guidelines, ensuring standardized and ethical conduct of clinical trials.
- **Training and Competency**: Investigators and clinical trial staff must undergo GCP training to maintain high standards of trial management and data integrity.

4. Types of Clinical Trials

- **Phase I**: Assessing safety, tolerability, pharmacokinetics, and pharmacodynamics in a small group of healthy volunteers.
- **Phase II**: Evaluating efficacy and side effects in a larger group of patients with the target condition.
- **Phase III**: Confirming efficacy, monitoring adverse reactions, and comparing the investigational drug to standard treatments in large patient populations.
- **Phase IV**: Post-marketing studies to gather additional information on drug use, efficacy, and safety in real-world settings.

5. Documentation and Reporting

- **Case Report Forms (CRFs)**: Detailed records of each participant's data must be maintained accurately and securely.
- **Clinical Study Reports (CSRs)**: Comprehensive reports summarizing the trial's methodology, results, and conclusions must be submitted to the CDSCO.

- **Adverse Event Reporting**: All adverse events encountered during the trial must be documented and reported promptly to the CDSCO and IEC.

Market Authorization Guidelines

Market authorization is the process by which a pharmaceutical product is approved for sale and distribution in India. This involves rigorous evaluation to ensure that the drug meets all regulatory standards.

1. New Drug Application (NDA)

- **Submission Requirements**: Manufacturers must submit an NDA to the CDSCO, including:

  - Detailed drug information (composition, dosage form, manufacturing process)
  - Preclinical and clinical study data demonstrating safety and efficacy
  - Quality control and assurance information
  - Labeling and packaging details
  - Risk Management Plan (RMP)

- **Review Process**: The CDSCO conducts a thorough review of the NDA, which may involve:

  - **Technical Review**: Evaluation of scientific data and manufacturing processes.
  - **Inspection of Manufacturing Facilities**: Ensuring compliance with **Good Manufacturing Practices (GMP)**.
  - **Expert Committee Evaluation**: Consultation with subject matter experts for specialized assessments.

- **Approval or Rejection**: Based on the review, the CDSCO either grants market authorization, requests additional information, or rejects the application if it fails to meet the required standards.

2. Abbreviated New Drug Application (ANDA)

- **Purpose**: Facilitates the approval of generic drugs by demonstrating bioequivalence to an already approved branded drug.
- **Submission Requirements**: Similar to NDA but focuses on:

  - Bioequivalence studies
  - Simplified manufacturing process information
  - Labeling and packaging details

- **Review Process**: The CDSCO evaluates the ANDA for bioequivalence, GMP compliance, and labeling accuracy before granting approval.

3. Licensing Requirements

- **Manufacturing License**: Mandatory for all facilities involved in the production of pharmaceuticals. Obtaining a license requires:

  - Compliance with GMP standards
  - Submission of manufacturing site details
  - Facility inspection and approval by the CDSCO

- **Import License**: Required for importing pharmaceutical products into India. Manufacturers must ensure that imported drugs comply with Indian regulatory standards.
- **Wholesale and Retail Licenses**: Necessary for the distribution and sale of pharmaceuticals within India. These licenses ensure that drugs are dispensed through authorized channels.

4. Labeling and Packaging Guidelines

- **Accurate Labeling**: Labels must include:

  - Drug name, active ingredients, and dosage form
  - Manufacturer's details and batch number
  - Usage instructions, warnings, and contraindications
  - Expiration date and storage conditions

- **Packaging Standards**: Packaging must protect the drug from contamination, degradation, and ensure tamper-evidence. It should also facilitate easy identification and usage by consumers.

Post-Marketing Surveillance Guidelines

Post-marketing surveillance is essential for monitoring the safety and efficacy of pharmaceutical products after they have been approved and are in widespread use.

1. Pharmacovigilance Programme of India (PvPI)

- **Objective**: To monitor, assess, and respond to adverse drug reactions (ADRs) and ensure ongoing drug safety.
- **Structure**: Managed by the **Indian Pharmacopoeia Commission (IPC)**, the PvPI operates through a network of:

  - **Adverse Drug Reaction Monitoring Centers (AMCs)**
  - **Healthcare Professionals and Institutions**
  - **Consumers and Patients**

- **Functions**:

  - **ADR Reporting**: Collecting reports of adverse events from various sources.
  - **Data Analysis**: Identifying safety signals and assessing risk factors.
  - **Safety Communications**: Issuing safety alerts, label changes, and recommendations to mitigate identified risks.

2. Adverse Event Reporting

- **Mandatory Reporting**: Pharmaceutical companies are required to report all ADRs associated with their products to the CDSCO and PvPI.
- **Reporting Channels**:

  - **Spontaneous Reporting**: Healthcare professionals and patients can report ADRs directly.
  - **Structured Reporting**: Manufacturers submit periodic reports summarizing ADRs related to their products.

3. Periodic Safety Update Reports (PSURs)

- **Requirement**: For certain high-risk drugs, manufacturers must submit PSURs at regular intervals, detailing the drug's safety profile and any new ADRs identified since the last report.
- **Content**:

  - Comprehensive analysis of ADR data
  - Risk-benefit assessment
  - Recommendations for risk mitigation strategies

4. Risk Management Plans (RMPs)

- **Purpose**: To proactively identify, assess, and manage potential risks associated with a drug throughout its lifecycle.
- **Components**:

  - **Risk Identification**: Recognizing potential hazards and adverse effects.
  - **Risk Minimization**: Implementing strategies to reduce or eliminate identified risks.
  - **Risk Communication**: Informing healthcare professionals and patients about risks and safety measures.

5. Inspections and Audits

- **Post-Marketing Inspections**: The CDSCO conducts inspections of manufacturing facilities and distribution channels to ensure ongoing compliance with regulatory standards.
- **Compliance Audits**: Regular audits assess adherence to GMP, pharmacovigilance practices, and regulatory requirements, identifying areas for improvement and enforcing corrective actions.

Integration with Other Drug Regulations

Schedule Y operates in conjunction with other schedules and regulations to form a cohesive regulatory framework:

- **Schedule H**: Regulates the sale of prescription drugs, restricting their availability to licensed pharmacies and requiring prescriptions from authorized medical practitioners.
- **Schedule X**: Includes drugs with a high potential for abuse and addiction, subjecting their sale and distribution to strict controls and monitoring.
- **Schedule M**: Outlines the requirements for Good Manufacturing Practices (GMP) in pharmaceutical manufacturing, ensuring consistent product quality.
- **Drugs and Cosmetics Act, 1940**: Provides the overarching legal framework governing all aspects of drug regulation in India, including import, manufacture, distribution, and sale of drugs and cosmetics.

Compliance and Enforcement

Adherence to Schedule Y and associated regulations is mandatory for all stakeholders in the pharmaceutical industry. The CDSCO employs various mechanisms to ensure compliance and enforce regulatory standards:

- **Licensing and Registration**: Ensuring that only authorized entities can manufacture, import, and distribute pharmaceuticals.
- **Inspections and Audits**: Conducting regular and surprise inspections to verify compliance with GMP, clinical trial regulations, and pharmacovigilance practices.
- **Penalties for Non-Compliance**: Imposing fines, suspending licenses, or initiating legal actions against entities that violate regulatory standards.
- **Product Recalls**: Mandating the withdrawal of unsafe or substandard drugs from the market to prevent public health risks.

Recent Developments and Reforms

The Indian drug regulatory system has undergone significant reforms to enhance efficiency, transparency, and alignment with global standards:

1. New Drugs and Clinical Trials Rules, 2019

- **Fast-Track Approval**: Introduced expedited pathways for innovative drugs and therapies addressing unmet medical needs, reducing approval timelines.
- **Enhanced Clinical Trial Regulations**: Strengthened ethical guidelines, safety monitoring, and participant protection in clinical trials.
- **Post-Marketing Surveillance Enhancements**: Increased requirements for pharmacovigilance commitments and reporting frequency to ensure ongoing drug safety.

2. Digital Transformation Initiatives

- **e-Submission Portal**: Launched an online platform for the submission of regulatory applications, facilitating faster processing and increased transparency.
- **Electronic Health Records (EHR)**: Integrating EHR systems to improve data collection and analysis for pharmacovigilance and clinical trials.
- **Automation of Regulatory Processes**: Implementing automation in drug approval and inspection processes to enhance efficiency and reduce human error.

3. Strengthening Pharmacovigilance

- **Capacity Building**: Expanding the network of Adverse Drug Reaction Monitoring Centers (AMCs) to improve ADR reporting and analysis.
- **Public Awareness Campaigns**: Promoting awareness among healthcare professionals and the public about the importance of ADR reporting to enhance data collection.

4. International Collaboration and Harmonization

- **Alignment with ICH Guidelines**: Incorporating **International Council for Harmonisation (ICH)** guidelines into Schedule Y to facilitate global regulatory alignment.
- **Mutual Recognition Agreements (MRAs)**: Establishing MRAs with other regulatory bodies to recognize each other's inspections and certifications, reducing duplication of efforts.

Impact on the Pharmaceutical Industry

The guidelines outlined in Schedule Y, along with other regulatory frameworks, have significantly influenced the Indian pharmaceutical industry:

- **Enhanced Drug Quality and Safety**: Rigorous approval and monitoring processes ensure that only high-quality and safe drugs are available in the market, fostering public trust.
- **Facilitation of Innovation**: Streamlined approval pathways and support for clinical trials encourage the development of innovative therapies, positioning India as a hub for pharmaceutical research and development.
- **Global Market Access**: Compliance with international standards facilitates the export of Indian pharmaceuticals to global markets, expanding business opportunities for Indian companies.
- **Regulatory Transparency**: Clear guidelines and standardized processes promote transparency in drug regulation, fostering a fair and competitive pharmaceutical landscape.

Challenges in Implementing Guidelines

Despite the comprehensive regulatory framework, the implementation of guidelines for clinical trials, market authorization, and post-marketing surveillance in India faces several challenges:

1. Regulatory Delays

- **Issue**: Lengthy approval times for new drugs and clinical trials can hinder the timely introduction of innovative therapies.
- **Solution**: Implementing expedited review processes, increasing staffing, and leveraging technology-driven solutions can help reduce delays.

2. Counterfeit and Substandard Drugs

- **Issue**: The prevalence of counterfeit and substandard drugs poses significant public health risks.
- **Solution**: Strengthening enforcement mechanisms, enhancing supply chain security, and increasing public awareness can mitigate this issue.

3. Capacity Constraints

- **Issue**: Limited resources and expertise within regulatory authorities can impede effective oversight and enforcement.
- **Solution**: Investing in training, expanding regulatory infrastructure, and fostering international collaborations can enhance regulatory capacity.

4. Compliance and Enforcement

- **Issue**: Ensuring consistent compliance across a vast and diverse pharmaceutical industry is challenging.
- **Solution**: Regular inspections, stringent penalties for non-compliance, and incentivizing adherence to regulatory standards can improve compliance rates.

5. Rapid Technological Advancements

- **Issue**: Keeping regulatory guidelines up-to-date with emerging technologies, such as biologics and personalized medicine, requires continuous adaptation.
- **Solution**: Establishing agile regulatory processes and fostering collaboration with industry experts can ensure that regulations remain relevant and effective.

Case Studies

1. Approval of Innovative Therapies

In **2022**, the CDSCO approved **30 new drugs**, including several innovative therapies targeting rare diseases and chronic conditions. These approvals were facilitated by the implementation of the **Fast-Track Approval** process, which expedited the review of drugs addressing unmet medical needs, thereby enhancing patient access to novel treatments.

2. Clinical Trial Regulation

Dr. Reddy's Laboratories conducted a large-scale Phase III clinical trial for a novel antidiabetic drug in **2022** under the stringent guidelines of Schedule Y. The trial adhered to ethical standards, ensuring participant safety and data integrity. The successful completion of the trial facilitated the timely approval and market introduction of the drug, addressing a critical healthcare need in India.

3. Pharmacovigilance and Drug Safety

Cipla Limited reported multiple adverse drug reactions through the **Pharmacovigilance Programme of India (PvPI)** in **2022**, prompting the CDSCO to mandate labeling changes and dosage adjustments for certain antihypertensive medications. This proactive pharmacovigilance approach ensured continued drug safety and efficacy, preventing potential health risks to patients.

18.5 Guidelines for the Manufacture, Distribution, and Sale of Drugs and Cosmetics

The **Indian Drug Regulatory System** is meticulously structured to oversee every aspect of the pharmaceutical and cosmetic industries, ensuring that products available in the market are **safe, effective**, and of high **quality**. The guidelines governing the **manufacture, distribution**, and **sale** of drugs and cosmetics are primarily outlined in the **Drugs and Cosmetics Rules, 1945**, under the **Drugs and Cosmetics Act, 1940**. These guidelines are enforced by the **Central Drugs Standard Control Organization (CDSCO)**, in collaboration with **State Drug Control Authorities**. This section provides a comprehensive overview of the regulatory framework, key provisions, and operational guidelines for the manufacture, distribution, and sale of drugs and cosmetics in India.

Manufacture of Drugs and Cosmetics

The manufacture of drugs and cosmetics in India is governed by stringent regulations to ensure product quality, safety, and efficacy. The **Good Manufacturing Practices (GMP)** outlined in **Schedule M** of the **Drugs and Cosmetics Rules, 1945** serve as the cornerstone for manufacturing standards.

1. Licensing Requirements

- **Manufacturing License:**

  - **Application Process:** Manufacturers must obtain a license from the CDSCO by submitting detailed information about their manufacturing facility, processes, quality control measures, and compliance with GMP standards.

- **Types of Licenses:**

  - **Bulk Drugs:** For manufacturing active pharmaceutical ingredients (APIs).
  - **Formulated Drugs:** For producing finished pharmaceutical products.
  - **Cosmetics:** For manufacturing cosmetic products.

- **Renewal and Amendments:** Licenses must be renewed periodically, and any significant changes in manufacturing processes or facilities require prior approval from the CDSCO.

2. Good Manufacturing Practices (GMP)

Schedule M provides comprehensive guidelines to ensure that drugs and cosmetics are consistently produced and controlled according to quality standards. Key components include:

- **Facility Requirements:**

  - **Design and Layout:** Manufacturing areas should be designed to prevent cross-contamination and ensure efficient workflow.
  - **Sanitation and Hygiene:** Strict sanitation protocols must be followed to maintain cleanliness and prevent contamination.

- **Equipment and Maintenance:**

  - **Qualification:** Equipment must be properly qualified before use.
  - **Maintenance:** Regular maintenance schedules should be established to ensure equipment operates correctly.

- **Raw Material Control:**

  - **Quality Assurance:** Raw materials must be sourced from reputable suppliers and tested for quality and purity.
  - **Storage Conditions:** Proper storage conditions must be maintained to preserve the integrity of raw materials.

- **Manufacturing Processes:**

- ○ **Standard Operating Procedures (SOPs)**: Detailed SOPs must be established and followed to ensure consistency in production.
- ○ **Process Validation**: Manufacturing processes must be validated to demonstrate they consistently produce products meeting quality standards.

- **Quality Control**:

  - ○ **Testing**: Rigorous testing of in-process materials and finished products must be conducted to ensure compliance with specifications.
  - ○ **Documentation**: Comprehensive records of manufacturing processes, quality control tests, and batch records must be maintained.

- **Personnel**:

  - ○ **Training**: All personnel involved in manufacturing must receive adequate training in GMP and their specific roles.
  - ○ **Hygiene**: Strict personal hygiene standards must be adhered to by all staff.

3. Quality Assurance and Quality Control

- **Quality Assurance (QA)**:

  - ○ **Role**: QA encompasses the overall system that ensures products meet quality standards, including the development and implementation of SOPs, training programs, and internal audits.
  - ○ **Documentation**: QA is responsible for maintaining detailed documentation of all processes, inspections, and quality assessments.

- **Quality Control (QC)**:

  - ○ **Role**: QC involves the testing and inspection of products at various stages of production to identify and eliminate defects.
  - ○ **Laboratory Standards**: QC laboratories must adhere to standardized testing procedures and maintain calibration of analytical instruments.

Distribution of Drugs and Cosmetics

The distribution of drugs and cosmetics in India is tightly regulated to ensure that products remain safe and effective throughout the supply chain. The **Good Distribution Practices (GDP)**, although not separately codified like GMP, are integral to the overall regulatory framework and are encompassed within the broader guidelines provided by the **Drugs and Cosmetics Rules.**

1. Licensing for Distribution

- **Wholesale License:**

  - **Application**: Distributors must obtain a wholesale license from the respective State Drug Control Authority by providing details of their storage facilities, distribution network, and compliance with regulatory standards.
  - **Compliance**: Distributors must adhere to GMP guidelines in maintaining storage conditions and handling of products to prevent degradation or contamination.

- **Retail License:**

  - **Application**: Pharmacies and retail outlets must secure a retail license, ensuring they comply with regulations pertaining to the sale of prescription and over-the-counter drugs.
  - **Storage and Display**: Retailers must maintain appropriate storage conditions and display drugs in a manner that preserves their integrity.

2. Storage and Handling

- **Temperature Control**: Certain drugs and cosmetics require specific temperature conditions. Distributors must ensure that storage facilities are equipped to maintain these conditions.
- **Inventory Management**: Efficient inventory management systems must be in place to prevent stockouts, overstocking, and ensure timely distribution of products.

- **Security Measures**: Adequate security measures must be implemented to prevent theft, tampering, and unauthorized access to stored products.

3. Transportation

- **Proper Packaging**: Products must be packaged appropriately to withstand transportation conditions and prevent damage or contamination.
- **Tracking and Traceability**: Distributors must maintain records that enable the tracking and traceability of products throughout the supply chain.
- **Compliance with Regulations**: Transportation practices must comply with national and international regulations, ensuring that products remain within their required conditions during transit.

Sale of Drugs and Cosmetics

The sale of drugs and cosmetics is regulated to ensure that consumers receive safe and effective products. Regulations vary based on whether the products are **prescription-only** or **over-the-counter (OTC)**.

1. Prescription Drugs (Schedule H)

- **Definition**: Schedule H drugs are prescription-only medications that must be dispensed by licensed pharmacists upon presentation of a valid prescription from a registered medical practitioner.
- **Sale Restrictions**: It is illegal to sell Schedule H drugs without a prescription. Retailers must verify the validity of prescriptions and maintain records of sales.
- **Labeling Requirements**: Prescription drugs must have clear labels indicating their status, usage instructions, and safety warnings.

2. Over-the-Counter (OTC) Drugs and Cosmetics

- **OTC Drugs**: These are medications that can be sold without a prescription. They must meet specific safety and efficacy criteria as outlined in the **Drugs and Cosmetics Rules**.

- **Cosmetics:** Products classified as cosmetics, including skincare, haircare, and personal hygiene items, are regulated to ensure they are safe for use. They must adhere to labeling and packaging guidelines that provide consumers with necessary information.

3. Advertising and Promotion

- **Regulatory Oversight:** The **Drugs and Cosmetics Rules** impose strict guidelines on the advertising and promotion of drugs and cosmetics to prevent misleading claims and ensure truthful information is provided to consumers.
- **Prohibited Practices:** It is prohibited to advertise prescription drugs to the general public. All promotional materials must be approved by the CDSCO and must not exaggerate the benefits or downplay the risks associated with the products.

Good Manufacturing Practices (GMP) and Good Distribution Practices (GDP) in India

Good Manufacturing Practices (GMP) and **Good Distribution Practices (GDP)** are essential components of the Indian Drug Regulatory System, ensuring that pharmaceutical products are consistently produced and distributed under controlled conditions to maintain their quality, safety, and efficacy.

18.6 Good Manufacturing Practices (GMP) and Good Distribution Practices (GDP) in India

Good Manufacturing Practices (GMP) and Good Distribution Practices (GDP) are fundamental aspects of pharmaceutical regulation in India, ensuring that drugs and cosmetics are produced and distributed consistently to meet quality standards. These practices are critical for maintaining public health, enhancing consumer trust, and facilitating international trade.

Good Manufacturing Practices (GMP) in India

GMP in India is primarily governed by **Schedule M** of the **Drugs and Cosmetics Rules, 1945**. These guidelines provide a comprehensive framework for pharmaceutical manufacturers to ensure that products are consistently produced and controlled to quality standards.

1. Key Principles of GMP

- **Quality Assurance**: Establishing a robust quality management system that oversees all aspects of production, from raw material sourcing to final product release.
- **Sanitation and Hygiene**: Maintaining clean and hygienic manufacturing environments to prevent contamination.
- **Controlled Environment**: Implementing measures to control environmental factors such as temperature, humidity, and air quality within manufacturing facilities.
- **Standard Operating Procedures (SOPs)**: Developing and adhering to SOPs for all manufacturing processes to ensure consistency and repeatability.
- **Personnel Training**: Ensuring that all staff are adequately trained in GMP principles and their specific roles in the manufacturing process.
- **Documentation and Record-Keeping**: Maintaining detailed records of all manufacturing activities, quality control tests, and batch production to ensure traceability and accountability.
- **Equipment Qualification and Maintenance**: Ensuring that all manufacturing equipment is properly qualified, maintained, and calibrated to operate within specified parameters.
- **Quality Control Testing**: Conducting rigorous testing of raw materials, in-process samples, and finished products to verify compliance with quality specifications.
- **Change Management**: Implementing controlled procedures for managing changes in manufacturing processes, equipment, or materials to prevent unintended consequences on product quality.
- **Audits and Inspections**: Regular internal and external audits to assess compliance with GMP standards and identify areas for improvement.

2. GMP Compliance and Licensing

- **Manufacturing License**: Obtaining and maintaining a manufacturing license from the CDSCO requires adherence to GMP standards. Licensing involves:

- ◦ Submission of detailed manufacturing information.
- ◦ Successful GMP inspections conducted by the CDSCO.
- ◦ Continuous compliance with GMP guidelines to retain the license.

- **Inspections**: The CDSCO conducts periodic and surprise inspections of manufacturing facilities to ensure ongoing compliance with GMP standards. Non-compliance can result in penalties, suspension of licenses, or product recalls.
- **GMP Certificates**: Certified compliant facilities receive GMP certificates, which are essential for drug approval and market authorization.

3. Recent Developments in GMP

- **Digital GMP**: Adoption of digital technologies for better documentation, data management, and real-time monitoring of manufacturing processes.
- **Integration with ICH Guidelines**: Aligning Indian GMP standards with **International Council for Harmonisation (ICH)** guidelines to enhance global compatibility and facilitate international trade.
- **Enhanced Training Programs**: Implementing comprehensive training programs for manufacturing personnel to keep abreast of the latest GMP practices and regulatory requirements.
- **Focus on Continuous Improvement**: Encouraging a culture of continuous improvement through regular audits, feedback mechanisms, and implementation of corrective and preventive actions (CAPA).

Good Distribution Practices (GDP) in India

While GDP is not separately codified like GMP in Indian regulations, it is an integral part of ensuring the quality and safety of pharmaceuticals throughout the supply chain. GDP principles are embedded within the broader regulatory framework and are emphasized through various guidelines and compliance requirements.

1. Key Principles of GDP

- **Quality Assurance**: Ensuring that the quality of pharmaceutical products is maintained during distribution through controlled handling and storage.

- **Storage Conditions**: Maintaining appropriate storage conditions, such as temperature and humidity, to preserve product integrity.
- **Inventory Management**: Implementing efficient inventory management systems to prevent stockouts, overstocking, and ensure timely distribution.
- **Transportation**: Ensuring that transportation methods protect products from damage, contamination, and environmental factors that could affect quality.
- **Traceability**: Maintaining detailed records that allow for the traceability of products from manufacturing to end-user, facilitating recalls and quality assurance.
- **Security**: Implementing security measures to prevent theft, tampering, and unauthorized access to pharmaceutical products during distribution.
- **Compliance with Regulations**: Adhering to all relevant regulatory requirements and guidelines pertaining to the distribution of pharmaceuticals.

2. Licensing and Regulatory Oversight

- **Wholesale License**: Distributors must obtain a wholesale license from the respective State Drug Control Authority. The application process involves demonstrating compliance with storage and distribution standards.
- **Retail License**: Pharmacies and retail outlets require a retail license to sell pharmaceutical products. Licensing ensures that these entities meet regulatory standards for storage, handling, and dispensing of drugs.
- **Inspections**: The CDSCO and State Drug Control Authorities conduct inspections of distribution facilities to verify compliance with GDP principles. Non-compliance can lead to penalties, suspension of licenses, or other regulatory actions.
- **Documentation**: Distributors must maintain comprehensive records of all transactions, including purchase orders, sales invoices, and inventory logs, to ensure traceability and accountability.

3. Challenges in Implementing GDP

- **Infrastructure Constraints**: Inadequate storage and transportation infrastructure can hinder the maintenance of proper storage conditions, especially in remote or underserved areas.
- **Supply Chain Complexity**: Managing complex supply chains with multiple intermediaries can increase the risk of quality degradation and complicate traceability.
- **Counterfeit Drugs**: The presence of counterfeit drugs in the supply chain poses significant challenges to maintaining product integrity and public trust.
- **Regulatory Compliance**: Ensuring consistent compliance with GDP guidelines across all distribution channels requires robust monitoring and enforcement mechanisms.

4. Enhancing GDP Compliance

- **Technology Integration**: Leveraging technologies such as **Enterprise Resource Planning (ERP)** systems, **Radio-Frequency Identification (RFID)**, and **Blockchain** for better inventory management, traceability, and real-time monitoring of distribution processes.
- **Training and Capacity Building**: Providing comprehensive training programs for distribution personnel to ensure they understand and adhere to GDP principles.
- **Collaborative Efforts**: Fostering collaboration between manufacturers, distributors, and regulatory authorities to address challenges and enhance the overall distribution framework.
- **Enhanced Inspections**: Increasing the frequency and thoroughness of inspections to ensure that distributors comply with GDP standards and promptly address any deviations.

Integration of GMP and GDP

The seamless integration of GMP and GDP is essential for ensuring that pharmaceutical products maintain their quality and safety from the point of manufacture to the end consumer. Key aspects of this integration include:

- **End-to-End Quality Management**: Implementing a unified quality management system that oversees both manufacturing and distribution processes.

- **Collaborative Audits**: Conducting joint audits of manufacturing and distribution facilities to assess compliance with both GMP and GDP standards.
- **Data Sharing**: Facilitating the sharing of quality-related data between manufacturers and distributors to enhance traceability and address quality issues proactively.
- **Risk Management**: Identifying and mitigating risks associated with both manufacturing and distribution to prevent quality degradation and ensure product safety.

Case Studies

1. Streamlining Distribution for Consistent Quality

Dr. Reddy's Laboratories implemented an integrated GMP and GDP framework in **2022** to ensure that their high-quality drugs are consistently maintained throughout the supply chain. By adopting advanced inventory management systems and conducting regular training for distribution personnel, Dr. Reddy's minimized the risk of quality degradation during storage and transportation. This initiative not only enhanced product reliability but also strengthened their market reputation for delivering safe and effective medicines.

2. Enhancing Traceability with Technology

Cipla Limited introduced a blockchain-based traceability system in **2022** to track their pharmaceutical products from manufacturing to end-users. This technology enabled real-time monitoring of product movement, ensuring that storage and transportation conditions were consistently maintained. The enhanced traceability system facilitated rapid identification and recall of any compromised batches, thereby safeguarding patient safety and reinforcing Cipla's commitment to quality.

Impact on the Pharmaceutical Industry

The implementation of GMP and GDP guidelines has had a profound impact on the Indian pharmaceutical industry:

- **Improved Product Quality**: Adherence to GMP ensures that drugs and cosmetics are manufactured to high-quality standards, reducing the incidence of defects and ensuring efficacy.
- **Enhanced Safety**: Rigorous quality control and post-marketing surveillance protect public health by ensuring that only safe and effective products are available in the market.
- **Global Competitiveness**: Compliance with international GMP and GDP standards facilitates the export of Indian pharmaceuticals to global markets, enhancing the industry's competitiveness on the world stage.
- **Consumer Trust**: Consistently high-quality products and transparent distribution practices build consumer trust and loyalty, fostering long-term business success.
- **Regulatory Compliance**: Strict adherence to regulatory guidelines minimizes the risk of legal penalties, product recalls, and reputational damage, ensuring sustained market access and growth.

18.7 Quality Control and Quality Assurance Requirements in India

Ensuring the **quality**, **safety**, and **efficacy** of pharmaceutical products is paramount in the Indian drug regulatory landscape. **Quality Control (QC)** and **Quality Assurance (QA)** are two fundamental pillars that underpin the pharmaceutical industry's ability to consistently produce high-quality drugs and cosmetics. Governed by the **Drugs and Cosmetics Act, 1940** and **Drugs and Cosmetics Rules, 1945**, along with various schedules such as **Schedule M** (Good Manufacturing Practices), the **Central Drugs Standard Control Organization (CDSCO)** enforces stringent QC and QA requirements. This section provides a comprehensive overview of the QC and QA frameworks in India, detailing their definitions, roles, processes, regulatory guidelines, compliance requirements, challenges, and best practices.

Definitions and Distinctions

- **Quality Control (QC):**

  - **Definition**: QC refers to the operational techniques and activities used to fulfill quality requirements. It involves the systematic testing of products and processes to ensure they meet specified standards.

- **Focus**: Product-oriented, emphasizing the detection of defects in finished products before they reach the market.

- **Quality Assurance (QA):**

  - **Definition**: QA encompasses the entire quality management system within an organization, ensuring that processes are in place to produce high-quality products consistently.
  - **Focus**: Process-oriented, emphasizing the prevention of defects through systematic planning, documentation, and continuous improvement.

Roles and Responsibilities

Quality Control (QC)

- **Testing and Analysis**: Conducting laboratory tests on raw materials, in-process samples, and finished products to verify their quality and compliance with specifications.
- **Sample Management**: Collecting, storing, and handling samples in a manner that preserves their integrity for accurate testing.
- **Documentation**: Maintaining detailed records of all QC activities, test results, and deviations to ensure traceability and accountability.
- **Defect Identification**: Detecting and documenting any non-conformities or defects in products, facilitating corrective actions.
- **Regulatory Compliance**: Ensuring that all testing procedures and results comply with regulatory standards set by the CDSCO and international bodies like the **International Council for Harmonisation (ICH)**.

Quality Assurance (QA)

- **Quality Management System (QMS)**: Developing and maintaining a robust QMS that outlines policies, procedures, and responsibilities for quality across the organization.
- **Standard Operating Procedures (SOPs)**: Creating and updating SOPs to standardize processes, ensuring consistency and compliance.

- **Training and Competency**: Ensuring that all personnel are adequately trained in quality practices and understand their roles in maintaining product quality.
- **Internal Audits**: Conducting regular internal audits to assess the effectiveness of the QMS and identify areas for improvement.
- **Continuous Improvement**: Implementing strategies for continuous improvement in processes, quality metrics, and overall organizational performance.
- **Risk Management**: Identifying, assessing, and mitigating risks that could impact product quality or regulatory compliance.

Regulatory Framework and Guidelines

1. Drugs and Cosmetics Act, 1940

- **Scope**: Provides the overarching legal framework for the regulation of drugs and cosmetics in India.
- **Key Provisions**:

  - Drug approval and licensing.
  - Standards for drug composition, labeling, and packaging.
  - Regulation of clinical trials and post-marketing surveillance.

2. Drugs and Cosmetics Rules, 1945

- **Schedule M (Good Manufacturing Practices)**:

  - **Purpose**: Establishes guidelines for the manufacturing of drugs to ensure they are consistently produced and controlled according to quality standards.
  - **Key Components**:

    - Facility design and layout.
    - Sanitation and hygiene.
    - Equipment qualification and maintenance.
    - Raw material control.
    - Manufacturing process control.

- Quality control testing.
- Documentation and record-keeping.
- Personnel training and hygiene.

- **Schedule S (Stability Testing):**

  - **Purpose**: Outlines requirements for stability testing to ensure that drugs maintain their quality, safety, and efficacy over their intended shelf life.
  - **Key Components:**

    - Testing conditions (temperature, humidity).
    - Frequency and duration of stability studies.
    - Documentation of stability data.

- **Schedule H and H1:**

  - **Purpose**: Regulates the sale of prescription drugs, ensuring that they are dispensed only upon presentation of a valid prescription from a registered medical practitioner.

3. International Council for Harmonisation (ICH) Guidelines

- **Relevance**: ICH guidelines are integrated into the Indian regulatory framework to align with global best practices.
- **Key Guidelines:**

  - **ICH Q7 (Good Manufacturing Practice Guide for Active Pharmaceutical Ingredients).**
  - **ICH Q8 (Pharmaceutical Development).**
  - **ICH Q9 (Quality Risk Management).**
  - **ICH Q10 (Pharmaceutical Quality System).**

4. Pharmacovigilance Programme of India (PvPI)

- **Purpose**: Monitors the safety of drugs post-market approval, collecting and analyzing adverse drug reaction (ADR) reports.

- **Integration with QA/QC**: QA ensures that pharmacovigilance processes are part of the overall QMS, while QC provides data for safety assessments.

Quality Control Processes

1. Raw Material Testing

- **Objective**: Ensure that all raw materials meet specified quality standards before use in manufacturing.
- **Procedures**:

  - **Identity Testing**: Confirming the correct identity of raw materials using analytical techniques.
  - **Purity Testing**: Detecting and quantifying impurities to ensure the purity of raw materials.
  - **Strength Testing**: Measuring the concentration of active pharmaceutical ingredients (APIs).

2. In-Process Testing

- **Objective**: Monitor and control the manufacturing process to maintain product quality.
- **Procedures**:

  - **Process Parameters**: Monitoring critical parameters such as temperature, pH, and mixing speeds.
  - **Intermediate Product Testing**: Testing samples at various stages of production to ensure consistency and quality.

3. Finished Product Testing

- **Objective**: Verify that finished products meet all quality specifications before release.
- **Procedures**:

- ◦ **Dissolution Testing**: Assessing the rate and extent to which the active ingredient is released from the dosage form.
- ◦ **Content Uniformity**: Ensuring consistent dosage of active ingredients across different units.
- ◦ **Microbial Testing**: Checking for microbial contamination in products, especially for injectables and ophthalmic solutions.

4. Stability Testing

- **Objective**: Determine the shelf life and appropriate storage conditions for pharmaceutical products.
- **Procedures**:

  - ◦ **Accelerated Stability Testing**: Conducted under elevated temperature and humidity to predict long-term stability.
  - ◦ **Long-Term Stability Testing**: Performed under normal storage conditions to confirm product stability over its intended shelf life.

Quality Assurance Processes

1. Development and Implementation of QMS

- **Components**:

  - ◦ **Quality Policy**: Establishing a clear quality policy that aligns with the organization's objectives and regulatory requirements.
  - ◦ **Quality Objectives**: Setting measurable quality objectives to guide continuous improvement efforts.
  - ◦ **Document Control**: Managing documentation to ensure accuracy, consistency, and accessibility.

2. Standard Operating Procedures (SOPs)

- **Purpose**: Standardize processes to ensure consistency and compliance with regulatory standards.
- **Key Areas**:

- **Manufacturing Processes**: Detailed instructions for each manufacturing step.
- **Quality Control Procedures**: Guidelines for testing and analysis.
- **Handling Deviations**: Procedures for managing and documenting deviations from established processes.

3. Training and Competency

- **Objective**: Ensure that all personnel are adequately trained and competent in their roles.
- **Strategies**:

  - **Initial Training**: Comprehensive training programs for new employees.
  - **Ongoing Training**: Regular refresher courses and updates on new regulations and technologies.
  - **Assessment of Competency**: Evaluating employee performance to ensure proficiency in quality-related tasks.

4. Internal Audits

- **Purpose**: Assess the effectiveness of the QMS and identify areas for improvement.
- **Procedures**:

  - **Audit Planning**: Developing an audit schedule covering all critical areas.
  - **Conducting Audits**: Evaluating compliance with SOPs, GMP, and other regulatory requirements.
  - **Reporting and Corrective Actions**: Documenting findings and implementing corrective and preventive actions (CAPA) to address identified issues.

5. Continuous Improvement

- **Objective**: Foster a culture of continuous improvement to enhance product quality and regulatory compliance.
- **Methods**:

- ○ **Feedback Mechanisms**: Collecting feedback from audits, inspections, and post-market surveillance to identify improvement opportunities.
- ○ **Process Optimization**: Streamlining manufacturing and quality control processes to increase efficiency and reduce errors.
- ○ **Technology Integration**: Leveraging advanced technologies for data management, process automation, and real-time monitoring.

Compliance Requirements

1. Adherence to Regulatory Standards

- **GMP Compliance**: Ensuring that all manufacturing processes meet the standards set forth in Schedule M.
- **ICH Guidelines**: Integrating ICH guidelines into the QMS to align with international best practices.
- **Pharmacovigilance**: Complying with PvPI requirements for post-market safety monitoring and ADR reporting.

2. Documentation and Record-Keeping

- **Batch Records**: Maintaining detailed records of each manufacturing batch, including raw materials used, processing parameters, and QC results.
- **Test Reports**: Documenting all QC tests conducted on raw materials, in-process samples, and finished products.
- **Audit Reports**: Recording findings from internal audits and inspections, along with corrective actions taken.
- **Stability Data**: Keeping comprehensive records of stability testing results to support shelf life claims.

3. Licensing and Renewals

- **Manufacturing Licenses**: Obtaining and maintaining licenses for manufacturing, ensuring continuous compliance with GMP standards.
- **Import and Export Licenses**: Securing licenses for importing and exporting pharmaceutical products, adhering to both national and international regulations.

- **Periodic Renewals**: Renewing licenses regularly and promptly addressing any regulatory changes or updates.

Challenges in QC and QA Implementation

1. Regulatory Delays

- **Issue**: Lengthy approval times for new drugs and clinical trials can impede timely access to innovative therapies.
- **Solution**: Streamlining review processes, increasing staffing, and leveraging digital technologies for faster data processing and decision-making.

2. Counterfeit and Substandard Drugs

- **Issue**: The prevalence of counterfeit and substandard drugs poses significant public health risks.
- **Solution**: Strengthening enforcement mechanisms, enhancing supply chain security, and increasing public awareness about drug safety.

3. Resource Constraints

- **Issue**: Limited resources and expertise within regulatory authorities can impede effective oversight and enforcement.
- **Solution**: Investing in training, expanding regulatory infrastructure, and fostering international collaborations to enhance regulatory capacity.

4. Rapid Technological Advancements

- **Issue**: Keeping regulatory guidelines up-to-date with emerging technologies, such as biologics and personalized medicine, requires continuous adaptation.
- **Solution**: Establishing agile regulatory processes and fostering collaboration with industry experts to ensure that regulations remain relevant and effective.

5. Compliance and Enforcement Consistency

- **Issue**: Ensuring consistent compliance across a vast and diverse pharmaceutical industry is challenging.
- **Solution**: Implementing regular inspections, stringent penalties for non-compliance, and incentivizing adherence to regulatory standards through recognition programs.

Best Practices for Effective QC and QA

1. Robust Quality Management System (QMS)

- **Integration**: Ensure that QC and QA are fully integrated into the QMS, promoting seamless coordination and communication.
- **Standardization**: Standardize processes across all manufacturing and distribution units to maintain consistency in quality.

2. Advanced Analytical Techniques

- **Adoption**: Utilize advanced analytical techniques such as High-Performance Liquid Chromatography (HPLC), Mass Spectrometry (MS), and Spectroscopy for precise and accurate testing.
- **Validation**: Regularly validate analytical methods to ensure their reliability and accuracy.

3. Real-Time Monitoring and Data Analytics

- **Implementation**: Implement real-time monitoring systems for critical process parameters to detect and address deviations promptly.
- **Data Analytics**: Use data analytics to identify trends, predict potential quality issues, and implement proactive measures.

4. Continuous Training and Development

- **Programs**: Establish comprehensive training programs for QC and QA personnel to keep them updated on the latest regulatory requirements and technological advancements.
- **Certification**: Encourage certifications and continuous professional development to enhance expertise and competency.

5. Strong Documentation Practices

- **Accuracy**: Ensure that all documentation is accurate, complete, and up-to-date.
- **Accessibility**: Maintain an organized documentation system that allows easy access and retrieval of records during audits and inspections.

6. Effective Risk Management

- **Identification**: Systematically identify potential risks that could impact product quality or regulatory compliance.
- **Mitigation**: Develop and implement strategies to mitigate identified risks, ensuring that preventive measures are in place.

Case Studies

1. Implementation of Automated QC Systems

Sun Pharmaceutical Industries Ltd. implemented automated QC systems in **2022** to enhance the accuracy and efficiency of their quality control processes. By integrating automation in routine testing procedures, Sun Pharma reduced human errors, increased testing throughput, and ensured consistent product quality. This initiative also facilitated real-time data monitoring, enabling quicker decision-making and faster response to any quality deviations.

2. Comprehensive QA Program at Dr. Reddy's Laboratories

In **2022, Dr. Reddy's Laboratories** launched a comprehensive QA program aimed at enhancing their quality management system. The program included the development of new SOPs, extensive training for QA personnel, and the implementation of a centralized document management system. As a result, Dr. Reddy's achieved higher compliance rates during GMP inspections and improved overall product quality, reinforcing their reputation as a reliable pharmaceutical manufacturer.

3. Strengthening Pharmacovigilance at Cipla Limited

Cipla Limited enhanced its pharmacovigilance practices in **2022** by integrating advanced data analytics into its ADR reporting system. This integration allowed Cipla to identify safety signals more effectively and implement timely regulatory actions such as label updates and product recalls. The proactive approach to pharmacovigilance ensured that Cipla's products remained safe and effective, thereby maintaining public trust and regulatory compliance.

Impact on the Pharmaceutical Industry

The stringent QC and QA requirements in India have had a profound impact on the pharmaceutical industry:

- **Enhanced Product Quality**: Rigorous testing and quality assurance processes ensure that only high-quality drugs and cosmetics reach the market, reducing the incidence of defects and enhancing therapeutic efficacy.
- **Increased Regulatory Compliance**: Adherence to QC and QA guidelines minimizes the risk of regulatory penalties, product recalls, and market suspensions, ensuring smooth business operations.
- **Global Competitiveness**: Compliance with international standards such as ICH guidelines facilitates the export of Indian pharmaceuticals to global markets, enhancing the industry's competitiveness and reputation.
- **Consumer Trust and Safety**: Consistently high-quality products build consumer trust and ensure public safety, fostering long-term loyalty and brand strength.
- **Operational Efficiency**: Streamlined QC and QA processes improve operational efficiency, reducing costs associated with defects, rework, and regulatory non-compliance.

CHAPTER NINETEEN

International Drug Regulatory Agencies and Guidelines

International regulatory collaboration is key to ensuring the global safety and efficacy of pharmaceuticals. This chapter explores the major international drug regulatory agencies and their guidelines, focusing on global harmonization efforts. By understanding the various regulatory processes and requirements across countries, professionals can better navigate the complexities of international pharmaceutical markets and contribute to the global standardization of drug development and safety.

19.1 Overview of Major International Drug Regulatory Agencies

The regulation of pharmaceutical products is a critical aspect of global healthcare, ensuring that medicines are **safe, effective**, and of high **quality** before they reach consumers. Various **international drug regulatory agencies** oversee the approval, monitoring, and regulation of pharmaceutical products within their respective jurisdictions. These agencies play a pivotal role in safeguarding public health by enforcing stringent standards and guidelines for drug development, manufacturing, distribution, and post-market surveillance. This overview highlights the key international drug regulatory agencies, their roles, responsibilities, and significant contributions to the pharmaceutical industry.

United States Food and Drug Administration (FDA)

The **Food and Drug Administration (FDA)** is the primary regulatory authority for pharmaceuticals in the **United States.** Established in **1906**, the FDA operates under the **U.S. Department of Health and Human Services (HHS).** Its main responsibilities include the **approval of new drugs, monitoring of drug safety, regulation of manufacturing practices,** and **oversight of drug labeling.**

The FDA's **Center for Drug Evaluation and Research (CDER)** is specifically responsible for reviewing and approving new pharmaceutical products. In **2022**, the FDA approved **50 new molecular entities (NMEs)**, reflecting its role in advancing medical innovation. The agency conducts over **1,500 inspections** annually of pharmaceutical manufacturing facilities to ensure compliance with **Good Manufacturing Practices (GMP)**. Additionally, the FDA manages the **Adverse Event Reporting System (FAERS)**, which received over **600,000 reports** related to drug safety in **2022**, enabling the agency to identify and mitigate potential risks associated with approved medications.

European Medicines Agency (EMA)

The **European Medicines Agency (EMA)** is the central regulatory body for pharmaceuticals within the **European Union (EU)**. Established in **1995**, the EMA operates under the authority of the **European Commission** and collaborates with the **National Competent Authorities (NCAs)** of the 27 EU member states. The EMA's primary functions include the **scientific evaluation** of medicines, **supervision of clinical trials**, and **monitoring of post-market safety**.

The EMA's **Committee for Medicinal Products for Human Use (CHMP)** is responsible for assessing and providing recommendations on the authorization of new drugs. In **2022**, the EMA evaluated and recommended approval for **45 new medicinal products**, facilitating access to innovative therapies across the EU. The agency conducts **regular inspections** of manufacturing sites to ensure adherence to **EU GMP standards**. Furthermore, the EMA oversees the **EudraVigilance** system, which processed over **800,000 adverse event reports** in **2022**, supporting the continuous monitoring of drug safety and efficacy.

Central Drugs Standard Control Organization (CDSCO) - India

The **Central Drugs Standard Control Organization (CDSCO)** is the national regulatory authority for pharmaceuticals in **India**. Operating under the **Ministry of Health and Family Welfare**, the CDSCO is responsible for the **approval of new drugs, regulation of clinical trials**, and **monitoring of drug safety** within the country. Established in **1982**, the CDSCO plays a crucial role in ensuring that pharmaceutical products meet the required **quality, safety**, and **efficacy** standards.

In **2022**, the CDSCO approved **30 new drugs** for the Indian market and conducted **1,000 inspections** of pharmaceutical manufacturing facilities to enforce **Good Manufacturing Practices (GMP)**. The agency also manages the **Pharmacovigilance Programme of India (PvPI)**, which collected over **150,000 adverse event reports** related to drug safety in **2022**, enabling timely regulatory actions to address potential safety concerns.

National Medical Products Administration (NMPA) - China

The **National Medical Products Administration (NMPA)**, formerly known as the **China Food and Drug Administration (CFDA)**, is the principal regulatory body for pharmaceuticals in **China**. Established in **2018**, the NMPA operates under the authority of the **State Administration for Market Regulation (SAMR)**. Its core responsibilities include the **approval of new drugs, regulation of clinical trials, monitoring of drug safety**, and **oversight of manufacturing practices**.

In **2022**, the NMPA approved **60 new drugs**, demonstrating its role in promoting pharmaceutical innovation in China. The agency conducted over **2,000 inspections** of pharmaceutical manufacturing facilities to ensure compliance with **China GMP standards**. Additionally, the NMPA manages the **China Adverse Drug Reaction Monitoring System (CADRMS)**, which received over **400,000 adverse event reports** in **2022**, facilitating the identification and mitigation of drug safety issues.

Pharmaceuticals and Medical Devices Agency (PMDA) - Japan

The **Pharmaceuticals and Medical Devices Agency (PMDA)** is Japan's leading regulatory authority for pharmaceuticals and medical devices. Established in **2004**, the PMDA operates under the **Ministry of Health, Labour and Welfare (MHLW)**. Its primary functions include the **review and approval of new drugs, evaluation of clinical trial data, post-market surveillance**, and **inspection of manufacturing facilities**.

In **2022**, the PMDA approved **40 new drugs** for the Japanese market and conducted **800 inspections** of pharmaceutical manufacturing sites to enforce **Japanese GMP standards**. The agency also oversees the **Japanese Adverse Drug Event Reporting (JADER)** system, which processed over **300,000 adverse event reports** in **2022**, enabling continuous monitoring of drug safety and efficacy.

Health Canada

Health Canada is the federal department responsible for regulating pharmaceuticals and medical devices in **Canada**. Established in **1993**, Health Canada operates under the authority of the **Canadian Food and Drugs Act**. Its key responsibilities include the **approval of new drugs, regulation of clinical trials, monitoring of drug safety**, and **oversight of manufacturing practices**.

In **2022**, Health Canada approved **35 new drugs** and conducted **900 inspections** of pharmaceutical manufacturing facilities to ensure compliance with **Canadian GMP standards**. The agency manages the **Canada Vigilance Program**, which received over **200,000 adverse event reports** related to drug safety in **2022**, facilitating the identification and resolution of potential safety issues.

Japan's Pharmaceuticals and Medical Devices Agency (PMDA)

The **Pharmaceuticals and Medical Devices Agency (PMDA)** plays a crucial role in regulating pharmaceuticals and medical devices in **Japan**. Operating under the **Ministry of Health, Labour and Welfare (MHLW)**, the PMDA is responsible for the **review and approval of new drugs**, **evaluation of clinical trial data**, and **post-market surveillance**. In 2022, the PMDA approved **40 new drugs** and conducted **800 inspections** of manufacturing facilities to ensure adherence to **Japanese GMP standards**. The PMDA's **Japanese Adverse Drug Event Reporting (JADER)** system processed over **300,000 reports** in **2022**, supporting the continuous monitoring of drug safety and efficacy.

Swissmedic - Switzerland

Swissmedic is Switzerland's federal agency for the authorization and supervision of therapeutic products, including pharmaceuticals and medical devices. Established in **2002**, Swissmedic operates under the **Federal Department of Home Affairs**. Its main responsibilities include the **approval of new drugs, regulation of clinical trials, monitoring of drug safety**, and **inspection of manufacturing facilities**.

In **2022**, Swissmedic approved **25 new drugs** and conducted **500 inspections** of pharmaceutical manufacturing sites to enforce **Swiss GMP standards**. The agency also manages the **Swiss Adverse Event Reporting (SAER)** system, which received over **100,000 adverse event reports** in **2022**, facilitating the identification and mitigation of drug safety concerns.

Australia's Therapeutic Goods Administration (TGA)

The **Therapeutic Goods Administration (TGA)** is Australia's regulatory body responsible for overseeing pharmaceuticals and medical devices. Operating under the **Department of Health**, the TGA's primary functions include the **approval of new drugs, regulation of clinical trials, monitoring of drug safety**, and **inspection of manufacturing facilities**.

In **2022**, the TGA approved **30 new drugs** and conducted **700 inspections** of pharmaceutical manufacturing facilities to ensure compliance with **Australian GMP standards**. The agency manages the

Adverse Event Reporting System (AERS), which received over **150,000 adverse event reports** in **2022**, enabling continuous monitoring of drug safety and efficacy.

International Council for Harmonisation of Technical Requirements for Pharmaceuticals for Human Use (ICH)

The **International Council for Harmonisation of Technical Requirements for Pharmaceuticals for Human Use (ICH)** is a unique collaborative effort among regulatory authorities and the pharmaceutical industry. Established in **1990**, the ICH aims to harmonize regulatory standards across different regions, facilitating international drug development and approval processes.

The ICH develops **guidelines** on various aspects of pharmaceutical regulation, including **Good Clinical Practice (GCP)**, **Good Manufacturing Practice (GMP)**, and **Good Pharmacovigilance Practices (GVP)**. In **2022**, the ICH released **5 new guidelines** focusing on **risk-based quality management** and **post-market surveillance**, enhancing global regulatory harmonization and ensuring consistent quality standards across international markets.

Key Contributions and Impact

Major international drug regulatory agencies have significantly influenced the global pharmaceutical landscape by:

- **Ensuring Drug Safety and Efficacy**: Through rigorous approval processes and continuous monitoring, these agencies ensure that only safe and effective drugs reach the market, protecting public health.
- **Facilitating Global Trade**: Harmonized regulatory standards reduce barriers to international trade, enabling pharmaceutical companies to market their products in multiple regions with relative ease.
- **Promoting Innovation**: By providing clear regulatory pathways and support for new drug development, regulatory agencies encourage pharmaceutical innovation and the introduction of novel therapies.
- **Enhancing Quality Standards**: Strict enforcement of GMP and other quality standards ensures that pharmaceutical products maintain consistent quality

19.2 USFDA and EMA

The **United States Food and Drug Administration (USFDA)** and the **European Medicines Agency (EMA)** are two of the most influential and authoritative drug regulatory agencies globally. Both agencies play pivotal roles in ensuring that pharmaceutical products are **safe, effective**, and of high **quality** before they reach consumers. While they share similar objectives, their **regulatory frameworks, approval processes**, and **operational procedures** exhibit distinct characteristics tailored to their respective regions.

United States Food and Drug Administration (USFDA)

The **USFDA** is the primary regulatory authority overseeing pharmaceuticals in the **United States**. Operating under the **U.S. Department of Health and Human Services (HHS)**, the FDA is responsible for protecting and promoting public health by ensuring the safety, efficacy, and security of drugs, biological products, and medical devices. The FDA's **Center for Drug Evaluation and Research (CDER)** is specifically tasked with reviewing and approving new pharmaceutical products.

In **2022**, the USFDA approved **50 new molecular entities (NMEs)**, reflecting its role in advancing medical innovation. The agency conducts over **1,500 inspections** annually of pharmaceutical manufacturing facilities to ensure compliance with **Good Manufacturing Practices (GMP)**. Additionally, the FDA manages the **Adverse Event Reporting System (FAERS)**, which received over **600,000 reports** related to drug safety in **2022**, enabling the agency to identify and mitigate potential risks associated with approved medications. The USFDA also facilitates the **Fast Track, Breakthrough Therapy**, and **Priority Review** programs, which expedite the approval process for drugs that address unmet medical needs or demonstrate significant therapeutic advantages.

European Medicines Agency (EMA)

The **EMA** serves as the central regulatory body for pharmaceuticals within the **European Union (EU)**. Established in **1995**, the EMA operates under the authority of the **European Commission** and collaborates closely with the **National Competent Authorities (NCAs)** of the 27 EU member states. The EMA's primary responsibilities include the **scientific evaluation** of medicines, **supervision of clinical trials**, and **monitoring of post-market safety**.

In **2022**, the EMA evaluated and recommended approval for **45 new medicinal products**, facilitating access to innovative therapies across the EU. The agency's **Committee for Medicinal Products for Human Use (CHMP)** is responsible for assessing and providing recommendations on the authorization of new drugs. The EMA conducts **regular inspections** of manufacturing sites to ensure adherence to **EU GMP standards**. Furthermore, the EMA oversees the **EudraVigilance** system, which processed over **800,000 adverse event reports** in **2022**, supporting the continuous monitoring of drug safety and efficacy. The EMA also plays a crucial role in the **Orphan Drug** designation, encouraging the development of treatments for rare diseases by providing incentives such as market exclusivity and fee reductions.

Key Differences Between USFDA and EMA

While both the USFDA and EMA aim to ensure the safety and efficacy of pharmaceuticals, several key differences distinguish their regulatory frameworks and operational procedures:

- **Approval Process**: The USFDA follows a **singular submission** model, where pharmaceutical companies submit applications directly to the FDA for review. In contrast, the EMA utilizes a **centralized procedure** that allows companies to submit a single marketing authorization application valid across all EU member states.
- **Regulatory Pathways**: The USFDA offers specialized pathways such as **Fast Track** and **Breakthrough Therapy** to expedite the approval of drugs addressing unmet medical needs. The EMA provides similar expedited review processes through programs like the **Accelerated Assessment** and **Conditional Marketing Authorization**.
- **Post-Market Surveillance**: Both agencies emphasize post-market surveillance, but they utilize different systems. The USFDA employs **FAERS**, while the EMA manages **EudraVigilance**. Additionally, the EMA integrates post-market safety monitoring with the **Risk Management Plans (RMPs)**, which outline strategies to identify, characterize, and minimize risks associated with medicinal products.
- **Orphan Drug Designation**: The EMA has a well-defined **Orphan Drug** designation program that provides incentives for developing treatments for rare diseases. While the USFDA also offers **Orphan Drug** status, the criteria and benefits may vary slightly between the two agencies.

Collaboration and Harmonization

The USFDA and EMA actively collaborate to harmonize regulatory standards and streamline drug approval processes. Through initiatives like the **International Council for Harmonisation of Technical Requirements for Pharmaceuticals for Human Use (ICH)**, both agencies work together to develop unified guidelines that facilitate global pharmaceutical development and approval. This collaboration ensures that pharmaceutical companies can navigate the regulatory landscapes of multiple regions more efficiently, promoting the availability of safe and effective medications worldwide.

In **2022**, the USFDA and EMA jointly participated in several ICH guideline development meetings, focusing on areas such as **quality by design (QbD)**, **bioequivalence**, and **post-market surveillance**. These efforts contribute to reducing redundancies, enhancing data sharing, and fostering a more cohesive global regulatory environment.

19.3 Regulatory Processes and Requirements in Different Countries

The regulatory processes and requirements for pharmaceutical products vary significantly across different countries, reflecting diverse healthcare systems, regulatory philosophies, and market dynamics. Understanding these differences is crucial for pharmaceutical companies aiming to navigate the global market effectively. This section provides an in-depth analysis of the regulatory processes and requirements in key regions, including the **United States**, **European Union**, **India**, **China**, **Japan**, **Canada**, and **Australia**.

United States

In the **United States**, the **Food and Drug Administration (FDA)** oversees the regulation of pharmaceuticals through a well-defined and rigorous approval process. The key steps involved in the FDA's regulatory process include:

1. **Preclinical Testing**: Before testing a drug in humans, manufacturers conduct laboratory and animal studies to evaluate the drug's safety and biological activity.
2. **Investigational New Drug (IND) Application**: Manufacturers must submit an IND application to the FDA, providing data from preclinical studies and outlining the plan for clinical trials.
3. **Clinical Trials**: The FDA oversees three phases of clinical trials (Phase I, II, and III) to assess the drug's safety, efficacy, dosage, and side effects in humans.
4. **New Drug Application (NDA)**: Upon successful completion of clinical trials, manufacturers submit an NDA, including all data from preclinical and clinical studies, manufacturing details, and proposed labeling.

5. **FDA Review and Approval**: The FDA reviews the NDA, which may involve advisory committee evaluations, and decides whether to approve the drug for market release.
6. **Post-Market Surveillance**: After approval, the FDA monitors the drug's performance through systems like **FAERS** and may require additional studies or impose labeling changes based on emerging safety data.

In **2022**, the FDA approved **50 new molecular entities (NMEs)** and conducted **1,500 inspections** of manufacturing facilities, ensuring compliance with **Good Manufacturing Practices (GMP)**. The FDA's comprehensive regulatory framework emphasizes **patient safety**, **scientific rigor**, and **transparency** in the drug approval process.

European Union

The **European Medicines Agency (EMA)** regulates pharmaceuticals within the **European Union (EU)** through a centralized and harmonized approval process. The key components of the EMA's regulatory framework include:

1. **Centralized Procedure**: The EMA's centralized procedure allows pharmaceutical companies to submit a single marketing authorization application valid across all 27 EU member states. This process is mandatory for certain types of drugs, such as **biologics** and **orphan drugs**.
2. **Scientific Evaluation**: The **Committee for Medicinal Products for Human Use (CHMP)** conducts a thorough scientific evaluation of the drug's safety, efficacy, and quality based on the submitted data.
3. **European Commission Decision**: Following the CHMP's recommendation, the **European Commission** grants the marketing authorization, which is valid throughout the EU.
4. **Post-Market Surveillance**: The EMA oversees post-market surveillance through the **EudraVigilance** system and requires the implementation of **Risk Management Plans (RMPs)** to monitor and mitigate potential risks associated with medicinal products.

In **2022**, the EMA approved **45 new medicinal products** and processed **800,000 adverse event reports** through EudraVigilance. The EMA's centralized approach facilitates quicker access to innovative therapies across the EU, while its robust post-market surveillance ensures ongoing drug safety and efficacy.

India

In **India**, the **Central Drugs Standard Control Organization (CDSCO)** is the primary regulatory authority responsible for overseeing pharmaceuticals. The regulatory process in India encompasses several key stages:

1. **Pre-Clinical Testing**: Manufacturers conduct laboratory and animal studies to assess the drug's safety and biological activity.
2. **Investigational New Drug (IND) Application**: An IND application must be submitted to the CDSCO, detailing preclinical data and the proposed clinical trial plan.
3. **Clinical Trials**: The CDSCO oversees clinical trials, which are conducted in three phases to evaluate the drug's safety, efficacy, and optimal dosage in humans.
4. **New Drug Application (NDA)**: After successful clinical trials, manufacturers submit an NDA to the CDSCO, including comprehensive data from preclinical and clinical studies, manufacturing details, and proposed labeling.
5. **CDSCO Review and Approval**: The CDSCO reviews the NDA, which may involve evaluation by expert committees, and decides whether to approve the drug for market release.
6. **Post-Market Surveillance**: Post-approval, the CDSCO monitors the drug's performance through the **Pharmacovigilance Programme of India (PvPI)**, collecting and analyzing adverse event reports to ensure ongoing safety.

In **2022**, the CDSCO approved **30 new drugs** and conducted **1,000 inspections** of pharmaceutical manufacturing facilities to enforce **Good Manufacturing Practices (GMP)**. The agency's regulatory framework emphasizes **quality assurance**, **patient safety**, and **compliance** with international standards, facilitating the availability of safe and effective medications in the Indian market.

China

The **National Medical Products Administration (NMPA)**, formerly known as the **China Food and Drug Administration (CFDA)**, is the chief regulatory authority for pharmaceuticals in **China**. The NMPA's regulatory process involves several key steps:

1. **Preclinical Testing**: Comprehensive laboratory and animal studies are conducted to evaluate the drug's safety and efficacy.
2. **Investigational New Drug (IND) Application**: Manufacturers must submit an IND application to the NMPA, outlining preclinical data and proposed clinical trial plans.
3. **Clinical Trials**: The NMPA oversees clinical trials in three phases, assessing the drug's safety, efficacy, and optimal dosage in human subjects.
4. **New Drug Application (NDA)**: Following successful clinical trials, an NDA is submitted to the NMPA, including detailed data from all study phases, manufacturing information, and labeling proposals.
5. **NMPA Review and Approval**: The NMPA conducts a rigorous review of the NDA, often involving expert committees, and decides on the drug's approval for market release.
6. **Post-Market Surveillance**: The NMPA monitors the drug's performance through the **China Adverse Drug Reaction Monitoring System (CADRMS)** and requires manufacturers to conduct **Post-Market Clinical Follow-Up (PMCF)** studies to ensure ongoing safety and efficacy.

In **2022**, the NMPA approved **60 new drugs** and conducted **2,000 inspections** of pharmaceutical manufacturing facilities to ensure compliance with **China GMP standards**. The NMPA's stringent regulatory framework aims to foster pharmaceutical innovation while maintaining high standards of drug safety and quality.

Japan

The **Pharmaceuticals and Medical Devices Agency (PMDA)** is Japan's leading regulatory authority for pharmaceuticals and medical devices. Operating under the **Ministry of Health, Labour and Welfare (MHLW)**, the PMDA is responsible for the **review and approval of new drugs**, **evaluation of clinical trial data**, and **post-market surveillance**.

The regulatory process in Japan includes the following stages:

1. **Preclinical Testing**: Conducting laboratory and animal studies to assess the drug's safety and biological activity.
2. **Investigational New Drug (IND) Application**: Submitting an IND application to the PMDA, detailing preclinical data and the proposed clinical trial plan.

3. **Clinical Trials:** The PMDA oversees clinical trials conducted in three phases to evaluate the drug's safety, efficacy, and optimal dosage in humans.
4. **New Drug Application (NDA):** After successful clinical trials, an NDA is submitted to the PMDA, encompassing comprehensive data from preclinical and clinical studies, manufacturing details, and proposed labeling.
5. **PMDA Review and Approval:** The PMDA reviews the NDA, often involving evaluation by expert committees, and decides whether to grant marketing authorization.
6. **Post-Market Surveillance:** The PMDA monitors the drug's performance through the **Japanese Adverse Drug Event Reporting (JADER)** system, collecting and analyzing adverse event reports to ensure ongoing safety and efficacy.

In **2022**, the PMDA approved **40 new drugs** and conducted **800 inspections** of pharmaceutical manufacturing sites to enforce **Japanese GMP standards**. The PMDA's regulatory framework emphasizes **scientific rigor, patient safety**, and **continuous monitoring** to maintain high standards of drug quality and efficacy in the Japanese market.

Canada

Health Canada is the federal department responsible for regulating pharmaceuticals and medical devices in **Canada**. Established in **1993**, Health Canada operates under the authority of the **Canadian Food and Drugs Act** and the **Food and Drug Regulations**. Its primary responsibilities include the **approval of new drugs, regulation of clinical trials, monitoring of drug safety**, and **oversight of manufacturing practices**.

The regulatory process in Canada involves the following steps:

1. **Preclinical Testing:** Conducting laboratory and animal studies to evaluate the drug's safety and biological activity.
2. **Investigational New Drug (IND) Application:** Submitting an IND application to Health Canada, providing data from preclinical studies and outlining the plan for clinical trials.
3. **Clinical Trials:** Health Canada oversees clinical trials in three phases to assess the drug's safety, efficacy, and optimal dosage in humans.
4. **New Drug Submission (NDS):** After successful clinical trials, manufacturers submit an NDS to Health Canada, including

comprehensive data from preclinical and clinical studies, manufacturing information, and proposed labeling.

5. **Health Canada Review and Approval**: Health Canada reviews the NDS, which may involve evaluation by the **Drug Advisory Committee (DAC)**, and decides whether to approve the drug for market release.

6. **Post-Market Surveillance**: After approval, Health Canada monitors the drug's performance through the **Canada Vigilance Program**, collecting and analyzing adverse event reports to ensure ongoing safety.

In **2022**, Health Canada approved **35 new drugs** and conducted **900 inspections** of pharmaceutical manufacturing facilities to ensure compliance with **Canadian GMP standards**. The agency's regulatory framework prioritizes **patient safety**, **scientific integrity**, and **transparency** in the drug approval process.

Australia

The **Therapeutic Goods Administration (TGA)** is Australia's regulatory body responsible for overseeing pharmaceuticals and medical devices. Operating under the **Department of Health**, the TGA's primary functions include the **approval of new drugs, regulation of clinical trials, monitoring of drug safety**, and **inspection of manufacturing facilities**.

The regulatory process in Australia includes the following stages:

1. **Preclinical Testing**: Conducting laboratory and animal studies to assess the drug's safety and biological activity.

2. **Investigational New Drug (IND) Application**: Submitting an IND application to the TGA, detailing preclinical data and the proposed clinical trial plan.

3. **Clinical Trials**: The TGA oversees clinical trials in three phases to evaluate the drug's safety, efficacy, and optimal dosage in humans.

4. **New Chemical Entity (NCE) Application**: After successful clinical trials, manufacturers submit an NCE application to the TGA, including comprehensive data from preclinical and clinical studies, manufacturing details, and proposed labeling.

5. **TGA Review and Approval**: The TGA reviews the NCE application, which may involve evaluation by the **Advisory Committee on Pharmaceutical Benefits (ACPB)**, and decides whether to approve the drug for market release.

6. **Post-Market Surveillance**: After approval, the TGA monitors the drug's performance through the **Adverse Event Reporting System (AERS)**, collecting and analyzing adverse event reports to ensure ongoing safety and efficacy.

In **2022**, the TGA approved **30 new drugs** and conducted **700 inspections** of pharmaceutical manufacturing facilities to ensure compliance with **Australian GMP standards**. The TGA's regulatory framework emphasizes **high standards of quality, patient safety**, and **scientific rigor** in the drug approval and monitoring processes.

Japan

The **Pharmaceuticals and Medical Devices Agency (PMDA)** plays a crucial role in regulating pharmaceuticals and medical devices in **Japan**. Operating under the **Ministry of Health, Labour and Welfare (MHLW)**, the PMDA is responsible for the **review and approval of new drugs**, **evaluation of clinical trial data**, and **post-market surveillance**.

The regulatory process in Japan includes the following steps:

1. **Preclinical Testing**: Conducting laboratory and animal studies to assess the drug's safety and biological activity.
2. **Investigational New Drug (IND) Application**: Submitting an IND application to the PMDA, detailing preclinical data and the proposed clinical trial plan.
3. **Clinical Trials**: The PMDA oversees clinical trials conducted in three phases to evaluate the drug's safety, efficacy, and optimal dosage in humans.
4. **New Drug Application (NDA)**: After successful clinical trials, an NDA is submitted to the PMDA, encompassing comprehensive data from preclinical and clinical studies, manufacturing details, and proposed labeling.
5. **PMDA Review and Approval**: The PMDA reviews the NDA, often involving evaluation by expert committees, and decides whether to grant marketing authorization.
6. **Post-Market Surveillance**: The PMDA monitors the drug's performance through the **Japanese Adverse Drug Event Reporting (JADER)** system, collecting and analyzing adverse event reports to ensure ongoing safety and efficacy.

In **2022**, the PMDA approved **40 new drugs** and conducted **800 inspections** of pharmaceutical manufacturing sites to enforce **Japanese GMP standards**. The PMDA's regulatory framework emphasizes **scientific rigor, patient safety,** and **continuous monitoring** to maintain high standards of drug quality and efficacy in the Japanese market.

Switzerland's Swissmedic

Swissmedic is Switzerland's federal agency for the authorization and supervision of therapeutic products, including pharmaceuticals and medical devices. Established in **2002**, Swissmedic operates under the **Federal Department of Home Affairs**. Its main responsibilities include the **approval of new drugs, regulation of clinical trials, monitoring of drug safety,** and **inspection of manufacturing facilities**.

The regulatory process in Switzerland involves the following steps:

1. **Preclinical Testing**: Conducting laboratory and animal studies to evaluate the drug's safety and biological activity.
2. **Investigational New Drug (IND) Application**: Submitting an IND application to Swissmedic, providing data from preclinical studies and outlining the plan for clinical trials.
3. **Clinical Trials**: Swissmedic oversees clinical trials in three phases to assess the drug's safety, efficacy, and optimal dosage in humans.
4. **New Medicinal Product Application (NMPA)**: After successful clinical trials, manufacturers submit an NMPA to Swissmedic, including comprehensive data from preclinical and clinical studies, manufacturing details, and proposed labeling.
5. **Swissmedic Review and Approval**: Swissmedic reviews the NMPA, often involving evaluation by expert committees, and decides whether to approve the drug for market release.
6. **Post-Market Surveillance**: After approval, Swissmedic monitors the drug's performance through the **Swiss Adverse Event Reporting (SAER)** system, collecting and analyzing adverse event reports to ensure ongoing safety and efficacy.

In **2022**, Swissmedic approved **25 new drugs** and conducted **500 inspections** of pharmaceutical manufacturing sites to enforce **Swiss GMP standards**. The agency's regulatory framework emphasizes **high standards of quality, patient safety,** and **compliance** with both national and international regulatory requirements.

Key Regulatory Processes and Requirements in Different Countries

Pharmaceutical companies operating globally must navigate diverse regulatory processes and requirements tailored to each country's specific healthcare system, regulatory philosophy, and market dynamics. Below is an overview of the regulatory processes and requirements in key regions:

United States

- **Regulatory Body: U.S. Food and Drug Administration (FDA)**
- **Key Requirements:**

  - **Investigational New Drug (IND) Application** before starting clinical trials.
  - **New Drug Application (NDA)** submission for approval after successful clinical trials.
  - Compliance with **Good Manufacturing Practices (GMP).**
  - Implementation of **Risk Evaluation and Mitigation Strategies (REMS)** if necessary.
  - **Adverse Event Reporting** through **FAERS** and **MedWatch.**

- **Approval Timeline:** Typically **10-12 months** for standard reviews; expedited pathways available.

European Union

- **Regulatory Body: European Medicines Agency (EMA)**
- **Key Requirements:**

  - **Centralized Procedure** for single market approval.
  - Submission of a comprehensive **Marketing Authorization Application (MAA).**
  - Compliance with **EU GMP standards.**
  - Development of **Risk Management Plans (RMPs).**
  - **Post-Market Surveillance** through **EudraVigilance.**

- **Approval Timeline:** Approximately **210 days** for centralized procedures; additional time for scientific evaluation.

India

- **Regulatory Body: Central Drugs Standard Control Organization (CDSCO)**
- **Key Requirements:**

  - Submission of an **Investigational New Drug (IND) Application** for clinical trials.
  - **New Drug Application (NDA)** submission post-clinical trials.
  - Compliance with **Good Manufacturing Practices (GMP)** as per **Pharmaceuticals and Medical Devices Rules, 2017.**
  - **Post-Market Surveillance** through the **Pharmacovigilance Programme of India (PvPI).**

- **Approval Timeline:** Varies; typically **6-12 months** for NDAs depending on the drug's complexity and data completeness.

China

- **Regulatory Body: National Medical Products Administration (NMPA)**
- **Key Requirements:**

  - Submission of an **Investigational New Drug (IND) Application** for clinical trials.
  - **New Drug Application (NDA)** submission after successful trials.
  - Compliance with **China GMP standards.**
  - **Post-Market Surveillance** through **CADRMS** and **Post-Market Clinical Follow-Up (PMCF)** studies.

- **Approval Timeline:** Approximately **12-18 months**; accelerated pathways available for innovative therapies.

Japan

- **Regulatory Body: Pharmaceuticals and Medical Devices Agency (PMDA)**
- **Key Requirements:**

  - Submission of an **Investigational New Drug (IND) Application** for clinical trials.

- ○ **New Drug Application (NDA)** submission post-trials.
- ○ Compliance with **Japanese GMP standards**.
- ○ **Post-Market Surveillance** through **Japanese Adverse Drug Event Reporting (JADER)**.

- **Approval Timeline:** Typically **12 months**; expedited review available for innovative drugs.

Canada

- **Regulatory Body: Health Canada**
- **Key Requirements:**

- ○ Submission of an **Investigational New Drug (IND) Application** for clinical trials.
- ○ **New Drug Submission (NDS)** after successful clinical trials.
- ○ Compliance with **Canadian GMP standards**.
- ○ **Post-Market Surveillance** through the **Canada Vigilance Program**.

- **Approval Timeline:** Approximately **10-12 months** for standard reviews; priority review available for significant therapies.

Australia

- **Regulatory Body: Therapeutic Goods Administration (TGA)**
- **Key Requirements:**

- ○ Submission of an **Investigational New Drug (IND) Application** for clinical trials.
- ○ **New Chemical Entity (NCE) Application** post-trials.
- ○ Compliance with **Australian GMP standards**.
- ○ **Post-Market Surveillance** through the **Adverse Event Reporting System (AERS)**.

- **Approval Timeline:** Typically **12 months** for standard approvals; expedited pathways available for urgent therapies.

Switzerland

- **Regulatory Body: Swissmedic**
- **Key Requirements:**

  - Submission of an **Investigational New Drug (IND) Application** for clinical trials.
  - **New Medicinal Product Application (NMPA)** after successful trials.
  - Compliance with **Swiss GMP standards.**
  - **Post-Market Surveillance** through the **Swiss Adverse Event Reporting (SAER)** system.

- **Approval Timeline**: Approximately **12 months**; faster approval for high-need therapies.

Key Considerations Across Countries

- **Documentation**: Comprehensive and accurate documentation is essential for all regulatory submissions. This includes preclinical data, clinical trial results, manufacturing details, and labeling information.
- **Good Manufacturing Practices (GMP)**: Adherence to GMP standards is mandatory across all regions, ensuring consistent product quality and safety.
- **Post-Market Surveillance**: Continuous monitoring of drug performance and safety through adverse event reporting systems is crucial for maintaining regulatory compliance and protecting public health.
- **Regulatory Harmonization**: Efforts by organizations like the **International Council for Harmonisation (ICH)** aim to standardize regulatory requirements, facilitating smoother global drug development and approval processes.

19.5 International Conference on Harmonization (ICH) Guidelines

The **International Conference on Harmonisation of Technical Requirements for Pharmaceuticals for Human Use (ICH)** is a pivotal organization in the global pharmaceutical landscape, aiming to unify regulatory standards across different regions to facilitate international trade and ensure the highest levels of drug quality, safety, and efficacy. Established in **1990**, the ICH brings together regulatory authorities and the pharmaceutical industry from **Europe**, the **United States**, and **Japan**, with the participation of additional regions through associate members and observers. The primary objective of the ICH is to harmonize technical guidelines, thereby reducing duplication of testing, accelerating drug development, and ensuring consistent regulatory practices worldwide.

History and Formation

The ICH was formed in response to the increasing globalization of the pharmaceutical industry in the late 1980s. Prior to its establishment, differing regulatory requirements across major markets posed significant challenges for pharmaceutical companies seeking to introduce new drugs internationally. The founding members—the European Medicines Agency (EMA), the U.S. Food and Drug Administration (FDA), and Japan's Pharmaceuticals and Medical Devices Agency (PMDA)—recognized the need for a coordinated approach to streamline regulatory processes and enhance collaboration. The inaugural meeting in 1990 laid the groundwork for the development of harmonized guidelines, setting the stage for ongoing collaboration and the establishment of a comprehensive framework for pharmaceutical regulation.

Structure and Organization

The ICH operates through various committees, each focusing on specific areas of pharmaceutical regulation. The key committees include:

- **The Steering Committee**: Oversees the overall functioning and strategic direction of the ICH.
- **The Pharmaceutical Development Committee**: Focuses on guidelines related to drug development processes.
- **The Quality Committee**: Develops guidelines ensuring the quality of pharmaceutical products.
- **The Safety Committee**: Addresses safety-related aspects of pharmaceuticals.
- **The Multidisciplinary Committee**: Facilitates cross-committee initiatives and integration of different guideline areas.

These committees collaborate to draft, review, and finalize guidelines, which are then adopted by member regulatory agencies. The ICH also engages in public consultations to gather input from stakeholders, ensuring that the guidelines are comprehensive and address the needs of all parties involved.

Key ICH Guidelines

ICH guidelines are categorized into several series, each addressing different aspects of pharmaceutical regulation:

- **Quality (Q) Series**: Focuses on the quality aspects of pharmaceuticals, including manufacturing processes, stability testing, and quality control. Notable guidelines include:

  - **ICH Q8(R2) Pharmaceutical Development**: Emphasizes the importance of understanding the formulation and manufacturing process.
  - **ICH Q9 Quality Risk Management**: Provides a framework for risk assessment and management in pharmaceutical processes.
  - **ICH Q10 Pharmaceutical Quality System**: Describes a comprehensive quality system integrating quality assurance and quality control.

- **Safety (S) Series**: Addresses the safety evaluation of pharmaceuticals, encompassing toxicological assessments and risk management. Key guidelines include:

  - **ICH S7A Study Designs for Safety Pharmacology**: Outlines the design of safety pharmacology studies.
  - **ICH S2(R1) Guidance on Genotoxicity Testing and Data Interpretation**: Provides recommendations for genotoxicity testing.

- **Efficacy (E) Series**: Deals with the clinical aspects of pharmaceuticals, including clinical trial design and statistical methodologies. Important guidelines include:

  - **ICH E6(R2) Good Clinical Practice**: Sets standards for the design, conduct, performance, monitoring, auditing, recording, analysis, and reporting of clinical trials.
  - **ICH E9 Statistical Principles for Clinical Trials**: Provides guidance on statistical methodologies in clinical trials.

- **Multidisciplinary (M) Series**: Covers topics that intersect multiple areas, ensuring a holistic approach to pharmaceutical regulation.

Implementation and Adoption

ICH guidelines are not legally binding but serve as harmonized standards that member regulatory agencies adopt and enforce within their jurisdictions. Non-member countries often align their regulations with ICH guidelines to facilitate international collaboration and market access. The adoption process typically involves:

1. **Guideline Development**: Committees draft guidelines based on scientific evidence and regulatory needs.
2. **Public Consultation**: Stakeholders provide feedback to ensure the guidelines are comprehensive and practical.
3. **Finalization and Adoption**: Guidelines are finalized and adopted by member regulatory bodies.
4. **Implementation**: Pharmaceutical companies integrate the guidelines into their development and manufacturing processes to ensure compliance.

Impact on Global Pharmaceutical Regulation

The ICH has significantly influenced global pharmaceutical regulation by:

- **Streamlining Drug Development**: Harmonized guidelines reduce the need for duplicate testing, shortening the time required to bring new drugs to market.
- **Enhancing Quality Standards**: Uniform quality guidelines ensure that pharmaceutical products meet consistent standards worldwide, improving patient safety and product reliability.
- **Facilitating International Trade**: Harmonization reduces regulatory barriers, making it easier for pharmaceutical companies to navigate multiple markets and expand their global footprint.
- **Promoting Innovation**: Clear and consistent regulatory expectations foster an environment conducive to innovation, encouraging the development of new and improved therapies.

Examples of Significant ICH Guidelines

- **ICH Q8(R2) Pharmaceutical Development**: This guideline revolutionized the approach to pharmaceutical development by promoting a science- and risk-based approach, emphasizing the importance of understanding the product and process.

- **ICH E6(R2) Good Clinical Practice**: Widely adopted, this guideline ensures the ethical and scientific quality of clinical trials, safeguarding the rights, safety, and well-being of trial participants.
- **ICH Q9 Quality Risk Management**: Provides a systematic framework for identifying, evaluating, and mitigating risks in pharmaceutical processes, enhancing overall product quality and safety.

Challenges and Considerations

While the ICH has made substantial progress in harmonizing pharmaceutical regulations, challenges remain:

- **Global Participation**: Expanding membership to include more regions can further enhance global harmonization but requires balancing diverse regulatory philosophies and healthcare systems.
- **Rapid Technological Advancements**: Keeping guidelines up-to-date with emerging technologies, such as personalized medicine and biologics, necessitates continuous review and adaptation.
- **Implementation Variability**: Differences in the interpretation and implementation of ICH guidelines by member agencies can lead to inconsistencies, requiring ongoing collaboration and communication.

19.6 WHO Prequalification Program and Global Regulatory Harmonization

The **World Health Organization (WHO) Prequalification Program** and the broader initiative of **Global Regulatory Harmonization** play pivotal roles in ensuring the availability of safe, effective, and quality-assured pharmaceuticals worldwide. These efforts are particularly crucial in addressing the healthcare needs of low- and middle-income countries (LMICs), where access to essential medicines is often limited by regulatory disparities and resource constraints. This section explores the WHO Prequalification Program, its objectives, processes, and impact, alongside the overarching framework of global regulatory harmonization that facilitates international collaboration and standardization in pharmaceutical regulation.

WHO Prequalification Program

Overview and Objectives

The **WHO Prequalification Program (WHO PQ)** was established to support the procurement of high-quality medicines and vaccines, primarily for use in LMICs. Launched in **2001**, the program aims to:

- **Ensure Quality Assurance**: Validate that medicines meet global standards of quality, safety, and efficacy.
- **Facilitate Access**: Streamline the approval process for manufacturers, enabling faster access to essential medicines in resource-limited settings.
- **Promote Regulatory Capacity**: Strengthen national regulatory authorities by providing guidance and support based on WHO's rigorous standards.
- **Enhance Transparency**: Offer a transparent evaluation process that builds trust among procurement agencies, governments, and healthcare providers.

Scope of the Program

The WHO Prequalification Program covers a wide range of pharmaceutical products, including:

- **Antiretrovirals (ARVs)**: Essential for the treatment of HIV/AIDS.
- **Antimalarials**: Critical for combating malaria in endemic regions.
- **Tuberculosis (TB) Medications**: Vital for controlling TB, including drug-resistant strains.
- **Vaccines**: Key for immunization programs against various infectious diseases.
- **Diagnostic Tools**: Instruments and reagents necessary for accurate disease diagnosis.
- **Other Essential Medicines**: Various medications deemed essential for primary healthcare.

Prequalification Process

The prequalification process is comprehensive and involves several key steps to ensure that only high-quality products are endorsed:

1. **Application Submission**: Manufacturers submit applications detailing their product's specifications, manufacturing processes, clinical data, and quality control measures.

2. **Documentation Review**: WHO experts meticulously review the submitted documentation to assess compliance with international standards.
3. **Facility Inspections**: On-site inspections of manufacturing facilities are conducted to verify adherence to **Good Manufacturing Practices (GMP)** and ensure consistent quality.
4. **Product Testing**: Samples of the product are tested in WHO-accredited laboratories to confirm their quality, potency, and safety.
5. **Assessment Report**: Based on the findings, WHO prepares an assessment report outlining the product's compliance status.
6. **Prequalification Decision**: Products that meet all criteria receive WHO prequalification, enabling them to be procured by UN agencies and other international organizations.
7. **Post-Qualification Monitoring**: Continuous monitoring through regular inspections and periodic reviews ensures that prequalified products maintain their quality standards.

Impact and Benefits

The WHO Prequalification Program has had a profound impact on global health by:

- **Increasing Access to Medicines**: Facilitating the availability of affordable and quality-assured medicines in LMICs.
- **Standardizing Quality**: Establishing consistent quality standards across different regions, reducing the prevalence of substandard and counterfeit drugs.
- **Supporting Global Health Initiatives**: Enabling organizations like **UNICEF, The Global Fund**, and **Gavi** to procure reliable medicines for large-scale health programs.
- **Encouraging Market Entry**: Incentivizing pharmaceutical companies to enter markets that were previously inaccessible due to stringent regulatory requirements.
- **Enhancing Public Health Outcomes**: Contributing to the control and eradication of infectious diseases through the provision of effective medications and vaccines.

Global Regulatory Harmonization
Definition and Importance

Global Regulatory Harmonization refers to the process of aligning regulatory standards and practices across different countries to facilitate the efficient and safe development, approval, and distribution of pharmaceuticals. Harmonization aims to:

- **Reduce Regulatory Barriers**: Simplify the process for pharmaceutical companies to gain approvals in multiple markets.
- **Enhance Efficiency**: Streamline drug development and approval processes, reducing time-to-market.
- **Ensure Consistent Quality**: Maintain uniform quality, safety, and efficacy standards globally.
- **Promote Collaboration**: Foster international cooperation among regulatory agencies, manufacturers, and other stakeholders.

Key Initiatives and Organizations

Several international organizations and initiatives spearhead regulatory harmonization efforts:

- **International Council for Harmonisation of Technical Requirements for Pharmaceuticals for Human Use (ICH)**: Develops harmonized guidelines on quality, safety, efficacy, and multidisciplinary aspects of pharmaceuticals.
- **WHO Global Benchmarking Tool (GBT)**: Assists countries in assessing and improving their regulatory systems.
- **Pharmaceutical Inspection Co-operation Scheme (PIC/S)**: Promotes uniformity in inspection procedures and facilitates mutual recognition of inspections.
- **TransCelerate Biopharma Inc.**: A collaborative initiative among major pharmaceutical companies to streamline clinical trial processes and regulatory submissions.
- **Global Regulatory Harmonization Forum (GRHF)**: Facilitates dialogue and cooperation among regulatory agencies and industry stakeholders to advance harmonization goals.

Benefits of Harmonization

Harmonizing regulatory standards offers numerous advantages, including:

- **Accelerated Drug Development**: Streamlined processes reduce redundancy, allowing faster development and approval of new drugs.
- **Cost Savings**: Decreased need for duplicate testing and submissions lowers overall costs for pharmaceutical companies.
- **Improved Access**: Enhanced regulatory alignment facilitates broader access to essential medicines in diverse markets.
- **Enhanced Quality Control**: Uniform standards ensure consistent product quality and safety across different regions.
- **Facilitated Innovation**: Simplified regulatory pathways encourage investment in research and development, fostering medical innovation.

Challenges in Harmonization

Despite its benefits, regulatory harmonization faces several challenges:

- **Diverse Regulatory Frameworks**: Countries have varying regulatory philosophies, legal systems, and healthcare priorities, making alignment complex.
- **Resource Disparities**: Regulatory agencies in LMICs may lack the resources and infrastructure needed to implement harmonized standards effectively.
- **Resistance to Change**: Institutional inertia and resistance from stakeholders accustomed to existing regulatory practices can impede harmonization efforts.
- **Maintaining Flexibility**: Balancing harmonized standards with the need for regional or country-specific adaptations to address local health needs and conditions.

Role of WHO in Regulatory Harmonization

The **World Health Organization (WHO)** plays a central role in promoting regulatory harmonization through:

- **Developing Guidelines and Standards**: Creating internationally recognized guidelines that serve as benchmarks for national regulations.
- **Capacity Building**: Assisting countries, especially LMICs, in strengthening their regulatory systems through training, technical assistance, and infrastructure support.
- **Facilitating Collaboration**: Acting as a facilitator for dialogue and cooperation among regulatory agencies, industry, and other

stakeholders.

- **Monitoring and Evaluation**: Assessing the implementation and impact of harmonization initiatives to ensure their effectiveness and sustainability.

Case Studies

1. ICH Guidelines Adoption

The widespread adoption of **ICH Q8 (Pharmaceutical Development), Q9 (Quality Risk Management)**, and **Q10 (Pharmaceutical Quality System)** guidelines by regulatory agencies globally has significantly enhanced the consistency and robustness of quality management systems in pharmaceutical manufacturing. These guidelines have been instrumental in integrating quality into the drug development lifecycle, promoting a proactive approach to quality assurance and risk management.

2. WHO PQ and Harmonization Synergy

The integration of the **WHO Prequalification Program** with global regulatory harmonization efforts has streamlined the approval process for essential medicines. By aligning prequalification standards with ICH guidelines and collaborating with regulatory agencies across different regions, WHO has facilitated the efficient dissemination of quality-assured medicines to underserved populations.

Impact on Global Health

The combined efforts of the WHO Prequalification Program and global regulatory harmonization have led to significant improvements in global health outcomes by:

- **Ensuring Consistent Drug Quality**: Uniform standards reduce the incidence of substandard and counterfeit drugs, enhancing patient safety.
- **Expanding Access to Medicines**: Streamlined regulatory processes enable faster access to essential medicines in LMICs, addressing critical health needs.
- **Supporting Global Health Initiatives**: Facilitates the effective implementation of global health programs by ensuring the availability of reliable pharmaceutical products.
- **Promoting Equity**: Bridges regulatory gaps between high-income and low-income countries, fostering equitable access to healthcare.

CHAPTER TWENTY

Canada Regulations

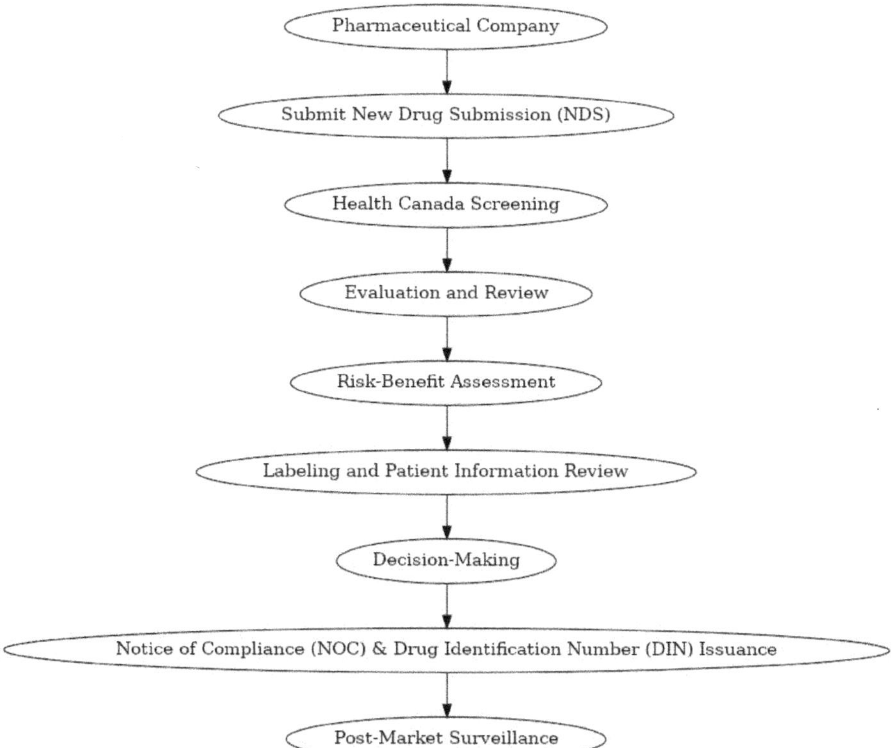

Drug Submission Process in Canada

CANADA REGULATIONS

In the field of **pharmaceuticals**, regulation is a crucial aspect to ensure the **safety, efficacy,** and quality of medicines. Canada is one of the leading countries with a well-structured regulatory framework for pharmaceuticals. This chapter provides a comprehensive overview of the regulations governing pharmaceuticals in Canada, focusing specifically on the regulation of clinical trials. Understanding the Canadian regulatory environment is essential for pharmaceutical companies, researchers, and healthcare professionals involved in developing, testing, and distributing new drugs in the country. This chapter will examine the key components of Canada's regulatory framework, its significance in protecting public health, and the processes involved in regulating clinical trials.

20.1 INTRODUCTION

Canada's **pharmaceutical regulations** are primarily overseen by **Health Canada**, the federal department responsible for national public health policies and programs. Health Canada's mandate is to ensure that **drugs** and health products are **safe, effective, and of high quality**. This is achieved through a comprehensive regulatory framework that governs the approval, marketing, and post-market surveillance of drugs. The regulatory framework in Canada is guided by the **Food and Drugs Act** and its associated regulations, including the **Food and Drug Regulations**, **Controlled Drugs and Substances Act**, and the **Natural Health Products Regulations**. These laws provide the legal basis for regulating the pharmaceutical industry and ensure that all products meet strict standards before they reach consumers.

One of the fundamental principles of Canadian pharmaceutical regulation is **risk management**. Health Canada assesses the risks and benefits of drugs and health products to ensure that their use is safe and effective. The **Canadian regulatory framework** is designed to protect the public from potential health hazards associated with drugs while allowing access to innovative therapies. The regulatory process in Canada is rigorous and involves multiple stages of evaluation and approval.

The regulation of pharmaceuticals in Canada begins with the **drug submission process**. Pharmaceutical companies seeking to market a new drug in Canada must submit a **New Drug Submission (NDS)** to Health Canada. The NDS contains detailed information about the drug, including its **chemical composition, manufacturing process, clinical trial data,** and proposed labeling. Health Canada evaluates the submission to determine if the drug is safe and effective for its intended use. This evaluation process involves a thorough review of scientific evidence and clinical trial data.

In addition to the **NDS**, Health Canada requires pharmaceutical companies to adhere to **Good Manufacturing Practices (GMP)**, which ensure that drugs are consistently produced and controlled according to quality standards. GMP compliance is essential for maintaining the integrity and quality of pharmaceutical products. Health Canada conducts regular inspections of manufacturing facilities to ensure compliance with GMP requirements.

Post-market surveillance is another crucial aspect of Canadian pharmaceutical regulation. Once a drug is approved and marketed, Health Canada continues to monitor its safety and effectiveness through **post-market surveillance** activities. This includes collecting and analyzing adverse drug reactions, conducting inspections, and reviewing safety data. If a drug is found to pose a risk to public health, Health Canada may take regulatory actions, such as issuing warnings, recalls, or product withdrawals.

Canada's regulatory framework also emphasizes transparency and public engagement. Health Canada provides information about approved drugs, safety concerns, and regulatory decisions to the public through its website and other communication channels. This transparency helps build public trust and confidence in the safety and effectiveness of pharmaceuticals.

20.2 REGULATING CLINICAL TRIALS

Clinical trials play a crucial role in developing new drugs and therapies, and Canada's regulatory framework ensures that these trials are conducted ethically and safely. Health Canada regulates clinical trials through the **Clinical Trials Regulations** (CTR), which provide guidelines for conducting trials in humans. The CTR is part of the broader **Food and Drug Regulations**, and it outlines the requirements for obtaining authorization to conduct clinical trials in Canada.

Before a clinical trial can begin in Canada, the sponsor must submit a **Clinical Trial Application (CTA)** to Health Canada. The CTA contains detailed information about the trial, including its objectives, design, methodology, and potential risks. Health Canada reviews the application to ensure that the trial is scientifically sound and that the risks to participants are minimized. This review process is rigorous and involves experts in various fields, including medicine, pharmacology, and ethics.

The **ethical conduct of clinical trials** is a cornerstone of the Canadian regulatory framework. Health Canada requires that all clinical trials be conducted in accordance with **Good Clinical Practices (GCP)**, which are internationally recognized ethical and scientific standards for designing, conducting, and reporting clinical trials. GCP ensures that the rights, safety, and well-being of trial participants are protected and that the trial data is reliable and accurate.

One of the key components of GCP is obtaining **informed consent** from trial participants. Informed consent is a process through which participants are provided with comprehensive information about the trial, including its purpose, risks, benefits, and alternative treatments. Participants must voluntarily agree to participate in the trial without any coercion or undue influence. This process ensures that participants understand their rights and the potential impact of the trial on their health.

Canada's regulatory framework also includes provisions for **monitoring and auditing clinical trials.** Health Canada conducts inspections of clinical trial sites to ensure compliance with regulatory requirements and GCP standards. These inspections assess the conduct of the trial, the integrity of the data, and the protection of participants' rights. If any deficiencies are identified, Health Canada may take corrective actions, such as suspending the trial or imposing fines.

In addition to regulatory oversight, clinical trials in Canada are subject to **research ethics review** by independent ethics boards. These boards, known as **Research Ethics Boards (REBs)**, review the ethical aspects of the trial, including the risks and benefits to participants and the adequacy of the informed consent process. REBs play a critical role in ensuring that clinical trials are conducted ethically and that participants' rights are respected.

Canada's regulatory framework also addresses the inclusion of **vulnerable populations** in clinical trials. Health Canada has guidelines for conducting trials involving special populations, such as children, pregnant women, and individuals with cognitive impairments. These guidelines emphasize the need for additional safeguards to protect the rights and welfare of vulnerable participants.

The regulation of clinical trials in Canada extends beyond the approval process. Health Canada requires sponsors to report **adverse events and safety concerns** that arise during the trial. This reporting is crucial for monitoring the trial's safety and identifying any potential risks to participants. If a serious adverse event occurs, the sponsor must promptly report it to Health Canada and the relevant REB.

20.3 REVIEWING DRUG SUBMISSIONS

The process of reviewing **drug submissions** in Canada is a meticulous and systematic procedure designed to ensure that all **medicinal products** entering the market are safe, effective, and of high quality. Health Canada is responsible for this critical task, and the process involves evaluating various aspects of a drug, from its scientific data and clinical trial results to its manufacturing processes and labeling. This section delves into the comprehensive procedures involved in reviewing drug submissions, highlighting the critical stages and considerations taken into account during the evaluation process.

20.3.1 Submission Types and Process

Pharmaceutical companies seeking to market a new drug in Canada must submit a **New Drug Submission (NDS)** to Health Canada. This submission contains extensive documentation detailing the drug's **chemical composition, clinical trial data, pharmacokinetics, pharmacodynamics, manufacturing process, and proposed labeling**. The NDS is the most common type of submission for new pharmaceuticals. However, there are other submission types depending on the nature of the drug or its intended changes, such as:

- **Supplemental New Drug Submissions (SNDS):** For modifications to an existing drug, like changes in formulation or manufacturing.
- **Abbreviated New Drug Submissions (ANDS):** For generic drugs, which require demonstration of bioequivalence to an existing approved drug.
- **Drug Identification Number (DIN) Applications:** For over-the-counter (OTC) drugs requiring a unique identification number to be marketed.

Once a submission is made, Health Canada begins the **screening process** to ensure the application is complete. This initial screening typically takes around **45 days**. If the application is deemed complete, it moves to the next phase of detailed evaluation. However, if deficiencies are found, the applicant is notified and required to provide additional information.

20.3.2 Scientific Evaluation and Review

The scientific evaluation is the heart of the drug submission review process. Health Canada's experts thoroughly examine the submission's data, focusing on several critical areas:

- **Clinical Efficacy and Safety:** Clinical trial data is analyzed to determine the drug's therapeutic benefits and potential risks. This includes reviewing **Phase I, II, and III trial results**, which provide insights into the drug's **safety profile, efficacy**, and appropriate dosage levels.

- **Preclinical Studies:** These studies involve in vitro (test tube or cell culture) and in vivo (animal) experiments that provide preliminary safety and efficacy data before human trials.
- **Chemistry and Manufacturing:** The manufacturing process is reviewed to ensure compliance with **Good Manufacturing Practices (GMP)**, ensuring that the drug is produced consistently and controlled for quality. This evaluation also covers the drug's stability, shelf life, and packaging.
- **Pharmacology and Toxicology:** An analysis of the drug's effects on the body and any toxicological concerns is conducted. This includes **pharmacokinetic (PK) studies**, which examine the drug's absorption, distribution, metabolism, and excretion (ADME), and **pharmacodynamic (PD) studies**, which assess the drug's mechanism of action.
- **Bioavailability and Bioequivalence:** For certain drugs, particularly generics, studies must demonstrate that the new drug is bioequivalent to an already-approved product, ensuring it has the same therapeutic effect.

This evaluation is conducted by specialized reviewers, including medical doctors, pharmacists, chemists, and statisticians, who ensure that the drug meets the standards set forth by Health Canada. The review process can take anywhere from **300 to 600 days**, depending on the complexity and type of submission.

20.3.3 Risk-Benefit Assessment

A pivotal aspect of the review process is the **risk-benefit assessment**. Health Canada's reviewers weigh the potential benefits of the drug against its risks. This assessment considers the drug's intended use, the severity of the condition it treats, and the available treatment options. Drugs that offer significant therapeutic advantages over existing treatments are often prioritized for approval, even if they carry certain risks, provided those risks are deemed manageable and well-documented.

The risk-benefit assessment also involves consultations with advisory committees and external experts, especially for novel or complex drugs. These consultations provide additional perspectives and ensure that the decision-making process is comprehensive and transparent.

20.3.4 Labeling and Patient Information

Proper labeling is crucial for ensuring that healthcare professionals and patients use the drug safely and effectively. Health Canada reviews the proposed labeling to ensure it contains clear and accurate information about the drug's indications, dosage, administration, contraindications, warnings, and potential side effects. The labeling must also comply with Canadian regulations and be available in both **English and French**, the official languages of Canada.

Patient information leaflets, which accompany the drug packaging, are also reviewed to ensure they provide understandable and accessible information to consumers. These leaflets must clearly explain how to use the drug, potential side effects, and what to do in case of an overdose or missed dose.

20.3.5 Decision-Making and Approval

Once the review process is complete, Health Canada makes a decision regarding the drug's approval. This decision is based on the cumulative findings of the scientific evaluation, risk-benefit assessment, and labeling review. If the drug meets all the necessary criteria, it is granted a **Notice of Compliance (NOC)** and assigned a **Drug Identification Number (DIN)**, allowing it to be marketed in Canada.

In some cases, a drug may receive conditional approval, requiring the manufacturer to conduct further studies or provide additional data post-approval. This is often the case for drugs that address unmet medical needs or provide significant clinical benefits but have outstanding safety concerns.

20.3.6 Post-Market Surveillance

The review process does not end with the drug's approval. Health Canada continues to monitor the drug's safety and effectiveness through **post-market surveillance**. This involves tracking adverse drug reactions, conducting inspections, and reviewing new safety data as it becomes available. Manufacturers are required to report any adverse events or new findings related to the drug, ensuring ongoing safety monitoring.

20.4 MONITORING POST-MARKET SAFETY

Monitoring post-market safety is a critical component of Canada's pharmaceutical regulatory framework. While pre-market evaluations and clinical trials provide valuable information about a drug's safety and efficacy, the full spectrum of a drug's effects often becomes apparent only after it has been widely used by the general population. Therefore, post-market surveillance plays a vital role in identifying and managing potential risks that may arise after a drug has been approved for use. This section explores the mechanisms and strategies employed by Health Canada to ensure the ongoing safety of pharmaceuticals in the Canadian market.

20.4.1 Importance of Post-Market Surveillance

Post-market surveillance is essential for several reasons. Firstly, it allows for the detection of rare or long-term adverse effects that may not have been identified during pre-market clinical trials. Clinical trials typically involve a limited number of participants and are conducted over a relatively short period, making it challenging to identify infrequent or delayed side effects. Once a drug is released into the market and used by a larger and more diverse population, new safety concerns may emerge.

Secondly, post-market surveillance helps assess the effectiveness of risk management strategies implemented during the drug's development and approval process. It ensures that any potential risks associated with the drug are adequately managed and that the benefits continue to outweigh the risks.

Finally, post-market surveillance supports informed decision-making by healthcare professionals and patients. By providing updated safety information, Health Canada enables healthcare providers to make evidence-based decisions about prescribing medications, and patients can make informed choices about their treatment options.

20.4.2 Adverse Drug Reaction Reporting

A key element of post-market surveillance is the reporting and analysis of **adverse drug reactions (ADRs)**. Health Canada encourages healthcare professionals, patients, and manufacturers to report any adverse events associated with drug use. This information is collected through the **Canada Vigilance Program**, which serves as a central repository for ADR reports.

The Canada Vigilance Program enables the identification of potential safety signals by monitoring trends and patterns in ADR data. When a safety signal is detected, Health Canada conducts a thorough assessment to determine whether a causal relationship exists between the drug and the reported event. This assessment may involve reviewing clinical data, consulting with experts, and collaborating with international regulatory agencies.

Healthcare professionals are required to report serious adverse drug reactions that result in hospitalization, disability, or death within 15 days of becoming aware of the event. Patients and consumers can also report adverse events directly to Health Canada through online forms, phone calls, or mail.

20.4.3 Risk Management Plans

Manufacturers are required to develop and implement **Risk Management Plans (RMPs)** as part of their post-market surveillance obligations. An RMP outlines the strategies and activities that will be undertaken to minimize the risks associated with a drug throughout its lifecycle. This includes monitoring for new safety information, implementing risk minimization measures, and evaluating the effectiveness of these measures.

RMPs are dynamic documents that evolve as new safety data becomes available. Manufacturers must periodically update their RMPs to reflect changes in the drug's safety profile and to incorporate new risk management strategies. Health Canada reviews and approves RMPs as part of its regulatory oversight.

Risk minimization measures outlined in an RMP may include additional labeling warnings, restrictions on use, educational materials for healthcare professionals and patients, and targeted monitoring of specific patient populations. These measures aim to reduce the likelihood of adverse events and ensure that the benefits of the drug continue to outweigh the risks.

20.4.4 Periodic Safety Update Reports

Another important aspect of post-market surveillance is the submission of **Periodic Safety Update Reports (PSURs)** by manufacturers. PSURs provide a comprehensive overview of a drug's safety profile over a specific reporting period, typically every six months to five years, depending on the drug's risk level.

PSURs include an analysis of all known adverse events, an evaluation of any new safety information, and an assessment of the overall benefit-risk balance of the drug. They also highlight any changes to the drug's labeling or risk management strategies. These reports allow Health Canada to monitor the ongoing safety of the drug and ensure that appropriate actions are taken to address any emerging safety concerns.

20.4.5 Pharmacovigilance Inspections

To ensure compliance with post-market surveillance requirements, Health Canada conducts **pharmacovigilance inspections** of pharmaceutical companies. These inspections assess the company's pharmacovigilance systems and processes, including their procedures for collecting, analyzing, and reporting ADRs. Inspections also evaluate the effectiveness of risk management plans and the accuracy of periodic safety update reports.

Pharmacovigilance inspections play a critical role in ensuring that manufacturers fulfill their obligations to monitor and report on the safety of their products. If deficiencies are identified during an inspection, Health Canada may require corrective actions or impose penalties to ensure compliance.

20.4.6 Safety Communications and Public Engagement

Transparency and public engagement are essential components of post-market surveillance. Health Canada provides timely and accurate safety information to healthcare professionals and the public through various channels, including safety communications, advisories, and updates on its website.

When a significant safety concern is identified, Health Canada may issue a safety communication to inform healthcare providers and patients of the potential risks and any recommended actions. These communications are designed to ensure that all stakeholders have access to the latest safety information, enabling them to make informed decisions about drug use.

Health Canada also engages with stakeholders, including healthcare professionals, patient advocacy groups, and the public, to gather feedback and promote awareness of post-market safety monitoring. This engagement helps build trust in the regulatory system and ensures that the voices of patients and consumers are considered in decision-making.

20.4.7 Collaboration with International Regulatory Agencies

In the globalized pharmaceutical market, collaboration with international regulatory agencies is crucial for effective post-market surveillance. Health Canada works closely with agencies such as the **U.S. Food and Drug Administration (FDA)**, the **European Medicines Agency (EMA)**, and the **World Health Organization (WHO)** to share safety information and coordinate responses to emerging safety issues.

This collaboration allows for the pooling of resources and expertise, enabling more comprehensive assessments of drug safety. It also facilitates harmonization of regulatory standards and practices, ensuring that safety concerns are addressed consistently across different regions.

20.4.8 Real-World Evidence and Post-Market Studies

In addition to traditional methods of post-market surveillance, Health Canada increasingly relies on **real-world evidence (RWE)** and post-market studies to evaluate the safety and effectiveness of drugs in real-world settings. RWE is derived from data collected outside of controlled clinical trials, such as electronic health records, insurance claims, and patient registries.

Post-market studies, including **Phase IV trials**, provide valuable insights into a drug's performance in diverse patient populations and under various conditions. These studies can identify rare adverse events, evaluate the long-term safety and effectiveness of a drug, and assess its impact on patient outcomes.

20.5 ENFORCING COMPLIANCE WITH THE REGULATIONS

Enforcing compliance with pharmaceutical regulations is a crucial aspect of ensuring that drugs and health products in Canada are safe, effective, and of high quality. Health Canada, the federal authority responsible for health policy, plays a pivotal role in overseeing the enforcement of these regulations. The enforcement process involves a range of activities, including inspections, audits, legal actions, and collaborative efforts with other regulatory bodies. This section explores the mechanisms and strategies employed by Health Canada to enforce compliance with pharmaceutical regulations and maintain public trust in the healthcare system.

20.5.1 Regulatory Framework and Authority

The regulatory framework for pharmaceuticals in Canada is governed by several key pieces of legislation, including the **Food and Drugs Act**, the **Controlled Drugs and Substances Act**, and their associated regulations. These laws provide Health Canada with the authority to regulate the development, manufacture, distribution, and sale of drugs and health products.

Health Canada's authority extends to various aspects of the pharmaceutical industry, including **Good Manufacturing Practices (GMP)**, **Good Clinical Practices (GCP)**, **Good Pharmacovigilance Practices (GVP)**, and labeling requirements. These standards ensure that drugs are manufactured consistently, clinical trials are conducted ethically, safety monitoring is robust, and product information is clear and accurate.

20.5.2 Inspection and Audit Processes

Health Canada's **Regulatory Operations and Enforcement Branch (ROEB)** conducts inspections and audits to ensure compliance with regulatory standards. Inspections are carried out at various stages of the drug lifecycle, including manufacturing facilities, clinical trial sites, and distribution centers. The primary objectives of these inspections are to assess compliance with GMP, GCP, and other relevant standards, identify potential risks to public health, and verify the accuracy of records and documentation.

Inspections are typically conducted on a **risk-based approach**, prioritizing facilities and products with a higher potential for non-compliance or safety concerns. Inspections can be routine, scheduled visits or **for-cause inspections**, initiated in response to specific safety signals or complaints.

During an inspection, Health Canada inspectors evaluate the facility's operations, review documentation, and interview staff to assess compliance with regulatory requirements. Inspectors may take samples of products for laboratory analysis to verify quality and compliance with specifications.

20.5.3 Enforcement Actions

When non-compliance is identified, Health Canada has a range of enforcement tools at its disposal to address the issue and ensure corrective actions are taken. The severity of the enforcement action depends on the nature and extent of the non-compliance, as well as the potential risk to public health.

1. **Warning Letters**: Health Canada may issue warning letters to companies or individuals found to be in violation of regulations. These letters outline the specific areas of non-compliance and require the recipient to address the issues promptly. Warning letters serve as an initial step in enforcement and provide an opportunity for corrective action without further penalties.

2. **Seizure and Detention**: In cases where products pose a significant risk to public health, Health Canada has the authority to seize and detain non-compliant products. This action prevents the distribution and sale of potentially harmful products and protects consumers from exposure to unsafe medications.

3. **Product Recalls**: If a product is found to be unsafe or of poor quality, Health Canada may initiate a product recall. Recalls can be voluntary, initiated by the manufacturer, or mandatory, directed by Health Canada. Recalls are categorized into three classes based on the potential risk to health, with Class I being the most severe.

4. **Monetary Penalties**: Health Canada can impose monetary penalties on companies that fail to comply with regulatory requirements. These penalties serve as a deterrent to non-compliance and encourage companies to adhere to regulations.

5. **License Suspension or Revocation**: In cases of serious or repeated non-compliance, Health Canada may suspend or revoke a company's license to manufacture, import, or distribute drugs. This action prevents the company from continuing operations until compliance is achieved.
6. **Legal Action**: For severe violations, Health Canada may pursue legal action against companies or individuals. This can include prosecution, resulting in fines or imprisonment, depending on the severity of the offense.

20.5.4 Collaboration with Other Agencies

Health Canada collaborates with other regulatory agencies, both nationally and internationally, to enhance enforcement efforts and share information on non-compliance. Within Canada, Health Canada works closely with agencies such as the **Canadian Border Services Agency (CBSA)** and the **Royal Canadian Mounted Police (RCMP)** to prevent the importation of counterfeit or unauthorized drugs and investigate criminal activities related to pharmaceuticals.

Internationally, Health Canada collaborates with regulatory agencies such as the **U.S. Food and Drug Administration (FDA)**, the **European Medicines Agency (EMA)**, and the **World Health Organization (WHO)** to harmonize standards and share intelligence on global supply chain risks. This collaboration helps identify and address non-compliance issues that may affect multiple countries and ensures that enforcement actions are consistent and effective worldwide.

20.5.5 Continuous Improvement and Training

To maintain high standards of compliance enforcement, Health Canada invests in continuous improvement and training for its inspectors and regulatory staff. Regular training sessions and workshops are conducted to keep staff updated on the latest regulatory requirements, inspection techniques, and enforcement strategies. This ongoing education ensures that Health Canada remains at the forefront of regulatory enforcement and can effectively respond to emerging challenges in the pharmaceutical industry.

Health Canada also conducts internal audits and reviews of its enforcement processes to identify areas for improvement and implement best practices. By continuously evaluating and refining its approach, Health Canada can enhance the effectiveness and efficiency of its compliance enforcement efforts.

20.5.6 Encouraging Industry Compliance

In addition to enforcement actions, Health Canada actively works to encourage industry compliance through education and guidance. The agency provides resources and support to help companies understand and adhere to regulatory requirements. This includes publishing guidelines, conducting webinars, and offering consultations with industry stakeholders.

By fostering a culture of compliance within the pharmaceutical industry, Health Canada aims to promote voluntary adherence to regulations and reduce the need for enforcement actions. Encouraging industry compliance also helps build trust between regulators and companies, ensuring a collaborative approach to safeguarding public health.

20.5.7 Public Engagement and Transparency

Transparency and public engagement are integral to enforcing compliance with pharmaceutical regulations. Health Canada is committed to providing the public with information about enforcement actions, safety concerns, and regulatory decisions. The agency publishes inspection reports, warning letters, and recall notices on its website, ensuring that consumers and healthcare professionals have access to the latest information on drug safety and quality.

Public engagement also plays a role in compliance enforcement. Health Canada encourages consumers and healthcare providers to report any concerns about drug safety or quality through the Canada Vigilance Program and other reporting channels. This feedback helps identify potential compliance issues and informs enforcement actions.

Key Points

- **Regulatory Authority**: Health Canada oversees pharmaceutical regulations to ensure drugs are safe, effective, and of high quality.
- **Legislative Framework**: Guided by the Food and Drugs Act, Controlled Drugs and Substances Act, and Natural Health Products Regulations.
- **Risk Management**: Evaluation of risks and benefits of drugs, emphasizing transparency and public engagement.
- **Drug Submission Process**: Includes New Drug Submissions (NDS), Good Manufacturing Practices (GMP) compliance, and post-market surveillance.

Regulating Clinical Trials

- **Clinical Trials Regulations (CTR)**: Guidelines for conducting trials in humans.
- **Clinical Trial Application (CTA)**: Detailed information required for trial approval.
- **Good Clinical Practices (GCP)**: Ethical and scientific standards for trials.
- **Informed Consent**: Ensuring participants understand the trial's purpose, risks, and benefits.
- **Monitoring and Auditing**: Health Canada conducts inspections to ensure compliance with GCP.
- **Research Ethics Boards (REBs)**: Independent boards reviewing ethical aspects of trials.
- **Vulnerable Populations**: Additional safeguards for special populations in trials.
- **Adverse Event Reporting**: Sponsors must report adverse events during trials to Health Canada and REBs.

Reviewing Drug Submissions

- **Submission Types**: New Drug Submissions (NDS), Supplemental New Drug Submissions (SNDS), Abbreviated New Drug Submissions (ANDS), and Drug Identification Number (DIN) Applications.
- **Scientific Evaluation**: Detailed assessment of clinical efficacy, preclinical studies, chemistry and manufacturing, pharmacology, and bioequivalence.
- **Risk-Benefit Assessment**: Weighing potential benefits against risks.
- **Labeling and Patient Information**: Ensuring clear and accurate labeling in both English and French.
- **Decision-Making**: Granting Notice of Compliance (NOC) and Drug Identification Number (DIN) for market approval.
- **Post-Market Surveillance**: Ongoing monitoring of drug safety and effectiveness.

Monitoring Post-Market Safety

- **Importance**: Detecting rare or long-term adverse effects and assessing risk management strategies.

- **Adverse Drug Reaction (ADR) Reporting**: Canada Vigilance Program collects and analyzes ADR reports.
- **Risk Management Plans (RMPs)**: Strategies to minimize risks throughout the drug's lifecycle.
- **Periodic Safety Update Reports (PSURs)**: Comprehensive safety profile overview.
- **Pharmacovigilance Inspections**: Assessing compliance with regulatory requirements.
- **Safety Communications**: Providing timely safety information to healthcare professionals and the public.
- **International Collaboration**: Sharing safety information with global regulatory agencies.
- **Real-World Evidence (RWE)**: Utilizing data from real-world settings to evaluate drug safety and effectiveness.

Enforcing Compliance with the Regulations

- **Regulatory Authority**: Health Canada enforces compliance through the Food and Drugs Act and other regulations.
- **Inspection and Audits**: Conducted by the Regulatory Operations and Enforcement Branch (ROEB) on a risk-based approach.
- **Enforcement Actions**: Warning letters, seizure and detention, product recalls, monetary penalties, license suspension or revocation, and legal actions.
- **Collaboration with Other Agencies**: Working with CBSA, RCMP, FDA, EMA, and WHO for effective enforcement.
- **Continuous Improvement**: Training and education for inspectors, internal audits, and best practices implementation.
- **Encouraging Industry Compliance**: Providing resources, guidelines, and support to promote voluntary adherence.
- **Public Engagement and Transparency**: Publishing inspection reports, recall notices, and encouraging ADR reporting.

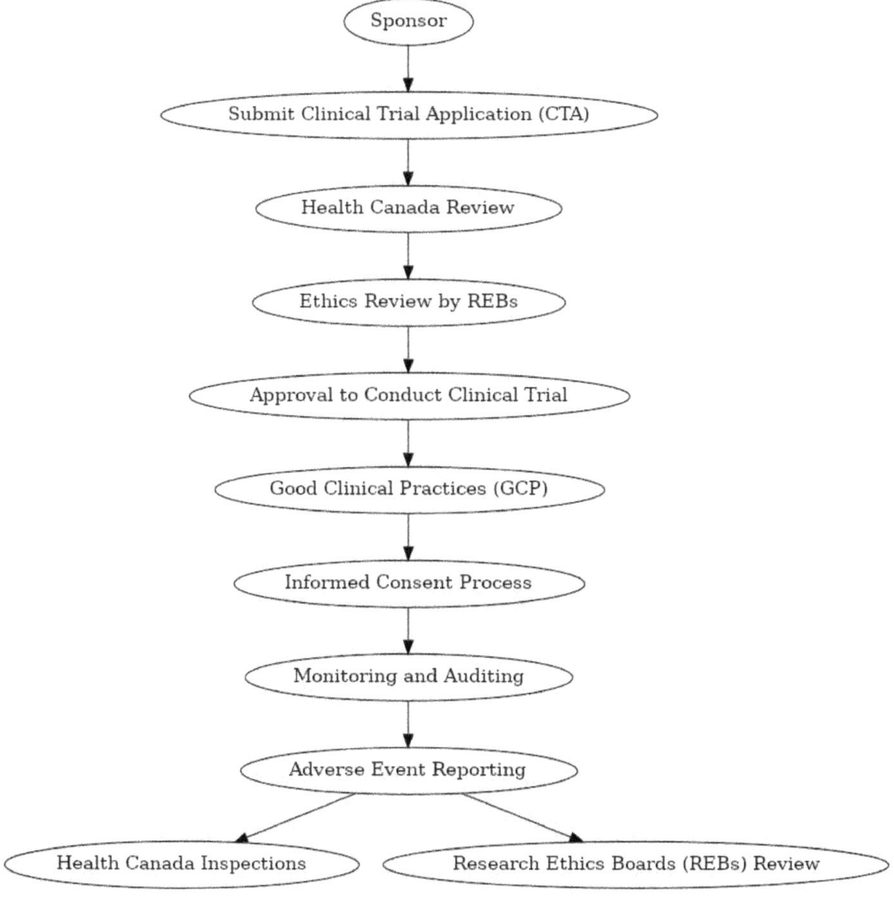

Clinical Trial Regulation Process in Canada

CHAPTER TWENTY-ONE

REFERENCES

1. **International Council for Harmonisation (ICH).** (n.d.). *ICH harmonised tripartite guideline: Good Clinical Practice E6(R2).* Retrieved from https://www.ich.org/page/ich-guidelines

2. **U.S. Food and Drug Administration (FDA).** (n.d.). *Code of Federal Regulations Title 21 - Food and Drugs.* Retrieved from https://www.ecfr.gov/current/title-21

3. **U.S. Food and Drug Administration (FDA).** (2016). *FDA guidance for industry: Acceptance of foreign clinical studies.* Retrieved from https://www.fda.gov/media/87236/download

4. **World Medical Association (WMA).** (2013). *Declaration of Helsinki: Ethical principles for medical research involving human subjects.* Retrieved from https://www.wma.net/policies-post/wma-declaration-of-helsinki-ethical-principles-for-medical-research-involving-human-subjects/

5. **U.S. Department of Health and Human Services.** (1979). *The Belmont Report: Ethical principles and guidelines for the protection of human subjects of research.* Retrieved from https://www.hhs.gov/ohrp/regulations-and-policy/belmont-report/index.html

6. **European Medicines Agency (EMA).** (2022). *EU Clinical Trials Regulation.* Retrieved from https://www.ema.europa.eu/en/human-regulatory/research-development/clinical-trials/clinical-trials-regulation

7. **Central Drugs Standard Control Organization (CDSCO).** (n.d.). *Schedule Y of the Drugs and Cosmetics Rules, 1945.* Retrieved from https://cdsco.gov.in/opencms/opencms/en/Clinical-Trials/

8. **Indian Council of Medical Research (ICMR).** (2017). *Ethical guidelines for biomedical research.* Retrieved from https://ethics.ncdirindia.org/ICMR_Ethical_Guidelines.aspx

9. **Therapeutic Goods Administration (TGA).** (n.d.). *Australian regulatory guidelines for prescription medicines (ARGPM).* Retrieved from https://www.tga.gov.au/publication/australian-regulatory-guidelines-prescription-medicines-argpm

10. **Health Canada.** (n.d.). *Clinical trials and drug submissions.* Retrieved from https://www.canada.ca/en/health-canada/services/drugs-health-products/drug-products.html

11. **ASEAN Secretariat.** (n.d.). *ASEAN Common Technical Dossier (ACTD) for the registration of pharmaceuticals for human use.* Retrieved from https://asean.org/?static_post=asean-common-technical-dossier-actd-for-the-registration-of-pharmaceuticals-for-human-use

12. **U.S. Food and Drug Administration (FDA).** (n.d.). *MedWatch: The FDA safety information and adverse event reporting program.* Retrieved from https://www.fda.gov/safety/medwatch-fda-safety-information-and-adverse-event-reporting-program

13. **World Health Organization (WHO).** (n.d.). *Guidelines on the quality, safety, and efficacy of herbal medicines.* Retrieved from https://www.who.int/medicines/areas/traditional/herbal_traditional/en/

14. **U.S. Food and Drug Administration (FDA).** (2006). *Guidance for industry: Quality systems approach to pharmaceutical cGMP regulations.* Retrieved from https://www.fda.gov/media/71023/download

15. **ISO.** (2015). *ISO 9001: Quality management systems—Requirements.* Geneva, Switzerland: International Organization for Standardization. Retrieved from https://www.iso.org/iso-9001-quality-management.html

16. **World Intellectual Property Organization (WIPO).** (n.d.). *Patent Cooperation Treaty (PCT).* Retrieved from https://www.wipo.int/pct/en/

17. **U.S. Food and Drug Administration (FDA).** (n.d.). *Hatch-Waxman Act and the Orange Book.* Retrieved from https://www.fda.gov/drugs/development-approval-process-drugs/orange-book-preface

18. **World Health Organization (WHO).** (n.d.). *Prequalification program for medicines, vaccines, and diagnostics.* Retrieved from https://extranet.who.int/pqweb/

CHAPTER TWENTY-TWO

Glossary

Accelerated Approval – A regulatory pathway that allows earlier approval of drugs treating serious conditions based on surrogate endpoints.

Active Pharmaceutical Ingredient (API) – The substance in a drug responsible for its therapeutic effect.

Adverse Event (AE) – Any undesirable experience associated with the use of a medical product.

Aggregate Report – A report combining data from multiple studies to assess the safety of a drug.

Amendment – A submission made to modify an existing regulatory application, often to add additional information.

ANDA (Abbreviated New Drug Application) – Application to the FDA for the approval of a generic drug.

Annual Report – A yearly update to regulatory agencies on the progress and status of drug development or post-marketing surveillance.

Article 58 – An EMA regulatory procedure allowing opinions on medicines intended for use outside the European Union.

Authorized Generic – A generic version of a branded drug produced by the brand company under an abbreviated NDA.

Biologics License Application (BLA) – Application for approval of biologic products like vaccines or gene therapies.

Biowaiver – A regulatory approval allowing a drug to be approved without conducting in vivo bioequivalence studies based on in vitro data.

Bioavailability – The proportion of a drug that enters the bloodstream and has an active effect.

Biosimilars – Biological products that are similar to already FDA-approved biologic products.

Bridging Data – Data used to extend clinical trial findings to a different population or formulation.

Bridging Study – A supplemental study used to extrapolate foreign clinical data to another regulatory region.

Breakthrough Therapy Designation – An FDA designation expediting the development of drugs for serious conditions.

CAPA (Corrective and Preventive Action) – A process for investigating and resolving root causes of deviations or non-conformances in drug manufacturing or clinical trials.

CDER (Center for Drug Evaluation and Research) – FDA division responsible for ensuring safe and effective drugs are available to the public.

Chemistry, Manufacturing, and Controls (CMC) – Regulatory information concerning the drug's manufacturing and quality control.

Class Labeling – A labeling practice where drugs in the same class must include the same safety information, based on data from other drugs.

Clinical Benefit – The positive effect of a treatment on a patient's condition.

Clinical Trial – A research study conducted to determine if a drug is safe and effective for humans.

CMC Filing – A portion of a regulatory submission that contains chemistry, manufacturing, and controls information.

Common Technical Document (CTD) – A harmonized submission format for regulatory authorities across several countries.

Compassionate Use – The use of investigational drugs outside of clinical trials for patients with no other options.

Conditional Approval – Temporary drug approval before all necessary evidence is available, often under accelerated pathways.

Consent Decree – A legal agreement between a company and the FDA addressing violations of regulatory requirements.

Controlled Substance – A drug whose manufacture, possession, and use are regulated by the government.

CRO (Contract Research Organization) – A company providing clinical trial management services on behalf of a pharmaceutical company.

Critical Path Initiative – An FDA initiative to modernize the development, evaluation, and approval of drugs.

Critical Quality Attribute (CQA) – A property or characteristic of a drug that must be controlled to ensure product quality.

Cross-Labeling – The practice of updating drug labels in combination therapy to reflect data from another drug.

Cumulative Exposure – The total exposure to a drug over time, often used to assess long-term safety risks.

Design Space – A multidimensional space of input variables and process parameters ensuring quality in drug development.

Dissolution Testing – A test measuring the rate at which a drug dissolves, often used to assess bioequivalence.

Distribution Protocol – A plan outlining drug distribution to ensure it reaches patients while maintaining product integrity.

Dose Escalation – A clinical trial process where the dose of the drug is gradually increased to find the optimal dose.

Dosage Form – The physical form of a drug (e.g., tablet, capsule, injection).

Double-Blind Study – A study where neither the participants nor researchers know who receives the active treatment or placebo.

Drug Development Tools (DDTs) – Tools like biomarkers or clinical outcome assessments used to streamline drug development.

Drug Efficacy Study Implementation (DESI) – A program evaluating the effectiveness of drugs approved before modern efficacy standards.

Drug Master File (DMF) – A submission to the FDA containing confidential information about the facilities or processes used in drug manufacturing.

Drug Product – The finished dosage form of a drug containing the active ingredient.

Drug Shortage – A situation where the supply of a drug is insufficient to meet demand.

Due Diligence – A thorough investigation and evaluation of a potential regulatory action or partnership.

E-labeling – Electronic labeling of drugs instead of traditional paper labels.

Early Access Program (EAP) – A program allowing patients to access investigational drugs before approval.

Efficacy – The ability of a drug to produce the desired therapeutic effect.

Electronic Common Technical Document (eCTD) – The electronic version of the Common Technical Document, used for regulatory submission.

EMA (European Medicines Agency) – The EU agency responsible for the scientific evaluation, supervision, and safety monitoring of medicines.

Essential Medicines – Medicines meeting the priority healthcare needs of the population, as defined by the WHO.

Expanded Access – A program allowing patients to access investigational drugs outside clinical trials.

Excipient – An inactive substance used as a carrier for the active ingredients in a drug.

Expert Report – A document written by experts providing scientific analysis on various aspects of drug development.

Fast Track Designation – An FDA process facilitating drug development and review for serious conditions.

FDA (Food and Drug Administration) – The US regulatory authority overseeing drug approval, safety, and monitoring.

First-in-Human (FIH) Study – The first clinical trial in which a new drug is tested in humans.

Foreign Clinical Study – A clinical study conducted outside the region where the drug is being registered.

Full Marketing Authorization – Regulatory approval for the full commercial release of a drug.

Generic Substitution – The practice of substituting a branded drug with its generic equivalent.

Good Clinical Practice (GCP) – International ethical and scientific quality standards for the design and conduct of clinical trials involving humans.

Good Distribution Practice (GDP) – Guidelines governing the proper distribution of medicinal products.

Good Laboratory Practice (GLP) – Principles ensuring the quality and integrity of non-clinical laboratory studies.

Good Manufacturing Practice (GMP) – Regulations ensuring proper drug design, monitoring, and control of manufacturing processes.

Good Pharmacovigilance Practices (GVP) – Guidelines for conducting pharmacovigilance and post-market surveillance.

Good Regulatory Practice (GRP) – Principles and practices ensuring high-quality regulation.

Health Authority Interaction – Communication between a pharmaceutical company and regulatory authorities during the drug approval process.

Health Technology Assessment (HTA) – The systematic evaluation of healthcare interventions.

Herbal Medicinal Products – Medicinal products derived from plants or plant extracts.

ICH (International Council for Harmonisation) – A body bringing together regulatory authorities and the pharmaceutical industry to discuss drug registration.

IND (Investigational New Drug Application) – Application to the FDA for approval to start human clinical trials.

In Silico Modeling – The use of computer simulations to predict a drug's behavior in the body.

In Vitro Study – Studies conducted outside a living organism, usually in a lab setting.

In Vivo Study – Studies conducted in living organisms, such as animals or humans.

Indication – The condition or disease a drug is intended to treat.

Integrated Summary of Safety (ISS) – A document summarizing the safety data collected during drug development.

Interim Analysis – An analysis of clinical trial data conducted before the study is completed.

Investigational Medicinal Product Dossier (IMPD) – A document providing information about the investigational medicinal product to regulatory authorities.

Juvenile Animal Study – Preclinical testing of a drug in young animals to assess safety before testing in children.

Label Comprehension Study – A study that evaluates whether patients can understand and correctly interpret drug labeling.

Label Expansion – Expanding the indications for which a drug is approved.

Last Patient In (LPI) – The date on which the last patient is enrolled in a clinical trial.

Late-Stage Development – The final stages of drug development, including Phase III clinical trials.

Lean Management – An approach to streamline operations and eliminate waste in drug development.

Licensure – Official authorization to manufacture and distribute a drug.

Life Cycle Management – Managing the entire lifecycle of a drug from development through post-marketing surveillance.

Lot Release – Testing each batch of product to ensure it meets quality standards before release.

MAA (Marketing Authorization Application) – Application submitted to the EMA for new product approval.

Market Authorization – Regulatory approval to sell a pharmaceutical product.

Medical Device – An instrument or machine used for diagnosis or treatment that does not achieve its primary effect through chemical action.

Mutual Recognition Procedure (MRP) – An EU regulatory procedure allowing a drug authorized in one member state to be recognized in others.

New Drug Application (NDA) – Application for the approval of a new drug.

NDA Resubmission – A revised application for new drug approval submitted after the original NDA was rejected.

Non-Clinical Study – Preclinical studies conducted in animals or in vitro before human clinical trials.

Non-Inferiority Trial – A trial designed to show that a new treatment is not worse than an existing treatment by a pre-specified amount.

Orphan Drug – A drug developed for the treatment of rare diseases.

Orphan Drug Designation – Status assigned to drugs for rare diseases, offering benefits like market exclusivity.

Off-Label Use – The use of a drug for an indication or age group not specified in the approved labeling.

Out-of-Specification (OOS) – Test results falling outside the set specifications for drug products.

Over-the-Counter (OTC) Drug – Drugs available without a prescription.

Parallel Import – The practice of importing a drug from one country to another where it is sold at a lower price.

Patient-Centric Drug Development – Involving patients in the drug development process to ensure treatments meet their needs.

Patient-Reported Outcome (PRO) – A report of a patient's health condition coming directly from the patient.

PDUFA (Prescription Drug User Fee Act) – A US law allowing the FDA to collect fees from drug manufacturers for new drug reviews.

Periodic Safety Update Report (PSUR) – A report summarizing a drug's safety profile submitted at regular intervals.

Pharmacodynamics – The study of the biochemical and physiological effects of drugs and their mechanisms of action.

Pharmacoeconomics – The study of the cost and value of drugs and therapies.

Pharmacokinetics – The study of how drugs are absorbed, distributed, metabolized, and excreted by the body.

Pharmacovigilance – The science and activities related to detecting and preventing adverse effects of medicines.

Phase 0 Study – A microdosing study conducted to gather early pharmacokinetic data on a drug.

Phase I Study – The first stage of clinical testing, assessing safety and dosage in healthy volunteers.

Phase II Study – Clinical trials testing drug efficacy and further assessing safety in patients.

Phase III Study – Large-scale trials confirming a drug's effectiveness, monitoring side effects, and comparing it to common treatments.

Phase IV Study – Post-marketing surveillance studies monitoring a drug's performance in the general population.

Pivotal Trial – A clinical trial providing the primary evidence used for regulatory approval of a drug.

Placebo-Controlled Study – A study comparing the effects of a drug to a placebo.

Post-Approval Studies – Studies conducted after a drug has been approved to gather additional safety or efficacy information.

Post-Market Surveillance – Monitoring the safety of a pharmaceutical product after it has been released.

PPQ (Process Performance Qualification) – Part of the validation process verifying that a manufacturing process meets requirements.

Preclinical Development – The stage of drug development involving laboratory and animal testing before human trials.

Pre-IND Meeting – A meeting between a sponsor and the FDA to discuss drug development plans before submitting an IND.

Prescription Drug – A drug requiring a doctor's authorization for use.

Priority Review – An FDA process reviewing drugs offering major advances in treatment or filling unmet medical needs.

Process Analytical Technology (PAT) – A system for designing, analyzing, and controlling manufacturing through timely measurements of critical quality attributes.

Product Monograph – A document providing essential information about a drug, including composition, pharmacology, indications, and warnings.

Protocol – A detailed plan for a scientific or medical experiment, treatment, or procedure.

Protocol Amendment – A modification to a previously approved clinical trial protocol.

QbD (Quality by Design) – A systematic approach to pharmaceutical development emphasizing product and process understanding.

Quality Agreement – A formal agreement defining each party's responsibilities related to quality and compliance.

Quality Assurance (QA) – Processes ensuring a product meets required quality standards.

Quality Control (QC) – Testing and verification activities ensuring products meet required specifications.

Quality Management System (QMS) – A system outlining policies and procedures to improve and control various processes.

Rare Disease – A condition affecting a small percentage of the population, often leading to the development of orphan drugs.

Real-World Evidence (RWE) – Information derived from real-world data (RWD), as opposed to controlled clinical trials.

Reference Listed Drug (RLD) – The approved drug to which a generic version is compared.

Reference Standard – A well-characterized substance used as a comparison in quality control and testing.

Regulatory Affairs – The profession ensuring pharmaceutical products comply with regulations and laws during development and marketing.

Regulatory Compliance – Ensuring that a product or process meets all legal and regulatory requirements.

Regulatory Inspection – An official review conducted by regulatory authorities to ensure compliance with regulations.

Regulatory Strategy – A plan for navigating the regulatory approval process.

Regulatory Submission – The package of documents submitted to regulatory authorities to obtain marketing approval.

Risk-Benefit Analysis – Evaluating the potential benefits of a drug against its risks.

Risk Evaluation and Mitigation Strategies (REMS) – An FDA-required strategy to manage the risks associated with certain drugs.

Risk Management Plan (RMP) – A document describing risk minimization measures for a medicinal product.

Route of Administration – The path by which a drug is introduced into the body (e.g., oral, intravenous).

Safety Signal – Information suggesting a new potential association between a drug and an adverse event.

Sampling Plan – A plan for collecting samples to test during drug manufacturing or quality control.

Scale-Up – Increasing the batch size during drug development and manufacturing.

Scientific Advice – Advice provided by regulatory authorities on drug development issues.

Serious Adverse Event (SAE) – An adverse event resulting in death, life-threatening effects, or hospitalization.

Shelf Life – The period during which a drug product remains within approved stability specifications.

Simultaneous Global Development – Developing a drug for multiple markets and submitting regulatory applications to different countries simultaneously.

Site Inspection – A regulatory inspection conducted at a clinical trial or manufacturing site.

Specification – A detailed description of the design and materials used to make a product, including its quality standards.

Standard Operating Procedure (SOP) – Step-by-step instructions for carrying out routine operations.

Statement of Investigator (Form FDA 1572) – A form completed by investigators conducting clinical trials under an IND.

Steering Committee – A group of experts providing oversight and advice for clinical trials.

Submission Ready – When all documents and data for regulatory submission are prepared and ready for review.

Substantial Evidence – Evidence supporting the approval of a drug or biologic.

Summary of Product Characteristics (SmPC) – A document containing essential information about a drug, including indications and side effects.

Surrogate Endpoint – A biomarker used in clinical trials as a substitute for a clinical endpoint.

Target Product Profile (TPP) – A strategic document outlining desired characteristics of a drug.

Targeted Therapy – A type of treatment using drugs to target specific molecules involved in disease, such as cancer.

Technology Transfer – Transferring knowledge, skills, and processes from one organization or facility to another.

Therapeutic Area – A category of diseases or medical conditions a drug is designed to treat.

Therapeutic Equivalence – When two drugs are bioequivalent and produce the same therapeutic effects.

Tiered Pricing – A pricing strategy setting different prices for different countries or markets.

Trial Master File (TMF) – A collection of documents and data related to the conduct of a clinical trial.

Type A Meeting – An FDA meeting requested to resolve a stalled development program or address an issue that has placed the program on hold.

Type B Meeting – A meeting between a sponsor and the FDA to discuss critical development milestones, such as an end-of-Phase II meeting.

Type C Meeting – A meeting to discuss additional development questions not addressed by Type A or B meetings.

Umbrella Trial – A clinical trial evaluating the effects of multiple drugs on a single disease.

Unblinding – Revealing treatment assignments in a clinical trial, typically after the study is completed.

Unmet Medical Need – A condition for which no satisfactory treatment exists or where available treatments are inadequate.

USPI (United States Prescribing Information) – The labeling document approved by the FDA accompanying a drug.

Validation – Documented evidence that a process or system produces consistent results meeting predetermined specifications.

Validation Master Plan (VMP) – A comprehensive document outlining the strategy and requirements for validating a manufacturing process or equipment.

Variance – A deviation from the expected process or result.

Waiver – An exemption from certain regulatory requirements.

White Paper – A document discussing the advantages or aspects of a specific drug or topic.

Xenobiotic – A substance foreign to the body or an ecological system.

www.ingramcontent.com/pod-product-compliance
Lightning Source LLC
Chambersburg PA
CBHW041300120726
48005CB00014B/1808